"Among the Heath and Harebells"

Northamptonshire County Golf Club
1909-2009

by NEIL SOUTAR
& BRUCE CLAYTON

FOREWORD

Although it is many years since my last visit, I have fond memories of Northamptonshire County Golf Club or "Church Brampton" as we mistakenly often called it. In the early 1970s I was living in Warwickshire and was a regular entrant to the Northamptonshire County Cup.

In those days the event attracted all the best players from the Midlands and often further afield and was always a most enjoyable affair. The golf course, one of Harry Colt's gems, was routinely in magnificent order – a true pleasure to play – and the welcome we received from so many enthusiastic members has not been erased from my memory. Although I rarely featured on the scoreboard, they were good times.

Little did I think in those days that I would be invited to contribute to the Club's centenary book and I am delighted to do so. Through our recent association, when the Club was a most popular venue for Open Championship Regional Qualifying, I well know that everything that was so good about Northamptonshire County all those years ago has been maintained and still characterises the Club to this day.

The members of the Royal and Ancient Golf Club of St Andrews join me in congratulating you on reaching your centenary and in wishing you well for the years ahead.

Peter Dawson
Secretary, The Royal and Ancient Golf Club of St Andrews

ISBN: 978-0-9561065-0-6

Published by Northamptonshire County Golf Club

© 2008

Dust jacket picture by: Brian Ball

Printed and bound in Great Britain
RiteTimePublishing.com

ACKNOWLEDGEMENTS

It must have been about 10 years ago when I first suggested to Michael Bairstow, who was then the Club Chairman and others that it might be a good idea if someone tried to assemble any anecdotes or tales of great deeds on and off the course before memory fades. Nothing much seemed to happen and the matter remained dormant as far as I know until about 18 months ago, when Chris Thompson, our current Chairman, said that it was the wish of the Management Committee to republish Neil Soutar's history of the first 85 years and that simultaneously an up-date to cover the next 15 years should be done. He said, with a twinkle in his eye, "Will you do it?".

Thus I came into the role of a co-author with Neil Soutar, which I am only too pleased to assume.

The colossus of this enterprise has been George Mobbs who has given me so much of his time. Advancing years have in no way dimmed his memory. George provided me with much background and many stories about incidents and members long deceased. To George, his brother Roger and nephew Edgar, I am eternally grateful.

Similarly, Peter Palmer saw me readily more than a year ago when I called to see him armed with a tape recorder. Peter is the "Father" of our Club, having become a member 88 years ago.

I thank our Chairman, Chris, for his endless patience, understanding and proof reading, as well as Marion Peel who not only proof read the text, but pointed the way where omissions might have occurred. John Beynon also helped to update the original book.

Stephanie McAra has always provided information concerning the Ladies' section whenever asked. To Richard Catlow and other contributors of articles and pen portraits in The County which I have pirated for posterity, I extend my heartfelt thanks. Brian Ball provided superb photographs, many of which are included.

Various others have provided me with contributions including Michael Learoyd on the "History of the Circus", Peter Arnold similarly as to "The Red Cats" and Lewis McGibbon as to the subject of the county cricket golfing society.

Peter Walsh and his staff have always co-operated in the most friendly way, as have members who have sent to me "tales" which I have been pleased to embrace.

I express my immense gratitude to my loyal and ever patient typist, Sally Carter, who prepared, typed, retyped and scanned endlessly my manuscript.

Finally I must thank Alex Corrin (daughter of José and the late Jack Corrin) who indexed Neil's book and who has undertaken this task for me embodying both books under one cover.

Bruce Clayton

Contents

Foreword by Peter Dawson, Secretary, Royal and Ancient Golf Club
Acknowledgements
Introduction by Bruce Clayton
Thoughts on Neil Soutar, author of the original narrative

Northamptonshire County Golf Club

Clubhouse 1912

Clubhouse 2009

INTRODUCTION

The Remaining Years … A Perspective
"To business that we love we rise betime,
And go to't with delight".

William Shakespeare

The invitation to update the late Neil Soutar's splendid history of the Club for the occasion of our centenary is not only a great personal honour but also a source of infinite pleasure, if only because of the opportunity to research names of members from times past on honours boards where the gilding has faded. I thus thank Chris Thompson and his Management Committee for this chance to cover the fifteen years since Neil's publication was written and presented to our members.

Part of this assignment is relatively straightforward. I have sought to add to the list of those who have served the Club. I have written accounts of course alterations and the additional new holes. I make mention of the Clubhouse extension and improvements and of changes of staff personnel. All such matters are rather routine in nature and are, in essence, matters of fact and easy to provide.

What I have sought to do as an imperative, is to enlighten us all as to something of the names from past eras, which are resplendent on the honours boards and refer to people known only to a few of us.

The catalyst for this quest was an occasion, some years ago, when I was chatting by chance to George Mobbs. I said "Tell me George, do you remember Brigadier R Osborne-Smith?", having spotted his name on one of the honours boards in the gentlemen's locker room. "Yes" said George, "Bobby Osborne-Smith, an old Radleian, with whom I used to play in the Halford Hewitt. This was just after the war in the late forties, early fifties. He retired to the Channel Islands". Who else will remember him or many others likewise who were once prominent members, now mere names, lost in time like those carved on gravestones? So it is my intention to provide a chapter on our forebears, some illustrious, some comparatively ordinary, like myself. Apart from names evoking past times, I have written about people, characters, some of their peculiarities, traits, queer habits, extraordinary and unusual feats.

A certain iconography inevitably seems to permeate all golf club histories. That is, I suppose, a path into which I myself have been led and have followed in the hope that it forms an eclectic and disparate overview of some of our own characters, which a hundred years have produced.

It is hoped that some will provide mirth. Some may raise a smile if such an anecdote recalls to memory a long forgotten incident. I have, unashamedly, co-opted help from such purveyors of humour as R B Catlow and others and indeed by imploring help from the membership in general. All are set out in my chapter which is entitled Tales from the Locker Room. In the late Neil Soutar's narrative, when dealing with the earliest days of the Club, I found one or two anecdotes which were highly amusing. Without doubt such material is almost inevitably destined to be lost if not written somewhere. Similarly, memories of people fade. So it has become my earnest endeavour to say something of past members and tell our current membership something of their forebears.

Thoughts on Neil Soutar 1918-93, Author of the Original Narrative
First, perhaps, I should say something of this book's original author.
Neil Soutar was always a modest man of quiet, dignified demeanour. His name is coupled in the annals of the Chamberlain Cup with that of George Mobbs. "Mobbs and Soutar" rolls off the tongue as easily as Marks & Spencer. They won this important foursomes trophy twice and in their heyday presented a formidable combination. In his book, Neil says very little of himself as one knew he would. In actual fact he had much style about him and was a person of enormous integrity and strength of character.
I first met Neil, I say with some blushes, in the Bantam Cock Inn on Abington Square, a pub that remains to this day. This early meeting took place over fifty years ago when I was prevailed upon to call in there after leaving my office in the early evening. It was then a prestigious tavern in which a group of professional and businessmen forgathered in order to "anaesthetise themselves" after the trials and tribulations of the day - from labour to refreshment, so to speak. The late Mr Bernard "Chub" Merry held court there every evening and I was introduced to this pleasant establishment by Mr R J (Dick) Cowling, who was a young partner at Merry and Sons, Auctioneers of Fish Street, Northampton, who were very long established in the Northampton Cattle Market. Amongst others to whom I was introduced was Mr Bob Heron, head brewer of the Northampton Brewery Company who owned the pub. His friends were apt to chide him if the beer was not up to their usual expectations of excellence, all of which he took in good humour. In those days Northampton boasted two top class breweries, N B C and Phipps, who vied with each other for the town and county trade and who in later years merged. Quite a few directors and key personnel from both were keen members of our Golf Club.
The pub was run by a husband and wife, as managers. The lady was an old trouper from the stage who took infinite care with her makeup in her twilight years, perhaps as a palliative. Every evening players performing that week at the New Theatre (the local palace of varieties) would dash from the theatre during the interval for a quick pint and again after the show. They knew of "mine hostess's" former connection with the stage and gravitated there, as if drawn by some compulsive magnetic force. She must have had something about her!
As we sat chatting, in walked Neil Soutar to whom I was introduced. He was, as could be seen at a glance, an assured and urbane patrician-like man. I took an instant liking to this attentive figure who talked good sense all of the time. It was thus that an enduring friendship began with many social contacts over many years until the very day that Neil died, when we met for lunch with other friends.
As it so happens, contemporaneously, at The Racehorse (the pub next door to the Bantam Cock) another similar school met most evenings in like circumstance featuring, among others, the Coker twins, Jack Shine and Harry Austin.
Neil was the son of the late Mr Gordon Soutar, born in 1918 and educated at Uppingham. Inevitably, whatever else Neil might have had in mind as a career, the demands of the family business prevailed and thus he was drawn inexorably to the leather trade, so much

part of the local scene before and during the war years. The "mandarins" of our staple industries - the boot and shoe trade and the leather trade - have always featured large in the Club membership from the very beginnings of our existence, as one might expect. Neil was always a fine sportsman, excelling in hockey (a county player for many years and some time captain of this side), a more than average tennis player and, later, a fine golfer who represented the county of Northamptonshire. He was a handy and enthusiastic bridge player and always an interesting conversationalist. I served on the Northamptonshire Bench for 30 years as did Neil, part of which time he was a Deputy Chairman. He was always fair and judicious but strict when it was necessary and he never suffered fools gladly. Neil joined the Territorial Army in 1939 as did many of his generation in the county regiment. Neil's autobiography Round Half the World in Eighty Months is a first class and compelling read. In it we learn that by 1942 Neil was adjutant of the 2nd Battalion of the Northamptonshire Regiment and served in the campaign of the invasion of Madagascar and its seizure from the Vichy French by force, thus denying the Japanese any chance of the establishment of a naval base in the western part of the Indian Ocean, a distinct possibility in the dark days of 1942. Sadly the Vichy French government had allowed the Japanese to walk straight through their colonies in French Indo-China (nowadays Vietnam), not that they could do much about it, in fairness. However, they were distinctly awkward about their possessions in the Lebanon and Syria which the British had to fight for and take off them, as they did French North Africa and Madagascar. Neil served with some distinction in Madagascar, India, Persia, Syria, Egypt, Sicily, Italy and ended up in Austria at the end of the war as a major with Brigadier Toby Low, later Lord Aldington.

As to his golfing prowess, Neil was a single figure handicap player over many years. A family man, his late wife, Margaret, was a Lady member of the Club and past Ladies' Captain and they had four daughters. During his business career, Neil was a much travelled man and regularly visited South Africa. He was a good churchman and a former warden at All Saints Church in the heart of Northampton. Neil survived a heart attack and lived a very full life until 1998 when he died. In 1984, Neil was the Club Captain.

Bruce Clayton

CHAPTER I

The Birth (1909-1913)

*"Never hurry, never worry and always remember
to smell the flowers along the way"*

Walter Hagen

In 1066, the village of Brampton together with 60 acres of land, belonged to a man called Wulfmer, but the greater part of the surrounding area comprising more than 1900 acres, was held by the Scandinavian Leofric and his son Osmund. After the Norman Conquest King William I began to dispossess all the landowners in the Midlands and South of England and give their lands to his relations and friends. All the land round Brampton and stretching from Sywell to Dodford and Guilsborough to Towcester was given to The Count of Mortain, a half-brother to King William.

At this time Northamptonshire was heavily wooded, but during the next 400 years, much of the forest was reclaimed for pasture and the raising of sheep became the main activity of the County.

During the 15th century the Spencer family were making large profits from this sheep grazing industry and buying land with the proceeds and in 1508 Sir John Spencer bought Althorp Manor for £800 and established it as the family seat, and it remains in the family to this day. Sir Robert Spencer was created a Baron in 1603 and was reputedly the wealthiest man in England at the time.

Towards the end of the 19th century the game of golf was enjoying a mini explosion and by 1900 there were already four 18 hole courses in the area - Northampton, Kingsthorpe, Rugby and Kettering, and two 9 hole courses at Wellingborough and Market Harborough. There was also a 9 hole course opposite the Harborough Road Hospital and Lord Annaly had a 9 hole hole course by his home at Holdenby Manor with holes ranging from 151 to 293 yards.

All this interest in golf prompted some of the County dignitaries to think of forming a new club in the Brampton area and as a consequence a meeting was convened at County Hall on January 14, 1909 to discuss the matter. At this first meeting the Chair was taken by the Hon E A Fitzroy and about 20 gentlemen attended, including Lord Annaly, Lord Lilford, Mr H C Boycott, Mr D C Guthrie, Mr O C Wallis, Mr Frederick Bostock and Mr H A Millington, who was the Clerk to the County Council and probably arranged the venue for the meeting. It seems that the Hon E A Fitzroy was the driving force of the undertaking, as he was the first captain of the Club, a post he held from 1910-1918.

Edward Algernon Fitzroy was born in London on 24 July 1869, the younger son of Charles Fitzroy, third Baron Southampton. He was descended through the Duke of Grafton from Charles II. His Mother was a Lady of the Bedchamber to Queen Victoria, to whom Edward was a page of Honour. He was educated at Eton and Sandhurst and gazetted to the 1st Life Guards in 1889, but two years later on his marriage to Muriel Douglas-Pennant, his preference for the life of a country gentleman led him to retire to Northamptonshire where

Left: professionals Tom Ball, James Braid, J H Taylor and Ben Sayers

Below: the car park on opening day

he became a noted breeder of shorthorn cattle. In 1909 he entered the House of Commons as Conservative member for Daventry, a seat he held until his death. After service in France from 1914-1918 he returned to politics and in 1922 became Deputy Chairman of the Ways and Means Committee. In 1928 he was unanimously elected Speaker of the House of Commons - a post he held until his death from pneumonia in 1943. He had three sons and a daughter. He was a County Councillor for 25 years, a Deputy Lieutenant for the County and a Justice of the Peace. Following his death his wife was raised to the Peerage with the title in her own right of Viscountess Daventry. She presented the Fitzroy Cup to the Club which is competed for by the lady members of the Club.

At the first meeting at County Hall it was decided:

1 To proceed with the formation of a Golf Club and Course on land at Church Brampton near Dallington Heath.

2 The name of the Club to be the Northamptonshire County Golf Club.

3 That negotiations be entered into with Lord Spencer for a lease of land of about 200 acres for 35 years if possible but not less than 25 years.

4 That the Trustees of the Club should be Lord Annaly, Lord Lilford, the Hon E A Fitzroy and Mr D C Guthrie.

5 That the Club be a members club.

6 That a sub-committee, consisting of the Hon E A Fitzroy, Mr Guthrie, Mr Wallis and Mr Millington be formed for the purpose of drawing up the form of invitation to gentlemen in the neighbourhood to support the undertaking financially.

7 It was suggested that the Annual Subscription be £4.20 and no Entrance Fee for the first 100 members.

A second meeting was held at Mr Guthrie's home East Haddon Hall - at which Lord Ludlow, Mr Guthrie, Mr Schilizzi, Mr Wallis, Mr Millington and Mr H C Boycott were present. It was reported that the following amounts had been promised.

	DONATION	GUARANTEE
Mr Schilizzi	£200	£100
Lord Annaly	£50	£50
Lord Ludlow	£50	£50
Hon E A Fitzroy	£50	£50
Mr O C Wallis	£50	£50
Mr D C Guthrie	£100	£100
Mr Monckton	£50	£50
Mr Craig	£50	£50

It was decided to instruct Harry S Colt to proceed to lay out the course on a scheme not to exceed £1500, the date of his visit being confirmed as February 23. The course to be of 18 holes.

The remarkable thing about the formation of the Club was the speed with which it was established. From the inaugural meeting on January 14 1909 to the Official Opening on April 4 1910 was a mere 15 months. As will be seen later, it was, perhaps, a case of more haste less speed.

Harry S Colt, a tall red-head was born in 1869. He was educated at Monkton Combe, a public school near Bath. Golf was not available to the boys, but Harry was in the 1st Cricket X1, the 1st Rugby XV and in the 1st Rowing IV. He was also a prefect. At Clare College Cambridge golf was available at Coldham Common and he was awarded his blue in 1889 and captained the side in 1890 against Oxford. In the same year he obtained his law degree, and went to Hastings where he practised as a solicitor. Together with other solicitors he became involved in the beginnings of Rye Golf Club, and as a scratch player was the first Captain of the Club which opened in 1895. He was Hon Secretary from 1896 to 1899 and played the major part in designing the course. He had been a member of the R & A Rules Committee since 1897, and when Sunningdale advertised the post of Secretary in 1910 at a salary of £150 per annum, he won the position against 434 other applicants.

As the years progressed he became more and more involved in course architecture. He wrote four lengthy essays on golf courses covering Architecture, Construction, Bunkering and Greenkeeping, works which will possibly never be surpassed. He regarded a golf course as "a natural haven for the eternal joys of true golf".

Amongst the best known of the 50 courses he designed in Britain are Wentworth, Sunningdale, Moor Park (West), Ham Manor, Trevose, Rye, St Georges Hill, Stoke Poges, Copt Heath, Prestbury and Tandridge. He also re-modelled Muirfield, Lytham St Annes, Hoylake, Ganton, Portrush, Porthcawl and Formby.

Present members of Brampton are privileged to-day to play on a course which, with only small alterations, was designed by such a giant in his profession.

Harry Colt came on February 23 as arranged and laid out the course in two days! On 25 February Rev E E Eddows, the Curate of Brampton, and Mr H C Boycott were appointed

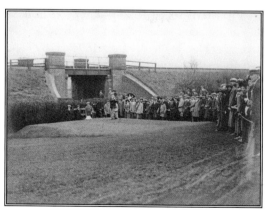

Top: Ben Sayers drives off the first tee
Middle: Bridge at the ninth hole
Bottom: J H Taylor drives off the tenth tee

joint Hon Secretaries and Mr A C Pearson was appointed Hon Treasurer. Harold Boycott lived at Pitsford and was a great sportsman. Besides being a 1 handicap golfer, he partnered L C (Turkey) Baillon at full back for England at hockey. He partnered J Faulkner Stops at tennis for the County, and he was a County cricketer. Alfred Pearson, who lived in Abington Park Parade, was an Accountant with the County Council for many years. He was also Treasurer for the County Cricket Club for 12 years, a keen sportsman and a violinist. He died in 1915 at the age of 61. There were two tenants on the land to be taken over for the course, a Mr Deacon and a Mr Morley. The main part of the land was leased by Mr Deacon who was paid compensation of £90 for giving up the land, but was allowed to graze his sheep free of charge until the Club rescinded the privilege. What are now the 1st and 18th fairways were under plough and had to be seeded, otherwise the land was pasture for grazing. Mr Morley leased some of the land adjacent to the new Practice Area, and this was taken over to enable a road to be built from Sandy Lane to the site of the course.

Construction of the course was to begin on March 8th with the clearing of hedgerows with the employed men on piecework which took four weeks. For the next three months the Committee met on the course every Sunday at 4.30 pm to monitor the work.

Construction of the rest of the course went ahead under the supervision of Mr Lucking who had been recommended by Harry Colt. The fairways were worked up and rolled (a heavy roller for the purpose had been loaned by Lord

Above: the sixth green. Below: the 10th fairway

Annaly) and a ton of Peruvian guano (dried bird droppings from seabirds on the coast of Peru) had been ordered as fertilizer for the fairways. Eight of the greens were turfed (Nos 1 2 7 8 9 11 17 & 18) and the remainder were worked up, cut, rolled and dressed. For the fairways of Nos 1 and 18 holes 80 bushels of Suttons best seeds were purchased for £80.35. Three small mowers - 2 x 14" and 1 x 16" were also bought from Shanks (the man who had invented the Lawn mower) and one 36" mower for the fairways. One horse and harness was also on the shopping list together with leather shoes so that the hooves did not spoil the turf. Discussion on construction of the bunkers was deferred until Mr Lucking and Rev Eddows had inspected the new course at Stoke. Rev Eddows must have been a versatile priest.

Whilst construction of the course went on apace, thoughts were given by the Committee to financing, and a General Meeting was called for July 3rd of donors and guarantors, but in the meantime plans were invited for the building of a Clubhouse.

On June 27th three sets of plans were submitted for the proposed Clubhouse by the Architects Mr H Norman, Mr F W Dorman and Mr G H Stevenson. Subject to the money being forthcoming, the plan of Mr Norman was accepted with minor alterations.

The Meeting of July 3rd held at County Hall was chaired by the Hon E A Fitzroy and Lord Annaly, Mr Guthrie, Mr J H Smith Mr Fred Bostock, Mr E R Bull, Mr C W Stringer, Rev Eddows and Mr H C Boycott (Joint Hon Secretaries) and Mr A C Pearson (Hon Treasurer) were present.

The statement of Accounts revealed that to June 30th donations totalled £805.50, Guarantees amounted to £1360, upon which the Club could borrow two thirds from the bank, and expenditure to date was £1008.24.

Spurred on by these financial results, the following week a sub-Committee drafted a circular inviting subscriptions by way of Debentures, to raise additional finance to cover the ongoing work on the course and the building of the Clubhouse.

At the same meeting an invitation to Len Holland, the Assistant Professional at

Harry Colt – course architect

Sheringham, to visit the course with a view to becoming the Club Professional was despatched. It was pointed out to Holland that his services would probably not be required until March 1st 1910.

It might be appropriate here to say a few words about Mr Guthrie who had been a tireless worker from the start of the undertaking.

David Charles Guthrie was born in 1861 and lived at East Haddon Hall, where he had beautiful gardens which he opened regularly to the public, not only to view, but also for picnics. Although greatly averse to public speaking, he was nevertheless persuaded to stand for South Northamptonshire in the General Election in 1893. Against all the odds he won the seat as a Liberal, but lost it 3 years later to the Conservative the Hon F E Douglas-Pennant. David Guthrie was obviously a great character. His family seat was at North Berwick, and returning from there with his chauffeur driving, they were reported for "furious driving at 30 mph".

The case came before the Magistrates at Carlisle. David Guthrie spoke on behalf of his chauffeur, and declared that he would not give a brass farthing for the testimony of the prosecution witness. In addressing the Chairman of the Bench as "My dear boy" which brought laughter in Court, he offered his car to anyone who could make it go at 30mph, extending the challenge to members of the Bench. The prosecution said that the worst feature of the case was that the car had killed a chicken. Mr Guthrie retorted "Chickens have no right on the road, they do not pay rates". The Magistrates were unimpressed with the defence and the chauffeur was fined £5 and

7

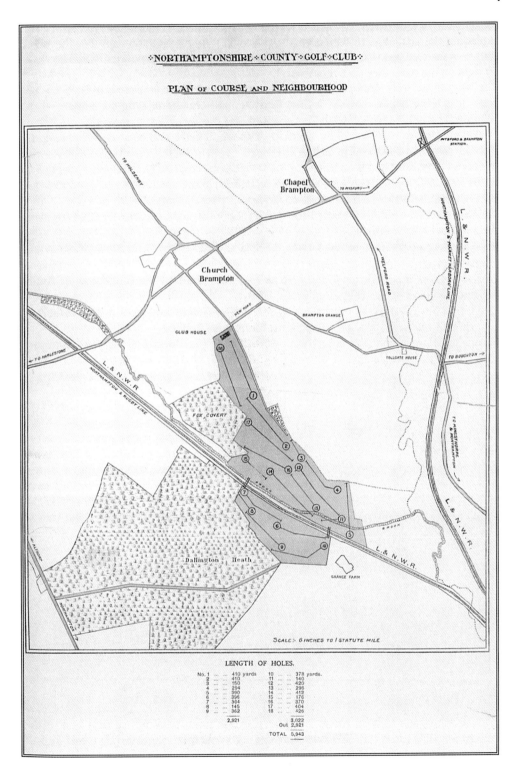

NORTHAMPTONSHIRE COUNTY GOLF CLUB

PLAN OF COURSE AND NEIGHBOURHOOD

SCALE:- 6 INCHES TO 1 STATUTE MILE

LENGTH OF HOLES.

No. 1	410 yards	10	378 yards.
2	410	11	140
3	150	12	420
4	294	13	296
5	390	14	412
6	396	15	176
7	364	16	370
8	145	17	404
9	362	18	426
	2,921		3,022
		Out	2,921
		TOTAL	5,943

costs. It is to be hoped that Mr Guthrie paid the fine, because relating the amount to the subscription rates of the Golf Club then and now, the fine would have amounted to £550! David Guthrie was High Sheriff for Northamptonshire in 1904, was an active member of the Pytchley hunt and a farmer. He died in 1918 aged 56.

By August 1st £1100 had been raised by the Debentures, and Len Holland was appointed as the Professional, but he was also expected to take an active interest in the upkeep of the course, a requirement which soon caused friction after his appointment.

The new road 9ft wide from Sandy Lane to the Clubhouse was approved for £200 to enable the builders to reach the site.

Rev Eddows reported that he was leaving the area so Mr H C Boycott was confirmed as sole Hon Secretary.

On October 1st the tender of William Heap for construction of the Clubhouse for £2299 was approved and work was to begin immediately.

On November 4th 1909 another General Meeting of donors and guarantors was held at County Hall where important matters for the future were decided.

32 original Donors and Guarantors were elected as original members and were exempted from paying an Entrance Fee.

A draft of the Rules of the Club was produced, discussed and approved. (At one meeting!)

The following appointments were made:

President Lord Spencer, Vice Presidents Lord Althorp, Lord Annaly, Lord Lilford, Captain Hon E A Fitzroy, Hon Secretary H C Boycott, Hon Treasurer A C Pearson Hon Auditor J E A Wyatt, Trustees Lord Annaly, Lord Lilford, Hon E A Fitzroy, Mr D C Guthrie, General Committee F Bostock H A Millington C W Stringer O C Wallis J H Smith.

It was resolved that the Committee be authorised forthwith to invite 170 gentlemen and 70 ladies to become members of the Club upon the following terms:

Gentlemen £3.15 Subscription, £4.20 Entrance Fee

Ladies £1.05 Subscription, £2.63 Entrance Fee

The Committee were authorised to borrow £3000 at an interest rate of no more than 4% upon the security of Debentures already given and charged on the Club property.

It will be obvious to anyone reading this account of the early years of the Club that the

William Berridge – greenkeeper

Northamptonshire County Golf Club was founded by the landed gentry and their friends for the landed gentry and their friends, and it is not surprising that Brampton has been regarded as the "snobs" Club by other Clubs in the town and county. The original members would not, however, have been embarrassed by having attracted this sobriquet. Despite the obvious wealth of a large number of its members, it is perhaps surprising that for many years the Club struggled to meet its financial obligations, and there are many instances of creditors being kept waiting for their money and indeed often being paid by instalments. The work, however, went on apace. The course was being constructed, the Clubhouse was being built, a Professional had been engaged and now applications were invited for the post of Steward to run the Clubhouse and the successful pair were Mr and Mrs Maisey. Stabling for two horses was built left of the 17th green in Fox Covert and plans submitted for a motor shed, stabling and Caddy shelter behind the Clubhouse.

By February 1910 there were 114 gentlemen and 52 lady members; a telephone was installed in the Clubhouse for an annual rate of £32 to make 900 calls during the year, and a Mr Brown had offered to provide a taxi service from Chapel Brampton & Pitsford Station to the Clubhouse for a return fee of 8p. Lord Annaly had a private 9 hole golf course at his home in Holdenby, where he employed a Mr Chart as Professional. As Len Holland was finding the work of Professional and course supervisor too onerous, Lord Annaly released Chart to become Assistant to Holland at Brampton but to be mainly concerned with course maintenance.

The total raised by Debentures was now £2200 and plans were laid for the Official Opening of the course on April 7th. By that date there were over 200 members and a sizeable crowd assembled for the occasion. J H Taylor of Mid Surrey, Tom Ball of West Lancs, Ben Sayers of North Berwick and James Braid of Walton Heath played singles matches in the morning. Tom Ball (82) beat J H Taylor (83) by one hole, but James Braid (80) comfortably beat Ben Sayer who took 86.

The Official Opening was made by HSH Prince Francis of Teck - brother to Queen Mary - and a luncheon was held in the Clubhouse at which there were many distinguished guests. In his speech Prince Francis said he was unique in that he had never sworn after playing a shot, had never sliced, hooked or topped a ball, and never missed a putt. The reason was he had never played golf.

The Treasurer reported that expenditure to date was £3643 of which £3009 had been subscribed: H C Boycott was highly praised for his work for the Club.

Len Holland –
Club professional

In the afternoon a foursome was played by the Professionals in which England (Taylor & Ball) defeated Scotland (Braid & Sayer) by 2 and 1.

The original clubhouse plan

And so, after the Official opening, members were free to practise their skills against the tests set by Harry Colt.

Let us try and conjure up a picture of what it was like in April 1910 to play round Brampton.

In the car park would have been a few fine examples of early motor cars, and in the stables (the wooden sheds still standing) would have been some members' horses who had ridden to the course. Others would have come by Mr Brown's taxi from Chapel Brampton & Pitsford Station; those members living in the Bramptons would have walked. There would be some caddies in the caddy shelter waiting to be hired at 8p per round, and organised by Jack Taylor the caddymaster, who would have been in his hut, which stood by the lst Championship tee.

The 18th green was not where it is now but was on the 9 hole putting green. The lst tee was immediately left of the present 18th green and the hole was 40 yards shorter than today. On the teeing ground would have been a container full of sand from which one made a mini sand castle upon which to place your ball before driving off. There were no such things as tee pegs in those days. Immediately ahead was a sizeable bunker about 100 yards from the tee. There were no stands of conifers between the 1st and 18th fairways and no spinney behind the 1st green.

The bunker on the right of the crossway was two small bunkers and a similar one corresponded on the left of the fairway. There was a bunker on the right about 280 yards from the tee and four bunkers guarded the green.

The selection of clubs that one had to attack the course were all hickory shafted, and there was a choice of four woods - a driver, brassie, spoon and baffie, corresponding to Nos 1, 2, 3 & 4 woods today, and the irons consisted of cleek, mid-iron, jigger, mashie, mashie-niblick, niblick and putter. There were no such things as a pitching wedge or sand wedge.

The men would have been playing in plus twos or knickerbockers as they were then known, and the ladies in long skirts. The par of the course at this time was 77, but as the spring turned to summer the rough would have got longer and longer because it was only cut once a year to make hay for the horses for winter feeding. When one considers these conditions and the 110 bunkers that were on the course as opposed to less than 50 today, the feat of Len Holland going round in 64 in 1923 was truly remarkable, especially as although being a superb iron player he was regarded as a poor putter by top standards.

The Committee were now giving thought to the arrangements within the Clubhouse. Lockers were charged at 25p per annum, and it was decided to instal radiators in the locker room and drying room costing £90

Jack Taylor (caddymaster), Len Holland (professional) and George Riches (assistant professional)

including hot water in the kitchen and lavatories. Perhaps it rained more in those days, but a drying room is not considered necessary today. There was no electricity laid on and the Clubhouse was lit by gaslamps. The following newspapers were available in the Gentlemen's lounge - The Morning Post, Daily Mail, Daily Chronicle, the Sportsman, the Field, Country Life, the Sporting Times and Hurst's Sporting & Dramatic. All the Ladies had were the Morning Post and Ladies Field. Male chauvinism was soon in operation, but it was decided to appoint a Ladies Captain and a Ladies Hon Secretary (who paid no subscription) and it was agreed to join the Ladies Golf Union and the Mens Midland Golf Union.

At this time – we are now in the summer of 1910 – Lord Annaly provided a Golf House to the left of the 13th green. It still exists today but is hidden by trees and shrubs and never used except perhaps in a sudden thunderstorm.

In May 1910 Mr F H Burn presented a £10.50 Cup which was to be for a Mens handicap

18 hole Knockout Competition limited to 24 handicap.

The arrangements by which the Club Professional was to be responsible for course maintenance as well as teaching duties, shoe and club cleaning and other chores came to a head, when Len Holland said he did not have time to attend to the supervision of the course, and as a result his assistant Mr Chart was appointed greenkeeper under the Greens Committee which was chaired by Mr Fred Bostock - an expert gardener.

Medal Competitions had been started in the summer for which the winner - both Lady and Gentleman - received a top golf ball priced at 13p. In July it was decided to hold a two-day Autumn Meeting, but by the middle of September, most of the greens had deteriorated to such an extent that 10 holes Nos 6, 7, 8, 9, 10, 11, 12, 14, 16 and 18 were closed and temporary greens established and the Autumn meeting was cancelled. It was, however to be replaced by a Knock Out Competition, similar to the Burn Cup but to be played in the Autumn, and was the Cup presented by Mr O C Wallis, now played for as a Medal Competition at our Autumn Meeting.

This closing of so many greens was a fairly drastic measure after only 6 months play, but it appears that the heavy iron roller was too severe and two wooden rollers were ordered to replace it. A further ton of Peruvian guano and 6 bushels of Suttons best Greens seed were also to be procured, so that the rested greens could be dressed and patch sown. 5 of the closed greens - Nos 7, 8, 9, 11 and 18 had originally been turfed, so one wonders whether the speed of construction mentioned in the first paragraph of this history had been too rapid to have been done properly. Another factor was whether the absence of a qualified greenkeeper from the outset had not been a false economy. With further treatment to other greens being recommended by Suttons, it was resolved to appoint an expert greenkeeper , and on 3rd November 1910 William Berridge, at that time Greenkeeper at Sudbrook Park, was engaged full time at £1.75 per week, the Club to pay his removal expenses. Initially Len Holland, William Berridge, his wife and baby Jim took lodgings in the farmhouse behind the 14th green, but later Lord Spencer gave £500 to build the greenkeeper's cottage, still in use today.

The story of the Stewards at Brampton between 1910 and 1914 could seemingly have been written about almost any period in the Club's 85 year history.

The first to be appointed in 1910 prior to the opening were Mr and Mrs Maisey, who had free board and lodging in the Clubhouse and were to provide meals for members as required, to keep the whole place clean and to run the bar. They lasted about 18 months, by which time there were many complaints about the value that the members were receiving, and by February 1912 they were given notice and the Committee decided to do their own catering, fixing prices to be charged. Following this decision, the Committee advertised for a Steward and Stewardess in the Daily Telegraph, the Morning Post, Golf Illustrated and the Field. Two Committee members travelled to London to interview a short list of seven. Prices were fixed at Hot Lunch 10p, Cold Lunch at 8p and Tea and Jam and Cake at 3p. Champagne was at 50p a bottle. As a result Mr and Mrs Allfrey were appointed at £1 per week. The Club engaged a Parlour maid at £35 per year with a boy from the village to help. The Steward was also responsible for collecting Green Fees from visitors. They took up their duties in March 1912. By May Mrs Allfrey had left her husband and Mr and Mrs Gardner were appointed on a months trial. At the end of July the trial was considered unsatisfactory and they were given notice. Then Mr Downton, butler to General Smith Dorian, and his wife were engaged from August lst at £60 per year and given £2 towards their removal expenses. All went well for a few months but then the ladies started complaining about the amount they were getting for their 3p tea and on May 4 1913 Downton, his wife and the Parlour maid all gave in their notice and the saga continued. "Plus ça change plus c'est la même chose" as the French would say.

During this period work was going on implementing the original design by Harry Colt. Bunkers were constructed and sand filled, the sand coming from the pit to the right of the 3rd green, and unwanted bumps on some of the greens were flattened out and returfed. There appears to have been trouble with the 15th green, perhaps due to flooding, because there was a strong proposal to do away with the 15th green and make a new par 3 hole parallel to the railway and going left of the 5th tee, and to move the 16th tee behind the stream to make a longer dog-leg hole. After Colt was consulted, however, the proposal was dropped. This was fortunate as the 15th has been regarded for years as one of the best par 3 holes in the Midlands. By now (the end of 1910) William Berridge had been appointed and the course work was much improved. It was an inspired decision to appoint Holland and Berridge (as against the stewards) who were both experts in their professions and got the Club off to a fine start.

Holland stayed with the Club for 14 years until he moved to Gerrards Cross, and Berridge remained at Brampton until his death in 1940.

In 1911 the Committee had approached the London and North Western Railway to ask whether they would build a Station at Church Brampton to enable golfers to use the facility, and surprisingly enough the request was agreed to and a Station was built between Church Brampton and Harlestone by the bridge over the Church Brampton / Harlestone road. The little Station, presided over by its own Stationmaster Mr T L Glass who had moved up from Euston to take command, was a mere half mile walk from the Clubhouse. The 120 yard long platforms each had their timber buildings flanking the tracks, and housed booking offices, waiting rooms and offices. The trip with joining from

Match v. Leamington County Golf Club.
September 28th 1911.

Singles

R.S.Lees	0	v	L.J.Bigg	1
H.C.Boycott	1	v	Gerald Osborne	0
E.Bostock	0	v	R.Curle	1
N.Bostock	1	v	A.C.S.Glover	0
H.C.Oldrey	0	v	H.Smith Turberville	1
L.H.Gay	0	v	Major Lloyd Carson	0
H.Mobbs	0	v	Captain C.French	1
C.Cooper	1	v	Leigh Hoskyns	0
	3			4

Foursomes

R.S.Lees and H.C.Boycott	1	v	L.J.Bigg and Gerald Osborne	0
E.Bostock and N.Bostock	1	v	R.Curle and A.C.S.Glover	0
H.C.Oldrey and L.H.Gay	0	v	H.Smith Turberville and Major L.Carson	1
H.Mobbs and C.Cooper	1	v	Captain C.French and Leigh Hoskyns	0
	3			1

An example of how early records were kept

Northampton Castle Station took 5 minutes and there were five trains a day in each direction. As the service was part of a rail link to Long Buckby and beyond, trains only stopped at the new station as required, so golfers had to notify the guard as they embarked at Northampton that their destination was the Golf Club.

Not surprisingly, for in 1912 participation in sport on the Sabbath was not encouraged, there were no trains on Sundays. The fare was under 2p each way.

The onerous work of Honorary Secretary, since the departure of Rev Eddows, was too much for Harold Boycott on his own, and it was decided to employ a paid Secretary, and in January 1911 Mr L H Gay from Exmouth was selected from 41 applicants at a salary of £120 per year. He was to have a table, typewriter, chair and filing cabinet. Lord Spencer, his sons and daughters, H A Millington and H C Boycott were elected Honorary Life members of the Club, together with A C Pearson as long as he held the post of Hon Treasurer.

At the AGM in April 1911 the Entrance Fees were increased to £5.25 for Gentlemen and £3.15 for Ladies and Subscriptions raised to £4.20 and £2.10 respectively.

As the summer matured, members were anxious to have water laid on to the greens and an estimate of £393 was obtained. The Committee decided they could not afford this, but a letter was sent to all members asking for donations to be given towards the cost of the work (almost the first levy!). Within 5 months £250 had been given, so it was decided to carry out the work this side of the railway, the work to begin after Christmas.

At the next AGM in April 1912 A C Pearson retired as Hon Treasurer owing to pressure of work (he was also Hon Treasurer of Northampton Golf Club and the County Cricket Club) and Mr B Cheney - an accountant with the local authority - was appointed. He subsequently became one of the Captains of the Club.

The Club was now gradually getting into profit although it still had an overdraft in excess of £2000, but was able to pay off £300 from the 1913-1914 accounts, leaving a profit of £9 on the year.

On April 29th 1914 we hosted the Midlands Professional Golf Championship, the first competition outside the County to be staged at Church Brampton.

At the AGM in April 1914 W J Watkins and A J Fraser, both brewers and both future Captains of the Club were elected to the Committee to join Sir Mervyn Manningham Buller and H A Millington, and H C Palmer of Palmer & Co was appointed Auditor.

Brampton Grange was farmed by Mr Bert Drage when the club first started. He was a farmer, but being a very keen horseman, he became more interested in this occupation and having extensive stabling at the farm, he became a well-known dealer in thoroughbred hunters, no doubt a more lucrative business. He was very friendly with Herbert Mobbs (father of Humphrey, George and Roger) and together they reminisced about pre-War hunting when the Pytchley had two packs of hounds and hunted Fridays, Saturdays and Mondays and the guests would play golf at Brampton on the Sunday.

In advancing years, it was Herbert Mobbs who persuaded Bert Drage to take up golf and he played almost every day at 10 30am on his own and usually just the first three and last two holes. It is ironic that now he was bitten with the golf bug, he realised his mistake that when the Golf Club was first established he had adamantly refused to allow a road across his land in order to build the proposed clubhouse in the region of the third green, and hence in the middle of the course to provide alternative starting places.

CHAPTER II

Childhood (1914-1925)

*"Golf, like measles, should be caught young, for if
postponed to riper years, the results may be serious"*

P G Wodehouse

The Club did not have a particularly happy early childhood. Storm clouds were gathering in 1914, and the chatter in the Clubhouse was of the possibility of the outbreak of war. William Berridge and his small band of men were working hard on the course and his wife and young family were well established in the Greenkeeper's cottage, but Len Holland had married and had moved into a house in Kingsthorpe Grove, almost opposite the Kingsthorpe Golf Club.

The war with Germany began in August 1914, and by October, the military had sited three rifle ranges on the far side of the railway line dividing the course, so that the 10th 11th 12th 13th and 14th holes were in the danger zone and the Army posted red flags to warn members when firing practice was in operation.

Men began to be enlisted, including one of the clubhouse staff - C Elliott - and the Committee generously agreed to pay his mother 50p per week for the duration of the war. Mr Gay, the Club Secretary, joined the East Lancs Regt and he was given leave of absence on November 4th, the Club to continue to pay his salary. This was subsequently rescinded in 1916 when he was appointed a Captain in the Regiment.

With the departure of Mr Gay, Mr Bertram Cheney took over his Secretarial duties and also kept the house books, but six months later, following the death of Mr A C Pearson, he was also appointed Treasurer. Len Holland was made responsible for ensuring that green fees were paid.

The Club minutes of Committee Meetings were now becoming very spasmodic, but it was soon apparent that with reduced play on the Course, and thereby reduced income from green fees and the Clubhouse, the Club began to run into financial difficulties, and measures had to be taken to reduce costs, and increase bar prices to boost the income. At the same time, it was resolved and accepted by the Debenture Holders that no dividends would be paid on the Debentures for the foreseeable future. An application for members serving on active service to have their subscriptions reduced was turned down by the Committee.

William Berridge was unfit for military service, so he remained as Head Greenkeeper with four men to help him together with two horses, but in appreciation of his hard work, he was given a £10 bonus at Christmas 1915 and his four men each received £2.

Meanwhile Len Holland, who had now little work to do teaching or selling in the shop, went to British Chrome Tanning Company, run by W P Cross, where he became reputedly one of the best Kidskin tanners in the County. He had also failed his medical. The loss on the year 1915 was £52, even though no Debenture interest had been paid, and in view of the large stock of cigarettes in the bar, they were offered for sale at 35p per hundred to clear the stock.

The Course was on occasion closed completely for Army manoeuvres and play was seldom possible on the far side of the railway. Early in 1916 the War Office asked for all the forage from grass cutting to be given to the Army, but after negotiations the Club was allowed to keep 6 tons.

In the middle of 1916 the Voluntary Aid Detachment (V.A.D) a branch of the British Red Cross Society, took over the Clubhouse as a military hospital and convalescent home. A small part of the North end of the Clubhouse was kept open as a Men's changing room, but otherwise the Clubhouse and all its facilities were closed to all members. It was staffed by what to-day we would call paramedics, and during the two years that it operated as a hospital 832 patients passed through it's doors. It took patients from Other Ranks from all branches of the Services, but the Berridges had to give up their front sitting room where they gave meals to Officers visiting their men in hospital, and to other Officers who were on the firing range. Mrs Berridge was responsible for the catering. The day

The Club's first tractor

before guests were due, a cart with two soldiers on board, drawn by two black horses used to bring the food, with white bread and butter and all the extra provisions that the Berridges never saw on their own menu. Mr and Mrs Berridge were both musical and entertained the patients with songs at the piano. Only one patient died during the war. He was a Canadian soldier who is buried in Church Brampton Churchyard.

William Berridge's other jobs were to keep the boilers going and dispense bandages used in the hospital.

The Steward - Jeffery - and the barmaid Miss Woolley were retained to serve the patients. The Red Cross paid the whole of Miss Woolley's salary and £30 per year against the salary of the Steward.

By March 1917 the Club's finances had further deteriorated showing a loss of £82 on the year and further economies were made. The Steward was dispensed with, the course on the far side of the railway was closed permanently and the area was let out to Mr Deacon for sheep grazing at £10 per year. As the rifle ranges were still in operation, it is to be wondered whether any wayward shooting resulted in the disappearance of the odd sheep. The outdoor staff was further reduced and one of the remaining horses was sold.

At the AGM in April 1917, there were no nominations for the Committee, so Mr Millington and Mr Wallis were co-opted to serve. There were only four members present at the meeting.

The operation of the Club as a Golf Club had by now almost ceased and there were no meetings until March 1918. In this year two of the Founder members of the Club, both of whom had done enormous work for the Club, died. Mr David Guthrie died early in January aged 56 and Lieut Harold Boycott was killed by a shell in France on March 21st. The AGM was held at the Grand Hotel in April.

On October 18th, just before the Armistice, Mr W A S Talbot was elected Hon Secretary and Hon Treasurer, and Lord Spencer agreed to extend the lease of the land for a further four years.

With the dawning of the New Year, the Club began to function again. Len Holland was re-engaged from March 28th at £150 per year, the Subscriptions were raised to £6.30 for Men and £4.20 for Ladies, and the Green fees were set at 25p for Sundays and 18p through the week. The Hon E A Fitzroy stood down after 8 years as Captain and Mr Neville Bostock was appointed Captain. A lot of damage had been done to the Clubhouse when in use as a hospital and £250 had to be spent on repair and refurbishment. Only £50 of this was paid by V.A.D. We also at this time hear mention of vandalism on the course, referred to in the minutes as "roughs" and Superintendent Buller of the Police was put in charge of the problem.

For the next 6 years, up to 1925, the Club struggled gamely to get back to viability after the war. The Clubhouse had needed extensive refurbishment, the course had had little work done on it and had been trampled by Army hob-nailed boots and the membership had dropped from 342 to 193 resulting in considerable loss of income. Prices on the other hand were escalating. Mr Neville Bostock was Captain for 1919, but then Mr Alfred Fraser had a spell of 5 years as Captain. Under his guidance with the considerable help of Herbert Millington, Fred Bostock and Bertram Cheney, the Club began to find it's feet again. Stringent economies were made, and in this respect none suffered more than the ground staff whose wages were cut three times in 15 months by a total of 18%. It does not appear that salaried staff suffered any similar reduction. A loss on the bar account was discovered and after a report from a professional stocktaker, it transpired that suppliers had been overcharging, members were being given credit at the bar and accounts had been carelessly supervised. As a result Mr Talbot, the Honorary Secretary resigned. Miss A G Hughes the paid Secretary took over the position. Miss Hughes and her sister, who helped in the office, lived at the Old House at Harlestone, and cycled daily to the club with wicker baskets on the handlebars of their machines to carry their handbags and other personal possessions. At the same time subscriptions were increased to £7.35 for Men and £4.20 for Ladies, no credit was to be given at the bar, and a drive to increase membership was put into operation.

The Club hierarchy seemed to be rather at odds with the R & A over some matters, for they rejected a new scheme for Men's handicaps proposed by the R & A, and also disagreed about the S.S.S of the course as assessed by the R & A. Following the latter incident, a representative from the governing body came down and played the course and pronounced the S.S.S. as 77 which figure was accepted by the Committee. Monthly medals were started on the 1st Thursday in each month. On the 3rd Saturday there was a Bogey competition. The Men's Spring and Autumn Meetings were both a three day affair of which a typical format was:

      Thursday AM 18 hole Medal
      PM 18 hole Foursomes
      Friday AM 18 hole Bogey
      Saturday 36 hole Medal

The Ladies were allotted two consecutive days for their Spring and Autumn Meetings.

In 1921 a letter was sent to Captain Drummond, who lived in the house now occupied by the Boys Grammar School at Pitsford, asking him to invite the Royal Princes to become Honorary members of the Club and to use it's facilities. Capt Drummond had a close connection with the Royal Family, and the Prince of Wales had a close connection with his wife. The Duke of York accepted the invitation but the Prince of Wales did not.

An Exhibition match was played on Sep 28th 1922 by the Professionals Vardon, Havers, Ray and Holland but no details of the results are available. Holland at this time was released occasionally to teach at the London Golf School at the request of the R & A.

The Committee now made a serious appraisal of the financial state of the Club and decided that something fairly drastic should be done to put the Club on a sound financial footing following the depradation of the war. There was a considerable overdraft about which the Bank was becoming anxious, but with the membership increasing (by 1922 it was back to pre-war levels) it was decided to try and buy the land from the Spencer Estate, reduce the overdraft, and make a Debenture flotation to pay for both these ambitions. After much deliberation and lobbying of the opinion of members and other parties, particularly the existing Debenture holders, the following package was put together:

1. A new issue of 1000 £5 Debentures at 5% interest would be floated to raise £5000.
2. Existing holders of the £10 4% Debentures would be offered 50% cash value of their holding or exchange them for £5 Debentures of the new issue.
3. To buy the land of the course (136 and a half acres) from the Spencer Estate for £3000 repayable over 30 years at 5% interest.
4. To relieve the existing Guarantors of their commitment.

This proposition was accepted unanimously by the existing Debenture holders on Feb 25th 1924, the purchase of the land was completed after many hiccups with the Estate's solicitors and the new issue of Debentures was approved at an Extraordinary General Meeting on Sep 11th the same year.

Trustees of the new issue were Miss Bouverie, Mr G H Winterbottom, Mr H W Dover and Mr A S Garrard. The deeds of the land were placed with the National Provincial Bank, but an occasional overdraft of £500 would be sanctioned without security.

This paragraph can be quickly written and read, but it required a tremendous amount of work, particularly by the Hon Treasurer Bertram Cheney who was offered a gratuitous payment of £25 for the extra work he had done. It is not recorded whether it was accepted.

The General Committee had also over this period streamlined it's work, by giving the House and Greens Committees authority to make their own decisions on expenditure subject to an annual budget which they each submitted to the General Committee for approval.

This policy was perhaps an early example of subsidiarity!

It is perhaps of interest at this point to show the membership statistics from pre-war to 1924.

Years	Gentlemen	Ladies	Total
1914	227	115	342
1918	121	72	193
1919	182	86	268
1920	218	103	321
1921	233	115	348
1922	256	125	381
1923	244	130	374
1924	250	131	381

And so, with 1925 just around the corner, the Club owned its own land, had a fine course and clubhouse, a membership approaching 400, the new issue of Debentures had been oversubscribed, and the profit for the year 1923/24 had been a record £325. All in all an achievement of considerable merit following the ravages of World War I.

The teenager had developed into a responsible Youth.

The Clubhouse during the first War

CHAPTER III

Youth (1926-1944)

"Golf is like a love affair. If you don't take it seriously it is not fun.
If you do take it seriously it breaks your heart"

Arnold Daly

T
he year 1926 was difficult, not only for the Golf Club, but for the country as a whole. There was dissatisfaction from employees with low wages that were being paid, Golf Club members were feeling the pinch and there were many applications from members to have their subscriptions reduced on various grounds, some reasonable and some spurious, but the Committee was taking a hard line on all financial matters. The Secretary Miss A G Hughes had put in her resignation and it was decided that the Club could not afford a straight replacement. A package deal was put to Mr Cheney who was acting as Hon Secretary and Hon Treasurer, for him also to do the work of Miss Hughes at a salary of £100 per year, subject to the consent of his employers, the County Accountants Department. This was agreed and he took on her responsibilities. It was proposed to Mr Bailey the Steward that if he was paid an extra £20 per year he would dispense with one of the maids. After discussion of the proposal he refused and resigned. At the same time the Committee discussed the possibility of dispensing with the Caddymaster, but this was not agreed.

There were over 30 caddies employed by the Club divided into lst and 2nd class, who were obliged to wear a badge. On booking a caddy each member had to pay 2p to the Caddymaster who allotted caddies, supervised car parking and generally kept the area tidy. The booking fees were paid to the Club which revenue just about covered the wages of the Caddymaster, there being over 200 caddie sorties per week. Members were advised not to give more than 2p as a tip to their caddy.

The close control of finances was brought about because for the year ending 28 Feb 1926 the Club made a loss of £14, but there was general unrest in the country about low wages and exploitation of labour particularly in the mining industry which led up to the General Strike on 29 April 1926, one day after the Club's AGM, which brought the whole country to a standstill. The strike in fact collapsed after 9 days, but the poor relations between employers and employees was plain for all to see.

Although work on redecoration of the Clubhouse was deferred, money was still spent on the course, and a motor tractor with tip cart and draw bars was purchased for £132. This was housed in the shed that used to stand on the left of the 7th fairway (the site is remembered by the copper beech tree planted by Mrs Beryl Harrison during her year of Captaincy). One of the horses thereby became redundant and was sold for £27.50.

Following the resignation of the Steward, Mr & Mrs Keay were appointed, he being the butler to Mr Guiness of Greens Norton.

In spite of an attempt still to dispense with one of the maids, this was not agreed by the new steward and two new maids were engaged at £30 and £24 per year respectively.

The Committee was, however, more helpful in other directions as judges at Assize and their families and home and visiting County cricketers when playing at Northampton or Kettering were given the courtesy of the course. The course was now, with its new tractor and gang mowers, getting into good shape following the War, but it must be remembered that in those days plantain weeds which were plentiful on the fairways, had to be removed singly by hand, there being no selective weedkillers as we enjoy today, although experiments were taking place with their production.

At the AGM in April 1927 The Duke and Duchess of York were elected Honorary Members. As far as is known that privilege has never been withdrawn, so HM The Queen Mother was an Honorary Member of our Club.

Sheep were again grazed on the course between 1st May and 1st October but had to be shepherded at all times.

The following year the Professional Midlands Foursome Competition was played at Brampton. Shortly afterwards the Caddymaster Taylor resigned to take up an appointment as Professional and Greenkeeper at St Neots GC and RSM Warren was appointed Caddymaster to succeed him.

For the next ten years the Club had a rollercoaster experience as far as finances were concerned. A Summary shows the picture.

YEAR	PROFIT £	LOSS £
1927	79	-
1928	52	-
1929	15	-
1930	195	-
1931	210	-
1932	-	105
1933	-	466
1934	349	-
1935	365	-
1936	40	-
1937	-	56
TOTAL	1305	627

So the Club was only averaging a profit of £61 a year over the period.

During the period of the 1930s there was turmoil both political and financial in many parts of the world. Japan invaded China in 1932. After the Wall Street crash in 1929 there was a period of many years of economic difficulty in industry, and the Shoe trade - the staple industry of Northampton - was on a 3-day week for most of the shoe factories. It was a time of the rise of the Dictators Stalin, Hitler, Mussolini and Franco and Italy's invasion of Ethiopia and the Spanish Civil War were all part of this troubled time. On the golfing front Len Holland had been appointed Professional at Gerrards Cross Golf Club and left in 1924. The following year he took William Berridge's son Jim as his Assisstant, and W G (Bill) Saunders from Brocton Hall came as Professional to Brampton. He had been Assistant to Len Holland when he was Professional at Sheringham, so no doubt Holland had recommended him. He was a good golfer and a popular member of the Staff, and was given leave to play in a Tournament in France and also to accompany the Duke

The Duke of York – captain 1931

of York on a golfing trip to Scotland and then to play in the Open Championship.

The supply of water round the course was unsatisfactory around 1930 and a new scheme of water distribution costing £450 and including the old Pump House to the left of the 5th tee was approved, but it was decided to try and raise the money by members' donations, a common practice in the Club up to World War 11. Within 3 months the money was raised. In 1930 Miss Hughes who had been helping as Competitions Secretary finally resigned altogether and out of 220 applications Col W K Bourne was appointed at £200 per year, and took his first meeting on 14th Sept. Bertram Cheney reverted to Hon Treasurer.

The Duke of York who was an Hononary Member with a handicap of 14 and a good golf swing took over the Captaincy of the Club in April 1931. It appears, however, that it was an Honorary position because he did not attend any meetings of the Committee during his term of office but did present a cup on it's conclusion.

In 1932 Lord Spencer - President of the Club - gave a lot of trees consisting of Scotch Firs, Douglas Firs and Norwegian Pines to the Club. These can be seen today at the back of the lst green, behind the 8th tee, behind the 13th green and to the left of the 18th green. In the Clubhouse, lighting was still by gas lamp but it was now decided to bring the Clubhouse and Cottage in to the Age of Electricity and tenders were invited for the Contract. The Electric Light Co installed the mains for £14.38, but the contract for all the wiring and fittings of the Clubhouse and Cottage went to V W C Jupp who had an electrical shop in St Giles Street, but was better known as captain of the Northamptonshire County Cricket Club, who in his career scored 13,656 runs and took 1078 wickets, six times doing the double of 1000 runs and 100 wickets. His price for the job was £32!

William Berridge, the Club's first Greenkeeper, had done a fine job over the years, although during the many financial crises in the Club, his wages and those of his staff were invariably the first ones to be cut. Conversely the Committees had always given the course priority over the Clubhouse where financial expenditure was concerned. This, happily, has been the policy throughout the Club's history, and remains so today. Brampton wants to be a first class golf course with Clubhouse facilities sufficient to support the people who play golf, rather than a Social Club where golf is one of the passing interests. The work which had been done on the course and in the Clubhouse in the early 1930s was to receive a big jolt when losses for 1932 and 1933 amounted to over £570. This was big money in those days and may have resulted from the rapid turnover of Secretaries during the period. Whatever the reason, Draconian measures of economy were put in hand once again including a cut in the green staff wages, the sacking of the Steward and Cook to replace them with a married couple, a suspension of Entrance fees for 6 months to encourage new members, a reduction in Green fees to encourage more visitors and a reduction in Debenture interest from 5% to 4%. Following these measures 76 new members were elected during the next 5 months, and by 1934 the Club was back in profit and membership had risen to 455.

Two stalwart original members died in 1934, Mr G H Winterbottom and Mr C C Marshall, both of whom had served many years on the Committee. Mr Winterbottom lived at Horton House, an estate he had bought from Mr Pickering Phipps, but following his death Horton House was dismantled brick by brick and rebuilt at Overstone Park by a Mr Gandy who opened it as a Restaurant and Reception Centre.

A period of prosperity followed the dark days of 1932/33 when Col Dening was given a 5 year Contract as Secretary at £250 p.a and the inevitable discussion on "Dogs on the Course" raised its head again which resulted in a good old English compromise when dogs were allowed, under control, on the course on Mondays Tuesdays Wednesdays and Fridays except on Match or Competition days. There were frequent appeals for money from Charities to the Club, but these were usually left to "lie on the table".

Male chauvinism took rather a knock in 1937 when a proposal was passed to extend the Clubhouse by making a mixed lounge, a new dining room, a new bar, two new bedrooms for the staff and improved serving conditions in the kitchen. This whole programme was scheduled to cost £1500 and a new Debenture at 5% interest was launched in April to cover the cost. The Architect was Mr Henson of Sir John Brown & Henson and the work was carried out by the builders Green & Son.

The year following his accession to the throne King George VI was graciously pleased to become Patron of the Club.

Following this appointment the Club made a request that it be granted a Royal Appellation. Such applications fall into the Intray of the Home Secretary, but he turned down the request in spite of our recent connections with the King.

The extensions to the Clubhouse, although bringing improved amenities to members, also brought increased charges to overheads, and although membership was a healthy 477 the accounts at the end of 1937 showed a loss of £251. So, once again, under the watchful eye of the Secretary Col Dening, fairly drastic economic measures were put into effect. An item about catering from the House Committee is of interest. Patum Peperium, or Gentleman's Relish (a strong anchovy paste) was a particular favourite on the tea menu, but a minute of the House Committee meeting of Sunday July 3rd 1938 reads: "After discussion it was decided that the only solution to the Patum problem was, as done elsewhere, to have this spread in the kitchen and not by members". It goes on to report "Mrs Lees again promised to make enquiries into the wholesale purchase of biscuits, shortbread etc. Further investigations were to be made into the price of purchased goods, but it was decided that the present prices of tinned plums could not be improved upon, and that as these were the cheapest form of tinned fruit, they should be provided fairly frequently. Suggestions were made that during the summer months particularly, pastry should be cut down, fruit served, not necessarily in a tart, fewer jam turnovers and scones. Care should be taken when carving, not to give excessively generous portions, and teas to be less standard in variety. It was decided to charge 10p for a two course lunch during the Ladies Autumn and Spring Meetings. It seems that our pre-war members had fairly healthy appetites, but that a period of belt tightening was to begin which lasted for almost 10 years. The House Committee also decided to buy one hair brush and one comb for the men's changing room. It was, however, to be a Maison Pearson brush - the Rolls Royce of brushes - and the comb would have been tortoiseshell, because the cheap plastic variety had not yet been invented.

The course itself was busy and for the first time, in May, Starting lists were introduced on Saturdays and Sundays. It must be remembered that at this time, with the holes played in a different order, there was no alternative starting place.

There was a proposal to make a track from the Clubhouse to the old horse paddock (to the left of the 6th green) to enable players to start at the 12th by going under the railway arch, but this was not carried out. The bunker behind the 12th green was grassed over,

Club House Interior

The Clubhouse during the first War

the Caddymaster resigned and was not replaced, and his job was handed over to the Professional.

In June 1939 the Ladies Midland Meeting was held at the Club and the Club gave a prize of £3.30 to the winner.

The threat of war again raised its ugly head which duly broke out on 3rd Sept and for the next seven years the Club struggled to maintain its existence. The 5 year contract of Col Dening expired in 1939 and he did not seek a further term, as he was probably asked to rejoin his Regiment. It was initially decided not to replace Col Dening and Committee members were put in charge of departments. J F Stops looked after secretarial work, L C Baillon took on the course, F F Parsons supervised the Clubhouse and B Cheney again took over all the finances.

As soon as war was declared, 9 evacuees were billeted on the Club - 2 women and 7 children - so the two extra bedrooms that had been added in 1937 would have been a considerable help.

Sheep were brought back onto the course for an annual rental of £100, and although shepherded, the greens had to be wired round which is always a nuisance. In 1940 William Berridge, the Greenkeeper died. He had held the job since the opening of the Club and had always received the highest acclaim from the Committee and members alike. It was now decided to employ a Secretary/Greenkeeper and the Club was fortunate in the choice of Mr R G Browne who took up his appointment on May lst 1940. He and his wife, who helped him, were also very popular with the members and he was largely responsible for guiding the Club through the difficult years of the war, and indeed, through to 1953.

In addition to the evacuees, the Clubhouse was made the Headquarters of the Home Guard with L C Baillon playing the part of Captain Mainwaring as he was the CO of the Unit. The Home Guard paid a rent of 25p per week for the privilege. Later on the course became an Infantry Training Centre, so what with sheep, soldier's hobnailed boots, 7 children in the clubhouse and Dad's Army doing their training, there could not have been much opportunity for serious golf. The captaincy during the war was shared between Bertram Cheney, J F Stops, Arthur Baxter and T E Manning. C S Catlow did a lot of design work on the course during the beginning part of the war. The Professional W G Saunders was offered the post of groundsman, because he had so little to do, but this came to nothing and he resigned in 1942.

Towards the end of the war, there was just a caretaker in the Clubhouse, and a locked drinks cupboard to which the Secretary held the key, but the receipts box was usually deficient. Membership had dropped from 475 to 231, members in the Forces paid no subscription and there was little income from green fees or the shop. Under these circumstances it was great credit to those in charge that the Club only lost £326 in the years 1941-1945.

So the war came to an end on May 8th 1945, the Club was 35 years old, and there was a mountain to climb to rebuild the condition of the course and Clubhouse, but the Committee and R G Browne set about the task with a will.

The men's lounge (whatever happened to the Grandfather clock?)

CHAPTER IV

Middle Age (1945-1966)

"The well-adjusted man is one who can play golf as if it were a game"

Anon

A formidable task faced the committee in 1945. Following the use of the clubhouse by evacuees and the Home Guard, the building was devastated with wet rot and damp, chairs and settees were in rags, carpets and curtains worn out. A carpet had been specially woven throughout the clubhouse with a border to fit all the nooks and crannies which it was not possible to replace until 1952 when coupons finally ended. There had also been special crested china with the NCGC design on it, but most had been chipped or cracked. Don Chamberlain and Pat Spencer sorted it all out, consigning most to the dustbin and slowly the club replaced it. The secretary, Bob Browne, who lived in the cottage with his blind wife, was a tower of strength in these difficult times.

In 1946 the grazing of sheep was cancelled, wiring round the greens was removed, and full subscriptions of £10.50p and £5.25p entrance fee and £6.30p and £3.15p for ladies were reintroduced. There was a suggestion that ladies with handicaps under 15 should be allowed to play in men's competitions, but this was one proposition that was left to lie on, or probably under, the table.

Owing to the continuance of petrol rationing, all committee meetings were held at the George Row club. Food rationing was also still in force and no club meal was allowed to cost more than 11p otherwise the club's food allowance would be cut.

The other problem was to find labour for the course and the clubhouse, and an approach was made to the Displaced and Disabled Soldiers Organisation for labour but met with no success. To help get to and from the club with the meagre petrol ration, York's Buses offered a coach service on Saturday afternoons and Sunday mornings from Northampton to the club at a cost of £2.50 per coach.

Late in 1946 James Braid was invited to visit the course and advise on a scheme of reconstruction. The cost of Braid's recommendations was £1646 and the amount was raised by a further Debenture and the work was ordered to be put in hand.

In 1947 a gas central heating system was installed throughout the clubhouse, half the cost being paid for by Don Chamberlain.

The course was in poor condition, especially the greens, following the hot summer of 1946 and severe winter of 1947, when 10 weeks work was lost on the course. It was not expected that the greens would recover before 1949. At this time the membership was 226 men, 84 ladies and 14 juniors, making a total of 324.

The provision of food for members was still a big problem; some members brought their own meat and poultry for their own consumption and Frank Parsons offered to provide food parcels to the club at 25p each to be sold to members at 50p.

To encourage new members, the entrance fee was temporarily suspended from March 1948, but green fees were increased to 25p Monday to Friday and 38p on Saturdays, Sundays and general holidays.

The main problem facing the management in the 10 years following the war was to increase membership which in 1950 was still only 349. The committee, however, continued to spend money on the course, buying a new tractor and a greens tining machine, and in spite of increasing the subscriptions to £12.60p for men and £7.35p for ladies, there was still a deficit of £262 for the year 1950-51. However, the quality of the course and the facilities of the clubhouse and the incentive of no entrance fee gradually began to wean a number of prominent golfers away from Northampton GC and to a lesser extent Kingsthorpe GC. Some of these were Tim Harley, Jack Corrin, Alfred and Edgar Coker, Canon Trevor Lewis, Gordon and Sydney Soutar and Reg Hammond. These moves did result in a small profit in 1952, but the forecasts for the next year were gloomy and an epic EGM took place on Friday, February 12, 1953, with the captain, Harry Lees, in the chair. In view of the financial state of the club, when a deficit of £300 was forecast for the year, the committee decided to recommend an increase from £12.60p to £14.70p for men and from £7.25p to £8.40p for ladies, and similar increases in other categories, which was proposed by Frank Roe and seconded by Geoffrey Adams.

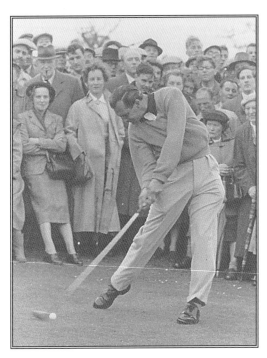

Max Faulkner (See page 30)

Twenty two members spoke either for or against the motion, and when Frank Roe accepted a small amendment to country members rates, the amendment was put to the meeting and defeated. The original motion was then put to the meeting and defeated by a substantial majority.

The chairman then said that the committee had an alternative suggestion of proposing a levy on each round played of 8p for men and 5p for ladies, and adjourned the meeting for 20 minutes for members to re-charge their glasses and consider the suggestion.

After another exhaustive discussion, it was finally agreed that the subscriptions should be £12.60p for men and £7.35p for ladies with the levy being implemented.

The meeting finally ended at 9 30pm, having been in session for four hours. Harry Lees must have wondered what he had let himself in for as captain. The levy was to remain for two years, but a Social Committee, including four ladies, was set up to organise functions to raise money, and together they did an excellent job raising over £1200 from 1953 to 1956. There was some discussion in committee at this time about the method of choosing future captains, and it was eventually decided that a committee of past captain, captain and vice captain should put forward to the general committee names which they recommended and who would be willing to stand.

It was also decided that the club could not afford a full time paid secretary, and by mutual agreement Bob Browne resigned and Norval Durham undertook the task of Honorary Secretary. The deficit for 1953 turned out to be £353 but this was covered by the efforts of the social committee, and from 1954 onwards there was a stable situation in the club with Norval Durham as Honorary Secretary, Mr and Mrs Parsons were appointed steward and stewardess in June 1954, and were great assets to the club, and the following year the services of Joe Carrick as head greenkeeper were secured.

1955 was a year of some distinction, owing to the generosity of the ever-helpful Don Chamberlain, and on this occasion supported by Alan Timpson, they offered to pay for the glassing in of the verandah and the heating of the new enclosed area. After many discussions the format was agreed, Messrs. Hawtin were commissioned to do the work, and the end product at a cost of £1600 to the donors was much appreciated by the membership.

Alf Padgham (See page 30)

Max Faulkner, Harry Weetman and Bobby Locke (See page 30)

On June 12, 1955, through the Lord Roberts Memorial Workshop, an exhibition by top professionals was organised at the club. Bobby Locke, Max Faulkner, Harry Weetman and Alf Padgham were the players. Bobby Locke first took a golf clinic in front of the first tee, in which he demonstrated how to draw, fade and hit a ball straight, together with other tips, and then the four men played a match, but none of them made the course look easy. Unfortunately, the weather turned wet and most of the spectators left after the match instead of coming into the clubhouse for refreshments, which had been arranged by Mrs Parsons. George Mobbs ran a competition on the scores and sent a cheque for £3.83p, being his profit on the enterprise, and Gordon Groome presented some good photographs of the occasion to the club. From the event £383 was raised for Lord Roberts Workshop. It was at this time that players were allowed to clean their golf balls on the green all the year round instead of just from October to March.

During the latter part of the 1950s and up to 1966 the committee made a much greater success of the finances of the club and became less dependent on the raising of money by the social committee to produce a reasonable profit figure. Although this was sufficient to keep the clubhouse in good repair and decoration, and buy the labour-saving equipment that was becoming available to the greens staff, there was no accumulation of funds for further expansion. The membership had risen to 484 by 1959 and had leapt to 575 by 1962, at which figure the membership list was closed. The better financial situation was not only brought about by good management, but was also considerably helped by the generosity of a few members who offered to pay for certain improvements in the clubhouse such as redecoration, face towels, new chairs in the men's lounge, new name boards for cup winners, new curtains in the dining room from the ladies section, a new carpet in the mixed lounge and so on. The gift of the glassing-in of the verandah has already been mentioned. Although Joe Carrick was now well established as greenkeeper and living in the cottage, it was difficult to get a trained second-in-command, who would certainly have to come from another area. Accordingly, a house in Whitehills was purchased in 1957 for £1450 and the new assistant, Lynch, was housed there rent free. This remained club property until 1961 when Lynch left and the house was sold for £1500. In the same year, the first Course Ranger was employed on some Saturdays and Sundays owing to public nuisances on the course. Rabbits were also causing some nuisance on the course, and although the committee at first decided that the greens staff could cope with the problem, this proved not to be the case, and for a sum of £6.40p per annum the club employed the Rabbit Clearance Society, a company set up by local farmers, to combat the nuisance which was successful. No doubt the committee of 1995 would appreciate the Society when the rabbit population exploded to Hiroshima proportions.

The annual dance at the Salon was a popular event which over 350 used to attend to the bands of Edmundo Ros, Victor Silvester, Nat Temple, the Temperance Seven, and once with Rolf Harris as entertainer. These numbers increased to 460 in 1964.

The Parsons, who had a very successful tour as steward and stewardess for four years, decided to leave in 1958, the same year that John Gubbins became Honorary Secretary, but they were persuaded without much pressure to return after a year away.

1960 was the club's Golden Jubilee Year and a dinner was held in a marquee in front of the clubhouse. To honour the occasion the past captains gave a wooden seat and starters hut for the first tee.

THIS PROGRAMME

is FREE, but Donations in the Boxes provided will be welcomed.

It is hoped that all will stay for the Auction (and Draw for the Raffle) which will start immediately the Match finishes.

All money raised will be for the Forces' Help Society and Lord Roberts' Workshops in aid of Disabled Soldiers. Your support at the Auction will therefore be greatly appreciated.

REFRESHMENTS

Licensed
Tea and Snack Bars

In the event of bad weather, the Auction will be held in the Marquee near the first Tee.

NORTHAMPTONSHIRE COUNTY GOLF CLUB

— Church Brampton —

EXHIBITION GOLF MATCH

Under the Distinguished Patronage of
Field - Marshal The Viscount Alanbrooke, K.G.,
G.C.B., O.M., G.C.V.D., D.S.O.

ON

Sunday, 12th June, 1955

In aid of **THE FORCES' HELP SOCIETY AND LORD ROBERTS' WORKSHOPS**

(Registered in accordance with the National Assistance Act, 1948)

—— NORTHAMPTONSHIRE COUNTY GOLF CLUB · CHURCH BRAMPTON ——

Exhibition Golf Match, Sunday, 12th June, 1955

BOBBY LOCKE · ALF PADGHAM · MAX FAULKNER · HARRY WEETMAN

(S. AFRICA)　　　**(SUNDRIDGE PARK)**　　　**(ST. GEORGE'S HILL)**　　　**(CROHAM HURST)**

A GOLF CLINIC will be arranged by Bobby Locke at 2 p.m. followed by a Four-Ball Match at 2.30 p.m.

AN AUCTION will be held by Alf Padgham at the end of Match when the Draw for the Raffle will also be made.

SCORE CARD

Hole	Length	Bogey	Stroke Index	Bobby Locke	Alf Padgham	Max Faulkner	Harry Weetman
1	459	5		4	4	4	5
2	457	5		4	5	4	5
3	163	3		3	3	3	3
4	300	4		4	4	3	3
5	377	4		3	4	4	4
6	415	4		4	4	4	4
7	371	4					
8	147	3		2	3	3	4
9	368	4					
OUT...	3057	36					

Professional Records. Old Course—Len Holland 64
New Course—G. Gledhill 67

SCORE CARD

Hole	Length	Bogey	Stroke Index	Bobby Locke	Alf Padgham	Max Faulkner	Harry Weetman
10	373	4					
11	173	3					
12	440	4					
13	321	4					
14	450	5					
15	180	3					
16	370	4					
17	408	4					
18	488	5					
IN ...	3203	36					
OUT	3057	36					
TOTAL	6260	72					

S.S.S. 71

Totals 18 Holes : Locke ....
Padgham ....
Weetman ....
Faulkner ....

There was a great need for an alternative starting point with the increased membership and the Bridle Road to the left of the first and second fairways was re-surfaced to enable members to start at the 10th tee as well as the first. Apart from a new starting point, there was also a demand for a practice ground and although a proposition to rent the field south of the greenkeeper's cottage was turned down on account of the cost of fencing, the rent was only going to be £3.50p per annum. Two years later, however, the matter was raised again, and at a cost of £700 for fencing, seven acres were leased from the Spencer estate at £35p.a. with £269 being paid in compensation to Lamont, who had farmed the area.

By the end of the 1950s, electric buggies began to appear on the market, and Mrs Deterding was perhaps the first 'Mobile Lady Member' on the course. Mr J P T Jeyes was given permission to use a moped and sidecar to take his golf equipment round the course in a Society meeting!

Looking ahead to the likely capital expenditure needed in the future to cater for almost 600 members, a new issue of 1000 £10 Debentures was launched in 1963. For the next three years, two major topics occupied the work of the general and sub committees. First was the threat of new housing developments to the east of the club's boundary, making the land on the far side of the railway a target for public intrusion and vandalism, and foreseeing the danger, Arthur Harris (club captain in 1963) and County Architect, produced a scheme for giving up the land on the far side of the railway and utilising our ground to the left of the fifth and sixth fairways and part of the Fox Covert.

The second proposal was for considerable alterations to the clubhouse to cater for the increased membership. An application to the County Education Dept. for a grant was turned down, and it was left to the club to find ways and means of raising the money to pay for the alterations at a cost of £9900.

At an Extraordinary General Meeting on January 19, 1966, under the superb chairmanship of the captain, Charles Gledhill, at which 143 members were present, the committee plans were passed and the clubhouse alterations confirmed with the tender of Bonsor & Wilding. The response to the Debenture Issue had been disappointing but subscriptions were raised from £18 to £21 for men and from £12 to £14 for ladies with similar increases in other categories. In the same year the Honorary Secretary, Dick Watkins, resigned owing to the pressure of the work, and it was decided to revert once again to a paid secretary, a post which was well filled by George Mobbs. All this work was a major step towards bringing the club up to the required standards of the leading club in the county, together with recognition nationally as a future venue for top amateur competitions.

CHAPTER V

Maturity (1966-1995)

"Golfers find it a very trying matter to turn at the waist, more particularly if they have a lot of waist to turn"

Harry Vardon

During the next 30 years the records of the activities of the Club underwent a major change. With the appointment of a paid full time secretary in the person of George Mobbs, followed by Geoff Morley and Michael Wadley, the minutes were much more detailed and provide an excellent record of the minutiae of the events which happen daily in any substantial club. There are details of all the problems with catering, finance, course upkeep, competitions, disputes between members, clubhouse improvements and other matters covering over 1,000 pages of typed minutes, all of which have been carefully read and digested, but in the hope of maintaining the interest of readers of this history, most of these have been discarded and emphasis placed on major events, which took place during the period.

The foundations had been laid for the Club to enter a new era of being recognised as one of the better inland courses in the country, and a suitable venue for major amateur competitions. Indeed, in May 1965, the Midland Amateur championship was held at Brampton, followed by the County Champions championship in September the following year, at which leading amateurs from all over the country sampled the delights and pitfalls of our course. It was the slopes on the greens that they found difficult to read with any certainty, and in 1968 Brampton was accepted as a member of the Golf Society of Great Britain - a significant status symbol.

The membership of the Club had by now risen to 675 but its finances were still very much on a knife edge, and there was a growing demand to replace the old water pipes round the course and install a pop-up watering system to the greens.

This was going to cost around £10,000 and a new issue of 1,000 £10 Debentures was launched to underwrite the cost, though the Club's finances went into the red by over £2,000 on the year.

During the 1960s a few mini Golfing Societies were formed within the Club, who held their meetings at Brampton or on other courses. They all still flourish.

The Dawn Patrol
The Society was formed in 1965 by Tony Hood, Peter Bennett and John Pendry. Other early members were Tony Wright, Sid Thornton, Bill Barron and Stuart Wilson.

The object was to play early in the morning, when the course was not crowded. There are today about 24 members and they foregather at 7.30am throughout the year on Tuesdays, Thursdays, Saturdays and Sundays, and make up fourballs among those who attend.

They play for four trophies during the year - the Todd Hood Memorial Trophy, the Sturdy Salver, the Clifford Packaging Cup and the Dawn Patrol Putter. They also hold an annual dinner.

The Red Cat Golfing Society
In 1959 Peter Arnold went to play in a benefit cricket match for George Tribe at Castle Rising, and was entertained at the Red Cat Hotel at North Wootton. He enjoyed it so much that the following year he organised a return trip for a golfing weekend.

Peter, Mike Warrington, Jack Parry, Jack Belson, Ron Bird, Dick Wells and Dick Hopkinson were in the vanguard. Over the years the headquarters have moved but the Red Cat is still their Alma Mater. There are 39 names on the all time members list, of which 20 are still active.

Play in the annual outing, which perforce has been before the cricket season, has always been in the east coast area from Thursday to Sunday, but Saturday has always been reserved for Brancaster and a medal round for the trophy - a handsome wooden model.

In November, another gathering takes place especially to count heads, which normally takes place at Brampton. All of the members have been cricketers, either at international, county or top club level, and include five past captains of Brampton.

The class of '69 – Norman Buswell (captain), George Mobbs (secretary), Janie Harley (lady captain) and Spriggs Baillon (chairman of greens committee)

St Botolph Golfing Society
A number of members, originally from Northampton GC, realised on joining Brampton that there was not normally a captain's weekend, and as a result Alf York arranged a party of eight in July, 1967, to stay at the Dormy House Hotel, Ferndown, and play Ferndown and Parkstone. Those eight were: Alf York, Don Barltop, Bruce Clayton, Colin Odds, Michael Rowe, Bernard Scott, Sydney Stewart and Alan Westley.

St Botolph, being the patron saint of Church Brampton, was adopted as the name of the society. They have a three night tour every year, and play on different, well known courses all over the country. In addition they meet Tuesday afternoons and dine in the evening at Brampton in the summer, and each Wednesday morning in the winter. They have no trophies but entertain their ladies to dinner once a year, and in 1994 donated the St Botolph Salver to the winner of the Seniors championship at Brampton.

The Agaric Golfing Society
This Society was founded in 1969 by Bruce Clayton and Jack Bell to form a small group to enjoy some of the best courses around the country. The first outing was to Brockenhurst at which Bruce Clayton, Jack Bell, Dickie Parr and Dick Stevens were present, and spent

so much time searching for balls in the forest that they came across the most marvellous displays of the Scarlet Fly Agaric fungi. It was in the autumn and the display promoted the name of the fungi for the Society.

Bruce Clayton was keen to visit a different course on each outing and throughout the years many famous courses have been visited including Gleneagles, Muirfield, St Andrews, Sandwich, Troon, Royal Harlech and Royal Porthcawl.

The membership has always been about 10 to 12 and include Jack Corrin, Tony Palfreyman, Dick Stevens, Peter Rudkin, John Barlow, John Gower, Neil Soutar, Ken Hammond, Ray Beirne, John Wilson, Dickie Parr, Simon Parr, Jim Chater, Alan Goddard and Bruce Clayton. Recent replacements are David O'Dowd, Chris Thompson and Jorgen Romose.

The Society entertain their ladies to dinner each year, and play during their tour for a modest trophy, but the real object is to enjoy each others company and have golfing fun.

The men's lounge – 1969

Three of the Societies have presented wooden seats to the Club.

The year 1971 was one of distinction when the Club was host to the British Youths championship, a 72 hole medal competition, which took place on August 5, 6 and 7. It had been preceded by an international match for the European Golf Association Trophy between Great Britain and Ireland against the Continent of Europe.

The Youths championship was won by Pip Elson from Coventry, the runner-up being Warren Humphreys of Royal Mid Surrey. Members were also able to see the golfing prowess of some of the stars of the future, including Howard Clark, Ian Mosey, Michael King, Mark James, Carl Mason and David Russell.

George Mobbs, the Club secretary, was finding some difficulty in fitting in the numerous societies, whose income greatly helped the finances of the Club, because we had only one satisfactory starting point. He therefore produced a scheme, heavily discussed in committee, to change the order of playing the course to give an alternative starting point away from the area of the railway bridge, which was a favourite for vandals from the public footpath, bisecting the course. After fervent opposition from the traditionalists, the new order was put into effect in 1973 and remains, apart from a brief period in 1988, the order of play of the holes to the present day.

In 1971 and 1973, the Club won the Hollingsworth Trophy (a foursome knock-out competition off handicap among all affiliated clubs in the county), and in the latter year Brampton played host to the Girls' British Open Amateur championship. It was a pleasure to see these girls play and an eye-opener to the male members when they saw how far they hit the ball. The event was won by Anne-Marie Palli from France, who defeated another French girl, Natalie Jeanson, in the final. The Championship was preceded by an international match between the home countries, which was won by Scotland.

Youths champion Pip Elson (above) receives the trophy from Brampton captain Edgar Coker

In 1975 the ladies were back again, this time for the finals of the inter County competition. Those qualifying were Glamorgan, Northumberland, Staffordshire and Surrey. Glamorgan turned out the champions, spearheaded by Welsh international, Tegwin Perkins.

From this time onwards, apart from hiccups in 1977 and 1978, the committee began to grasp the financial nettle and good profits started to be made and money put into capital account to go towards inevitable future requirements.

Inflation, however, was a blight on the economy and from 1974 to 1981 subscriptions rose from £56 to £172 for men and from £40 to £126 for ladies, not without some squeals from some of the members. There have always been opposing schools of thought among members as to the need for visiting societies. The need for these for increased income to the Club is always questioned by those members who are prepared to pay more and have unhampered use of their course at all times. It is a vexed question, but over the years the Club has probably got the balance about right.

The ninth green had for some years caused concern over its quality and drainage, and in 1978, under the direction of Charles Catlow, it was dug up and completely re-laid, but with the same contours as before. The area in front of the green was also remodelled under Eric Kottler, the civil engineer, to help to minimise flooding from the stream. These alterations appeared to be completely satisfactory at the time, but although the remedy for flood control has stood the test of time, the condition of the green has not, and in 1994/95 it was completely re-designed and re-laid under the Club's member/course architect, Cameron Sinclair. By the turn of the century we shall probably know if this time the medicine has worked.

On the clubhouse front, in order to provide more changing room for the men, the pro's shop was enlarged into the locker room and a Portakabin erected near the first tee as a shop

*Top: Anne-Marie Palli is presented with
her cup by 1972 lady captain,
Dorothy Cooch*

*Above: 1972 county champions,
Glamorgan*

for the professional. Although hardly an architectural feature in keeping with the clubhouse, it was, at the time, a financial expediency, at a total cost of £7,000. This was in 1975, the year when interest dwindled in the Annual Dance making it impossible to continue it, and male chauvinism was at last broken down, when the lady captain and lady vice captain were invited to join the general committee. The vice captain was later replaced by the lady secretary.

Following the losses of 1977 and 1978, the Club made good profits for the next few years, the County Scratch League was entered, and in 1980 the English County Championship finals were held at Brampton, but in 1981 there was a complete upheaval in the organisation. Under Eric Kottler's captaincy, but certainly not because of it, the secretary, steward and stewardess, professional and head greenkeeper all left in the space of 12 months, and Eric, always at his best under pressure, faced the crisis and supervised the installation of a completely new team. George Mobbs was now finding his post of secretary too onerous, and Geoff Morley, an executive from the food industry and former member of Formby GC, was appointed. Stuart Brown replaced Robin Day as club professional, and Mike Lake succeeded Joe Carrick, who retired after 27 years devoted service, and the Marriotts replaced the Gibbons as steward and stewardess.

Following these changes, the management structure was also changed in that Geoff Morley was styled as Secretary-Manager, and was to be responsible to the general committee for the operation of the greenkeeper, steward and professional, and that the 'titles' of chairman of the greens, house, competitions and social committees would disappear.

The general committee was to consist of the captain, vice captain, two Trustees, lady captain, lady secretary and six elected members. Although this was a cosy blueprint for a streamlined organisation, it did not work out quite like that over a period of time. No one man can be expected to be an expert in administration, finance, agronomy, all aspects of golf, a caterer and social organiser, which was in theory to be the role of the secretary-manager. Inevitably, committee members gradually took over the duties of greens, house, competitions and social events as before, and the executive committee was born, which comprised the captain, vice captain, secretary, treasurer and chairmen of house, greens, competitions and social committees: this committee was answerable to the general committee for major decisions.

Two good new appointments were made in 1984, those of course ranger and forester. There was regular vandalism to parts of the course, not only to those areas adjacent to the bridle path dividing the course, especially at weekends, and a course ranger, in the person of a former paratrooper, was a good match for any troublemakers.

The appointment of a full time forester has seen a great improvement in the tidiness of the course, especially in remoter areas. He is responsible for the pruning of trees, the layering of hedges, the maintenance of fences and the clearing of unwanted undergrowth, and does an excellent job.

On the course, £16,000 had been spent on new machinery and it had now become an unusual sight to see any of the greens staff actually walking on the course. By 1995 a pedestrian member of the greens staff was a phenomenon.

The year 1985 saw the Club's 75th anniversary, and the committee arranged a number of functions to celebrate the event. It was a happy coincidence that the English Ladies StrokePlay championship was due to be played at Brampton from August 5-8, which was followed on the 10th by a Dinner-Dance in a marquee by the 18th green, and on August 12, an exhibition match by four professionals was played before a good crowd. Sandy Lyle had promised to play in this match, but having won the Open the previous month, he found he had other engagements, and his place was taken by Bernard Gallagher.

Miss Patricia Johnson was the star of the ladies competition, winning the championship itself and being champion of the Under 23 and Under 21 competitions. She is today a leading professional on the ladies world tour.

The Dinner-Dance was attended by the Lord Lieutenant, Mr John Lowther, and his wife, Mr John Wilde, President of the English Golf Union, and his wife, and Lord and Lady Boardman. Lord Boardman was Chairman of the National Westminster Bank, which had sponsored the ladies competition. There were about 150 members and friends at the Dinner. In the professional exhibition match, which also included a clinic by Tommy Horton, Stuart Murray returned the best score with 71, followed by Stuart Brown with 72. Bernard Gallagher scored 75 and Tommy Horton 76, so local knowledge had the edge. Apart from their fee, each player was presented with a glass tankard, suitably inscribed with the 75th anniversary. A number of these had been ordered for prizes for the year's competitions, and for sale to members. Anniversary ties and ladies scarves were also available. Another highlight of the year was the winning of the Hollingsworth Trophy for the first time for many years.

Just before the anniversary celebrations, the car park had been extended and new machinery sheds built costing £35,000. The offices had been computerised and the GSGB held their autumn meeting at Brampton in October, 1986.

From now until 1994, major alterations were made to the clubhouse in phases, dependent on finance being available. These included the replacement of the pro's Portakabin, a new pro's shop within the main clubhouse building, the extension of the men's changing room, a new office for the secretarial staff, a covered way into the clubhouse, the extension of the veranda in two stages, the enlargement of the dining room to allow two societies to be accommodated on the same day, the enlargement of the ladies dressing and locker rooms with showers and other necessary amenities, and a new practice ground with ball dispenser and a machine for ball collection. The total costs were in excess of £300,000 and were financed by increased profits, the issue of new Debentures, many gifts and free loans from members and a capital levy of £100 per playing member with lesser amounts for social and junior members. Needless to say, this all entailed a huge amount of work for the various committees, largely guided by the Club's architect, Peter Haddon, the captain in 1994. The final outcome, now being enjoyed by members and visitors alike, must be regarded as a great success, bringing the Club up to the standard expected of the leading club in the county.

Trish Johnson – 1985 English Ladies stroke play champion

During these alterations, the course had not been neglected. Under Cameron Sinclair, some of the old tiger tees were brought back into play and new winter tees were constructed at the 5th, 9th, 13th, 14th and 15th. The water pop-up system had been extended to all the tees, and a lot of money was spent on new and replacement machinery now housed in the new machinery sheds already mentioned. New tee markers were made for all the tee positions.

In 1991 the committee had deliberated at considerable length over the possible purchase of Fox Covert to make an additional three, five or nine hole extension to the course. Preliminary meetings were held with the Spencer Estate concerning the possibility of the purchase, and, if positive, a likely price per acre. Cameron Sinclair produced alternative

Local knowledge came out on top in the 75th anniversary exhibition match

The exhibition match (from left): Neil Soutar (men's captain), Jenny Preston-Jones (ladies captain), Bernard Gallagher, Bruce Clayton (greens chairman), Stuart Murray, Tommy Horton, Stuart Brown and Geoff Morley (Secretary-Manager)

plans, either including the practice ground if a new one could be procured, or excluding it. It was inevitable that protracted negotiations on price and restrictive covenants had to be made prior to any plan or proposal being put to the members. Unfortunately, however, rumours began to circulate among members that the committee was making plans

The Anniversary Party

and negotiating options without members being consulted. A number of members, therefore, called an EGM to clear the air and prevent the committee from taking unilateral action without the members consent.

This meeting took place on March 20, 1992, at which 209 members were present, and the motion that the committee was acting precipitously without consent of the members was carried by 126 to 72 with a few abstentions. There is little doubt that a golden opportunity of acquiring a most desirable extra loop of holes to avoid congestion on the course was lost, and indeed in 1993 when the matter was raised again with the Spencer estate, any future proposals for the purchase of land were turned down.

In 1993 a small committee, chaired by John Duffy, drew up a revised set of rules for the Club, which were accepted by members after a prolonged discussion on the question of dogs on the course, which had been an emotive subject for the last 80 years.

The main event of 1992 was staging the British Girls Open Amateur championship, which took place from August 11-14. Competitors came from France, Spain, Italy and Sweden apart from the British Isles. Spain won the team prize, but the individual winner was Mhairi McKay from Turnberry. In the first round she broke the ladies course record with a 72. Robert Duck, who was caddying for her, must have had mixed feelings because the record she broke had been held by his mother, Angela.

Reference has often been made in this history to the goings and comings of stewards and

*Tommy Horton from the bunker at the 18th –
and some unusual stroke play during his clinic
(inset)*

stewardesses, and in 1993 a new departure was tried by the granting of a catering franchise to a male chef and the employment of a clubhouse and bar steward by the Club.

This was successful for a few years but with the advent of new legislation concerning employment and health and safety laws, the Club has reverted to in-house catering and currently employs two chefs!

On the financial side, under the guidance of Bill Stephenson and John Wilson, the Club is in a healthy economic state with accurate quarterly budgets and good profits being maintained. All Debentures were paid off in 1994 and VAT refunded to members who were given options of either total, partial or no repayments.

In 1994 the Club was privileged to play host to the Carris Trophy, a prestigious national 72 hole stroke play competition for amateurs under 18. The competition was played on July 19-21 and members were all delighted that it was won by our junior member, Robert Duck, with a total of 280 for the four rounds. Robert spreadeagled the field with a brilliant record 65 in the third round. He had rounds of 72 73 65 and 70 to win by two shots from James Harris, S P Nightingale and B J J Barham, who all scored 282 against a par of 284 for the four rounds.

Brampton has never been renowned as a social club, but over the past 10 years or more there has been an increase in social activities outside golf. Through the enthusiasm of the late John Burnett, Sidney Drown and latterly, Don Lamb, there is today an active participation in bridge for rubber and duplicate varieties of the game, especially during the winter months. An evening of cribbage is also organised by Don Lamb. On the catering side, there have been evenings with different national flavours such as Danish, Spanish and Italian, and candlelight suppers have been held. Sunday luncheons are also especially popular with social members and their guests.

Pro-am competitions to raise money for charity have become an annual event, and many thousands of pounds have been given away. Experiments have been made with Nite Golf but this has had minimal appeal.

The late Ken Hunter began to organise the seniors to play regularly together, and this work has been carried on by Robert Grigg and John Fearn. The seniors (or geriatrics as they are rather derisively called) meet each Monday, Wednesday, Thursday and Friday morning at 10.30am, when they draw lots and play either three or four ball matches. 'Tea and tea cakes' is the usual penalty for the losers to pay. Matches are arranged against many other clubs and a Christmas competition and party is a popular event.

The hot spell of July, 1995, brings this history to its conclusion. It is satisfactory to report that with 865 members the Northamptonshire County Golf Club at Church Brampton is in a very healthy state structurally, financially, sportingly and agronomically. The next major milestone will be the centenary of the Club in 2010, and it is to be hoped that the future committees will have the foresight to plan well ahead to make the occasion worthy of the aspirations of the early pioneers, who founded it, and the traditions which subsequent captains, committees and members have established.

For the future, the committee is trying to set up a Future Developments committee to look at long term prospects for the Club into the next century. They will have plenty of scope to discuss the removal of the wooden sheds behind the pro's shop, the resurfacing of Golf Lane and track down to the railway, the acceptance of buggies as an inevitable service for members and visitors, together with a place to house them, the use of the old practice ground (perhaps a nine hole pitch and putt course?), and many others.

The victorious Hollingsworth team, 1985: Back row (left to right): Malcolm Pounds, Richard Halliday, Tony Bishop, Tony Lord, Richard Aitken, Michael Duck. Front row: Cameron Sinclair, Jack Humphries, Neil Soutar (club captain), Dick Biggin, Ken Nokes

Top: Club captain Graham Underwood presents the cup to the winning Spanish team (1992)
Right: Robert Duck receives the Carris Trophy from EGU president, Stuart Cookson (1994)
Above: Jimmy Tarbuck at the pro-am for Guide Dogs for the Blind

Brampton high spots

CHAPTER VI

A History of the Course
compiled & written by G E MOBBS

*"I'd like to see the fairways more narrow Then everybody
would have to play from the rough, not just me"*

Seve Ballesteros

*The original lay-out of the course, designed by the famous architect, H S Colt, was commenced in
1909, and the opening took place in April 1910. The 85 years that the course has been in
existence may be conveniently divided into five periods.*

1910-1939

Although many members served on the Greens Committee for short intervals from time to time, during this period the chairmanship was usually in the hands of the writer's grandfather, Fred Bostock, an original founder member, who had a local reputation for his knowledge of horticulture. The head greenkeeper, Berridge, normally had, in those unmechanised days, a staff of up to 8 under his control.

The membership was largely drawn from local country gentry and their families, together with a leavening of professional and business men. With the Great War breaking out 4 years after the opening, followed by the financially depressed 1920's and 1930's, there was never much money to spare for improvements to the course, so that we find that few alterations to the original lay-out took place during this period. However the course was gradually lengthened, by the creation of new tees further back, from its original 5,943 yards in 1910 until it had reached 6,321 yards by 1939. This lengthening was obviously brought about by the improvements in golf balls and clubs which had made the ball fly considerably further.

It may be of interest to members to learn that originally the fairways consisted mostly of fine heathland turf, as at present exists on the best parts of the 5th, 7th, and 16th holes, and consequently over most of the course the ball ran further than it does now. Only the 1st and 18th holes had been under plough in 1910 and had required to be seeded, the rest consisted of the original heathland turf, but, as on so many courses, they have gradually reverted to a lusher type of grass.

1940-1951

The early part of this period covered the years of the Second World War, when, not unnaturally, the Club had a struggle to continue. Mercifully, by agreeing to allow sheep to graze on the course (which brought in much needed revenue), the club escaped the devastation which would have resulted if a compulsory ploughing-up had been ordered but all the greens had to be wired against the sheep, and only the minimum maintenance could be afforded. So the end of the War found the course in a run-down condition, with

46

Splendid aerial views of (in clockwise order from top left):
A) The 4th hole; B) the 5th green and 17th hole; C) greens 10, 11 and 12;
D) the 9th green and 5th and 16th holes

much long grass and hay in the rough, and the sand bunkers falling into decay.

It is an interesting fact that, during the War period the Chairman of the Greens Committee was "Turkey" Baillon, a pillar of the local Home Guard who used the clubhouse as their headquarters, and that 30 years later his son, Spriggs, followed his father's footsteps in supervising the work of the greens staff on the golf course.

R G (Bob) Browne had been appointed Secretary-Greenkeeper in 1940, and it was largely due to his devoted efforts that the course survived at all, and the club owes an immense debt to him. He continued as Secretary until 1952 when the club was in such financial straits that it could no longer afford to pay his salary, small though it was.

Around that time, it was even necessary to have a whip-round amongst the members to keep things going.

So, at the end of the War, it was decided that steps must be taken to reduce the amount of upkeep of the course. In addition it was realised that the old system of bunkering, with cross-bunkers at regular intervals and further penal bunkers down each side to catch slices and pulls, was now out of date.

Accordingly James Braid was consulted in 1946 and he produced a plan for the closing of unnecessary bunkers, modernising the lay-out, and consolidating the teeing-grounds, the prime objective being to reduce the cost of maintenance.

Whilst he was present, Braid was asked if he had any other ideas for improving the course, and he suggested that the 18th should be altered from a straightaway hole to one dog-legged right to a new green in front of the clubhouse. It is probable that no single alteration has given more pleasure to members than this one, not only because it made a far better hole, but it brought the action approaching the 18th green under the critical gaze of the onlookers on the Clubhouse verandah.

1952-1968

This period was notable for the able Chairmanship of the Greens Committee by Frank Roe. In 1952, another golf architect, C. K. Cotton, was called in to accelerate the reduction of the bunkers, and in many cases these were replaced by the planting of trees and broom bushes as alternative hazards.

By the mid-fifties this plan had been completed, and from a total of 110 sand traps in 1939, the number had been reduced to about 50; moreover the club's source of sand from the pit to the right of the 3rd hole was now running out, and hereafter it became necessary to purchase from Leighton Buzzard.

At this time Joe Carrick was engaged as head greenkeeper. Trained at the Championship Course of Portmarnock, he brought a wealth of knowledge of the art of greenkeeping with him, and the club has been fortunate indeed over the last 20 years to enjoy the services of such a loyal and experienced head greenkeeper.

With the coming of the affluent society and the expansion of motoring, the game of golf boomed in the late Fifties and increasing membership at last enabled money to be available for the purchase of labour-saving machinery and the installation of an automatic pop-up sprinkler system for watering the greens.

In 1964, at the instigation of Charles Gledhill, it was decided that there was no administrative machinery in existence to keep the course under constant review for the carrying out of improvements.

Accordingly, a report was compiled which emphasised two main defects.

(1) That many of the approaches to the greens were too wide open - the areas of the cut surface of most of the greens had contracted in the past to save maintenance, consequently the guarding bunkers were mostly by now far out from their perimeters.

(2) That many of the two-shot holes played too straight and there was insufficient emphasis on the placement of the tee-shot.

The Gledhill report recommendations for the tightening of many holes were completed, with one or two exceptions, by the end of this period.

In 1966, C. K. Cotton was again called in to comment on what had been done, but, unfortunately, his report was largely ignored.

By 1968, traffic of horses and pedestrians on the bridle road traversing the course was beginning to become so heavy, particularly at weekends, that it was causing delays and interference with play. A past Captain, Arthur Harris, therefore produced a plan to alter those holes affected by the bridle path so that they would no longer cross it. The Harris plan produced another counter-plan, and, in an attempt to resolve the situation,

From tee to green – the 13th hole

Start to finish – the 1st and 18th holes

another course architect, F. W. Hawtree, was called in for consultation.

Although Hawtree came down strongly in favour of the Harris plan, the Committee failed to reach agreement, and consequently nothing was done. In retrospect, perhaps a great opportunity was missed, as the plan could then have been carried out at a cost of £5,000, well within the means of the Club at the time.

1969-1975

After nearly 60 years of continued and increasing use, the condition of the greens now began to cause anxiety because of their poor colour, sparse herbage, and failure to respond to fertilisers for any length of time.

The Club's turf advisers were changed, and Sutton's of Reading were called in to report. They confirmed our worst fears and a 5-year programme of remedial treatment was started. This involved massive use of expensive organic fertiliser, laborious deep hand-forking and frequent surface-slitting, all to remove the dead fibre-layer which had been revealed and which was blocking drainage and encouraging the wrong type of shallow-rooting grass. This poor grass condition was becoming widespread all over the country, and affecting many of the greatest championship courses, and was due to nature being unable to recover to natural humus the heavy quantity of artificial fertilisers being used to cope with the increase in the amount of golf being played. The remedial treatment carried out caused the green surfaces for much of the year to be in an indescribably bad condition for proper putting. Under the lead of Charles Catlow, backed by the advice of Sutton's, the Club members were persuaded into the understanding that, however distasteful the medicine being prescribed, it was nevertheless for their ultimate benefit; there was probably no other member of the Club whose enthusiasm and knowledge could have carried the members along with this policy, and the Club should indeed be grateful to him for his leadership during this difficult period. The Club had, from time to time, been host to Midland Tournaments, and comment had been recently made by one of their officials, that, although we had a fine golf course, it really was rather short by modern standards. Accordingly, when the Club was invited to host its first National Championship, the British Youths, in 1971, the opportunity was taken to remedy this defect by re-opening or making new back tees to bring the length up to 6,462 yards, and thereafter having a special Championship Course only to be used for major events. When the course was re-surveyed in 1972 with modern equipment, this actually turned out to be only 6,397 yards.

1976-1994

At the beginning of this period, the eminent Golf Architect, Donald Steel, was invited to report on the course architecture to see whether any further improvements should be made. Some, but not all of his recommendations were carried out.

It has been an unfortunate fact through the years, that, when a Professional Golf Architect has been consulted to report on the course, much of what has been recommended has not been carried out as a result of the Committee's opinions being against what has been suggested. However, the Club is now in the fortunate situation of having, in Cameron Sinclair, an experienced Golf Course Architect who is also a member, so that he is available for consultation at any time.

With the retirement of Joe Carrick as Head Greenkeeper, his position was taken up by his deputy, Michael Lake, so continuity was maintained. He, however, left in 1988, since when David Low has been in charge, and, thanks also to the Club having sufficient funds to be able to purchase the most modem greenkeeping machinery, it cannot be disputed that he has been able to maintain a standard of excellence in the upkeep of the course better than anything previously achieved. In particular the putting surfaces have been truer and faster for longer periods annually than ever before, largely due to the Club having been able to hire verticutting machinery to improve the drainage.

There was an unfortunate hiatus in 1983, when for some inexplicable reason, all the rough was allowed to grow to knee height. This resulted in howls of anguish from members and visitors alike as they spent ages searching for their lost golf balls, which contributed to making play even slower (the curse of modern golf). It is difficult to understand why this was allowed to happen, the only beneficiary being the Club Professional in boosting his sales of golf balls! It is to be hoped that such a misguided policy will never be allowed to happen again.

As a tribute to the excellence of the course, the following National Championships have been held at Brampton during the last 15 years.

1985 English Ladies Strokeplay
1986 English Mens Senior Strokeplay
1992 British Girls Matchplay
1994 English Boys Strokeplay (Carris Trophy)

It is probable that, after 85 years, the course has reached such a degree of maturity that any more major alterations are unlikely to be made to it. Consequently the emphasis on management of the course has been of recent years concentrated on keeping it in as excellent condition as possible. Contributing to this has been a policy of maintaining or even restoring where necessary, the original heathland characteristics of the course. In 1984 a forester was therefore added to the staff and his employment has been beneficial in removing unwanted quantities of brambles, nettles, elder, rosebay willowherb etc and encouraging the natural indigenous broom, gorse and heather. This work has been most ably supervised by Bruce Clayton.

In 1988, an attempt was made to revert to the original order of holes which had existed until 1973. The promoters of this idea were probably not sufficiently aware that the 1973 change was not made because anyone thought that the course played better that way round, but because administratively it had become necessary to have a proper alternative Starting Tee down the course at the 8th (previously 4th) and thus be able to separate 2 and 4 Ball play. Happily a referendum of the members was held with the result that the 1973 change was confirmed.

It had long been considered desirable to negotiate with the Althorp Estate the sale of the Fox Covert to the left of the 18th hole, either to acquire 60 acres to build 9 further holes to relieve the pressure of so much golf being played on the 18 hole course, or sufficient land to have 3 new extra holes available after playing the 6th, to give a 9 hole circuit returning to the Clubhouse, thus eliminating the necessity of cutting in at the 17th Tee by those who wished to play 9 holes only. However, the membership decided that the cost of acquiring Fox Covert would be prohibitive, assuming that a satisfactory arrangement could be agreed with the Althorp Estate. At the present time the Estate is not anxious to sell any of Fox Covert, but perhaps in the future this idea may not be finally dead and buried.

So, in 1995, the Club has a Championship Course of 6503 yards, still a trifle on the short side compared with other major Courses in the Midlands which are mostly in the 6,500 to 6,900 yards bracket, a Summer Medal Course of 6233 yards and a Winter Medal Course of 5820 yards, both the latter probably about right for general play.

The Ladies Course measures 5833 yards, which is comparatively quite long, and reference to this aspect is discussed below.

A programme of enlarging those tees which were too small to absorb the amount of play taking place has been completed. Also, under Cameron Sinclair, a number of new Winter Tees have been constructed, notably at the 4th 5th 9th 13th and 14th holes.

As the Club approaches its Centenary in 2010, the membership have the knowledge that they possess one of the finest courses in the Midlands, maintained in excellent condition for their enjoyment, and worthy of hosting National Championships.

The Ladies

In designing a Golf Course, consideration must be given to all classes of players in that hazards must not be allowed to make things too diffcult for the shorter players. Particular attention must be paid to the requirements of the Ladies, as usually they hit the ball a shorter distance and they must not be penalised by being asked to make impossible carries over hazards that are no problem to longer-hitting men. This is usually achieved by intelligent siting of their tees. Conversely, fairways on the longer holes should not be so devoid of hazards that they are compelled to play several successive strokes with nothing to sustain their interest, and criticism has been heard from our Ladies in the past that this does apply to several of our holes (e.g. Nos. 2, 5,10, 16,18), and it may well be justified in that perhaps, in the past, too many fairway hazards were removed from these particular holes.

When the course was remeasured in 1972, it was found that the total yardage was now too short to justify their S.S.S. of 74, and consequently their tees at the 11th and 14th holes were brought back. On reflection, it would appear that they might have been better advised to have accepted the S.S.S. of 73 and utilised the advantage of some spare yardage to reduce some of their particular difficulties with more forward tees, e.g. at holes 5, 7, 8, 9,11,14 and 15.

A comparison of total lengths of mens and ladies yardages at 30 courses sampled reveals that the ladies courses average 615 yards shorter than the mens; at ours it is 400 yards only. It appears that our ladies have a larger number of long (comparatively for them) par 4s than most courses.

It therefore seems that there is a strong case for considering whether something should be done by providing more forward tees for them than they have now, particularly at the long par 4 holes. If they wished to maintain the total length of their course, they would do better to move back on their par 5 holes.

COURSE LAY OUT

The following 18 pages contain a diagram of each hole with a history of each hole and how each has evolved over the years. The names in the text refer to the following:

JAMES BRAID   – 1946 plan
C. K. COTTON   – 1952 report
CHARLES GLEDHILL   – 1964 recommendations
ARTHUR HARRIS   – 1968 plan
CHARLES CATLOW   – 1969 recommendations

COMPETITION	CARRIN TROPHY									Indicate which tee used	
DATE 21/7/94	TIME						Handicap	Strokes Rec'd		PAR 70 SSS 71	
PLAYER A										PAR 70 SSS 70	
PLAYER B										PAR SSS	
Hole	Marker Score	White Yards	Par	Yellow Yards	Par	Green Yards	Par	Stroke Index	Gross Score A	B	Points
1		454	4	443	4	415	4	5	5		
2		519	5	486	5	457	4	10	4		
3		180	3	171	3	135	3	14	2		
4		317	4	317	4	304	4	17	4		
5		442	4	442	4	404	4	1	3		
6		204	3	198	3	179	3	12	2		
7		378	4	360	4	349	4	4	3		
8		312	4	291	4	271	4	16	4		
9		396	4	379	4	339	4	8	3		
		3202	35	3087	35	2853	34	OUT	30		
PLEASE AVOID SLOW PLAY AT ALL TIMES											
10		413	4	413	4	381	4	3	5		
11		384	4	375	4	338	4	11	4		
12		142	3	136	3	117	3	18	3		
13		396	4	383	4	361	4	6	5		
14		380	4	365	4	322	4	9	3		
15		179	3	167	3	142	3	15	3		
16		434	4	426	4	415	4	2	5		
17		466	4	410	4	395	4	7	4		
18		507	5	478	5	465	5	13	3		
		3301	35	3153	35	2967	35	IN	35		
		3202	35	3087	35	2853	34	OUT	30		
		6503	70	6240	70	5820	69	TOTAL	65		
HOLES WON	PLUS STROKE HOLES	HANDICAP									
HOLES LOST	+1 HOLE 18										
BOGEY RESULT	+2 HOLE 4	NETT									

Markers Signature   Players Signature *RHDuck*

BLUE MARKER POSTS INDICATE 150 YARDS TO CENTRE OF GREEN

The card of the course, and the score shot by
Robert Duck to set a new amateur record in July, 1994

1st HOLE 454 yards LGU: 435

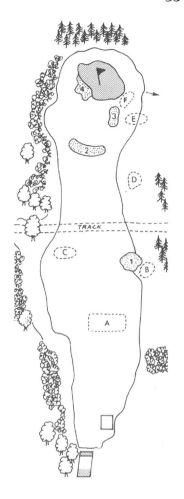

HISTORY

1932   Spinney planted at back of green

BRAID   2 spinneys planted in rough on right
Out - bunkers B, C, D
Enlarged - bunker 1
Extended - closer to green - bunkers
4, F

COTTON   Out - bunker E
Reduced - area of bunker A

GLEDHILL Out - bunkers A, F
New - Bunker 3
Bank lowered - bunker 2
Reduced (brought closer to green) -
bunker 4

DESCRIPTION

An adequate opening hole with plenty of space for
the drive for players to get away comfortably. Used to
play very straight and was rather dull but was much
improved by Gledhill work.

2nd HOLE 519 yards LGU: 440

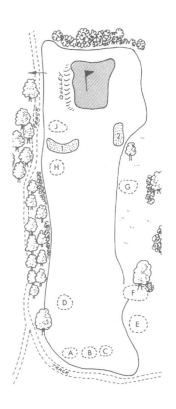

HISTORY

BRAID	OUT - bunkers A, B, C, H, J
COTTON	Out - bunker D
	Out and planted with broom etc.
	bunkers E, F, G
1963	Spinneys planted in rough on right
GLEDHILL	Gulley created left of green
1970	Summer medal tee constructed
1972	Championship tee constructed

DESCRIPTION

This hole should now be regarded as a par 5 and bunkered accordingly. To be successful, a par 5 needs to ask the question of the player being compelled to make a long carry for either the drive or second shot, or alternatively play short - also the green should be tightly trapped as the 3rd shot is usually a short one.

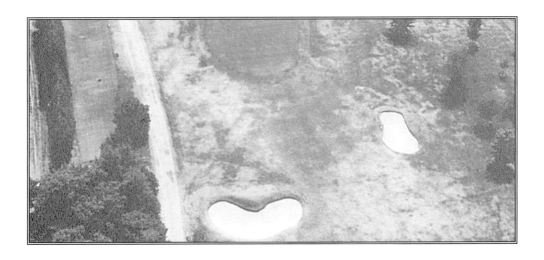

3rd HOLE 180 yards LGU: 142

HISTORY

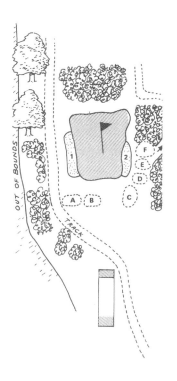

1932	Out - bunkers E, F; replanted with broom
BRAID	Out - bunkers A, B, C, D. Extended closer and lengthened - bunker 1. Widened closer to green - bunker 2. Tee enlarged and gorse in front removed.
GLEDHILL	Slope into bunker 2 accentuated.
CATLOW	Bunker 2 made more visible.
1975	Tee extended 20 yards to rear,

DESCRIPTION

A more difficult par 3 than it looks - due to problems in recovering if the green is missed from the tee shot.

4th HOLE 317 yards LGU: 288

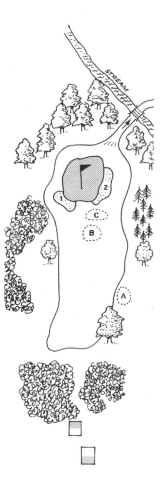

HISTORY

1923   New bunker in - B

BRAID   Out - bunkers A, C
Grass - bunker B
Front extended and closer to green -
bunker 2

GLEDHILL   Bunkers 1 and 2 extended round front
of green and valley constructed
between.

1976   Grass bunker B lowered and re-
shaped to form mound

DESCRIPTION

Suggestions have been made to lengthen the hole by
constructing a new tee further back to the right - this
is not favoured as it would make an enormous carry,
and probably lead to more drives landing on 5th fairway. The hole has been greatly improved by the
Gledhill work.

5th HOLE 442 yards LGU: 418

HISTORY

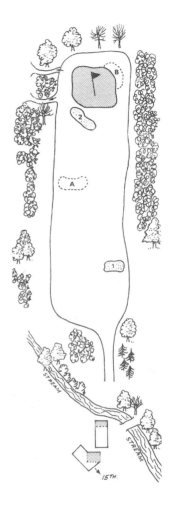

1930s	Front tee put in
BRAID	Extended back tee In - new bunkers 1, 2, B Lower bank of bunker A
COTTON	Out - bunker A
GLEDHILL	Out - bunker B
1968	Gorse at 80 yards - out
1969	Broom replanted at 80 yards
1970	Championship tee shared with 15th tee (no longer the case)
1976	Bunker A restored

DESCRIPTION

A tough par 4 test, even for the scratch man. Bunkers 1 and 2 are well placed, as a drive on the right gets rewarded by opening up entry into the green from right. Catlow suggestion to restore bunker A improves hole visually and provides interest in a long, plain uphill fairway.

6th HOLE 204 yards LGU: 149

HISTORY

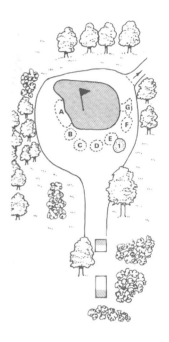

1913	In - bunkers C, D, E
BRAID	Join up as one - bunkers C, D, E In - bunker B Out - bunkers F, G
COTTON	Out - bunkers A, B, C, D, E. Approach broken up by creation of severe mounds In - bunker 1
1960s	New back tee

DESCRIPTION

Although a long par 3, the average scoring is as low as on the shorter par threes at 3rd and 15th - due to the easy recovery work from around the green. Three major alterations to try and improve the hole have been attempted, none of them very successful - the fault lies in the exceptionally large green (35 yards at its widest point) and width of approach (6 yards too wide), together with the too severe undulations in front which penalises unfairly the shorter player without incommoding the long-hitting player.

7th HOLE 378 yards LGU: 354

HISTORY

1959 Reduce bank on bunker 3

1963 Broom spinney planted at 200 yards 250 yards on left

GLEDHILL Tee enlarged - lengthened by 5 yards Bunker 6 brought in 5 yards nearer green

1966 Bunker 6 brought in 4 yards nearer and 'Scottish' type revetting with turf experimented with

1968 Bunker 6 restored to Gledhill position

DESCRIPTION

This hole has stood the test of time, the original six sand bunkers being more or less as originally constructed.

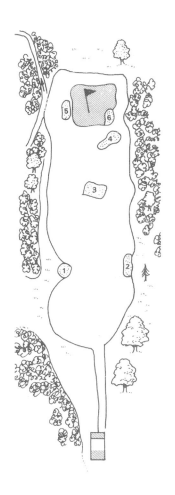

8th HOLE 312 yards LGU: 284

HISTORY

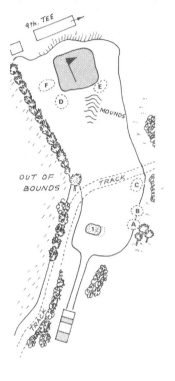

BRAID	Tee at back of 3rd green closed Out - bunkers B, F New - bunker C Bunker 1 - right half removed Enlarged - bunker E
COTTON	Out - bunkers A, C, D, E
1958	Bank at back of green made less severe
1959	Bumps in - short, right of green
1963	Spinney planted right at 180 yards
GLEDHILL	Reshape green more to right

DESCRIPTION

A thoroughly unsatisfactory hole:

l. Interference of play by traffic on bridle path.

2. Play held up by long hitters waiting for green to clear.

3. Green does not conform to built-up surrounds and is very open for a short par 4.

Further mounds at the approach and sides have been made round the green.

9th HOLE 396 yards LGU: 364

HISTORY

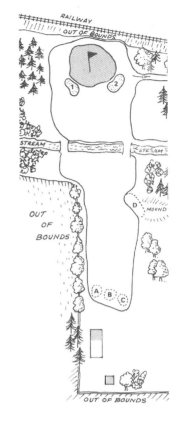

1931	Bunkers A, B, C turned to grass (and water!)
1932	Spinney left of tee planted
BRAID	Out - bushes across fairway at 240 yards New - bunker D Bunkers 1 and 2 enlarged
COTTON	Out - bunkers D and l. Grass bank replaced by spinney on right at 175 yards
1963	Trees left of green planted
CATLOW	Bunker 1 restored
1975	Old back tee re-opened
SINCLAIR	New green (1995)

DESCRIPTION

A fine hole but a very tough par 4 for ladies. Drive needs careful placing, and green area has been much improved by extension. The old tee re-opening gives 155 yards extra and a better view of the hole.

10th HOLE 413 yards LGU: 393

HISTORY

1923	New - bunker 2
1934	New - tee left (up the slope)
BRAID	Out - new tee left Out - bunkers D, E Out - right half of bunker A New - bunker F Bunker 4 re-shaped and brought closer in
COTTON	Out - bunkers C, F Grassed - bunkers A, B, G
1963	Spinneys planted left and right
GLEDHILL	Bunker 2 extended left

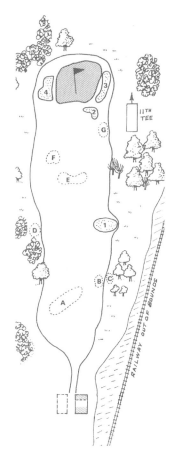

DESCRIPTION

A good par 4, much improved by extending bunker 2, requiring the drive to be placed left.

11th HOLE 384 yards LGU: 352

HISTORY

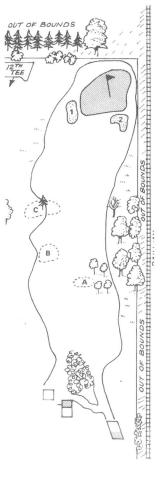

1923	New - bunker A
1933	New - ladies tee back of 10th green
1938	Suggestion of cross-bunker in face of bank short of green not carried out. Experimented with fairway between top of hill and green made into semi-rough. Not successful, later removed.
BRAID	Enlarged - bunkers A, C New - bunker B Green re-shaped, front flattened and extension made to right rear. Bank on right of green re-shaped and present bunker 2 inserted
COTTON	Out - bunkers A, C. Bunker C replaced by broom bushes
1963	New - back tee beside railway. Spinney planted on right at 250 yards.
GLEDHILL	Out - bunker B Extended left - bunker 2

DESCRIPTION

A superb par 4, especially from the bottom tee by the railway. The fairway is very wide, but this does not matter due to the exceptional tightness of second shot. The left side is masked by replanting of trees at brow of hill.

12th HOLE 142 yards LGU: 135

HISTORY

1938   Out - bunker F

BRAID   Separate tees combined into one level
                Out - bunkers A, D
                Enlarged - bunker 1

COTTON   Out - bunker 2

GLEDHILL Out - bunker E
                Enlarged - bunker 3

COTTON   In - bunker 2

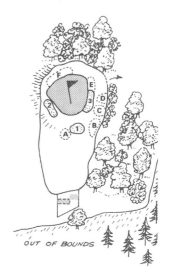

OUT OF BOUNDS

DESCRIPTION

Well designed short par 3, much improved by restoration of bunker 2. Looks somewhat unbalanced, particularly from right half of tee, due to density of trees on the right and open aspect on the left. This should be improved in time by the replanting of trees back left to the green.

13th HOLE 396 yards LGU: 320

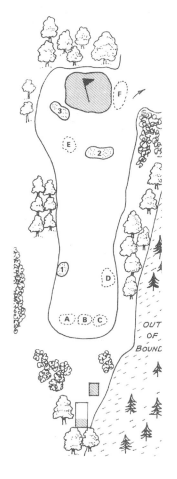

HISTORY

1928	Out - bunkers A, B, C
1932	Spinney at back of green planted
1933	New forward ladies tee
BRAID	Back tee closed Out - bunker F Bank of bunker 2 lowered Bunker 3 enlarged to become visible New - bunker E
COTTON	Out - bunkers D, E
1963	Silver birch spinney on left planted
1975	Back tee re-opened for championship play

DESCRIPTION

Straightforward par 4 - perhaps too straight - the entrance to the green being nine yards too wide (the green has shifted position down and up the slope). Blindness of green induces many second shots to be played short

14th HOLE 380 yards LGU: 359

HISTORY

BRAID	Out - bunkers A, D In - bunker C
COTTON	Out - bunkers B, C Re-shape - bunker 2
1960	New tee (left) in the woods
1961	Bunker 3 extended closer to green
1963	Spinney on right at 200 yards planted
1966	New back tee constructed Hollow at back of green constructed owing to contraction of out-of-bounds fence
CATLOW	Close tee in the woods (left)

DESCRIPTION

Visually good looking par 4, much improved by spinney planted on right and new back tee. The tee on the left in the woods, though admirable in conception, made the hole play too short - 30 yards back would have been splendid. Now re-opened for winter play.

15th HOLE 179 yards LGU: 157

HISTORY

1921 Experimented playing from tee in area of ninth green with 16th tee on 15th fairway. (not pursued - but similar idea was part of HARRIS plan to avoid the road).

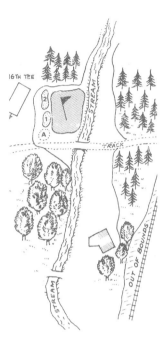

1923	In - bunker A
1928	Island in stream cleared away
1950s	Spinney at back planted
COTTON	Reduce - bunker A
GLEDHILL	Out - bunker A
CATLOW	Cleared out bushes short of bridle path

DESCRIPTION

Probably the most well known and remembered hole on the course.

16th HOLE 434 yards LGU: 401

HISTORY

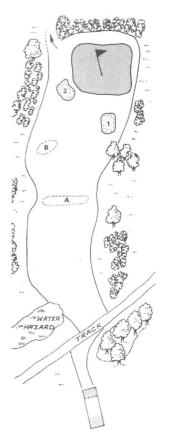

BRAID   Reduce size of bunker A
New - bunker B

COTTON   Out - bunker A

1932   Spinney planted right at 320 yards

GLEDHILL Out - bunker B
Bunker 2 brought closer to green
Water hazard reduced in size

DESCRIPTION

A tough par 4, especially into the prevailing wind; the drive has to be held against the slope of the ground, and the green has its peculiarities, to say the least!

17th HOLE 466 yards LGU: 386

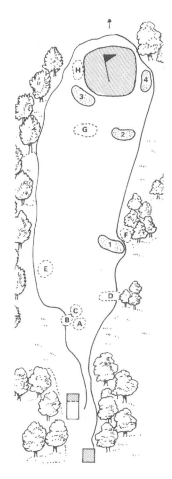

HISTORY

1926	New back tee
1932	Trees planted left at 350 yards
BRAID	Back tee closed Out - bunkers A, B, C, F, G New - bunker 1
COTTON	Out - bunkers D, E, H Enlarged - bunker 3
1963	Spinneys planted right at 140 yards, 250 yards, 320 yards
1970	Championship tee re-opened
CATLOW	Bunker 1 extended left, fairway extended on left Bunker G re-opened and shape altered

DESCRIPTION

Now an exceptionally good par 4 from the championship tee. The green is poorly shaped, being roughly a featureless circle. It has also too wide an approach for the length of the hole and needs to be tightened on the right.

18th HOLE 507 yards LGU: 456

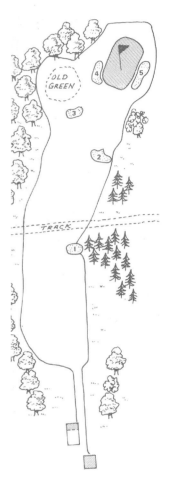

HISTORY

1926	New back tee
1932	Spinney planted at back of green
BRAID	Major re-construction to dog-leg
COTTON	Reduced - bunker 1
GLEDHILL	New - Bunker 3
1970	Championship tee re-opened

DESCRIPTION

A very tough birdie 4, but a very easy par 5 if played as such.

SUMMARY OF YARDAGE AND BOGEY/PAR

Hole No.	1910	1922	1933	1949	1961	1968	1971
		Bogey	Bogey	Bogey	Par	Par	Par
1	410	408-5	458-5	449-5	459-5	459-4	459-4
2	410	445-5	445-5	457-5	457-5	457-4	457-4
3	150	150-3	160-3	163-3	163-3	163-3	163-3
4	296	296-4	326-4	321-4	321-4	321-4	321-4
5	412	432-5	432-4	450-5	450-5	450-4	450-4
6	176	176-3	176-3	180-3	180-3	200-3	200-3
7	370	370-4	370-4	370-4	370-4	370-4	375-4
8	294	294-4	294-4	300-4	300-4	300-4	300-4
9	390	390-5	390-4	377-4	377-4	377-4	377-4
	2908	2961-38	3051-36	3067-37	3077-37	3097-34	3102-34
10	396	396-5	426-5	415-5	415-4	415-4	415-4
11	364	364-5	364-4	371-4	371-4	381-4	381-4
12	145	145-3	160-3	147-3	147-3	147-3	147-3
13	362	362-4	377-4	368-4	368-4	368-4	368-4
14	378	378-4	378-4	373-4	373-4	391-4	391-4
15	140	140-3	175-3	173-3	173-3	173-3	173-3
16	420	440-5	440-5	440-5	440-4	440-4	440-4
17	404	404-5	474-5	408-4	408-4	408-4	408-4
18	426	426-5	476-5	488-5	488-5	488-5	488-5
	3035	3055-39	3270-38	3183-37	3183-35	3211-35	3211-35
Total	5943	6016-77	6321-74	6250-74	6260-72	6308-69	6313-69
					S.S.S.-71	S.S.S.-70	S.S.S.-70

Hole No.	1974 (Re-measured)		1976			1995	
	Medal	Championship	Medal	Championship	Winter Medal	Summer Medal	Championship
	Par	Par	Par	Par	Par	Par	Par
1	454-4	454-4	454-4	454-4	415-4	443-4	454-4
2	486-5	519-5	486-5	519-5	457-4	486-5	519-5
3	160-3	160-3	171-3	180-3	135-3	171-3	180-3
4	317-4	317-4	317-4	317-4	304-4	317-4	317-4
5	442-4	463-4	442-4	463-4	404-4	442-4	442-4
6	204-3	204-3	204-3	204-3	179-3	198-3	204-3
7	367-4	367-4	367-4	367-4	349-4	360-4	378-4
8	296-4	296-4	296-4	296-4	271-4	291-4	312-4
9	379-4	379-4	396-4	396-4	339-4	379-4	396-4
	3105-35	3159-35	3133-35	3196-35	2853-34	3087-35	3202-35
10	413-4	413-4	413-4	413-4	381-4	413-4	413-4
11	384-4	384-4	384-4	384-4	368-4	368-4	384-4
12	128-3	128-3	128-3	128-3	117-3	136-3	142-3
13	370-4	370-4	383-4	396-4	361-4	383-4	396-4
14	380-4	380-4	380-4	380-4	322-4	365-4	380-4
15	167-3	167-3	167-3	167-3	142-3	167-3	179-3
16	434-4	434-4	434-4	434-4	415-4	426-4	434-4
17	403-4	455-4	410-4	455-4	395-4	410-4	466-4
18	478-5	507-5	478-5	507-5	466-5	478-5	507-5
	3157-35	3238-35	3177-35	3264-35	2967-35	3146-35	3301-35
Total	6262-70	6397-70	6310-70	6460-70	5820-69	6233-70	6503-70
	S.S.S.-70	S.S.S.-70	S.S.S.-70	S.S.S.-71	S.S.S.-68	S.S.S.-70	S.S.S.-71

CHAPTER VII

Past Captains

"But his Captain's hand on his shoulder smote –
Play up, play up and play the game"

Sir Henry Newbolt

1910-1918   **Hon Edward Algernon Fitzroy**
See Chapter 1

1919   **Neville Frederick Bostock**
Managing Director, Lotus Shoes. Son of Frederick Bostock. Good at all sports especially fly fishing and shooting. Low handicap golfer. Neville served in the 1914-18 War and remained a bachelor who lived in Spratton. Brother of Norah Bostock, who married Herbert Mobbs, (father of Humphrey, Rachel, George and Roger) who was the brother of Lieutenant Colonel Edgar Richard Mobbs DSO, the great sporting hero of rugby football fame and who played for the Saints, East Midlands and England. He was killed in Flanders in 1917 commanding the Northamptonshire Battalion which he raised at Franklin's Gardens. Noel Mobbs was another brother who founded Slough Estates (the property company) after the 1914-18 War and who lived in and owned, what is now, Stoke Park Golf Club, as his private residence, near Slough. Herbert and Norah Mobbs begat four children: Rachel, John Humphrey, Graham Eric (alias George) and Roger Linnell Mobbs, the last three great stalwarts of Brampton and all fine golfers.

1920-1925   **Alfred James Fraser DSO**
Chairman & Managing Director Phipps Brewery. Awarded DSO in World War I. Had been a tea planter in Borneo until 1902. Founder member of NCGC.

1926   **Thomas Edgar (TEM) Manning**
Managing Director of T Manning & Co Castle Brewery. Founder member and Trustee of NCGC. Won the Boycott Trophy 13 times. Captain & President Northamptonshire County Cricket Club. Uncle of Peter Palmer and father of Tom Manning. Born 1884 and died in 1975. Educated at Wellingborough School.

T E Manning

Dick Watkins   1968

Jack Belson   1976

Bruce Clayton   1977

Jack Corrin   1978

1927   **J Faulkner Stops**
Solicitor with Becke Green & Stops. Clerk to
Northampton Divisional Bench. Under Sheriff.
Deputy coroner. Election agent to Hon E A Fitzroy.
Coldstream Guards. Played rugby for Saints &
East Midlands and hockey for Northampton &
Midlands. 4 handicap golfer. Present at the
execution at Bedford Prison of Alfred Rouse, the
blazing car murderer at Hardingstone, tried at the
Northampton Assizes. Played cricket and hockey for
Northamptonshire.

1928   **William John Watkins**
Head Brewer at Northampton Brewery Co. then followed L C Baillon as
Managing Director. Awarded BEM in 1946. Died at
home in Dallington in tragic circumstances aged 74.

1929   **Lancelot Bostock DSO**
Another son of Fred Bostock. Buyer for Lotus
Shoes. Fine sportsman at all sports including
scratch golfer. Won DSO with 7th Northamptons
in World War I. Resided at Pitsford House with his
parents. Unmarried and died of septic pneumonia
in 1935 aged 43.

Lancelot Bostock

1930   **Fred Bostock**
Born in 1860 became head of Lotus Shoes and lived at
Pitsford House. Deputy Lieutenant in 1937.
Chairman of Northampton Gas Co and St
Matthews Nursing Home and former captain of
Northampton Golf Club and founder member of
NCGC. An expert horticulturalist. Father of
Neville and Lancelot. Preceded HRH Duke of
York. (Are there other precedents whereby sons
precede their father in the tenure of an office of some
distinction in our Club as happened in this case?)

1931   **HRH Duke of York**
HRH Duke of York who became King George VI when his brother,
Edward VIII abdicated. Queen Elizabeth his consort (known to our
generation as the Queen Mother and who lived to be 101) shared her
husband's love of golf. Each season the couple took possession of a
hunting lodge at Thornby (later the home of the eccentric Captain Wills
of the tobacco family from Bristol) to hunt regularly with the Pytchley
and Quorn. They would hunt on Saturdays and play golf on Sundays
and were frequent visitors to Althorp.

Eric Kottler   1980

John Duffy   1981

Jack Bell   1982

Eric Sleath   1985

1932   **Captain J C Grant Ives**
Regular officer with the Rifle Brigade. The family home had been at Bradden House near Towcester since the 17th century. Chairman of Towcester RDC 1950-54 and on the Grafton Hunt Committee and expert on greyhound coursing. Died 1955 aged 69. The estate is now the home of Keith Barwell, the Saints' Rugby Football Club benefactor and well-known local businessman.

1933   **Arthur Gerald Seward**
Joined Phipps Brewery in 1899. Became head brewer in 1906 and a director in 1933. Lived near the Cock Hotel and died in 1956. Arthur was given the nickname "closet crouch" by fellow golfers because of the posture he adopted whilst playing every shot. Played regularly in a foursome which was given the soubriquet the "brewery four" comprising Tem Manning, Turkey Baillon, Major Fraser and Arthur Seward. The formidable quartet played every week and woe betide any rank and file member who got in front of them and delayed them for a second or appeared to be approaching rapidly from behind.

1934   **William Lees**
Wholesale and retail tobacconist. Alderman of the Borough 1925-61. Mayor of Northampton 1942. Honorary Freeman of the Borough. Also captain of Kingsthorpe GC and President of NGU. Died in 1965 aged 67. Resided at Cliftonville, Northampton, one of the first gentlemen of "trade" who became a member of the Golf Club. Built up a fine business, located at the top of Bridge Street, now occupied by the firm of Michael Jones, Jewellers. His son Harry Lees, daughter Mrs Dorothy Cooch, and son-in-law John Cooch, were all Captains of the Golf Club.

1935   **Lancelot Bostock DSO**
Second term of office. See 1929.

1936   **Leslie H Church DSO**
Chairman of Church's Shoes for 25 years. Also chairman of St Matthews Nursing Home and the Northampton Electric Light Co. Resided at Holly Lodge, Church Brampton and Broom Hill, Spratton.

1937-38   **Louis Charles (Turkey) Baillon**
Born in the Falkland Islands in 1851. Chairman and Managing Director of the Northampton Brewery Co. A founder member of the County Golf Club, the Northampton Hockey Club and the Northampton Tennis Club. Won a gold medal at the 1908 Olympic Games as captain of the England hockey team. Partnered Harold Boycott at full back for England at hockey and played tennis for Northamptonshire. Father of Spriggs Ballion, Brabs Ballion (architect) and two other sons, both killed on active service in the RAF during World War II.

Alf York   1987

Clive Blackburn   1988

Roger Martin   1989

Peter Arnold   1990

1939-40   **Bertram Cheney**
County Treasurer of Northamptonshire County Council. Acted both as secretary and treasurer to the County Golf Club and did much to keep the Golf Club running during the war years.

1941   **J Faulkner Stops**
Second term of office. See 1927

1942-43   **Arthur Spencer Baxter OBE**
Led the London Central Meat Company to become one of the most important national multiple retailing butchery companies, with its own abattoirs and over 500 shops throughout the United Kingdom. Keen golfer and a man of great charm who did much for the Club during the war. Under Arthur's chairmanship his company, Baxter's, became a public company and after his death was taken over by Brooke Bond Liebig. The sand bunker, just short and to the right of the sixth green, became affectionately known as "Baxter's crack".

1944   **Thomas Edgar Manning**
Second term of office. See 1926.

1945   **Alfred Samuel Garrard**
Managing Director of shoe manufacturers Manfield & Sons. Member and past captain of Kingsthorpe Golf Club. Father of Mrs Beryl Harrison, past Ladies' Captain.

1946   **Frank Flintham Parsons JP**
Managing Director of Pork Pie Co. Played cricket and football for Irchester. County Councillor for 22 years and County magistrate.

1947-48   **Richard Augustus Palmer OBE JP FCA**
Senior partner with A C Palmer auditors to the club since its foundation. Played golf for the county and rugby for East Midlands. Justice of the Peace and Deputy Lieutenant 1977. Trustee and Vice President of NCGC. President of NGU, County Chamber of Commerce and Northampton Rugby Football Club.

1949   **Donald Chamberlain**
Chairman of W W Chamberlain. Scratch golfer and also member of Clapham, Sheringham and Rushden golf clubs. Committee member and benefactor of Northamptonshire County Cricket Club. Together with Alan Timson donated the veranda at Brampton. Commandant of Wellingborough Division of Northampton Special Constabulary.

1950   **Dr J Lyon-Brown OBE**
Doctor in general practice in Northampton. Received OBE for services in Hankow during 1926 riots. President of the Royal Medical Society of Edinburgh and Senior Medical Officer for Coastal Command in 1939-45 war. Lived at the Red House at Chapel Brampton.

1951   **Percy George Jones**
Chairman of Crockett & Jones shoe manufacturers and President of Northampton Shoe Manufacturers Association. Also captain of Northampton GC. County and Midlands hockey player.

1952   **Harry Allen Lees**
Son of William Lees. Managing Director William Lees (Tobacconists). President Wholesale Tobacco Association 1968. Captain Oakham School Rugby XV, also in cricket XI and half blue for billiards at Cambridge. Committee member of General Hospital and Church Charities (St Giles).

1953   **Stuart Harold Guise Humfrey**
Educated at Oakham and Gonville & Caius Cambridge. Public Schools national champion at high and long jump. Played for Barbarians 1912 alongside Edgar Mobbs. Played county cricket 1913-26. An eye surgeon in partnership with Mr Harries-Jones.

1954   **Charles Stanley Catlow**
Company director with BB Vos Leather Merchants. (see chapter on Sporting Personalities for further details).

1955   **John Henry Cooch**
Managing Director of agricultural machinery company. Played rugby for Old Northamptonians. Chairman of Northampton Divisional Tax Commissioners.

Charles Catlow

1956   **Stewart Filshill Kennedy OBE**
Chairman of Church & Co 1962-76. Vice President of Northampton Rugby Football Club. Awarded OBE for services to export.

1957   **Gerald John William Wareing**
Managing Director of clothing manufacturing company. Chairman of Parish Council for Great Houghton and Churchwarden of the local church. Lived next door to the Cherry Tree Inn at Great Houghton to which he reputedly had a connecting door.

1958   **Thomas Faulkner Gammage**
Solicitor and clerk to the magistrates of Northampton and Daventry. Area

Spriggs Baillon, the 1969 captain, with his companion, George, and displaying a picture of the 1908 England Olympic hockey team. His father L C Baillon, Brampton captain in 1937/38, led the English team to the gold medal at the White City Stadium

coroner to Northampton and Daventry. Keen and highly competent rock climber in Wales and Skye. Secretary of the Northampton Symphony Orchestra for many years.

1959 **Norval Gibson Durham**
Director of Northampton chemical company which he established. Hon Sec of the golf club 1953-60. President of the Northampton Chamber of Commerce. Enlisted in Royal Flying Corps in 1914-18 War. RAFVR 1918-38.

1960 **Henry Makin Draper CBE**
Solicitor. County Court Registrar for Northampton court. Chairman of the registrars Committee for which he received a CBE.

1961 **John Charles Jennings Legge JP**
Chartered Auctioneer and Surveyor. Justice of the Peace on the Northampton Bench. Chairman of the Council for Voluntary Services. President of the Northampton Orpheus Choir.

1962 **Thomas Faulkner Gammage**
See 1958.

1963 **Arthur Noel Harris**
County Architect for Northamptonshire 1948-69. Came from a family of architects. His father came from the same profession and his brother was County Architect for Somerset.

1964 **Wilfred H Orbell**
Managing Director of Mulliners Coach Builders in Bridge Street. A man of sartorial elegance. It probably took him as long to change after a round of golf as it took him to play the round.

1965 **Walter Charles Gledhill MBE**
Born in Australia. Came to Northampton after the War as consultant Ear, Nose and Throat surgeon. Won an MBE in the War. After retirement, returned to Australia.

1966 **Richard John Ward Gubbins**
Managing Director of leather manufacturing company. Hon Sec of the golf club 1958-64. Vice President of the club and Trustee since 1989.

1967 **Jesse Lionel Harrison**
Solicitor with family firm of Shoosmiths & Harrison. President of the Northampton Law Society. Honorary solicitor to the club for many years.

1968   **Richard Francis Watkins**
Chartered Accountant and senior partner with Coopers & Lybrand. Hon
Sec of the golf club 1964-66. Hon Auditor and Trustee of the club.

1969   **Richard Obie (Spriggs) Baillon**
Son of founder member L C Baillon. Sales Director of Northampton
Brewery company. County tennis player before and after World War II.
Partnered Billy Knight in 1954. Full back for Northampton Rugby
Football Club and East Midlands. Chairman of greens committee at
Brampton for ten years.

1970   **Charles Norman Buswell OBE, MC and Bar, Croix de Guerre**
Wholesale butcher. President of National Wholesale Butchers
Association. Played for Northampton Saints Rugby XV. (see separate
narrative)

1971   **Edgar Coker JP**
Joint Managing Director with brother in family shoe supply company.
Town councillor 1965-79. Justice of the Peace on Northampton Bench
1967-90. School Governor of Spratton School. County golfer.

1972   **William Geoffrey Palmer**
Solicitor and Clerk to Wellingborough Urban District Council. Member
of Wellingborough Golf Club and prime mover in the plan to sell the nine
hole course and move to Harrowden Hall and construct the 18 hole
course being played today.

1973   **Kenneth Clarke Hunter**
Schoolmaster. Headmaster at a British school in Jerusalem. Founded and
was Headmaster of Spratton Hall Preparatory School 1951-1975;
Churchwarden of Pitsford Church and ran the Seniors "Tour" at
Brampton.

1974   **Andrew Roy Banham**
Surgeon at Northampton General Hospital 1935-69 and was on the
Oxford Hospital regional Board 1947-59. President of the Northampton
Medical Society. County squash player and Chairman of the Brington
Parish Council 1972-80.

1975   **Dennis Laverick**
Dental surgeon. Chairman of the Health Authority 1967. Played rugby for
the London Hospitals in the Thirties.

1976   **Leslie John Belson**
Wholesale newsagent. Worked for the News Chronicle before World War

II and promoted the Mr Lobby Ludd competition. Keen cricketer and member of the Saints XI for many years.

1977   **Bruce John Clayton JP**
Chartered surveyor and auctioneer. After 41 years in the estate profession and retirement joined Christie's, the Fine Art Auctioneers, in the Midlands. Justice of the Peace on Northampton Bench for 30 years. Trustee and former Chairman of Greens, honoured with Presidency of the Club, following the death of Spriggs Baillon.

1978   **John Bowes Corrin OBE**
Accountant and senior partner with Grant Thornton. Alderman of the Borough. Leader of the council and Mayor of Northampton 1964. Honorary Freeman of the Borough. Chairman of Anglia Building Society and Northampton High School.

1979   **Edward Victor Corps**
Senior geologist with Burmah Oil Company. Spent many years before and after World War II in Burma, India and Pakistan where he played polo. After retirement in 1956 became English representative of Dallas oil firm of consultant geologists.

Lionel Harrison   *1967*   *R A (Peter) Palmer*   *1947-1948*

1980   **Eric Cecil Kottler**
Civil Engineer and Managing Director of Kottler & Heron. Member of National Executive Council of Federation of Civil Engineers. Chairman of Midlands Federation of Civil Engineers and Chairman of Birmingham Training Centre. Skilled amateur wood carver.

1981   **John Rutherford Duffy**
Born in Rugby where his father was town clerk and educated at Rugby School. Solicitor and partner at Bretherton Turpin and Pell, both in Rugby and Lutterworth. Until retirement was Chairman of the local Income Tax Commissioners and served as Chairman of the Social Security Appeals Tribunal in Coventry. From school days onwards, played golf to a low handicap and was Honorary Secretary to Rugby Golf

Above left: David Deane, 1992

Above: Peter Haddon, 1993

Left: Bill Stephenson, 1994

Club. His wife used to play golf but happily for him gave it up in favour of gardening. John was once the proud possessor of the Alpine Cup, played for in Iglis in Austria – golf, you understand, not skiing. A Trustee of the NCGC and holds honorary membership at both Northants County and Rugby Golf Clubs.

1982   **John Frederick Norman Bell**
Tall, quiet, dignified and the personification of a gentleman, educated at Berkhamsted School. Called up in 1939 and joined the County Regiment. Commissioned into Indian Army Infantry Regiment and fought with the 14th Army from the Arakan down the length of the Irrawaddy River until the final defeat of the Japanese. Keen sportsman, former rugby footballer, cricketer with Northampton Saints XI, member of the Red Cat and Agaric Golfing Societies. President of the Northants Amateurs, Managing Director of A Bell and Co and Chairman of the National Fireplace Council.

1983   **Richard Gibson Aitken**
Consultant Clinical Biochemist at Kettering General Hospital. President of Northampton & County Scottish Association (see separate chapter on Sporting Personalities).

1984   **Arthur Neil Soutar JP**
Managing Director of leather manufacturing company. County and Midlands hockey player and county golfer. Justice of the Peace on Northampton Bench. Trustee for the Debenture Holders for NCGC. Churchwarden All Saints, Northampton.

1985   **Eric David Sleath**
Export manager for Church & Company and Sales Director of H R Marrun Ltd. President Northampton & County Shoe Trades Golfing Society. Chairman of Boughton & Whitehills Conservative Association.

1986   **Jack H Humphries**
See chapter on Sporting Personalities.

1987   **Frederick Alfred York**
Managing Director Yorks Travel. General Commissioner for Taxes. Trustee of St John's Hospital and Churchwarden for All Saints Church, Northampton.

1988   **Clive Taylor Blackburn**
Area Manager National Life Assurance & Pensions Company. President Northamptonshire Society of Golf Club Captains. NGU Selector.

1989   **Keith Roger Martin**

Graduate of Oxford and Reading universities. Served as a naval officer. Held a distinguished career in education as headmaster, inspector of schools and consultant participating actively in a number of important national projects.

1990   **Peter Arnold**

Played cricket at first class level in New Zealand before joining Northamptonshire County Cricket Club in the late 1940's at a time when several colleagues from the antipodes were attracted to the Club. Strengthened it enormously and turned it from an indifferent side into one of the best in the championship. Peter was an opening batsman who showed patience, resilience and aggression when needed. His patience was of virtue in as much as two seasoned professionals in Dennis Brookes who later captained the side (and played in one Test Match for England) and Percy Davies were the established opening batsmen and for whose retirement he had to wait. Whilst playing for Northamtonshire Peter achieved five centuries and is proud to have served under the captaincy of F R (Freddie) Brown.

Whilst playing cricket Peter, in common with others, worked for British Timken during the winter months, under the patronage of Sir John Pascoe. On retiring from cricket, formed his own company Arnold (Hose) Limited. Played cricket for Northampton Saints' Cricket Club and took up golf at which he excelled and played to a single figure handicap. Devoted much time in RC Church affairs and is a governor of Thomas Becket RC School.

1991   **Graham Neil Underwood**

Youngest of three sons of the late "Briff" and Dora Underwood. A family passionate about sport, Graham played all team games at Northampton Grammar School and represented Northamptonshire at cricket (schools) and at senior level tennis, badminton and squash. A chartered surveyor by profession, which for Graham was inescapable, joining the practice set up by his father with brother, Trevor, as another partner who ran the residential side of the business, whilst Graham founded the commercial side and took it to the much respected practice that it is today.

1992   **David W G Deane**

David Deane was a very successful businessman in the town and Captain of the Club in 1992. He spent two three-year terms as a hardworking member of the Committee and his advice, with his craftsman's expertise, was invaluable in work carried out on the Clubhouse. During his year of Captaincy he oversaw the extension to the dining room and he and his Co-Director, Tony Amos, donated the fine oak doors to the entrance of the Clubhouse.

A very popular club member and much respected who still takes an active part in club activities. His wife Delia is also a lady member.

1993   **Peter Haddon JP**

An architect by profession who trained in Northampton before opening his own practice. A fine chorister, Peter sang as man and boy in the distinguished choir of All Saints Church, Northampton. He served as National Service Officer in the Royal Engineers and as a magistrate on the Northampton petty sessional division for some 25 years. For many years Peter played back row and prop forward for Northampton Rugby Football Club (the Saints) with over 100 appearances for the First XV. He also played for the Army and the East Midlands. During national service played for the Harlequins and Leicester Tigers. Peter still retains his good looks despite his risky and accident-prone antecedent history, and remains a keen golfer!

1994   **W A (Bill) Stephenson**

Retired bank manager whose career was with the National Westminster Bank. Like several other Club treasurers before and after him, this background provided Bill with the wisdom and experience to run the Club's finances extremely well for ten years, relinquishing this important office when he assumed the role as Club Vice-Captain and ultimately Captain, a distinction genuinely deserved. Keen golfer for many years and a regular with the Whisky Macs and avid supporter of the past Captains' day when the Corrin Cup is played for. A positive outlook and attitude helped Bill overcome major surgery in recent years and return to regular golf. He was honoured with Honorary Life Membership for his infinite services to the Club.

Past Captains and a Few Further Facts About Them

"The shouting and the tumult dies, the captains and the kings depart".

Rudyard Kipling

Neil Soutar listed the past captains from the very first year right up to 1994 and catalogued brief and cryptic facts about all of them. I am providing additional information wherever I can, in order to paint a broader canvas of eminent names from the past and present.

1995   **Alan Goddard**
Doyen of the leather trade, acting as an importer/factor dealing mainly with the Indian sub Continent and therefore a much travelled man. Served with the 11th Hussars during the war years and afterwards joined the same company of which his father was a Director - B B Vos. Finally settled in Northampton in the village of Boughton (see separate narrative).

1996   **Les Cantrell**
Successful local businessman in the printing trade with business interests in leisure abroad. Played Rugby League to a high standard as a young man. Very competent single figure golfer, former county junior player for Yorkshire and Nottinghamshire, served as Northamptonshire Golf Union County Team Captain from 1996-01. Member of Northamptonshire Golf Union County Seniors Team 2006 and 2007. NGU President 2006-08. Sponsor of Northamptonshire PGA Order of Merit from 1985 to 1996, President of Northamptonshire PGA 2003-06.

1997   **Alexander Cameron Sinclair**
Born at Coatbridge, Scotland and graduated at Heriot Watt University, Edinburgh in landscape architecture. Played early golf at Bothwell Castle Golf Club and represented his university side. Golf architect who gained experience working with Cotton, Pennink, Steele and Partners and Graham Marsh in Australia. Designed Whittlebury Park Golf Club, Rutland County, Bedfordshire Golf Club and our own additional three holes. Fine track record in club competitions, played golf for Northamptonshire and is a member of the Royal and Ancient Golf Club.

1998   **Michael T Bairstow**
Keen rugby footballer in his younger days who took up golf having finished playing rugby and thereafter refereeing. Michael joined the paper distribution company Robert Horne when it only boasted 20 employees, later to become a large and formidable firm. When the company moved from London to Northampton in the 1970s, he became joint Managing Director, eventually succeeding the late Mr Kenneth Horne (also a member of this Club) as Chief Executive and Chairman. The first Chairman of Northamptonshire County Golf Club, a position Michael held for six years (see separate narrative).

1999   **Christopher Thompson**
Born in Newcastle-on-Tyne thus qualifying as a "Geordie" and was educated at Durham School, which his own two sons attended later. Excelling at sport, Chris played first class rugby for Gosforth Park in the 1960s. Chris followed his father in the career of banking which took him via the itinerant route of management training with Lloyds Bank, southwards to regional offices and to head office in Threadneedle Street in London during the time of Sir Jeremy Morse's heyday. Lloyds Bank later merged with the Trustee Savings Bank.
A golfer since boyhood, Chris joined Northamptonshire County Golf Club when he came to the George Row branch of the bank as Assistant Manager in 1987. Moving on to greater things, he concluded his career as a Regional Commercial manager. Chris served on the general committee and became Club Treasurer and later Club Captain and is currently the Club Chairman succeeding Michael Bairstow in this role. Meanwhile Chris plays to a single figure handicap which seems to present no undue problems to him or to those fortunate to be drawn as his playing partners.

2000   **John Leonard Bernstein**
Product of Northampton Grammar School and Oakham. Ran E & J Bernstein (Sylvan) Ltd, light clothing manufacturers. Keen sportsman, having played rugby for Hendon RFC and hockey for Northampton Hockey Club and a keen golfer most of his life. (see Pen Portrait)

2001   **Richard G Halliday**

In his young days Richard joined Northamptonshire County Council as trainee local government officer. He soon turned to banking and joined Lloyds Bank and remained at the main branch for the rest of his professional career. Over a period of many years Richard excelled as a golfer, starting as a young player at Northampton Golf Club at Kettering Road and later at Church Brampton. He represented the county side for many years and served as Captain and President of the Union. (see separate narrative)

2002   **Keith Archbold**

Keith came to Northampton working as a Chartered accountant for John Blackwood Hodge and Company at Hunsbury, Northampton. Keith is a Yorkshireman, born and educated in Sheffield where he qualified professionally. Served national service in the RAF. Keith is a Rotarian (past president), a keen bridge player and a fine golfer. For many years he has been a stalwart of the "Dawn Patrol", since its formation by Peter Bennett and John Pendry and is present on the course early several times every week, which probably explains his single figure handicap since retirement. Keith was former Club Treasurer - one of the most important roles in the management of the club's affairs.

2003   **Peter Lock**

Devonian by birth, and previous member of Ramsey Golf Club (Cambridgeshire), John O'Gaunt (Bedfordshire), Karen and Limuru (Kenya) before finally joining Brampton in 1989. Winner of the Chamberlain Cup and Clayton Rose Bowl. Ran own packaging company very successfully.

2004   **Malcolm Peel**

Born in Harrow and read physiology at Worcester College, Oxford. Served as young officer in the Seaforth Highlanders in BAOR, Germany. Career in the paper trade and printing, joining Clarke & Sherwell, the well known Northampton firm in 1971 which brought him to Church Brampton. Fine golfer, former Oxford Blue, still plays in the President's Putter every January (to date 45 times). Married to Marion, former Lady Secretary. Elected as a member of the R & A Golf Club, current handicap 9.

2005   **Robin Patterson**

Robin was born in Trinidad where his father was an oil engineer. Educated partly in Trinidad and later at Eastbourne College where he learnt his rugby football and achieved distinction in that and many other sports, later playing rugby for Blackheath, Rosslyn Park, Metropolitan Police, Solihull and other clubs. Lowest handicap 7.

2006   **John Beynon**

A Chartered Surveyor by profession and now residing in East Haddon Hall, formerly the distinguished home of Mr David Guthrie, a founder member of this Golf Club (see Chapter 1). A keen golfer and highly competitive sportsman.

John read Estate Management at London University and thus entered the estate profession, at first with the District Valuers' Office in Staffordshire.

Then through the estate offices of various commercial firms, he entered a partnership and practised in London for 25 years, through the vicissitudes of good times and bad.

John is married to Dorothy and they have two sons, both in the estate profession.

2007   **Brian O'Connell**

Dedicated fine golfer, to whom practice seems no chore and leads to near perfection. Northamptonian by birth who took up golf late (aged 33) and who has achieved a handicap of 1 and is currently 3. Winner of 20 trophies to date with every prospect of more to come. Businessman who resides in Golf Lane in close proximity to the Club.

2008   **David Green**

Club Treasurer and Centenary Captain 2008-09. Quiet, dignified and shrewd Chartered accountant who followed a succession of hard working and devoted Treasurers looking after the Club's affairs and providing wise counsel. Born in Dublin where he qualified as an Accountant. Now runs Target Furniture, the family firm. Gifted golfer (see separate cameo - Centenary Captains).

CHAPTER VIII

The Ladies Section

"Anon comes home my wife from Brampton, not looked for till Saturday, which will hinder me of a little pleasure, but I am glad of her coming"

Samuel Pepys

The Ladies Section at Brampton has always been of a high calibre, and whereas the men in the early days could boast the names of Lord Spencer, Lord Annaly, Lord Ludlow and the Hon. Edward Fitzroy among their members, the ladies could counter with Lady Dawnay, Lady Annaly, Countess Spencer, Miss Bouverie and Mrs Deterding, all formidable ladies in the county hierarchy.

The management of the club, however, has always been male dominated and it was not until 1949 that two ladies were invited on to the Club management committee. The men may have been shamed into this decision because in that year when the Club was in dire financial straits, the ladies section donated £100 to the Club which was a considerable sum in those days, and the men's committee was 'staggered by the generosity' as recorded in their minutes. The relationship was still, however, a little strained as the men originally made their own choice of which ladies should serve. This decision was later reversed but on one occasion the men refused the ladies' selection because it had not been made three clear weeks before the AGM. It was not until 1975 that the Lady Captain and Ladies' Secretary were automatically a permanent fixture on the Club management committee.

The ladies have always been able to look after their own affairs particularly on the financial front, and it appears that they were always able to make a profit on their section. Apart from the gift mentioned above there have been many small items such as redecoration, new curtains and so on that the ladies have paid for without coming to the main committee for money. They were also of great value to the social committee in the 1950s, when a lot of much needed revenue was raised through the Annual Dance. This was noteworthy when you consider that in 1959 the price for the Annual Dance at the Salon with Tommy Kinsman and his band and a buffet supper was only £1.25p per ticket!

On the golfing scene, from early days Brampton has played host to a number of ladies events, one of the first being the LGU Handicap Challenge Bowl in 1923, which also included the Barnehurst Scratch Challenge Bracelet and Golfing Bowl, which was won by Mrs R D Fowler, who went round in 83 (including a 7 at the fifth), a ladies record for the course.

In 1924 Miss Cecil Leitch - one of five sisters - played in the Brampton Open Ladies Meeting off a +2 handicap and scored a gross 81 to win the scratch prize and lower the course record. Miss Leitch was very fond of Brampton and often played there when visiting relatives in the area, and in 1926 gave a cup to be played as an inter Club competition within the county with handicaps limited to 12-36. This Cecil Leitch Cup is still played for today, but whereas it originally was always played at Brampton, other clubs in the county also stage matches. Brampton have won the cup on 16 occasions. Cecil Leitch herself was a very distinguished golfer, winning the British Ladies Open championship four times.

Margaret Musgrave and Peggy Coker

In 1939 the Ladies Midland championship was played at Brampton, but with the outbreak of war in September, all competitions and fixtures were cancelled, the ladies in office continued until the end of hostilities, and ladies golf ceased to exist until 1946.

In 1946 everyone was mad keen to play golf again. Bridge drives were organised to raise some money, and eventually 10 to 15 players, including country members from Rugby, formed teams to play Luffenham, Stoneygate, Finham and Tadmarton. It was very much a family affair with everyone knowing everyone else. Occasionally, Mrs Deterding, who was the owner of a white Rolls Royce, would take an entire team to play a match, fortified with packed lunches. On one occasion the car died on the railway line at Brampton near the Boughton Road turn. The team endeavoured to push it off but to no avail and eventually it was towed clear with a rope. Fortunately there were only three trains a day at that time.

In the 1950s structural alterations to improve the cloakroom facilities were made and life in the section gradually began to return to some form of normality, and the membership had risen to 96.

Since the war up to the present day, the ladies section maintained meticulous records of their meetings, and these provide an interesting insight into the deep and earnest discussions that have taken place over large as well as small matters, all in a most democratic manner. A team of ladies have always arranged the flowers throughout the clubhouse, which has added a touch of homeliness to the surroundings.

Throughout the period important national ladies events have been held at Brampton, and club members have always come forward with offers of accommodation for visiting contestants, trolley pullers and all the small details which go to make a success of any championship. This was especially noteworthy during all the 75th Anniversary celebrations under the Lady Captain of the day, Jenny Preston-Jones.

Many Midland competitions for ladies have been held at Brampton over the years, but the main national events, which are chronicled in earlier chapters, were the Girls British Open Amateur championships in 1973 and 1992, the County team Finals in 1975, and the English Ladies Stroke Play championship in 1985.

In 1995, with much improved and rather overdue facilities in their dressing rooms having been completed, the Ladies Section is in good heart and with a membership of 160 is looking forward to the future with pleasure and confidence.

Glenys Wild, Angela Duck and Heather Williams –
winners of 66 Club cups between them

Lady Captains

1910-21 No records
1922 Mrs R T Phipps
1923-26 No records
1927 Miss J Greig
1928 Miss J Greig
1929 Miss B Harvey
1930 Mrs H Mobbs
1931 Mrs R T Phipps
1932 Mrs E H Lankester
1933 Mrs S H G Humfrey
1934 Mrs G W Baldwin
1935 Miss E D Lees
1936 Mrs H Mobbs
1937 Mrs S H S Cook
1938 Mrs H Deterding
1939-46 Mrs R T Phipps
1947 Mrs E F Adnitt
1949 Mrs W T Swannell
1950 Mrs H Deterding
1951 Mrs J Cooch
1952 Mrs A Wilson
1953 Miss M P Spencer
1954 Mrs R Morton
1955 Mrs A Wilson
1956 Mrs H M Draper
1957 Mrs A G Timpson
1958 Mrs R A Palmer
1959 Miss N Askew
1960 Mrs M Tennent
1961 Mrs E F Adnitt
1962 Mrs C S Catlow
1963 Mrs C Gledhill
1964 Mrs T McLardy
1965 Mrs M Tennent
1966 Mrs J H Mobbs
1967 Mrs E F Adnitt
1968 Mrs W G Palmer
1969 Mrs E G Harley
1970 Mrs R J W Gubbins
1971 Mrs E Coker
1972 Mrs M Tennent
1973 Mrs J Cooch
1974 Mrs A R Banham

1975 Mrs M H Hollingsworth
1976 Mrs A N Soutar
1977 Mrs R A Benbow
1978 Mrs J D Haig
1979 Mrs J G White
1980 Mrs R B Catlow
1981 Mrs D Laverick
1982 Mrs J L Harrison
1983 Mrs E D Sleath
1984 Mrs M Logan
1985 Mrs J Preston-Jones
1986 Mrs E K Williams
1987 Mrs R Bell
1988 Mrs R Champness
1989 Mrs M Musgrave
1990 Mrs S Aitken
1991 Mrs D Reason
1992 Mrs V A Parker
1993 Mrs B Austin
1994 Mrs M McDougall
1995 Mrs P Parsonson
1996 Mrs G Morley
1997 Mrs J Wild
1998 Mrs P M Warrington
1999 Mrs R G Halliday
2000 Mrs M A Savage
2001 Mrs E K Thompson
2002 Mrs S K Jones
2003 Mrs S J Sumpton
2004 Mrs R A Haig
2005 Mrs D Saunderson
2006 Mrs J Morris
2007 Mrs W J Devereux
2008 Mrs P Toseland
2009 Mrs S Aitken

County Captains

1930 Mrs R T Phipps
1931 Mrs H Mobbs
1934 Mrs R T Phipps
1947 Mrs D Cooch
1951 Miss M P Spencer
1953 Mrs R T Phipps
1955 Mrs K Swannell
1957 Marchioness of Northampton

1959 Miss M P Spencer
1961 Mrs A Wilson
1965 Mrs P Clarke
1967 Mrs M Hollingsworth
1975 Mrs A Duck
1977 Mrs J Gubbins
1981 Mrs G Wild
1991 Mrs G Wild
2001 Mrs S Aitken
2005 Mrs H Williams

Lady Presidents

1910 Miss Bouverie
1929-30 The Hon Mrs Fitzroy
1931-38 Lady Annaly
1946-51 Countess Spencer & Mrs W
                    Deterding
1984 Mrs K M Swannell
1987 Mrs M H Hollingsworth
1990 Mrs E D Cooch
1993 Mrs A Catlow
1995 Mrs E Coker
1998 Mrs D Laverick

2000 Mrs R J Gubbins
2003 Mrs A R Banham
2005 Mrs J G White
2007-2009 Mrs R B Catlow

Lady Secretaries

1926-30 Miss A G Hughes
1930-32 Mrs R T Phipps
1932-33 Mrs E H Lankester
1933-34 Mrs S H G Humfrey
1934-38 Mrs G W Baldwin
1938-51 Mrs F G Coales
1951-64 Unknown
1964-75 Mrs W T Swannell
1975-83 Mrs E G Harley
1983-88 Mrs R G Halliday
1988-92 Mrs M Logan
1992-97 Mrs E K Williams
1997-99 Mrs E Caldow
1999-00 Post Vacant
2000-01 Mrs N McClurg
2001-06 Mrs M Peel
2006-   Mrs S McAra and Mrs M Gooch

Outstanding lady club golfers

The Club has boasted many high quality lady golfers over the years, including Mrs R T Phipps, Miss M Troup, Mrs Herbert Mobbs, Mrs L V Everard, Mrs L C Baillon and the Marchioness of Northampton, but special mention should be made of three of our current members.

Mrs Kath Swannell:

Kath Swannell was born in 1904 and began playing golf at 13, and has been an outstanding golfer at Northampton GC and Brampton, which she joined in 1935. She played her first county match in 1925 and was Ladies County champion five times between 1937 and 1950, and was Ladies County captain in 1956/57 and president from 1974/78.

Her many competition wins at Brampton are listed in the cup winners section. Kath was also Honorary Secretary and Treasurer for the Northamptonshire Ladies County Golf Association from 1930/64, so she has put back into the game every bit as much as she has taken out of it.

Kath Swannell

Mrs Angela Duck:

Angela Duck has certainly been the top lady golfer in the history of the Ladies Section at Brampton: Originally from Staffordshire, Angela was a member of Brocton Hall GC where as Angela Higgott, she twice won the Midlands Ladies championship, the Spanish Open in 1969, and the Swiss championship in 1972. Since coming to Northampton and joining Brampton she has been County champion in 1972, 1984, 1985 and 1988, and has won the Ladies Club championship every year since 1985. In 1991 she played for England in the Senior Ladies International against Europe in France. Together with her husband, Mike, she has taken a lively interest in the training of the juniors at Brampton, including her two talented sons, Robert and Thomas.

Mrs Glenys Wild:

Glenys is of a sporting family. Her husband, John, and son, Duncan, both played cricket for Northamptonshire for many years, but Glenys has been the golfing star of the family. She made her County debut in 1977 and was Club champion in 1980, 1981 and 1983 and County captain in the 1981/82 and 1991/92 seasons.

LADY CUP WINNERS
GUTHRIE CUP

Presented by Mr David Guthrie. Matchplay under handicap limited to 25 after qualifying round for best 8 scores. Played for in the summer months.

Winners

1910 Mrs C Cooper
1911 Mrs D K Courage
1912 Mrs C L Mason
1913 Mrs C Cooper
1914 Mrs E Courage
1915-18 Not played
1919 Mrs H Mobbs
1920 Mrs H Mobbs
1921 Mrs Phillips
1922 Mrs Mursell
1923 Mrs T E Manning
1924 Mrs Lankaster
1925 Miss Loam
1926 Mrs H Mobbs
1927 Mrs R T Phipps
1928 Mrs H Mobbs
1929 Miss Harries Jones
1930 Mrs Lees
1931 Miss D Lees
1932 Mrs R T Phipps
1933 Mrs E H Johnson
1934 Miss Kittermaster
1935 Mrs Deterding
1936 Mrs A C Timpson
1937 Miss D Lees
1938 Miss D M James
1939 Mrs R T Phipps
1940-45 Not played
1946 Mrs W T Swannell
1947 Miss Spencer
1948 Miss M Troup
1949 Mrs B Reynolds
1950 Mrs W T Swannell
1951 Mrs H Garrard

1952 Mrs D J Jones
1953 Mrs H Lock
1954 Marchioness of Northampton
1955 Mrs A Timpson
1956 Mrs J T Hawkes
1957 Mrs L V Everard
1958 Mrs L V Everard
1959 Mrs D Robinson
1960 Mrs H Lock
1961 Mrs T McLardy
1962 Mrs C S Catlow
1963 Mrs H Lock
1964 Mrs L V Everard
1965 Mrs D Jones
1966 Mrs J G Sugden
1967 Mrs H Lock
1968 Miss J Dicks
1969 Mrs J G Sugden
1970 Mrs W T Swannell
1971 Mrs R G Halliday
1972 Mrs M E Tennent
1973 Mrs R G Halliday
1974 Mrs I Green
1975 Mrs D G T Russell
1976 Mrs R H Benbow
1977 Mrs I Green
1978 Mrs J Wild
1979 Mrs J Wild
1980 Mrs N Taylor
1981 Mrs M Hollingsworth
1982 Mrs A Cullen
1983 Mrs I Green
1984 Mrs E D Sleath
1985 Mrs M D Duck
1986 Mrs M Logan
1987 Mrs A Minor

1988 Mrs S G Wright
1989 Mrs M D Duck
1990 Mrs J Russell
1991 Mrs J Wild
1992 Mrs E K Williams
1993 Mrs J Wild
1994 Mrs M D Duck
1995 Mrs A M Henley
1996 Mrs P Coles
1997 Mrs R M Gimson
1998 Mrs D Saunderson
1999 Mrs L Harte
2000 Mrs E K Williams
2001 Miss E Parr
2002 Mrs S Barrick
2003 Mrs G Curley
2004 Mrs S McRae
2005 Mrs L Harte
2006 Miss A Shine
2007 Miss K Hanwell
2008 Mrs S McRae

FITZROY CUP

Presented by the Hon Mrs E A Fitzroy
(President). Singles matchplay under
handicap limited to 25. Played for in the
summer months.

Winners

1910 Mrs M G Smith
1911 Mrs C Cooper
1912 Mrs M G Smith
1913-21 Not played
1922 Mrs L Baillon
1923 Mrs R T Phipps
1924 Mrs L Baillon
1925 Mrs H Mobbs
1926 Mrs C L Mason
1927 Mrs L Harvey
1928 Mrs R T Phipps
1929 Mrs R T Phipps
1930 Mrs B Harvey
1931 Mrs T E Manning
1932 Mrs T E Manning
1933 Mrs H Mobbs

1934 Mrs R T Phipps
1935 Mrs A C Timpson
1936 Mrs H Deterding
1937 Mrs L Baillon
1938 Mrs M Strang
1939 Mrs W T Swannell
1940-46 Not played
1947 Mrs J Cooch
1948 Mrs H Deterding
1949 Mrs B Reynolds
1950 Miss M Troup
1951 Mrs R T Phipps
1952 Miss M Troup
1953 Marchioness of Northampton
1954 Marchioness of Northampton
1955 Mrs A Wilson
1956 Mrs H Lock
1957 Mrs D Robinson
1958 Mrs Collins
1959 Mrs D Robinson
1960 Miss M Troup
1961 Mrs T McLardy
1962 Mrs R W Clarke
1963 Mrs W T Swannell
1964 Mrs W T Swannell
1965 Mrs I Green
1966 Mrs J H Mobbs
1967 Mrs J G Sugden
1968 Mrs H Lock
1969 Mrs W T Swannell
1970 Mrs C N Buswell
1971 Mrs C N Buswell
1972 Miss J Dicks
1973 Mrs W T Swannell
1974 Miss J Douglas
1975 Mrs E G Harley
1976 Mrs J D Frame
1977 Mrs M Robertson
1978 Mrs R V Rawlins
1979 Mrs J D Frame
1980 Mrs J Wild
1981 Mrs J A Cox
1982 Mrs C Phillips
1983 Mrs A Cullen
1984 Mrs G Austin

1985 Mrs J G White
1986 Mrs E K Williams
1987 Mrs R V Rawlins
1988 Mrs G G Morley
1989 Mrs R J W Gubbins
1990 Mrs M D Duck
1991 Mrs M D Duck
1992 Mrs G G Morley
1993 Mrs A Minor
1994 Mrs A Palmer
1995 Mrs E K Williams
1996 Mrs M D Duck
1997 Mrs M Brown
1998 Mrs L Harte
1999 Mrs K Lobb
2000 Mrs B J Chater
2001 Mrs S Barrick
2002 Mrs S Barrick
2003 Mrs K Jennings
2004 Mrs L Harte
2005 Mrs G Curley
2006 Mrs C M James
2007 Mrs L Harte
2008 Miss R Smith

MILLS CUP

Presented by Mrs T H Mills. 18 hole medal play handicap limited to 20. Played for in the summer months.

Winners

1911 Miss G Hughes
1912 Miss N G Bostock
1913 Mrs H C Boycott
1914 Mrs H C Boycott
1915-18 Not played
1919 Mrs H Mobbs
1920 Miss Eunson
1921 Mrs R Manning
1922 Mrs L Baillon
1923 Mrs Dulley
1924 Mrs J O Greig
1925 Mrs L Baillon
1926 Mrs R T Phipps
1927 Miss B Loam

1928 Mrs Toller-Eady
1929 Mrs L Baillon
1930 Miss Logan
1931 Miss Kittermaster
1932 Mrs C C Holman
1933 Mrs E F Adnitt
1934 Mrs B Harvey
1935 Miss Hipwell
1936 Miss Askew
1937 Mrs Strang
1938 Mrs S H G Humfrey
1939 Miss Spencer
1940-46 Not played
1947 Mrs J Cooch
1948 Mrs J H Mobbs
1949 Mrs H Garrard
1950 Mrs A Wilson
1951 Mrs H Garrard
1952 Mrs J Cooch
1953 Mrs A Wilson
1954 Marchioness of Northampton
1955 Miss P Spencer
1956 Miss P Spencer
1957 Mrs R T Phipps
1958 Mrs D Robinson
1959 Mrs J L McDougall
1960 Mrs J L McDougall
1961 Mrs D Jones
1962 Mrs J H Mobbs
1963 Mrs J Hawkes
1964 Mrs I Green
1965 Mrs A Wilson
1966 Mrs E T Harris
1967 Mrs J G Sugden
1968 Mrs R V Rawlins
1969 Mrs J M Harris
1970 Mrs D Jones
1971 Mrs F W Coles
1972 Mrs E G Harley
1973 Mrs M F Allott
1974 Mrs R J W Gubbins
1975 Mrs R G Wilcock
1976 Mrs W T Swannell
1977 Mrs E G Harley

1978 Mrs E G Harley
1979 Mrs M Robertson
1980 Mrs R G Chandler
1981 Mrs R G Halliday
1982 Mrs J G White
1983 Mrs J Wild
1984 Mrs J G White
1985 Mrs S Tookey
1986 Mrs D J Barber
1987 Mrs A Minor
1988 Mrs M McDougall
1989 Mrs A Stevens
1990 Mrs R V Rawlins
1991 Mrs R G Halliday
1992 Mrs V A Parker
1993 Mrs R G Halliday
1994 Mrs V A Parker
1995 Mrs J Russell
1996 Mrs D Arrowsmith
1997 Mrs J Preston-Jones
1998 Mrs L Harte
1999 Mrs S Barrick
2000 Mrs G G Morley
2001 Mrs L Harte
2002 Mrs S Barrick
2003 Mrs G Austin
2004 Mrs B Chater
2005 Mrs K Jennings
2006 Mrs M C Wetherly
2007 Mrs M McDougall
2008 Mrs M McDougall

DETERDING CUP

Presented Mrs H Deterding in 1939 as a memento of her year as captain but owing to World War II was not played for until 1947. Foursomes matchplay originally handcap limited to 24.

Winners

1947 Mrs E F Adnitt & Mrs R Morton
1948 Mrs F Roe & Miss M Troup
1949 Mrs R Morton & Mrs H Garrard
1950 Mrs F Roe & Miss M Troup
1951 Mrs H Garrard & Mrs R Morton

1952 Mrs F Roe & Miss M Troup
1953 Mrs S Collier & Mrs R T Phipps
1954 Marchioness of Northampton & Mrs W T Swannell
1955 Mrs J Cooch & Mrs A Wilson
1956 Marchioness of Northampton & Mrs W T Swannell
1957 Mrs F Roe & Mrs Robinson
1958 Mrs D Jones & Mrs J Mitchell
1959 Mrs D Robinson & Mrs F Roe
1960 Mrs Edwards & Mrs L McDougall
1961 Mrs H Draper & Mrs D Jones
1962 Mrs L V Everard & Mrs H Lock
1963 Mrs A Allebone & Mrs E T Harris
1964 Mrs L V Everard & Miss J Tebbs
1965 Mrs L V Everard & Mrs H Lock
1966 Mrs E G Harley & Mrs C N Buswell
1967 Mrs J H Mobbs & Mrs H Lock
1968 Mrs M Tennent & Mrs D Jones
1969 Mrs E G Harley & Mrs W T Swannell
1970 Mrs J F Mitchell & Mrs W G Palmer
1971 Miss J Douglas & Mrs R W Clarke
1972 Mrs D Jones & Mrs L J Belson
1973 Mrs M D Duck & Mrs R G Halliday
1974 Mrs M D Duck & Miss J Lee
1975 Mrs M D Duck & Mrs C T Higgott
1976 Mrs J G White & Mrs D G T Russell
1977 Mrs R H Benbow & Mrs R G Chandler
1978 Mrs R J W Gubbins & Mrs J Wild
1979 Mrs J F Bell & Mrs E D Sleath
1980 Mrs D Laverick & Mrs V Fielding
1981 Mrs M Hollingsworth & Mrs R W Clarke
1982 Mrs R J W Gubbins & Mrs J Wild
1983 Mrs J L Harrison & Mrs S Tookey
1984 Mrs J Preston-Jones & Mrs L M Hudson
1985 Mrs R G Aitken & Mrs R B Catlow
1986 Mrs J L Harrison & Mrs S Tookey
1987 Mrs M D Duck & Mrs A Stevens
1988 Mrs J Wild & Mrs R J W Gubbins
1989 Mrs M McDougall & Mrs M Logan
1990 Mrs E K Williams & Mrs R G Halliday

1991 Mrs J Wild & Mrs R J W Gubbins
1992 Mrs J Wild & Mrs R J W Gubbins
1993 Mrs M D Duck & Mrs G G Morley
1994 Mrs J Russell & Mrs R Gimson
1995 Mrs R B Catlow & Mrs R G Aitken
1996 Mrs E K Williams & Mrs R G
    Halliday
1997 Mrs E K Williams & Mrs R G
    Halliday
1998 Mrs S Goodings & Mrs S Barrick
1999 Mrs L Whalley & Mrs L Harte
2000 Mrs M McDougall & Mrs W
    Devereux
2001 Mrs M C Edmonds & Miss A Shine
2002 Mrs A Duck & Mrs R G Aitken
2003 Mrs S Goodings & Mrs S Barrick
2004 Mrs K Jennings & Miss S L Carter
2005 Mrs A Duck & Mrs R G Aitken
2006 Miss A Shine & Mrs M C Edmonds
2007 Mrs K Jennings & Miss K Hanwell
2008 Mrs K Jennings & Miss K Hanwell

THE GLEDHILL CUPS

Presented by Mrs C Gledhill. An American tournament played in sections. 18 hole Foursome matchplay off handicap. Played for in the winter.

Winners

1960 Mrs M Tennent & Mrs Robinson
1961 Mrs D Cooch & Mrs Wilkin
1962 Mrs M Tennent & Mrs J Draper
1963 Mrs M Hollingsworth & Mrs N Lacey
1964 Mrs W T Swannell & Mrs R Clarke
1965 Mrs I Green & Mrs S Dickens
1966 Mrs W T Swannell & Mrs D Russell
1967 Mrs W T Swannell & Mrs D Russell
1968 Mrs Adnitt & Mrs E Harley
1969 Mrs W T Swannell & Mrs D Russell
1970 Mrs N Buswell & Mrs E Harley
1971 Mrs W T Swannell & Mrs D Russell
1972 Mrs J Sugden & Mrs M D Duck
1973 Mrs R Chandler & Mrs R Benbow
1974 Mrs M D Duck & Miss J Lee
1975 Mrs W T Swannell & Mrs D Russell
1976 Mrs M Musgrave & Mrs N Taylor

1977 Mrs W T Swannell & Mrs D Russell
1978 Mrs P Spokes & Mrs L Wakeford
1979 Not played for owing to bad weather
1980 Mrs L Goode & Mrs A Thompson
1981 Mrs M Hollingsworth & Mrs R Clarke
1982 Mrs R J W Gubbins & Mrs R Haig
1983 Mrs E K Williams & Mrs R Costin
1984 Mrs D Russell & Mrs A Turner
1985 Mrs M Austin & Mrs R Aitken
1986 Mrs M D Duck & Mrs D Higgott
1987 Mrs M D Duck & Mrs S Wright
1988 Mrs M D Duck & Mrs S Wright
1989 Mrs M D Duck & Mrs S Wright
1990 Mrs M D Duck & Mrs E K Williams
1991 Mrs M D Duck & Mrs J F N Bell
1992 Mrs E D Sleath & Mrs J Preston-Jones
1993 Mrs E K Williams & Mrs M Austin
1994 Mrs S Wright & Mrs J Wild
1995 Mrs E K Williams & Mrs R G
    Halliday
1996 Mrs J Halliday & Mrs B Forrest
1997 Mrs P Coles & Mrs E Caldow
1998 Mrs J Halliday & Mrs M Bland
1999 Mrs V Parker & Mrs S Aitken
2000 Mrs M Morley & Miss A Shine
2001 Mrs R Gimson & Mrs J Matthews
2002 Mrs M Bland & Mrs E Brooks
2003 Mrs A Haig & Mrs G Curley
2004 Mrs A Haig & Mrs G Curley
2005 Mrs J Matthews & Mrs C Nickson
2006 Mrs M D Duck & Mrs M Edmonds
2007 Mrs M McLain & Mrs J Slinn

HIGH HANDICAP CUP

Presented by Mrs J H Cooch. Singles matchplay off handicap limited to 26 and over.

Winners

1969 Mrs R J W Gubbins
1970 Mrs E F Adnitt
1971 Mrs A R Harris
1972 Mrs R G Aitken
1973 Mrs B W Scott
1974 Mrs D M Bryden
1975 Mrs R J Wilcock

1976 Mrs S Cooper
1977 Mrs P T Logan
1978 Mrs D Coley
1979 Mrs J F N Bell
1980 Mrs D J Barber
1981 Mrs R A Haig
1982 Mrs P Rudkin
1983 Mrs L M Hudson
1984 Mrs L M Hudson
1985 Mrs B Smith
1986 Mrs B Smith
1987 Mrs M Stevenson
1988 Mrs K Sturgess
1989 Mrs S Ashley
1990 Mrs S Cooper
1991 Mrs J M Neal
1992 Mrs S H Goodings
1993 Mrs D Amos
1994 Mrs R D Waller
1995 Mrs P A Parsonson
1996 Mrs L Whalley
1997 Miss A Shine
1998 Mrs K Billson
1999 Mrs Y Forster
2000 Mrs M C Edmonds
2001 Mrs B C Forrest
2002 Mrs D Deane
2003 Mrs K Kennedy
2004 Mrs K Kennedy
2005 Mrs K Billson
2006 Mrs U M Morris
2007 Mrs S Cook
2008 Mrs U M Morris

JUBILEE BOWL

Presented by Mrs J M Gubbins. Lowest aggregate of the three best net medal scores and extra medal scores between February and January.

Winners

1970 Mrs E Coker
1971 Mrs C N Buswell
1972 Mrs P W Stiles
1973 Mrs E Coker

1974 Mrs B C Scott
1975 Mrs I Green
1976 Mrs R Wilcock
1977 Mrs J F N Bell
1978 Mrs I Flowers
1979 Mrs S Ashley
1980 Mrs J Wild
1981 Mrs M Barber
1982 Mrs R G Halliday
1983 Mrs R G Aitken
1984 Mrs E D Sleath
1985 Mrs A J Minor
1986 Mrs L Goode
1987 Mrs B Willmoth
1988 Mrs P Coles
1989 Mrs A A Palmer
1990 Mrs J Bernstein
1991 Mrs R G Aitken
1992 Mrs D J Deane
1993 Mrs S Barrick
1994 Mrs J Bradley
1995 Mrs L M Whalley
1996 Mrs L Harte
1997 Mrs A Duck
1998 Mrs M Logan
1999 Mrs V A Parker
2000 Dr D Pratt
2001 Mrs L Harte
2002 Miss E Parr
2003 Mrs M C Edmonds
2004 Mrs C M James
2005 Mrs E Brooks
2006 Mrs C M James
2007 Miss S A Williams

ECLECTIC CUP

Presented by Mrs M Gammage. Treasurer of the Ladies section for 11 years. Total of lowest scores on medal and Stableford scores on summer cards.

Winners

1971 Mrs W T Swannell
1972 Mrs R V Rawlins
1973 Mrs W T Swannell

1974 Mrs J R Hurley
1975 Mrs J R Hurley
1976 Mrs J R Hurley
1977 Mrs G Austin
1978 Mrs P T Logan
1979 Mrs V Fielding
1980 Mrs G Austin
1981 Mrs V Fielding
1982 Mrs G Austin
1983 Mrs S Ashley
1984 Mrs J Preston-Jones
1985 Mrs E K Williams
1986 Mrs A Minor
1987 Mrs A Minor
1988 Mrs G G Morley
1989 Mrs R G Aitken
1990 Mrs E K Williams
1991 Mrs E K Williams
1992 Mrs D Arrowsmith
1993 Mrs E K Williams
1994 Mrs J M Morton
1995 Mrs S Barrick
1996 Mrs J Halliday
1997 Mrs A Duck
1998 Mrs S Aitken
1999 Mrs S Barrick
2000 Mrs G Curley
2001 Mrs E Thompson
2002 Mrs G Curley
2003 Mrs G Curley
2004 Mrs L Harte
2005 Mrs G Curley
2006 Mrs S Aitken
2007 Mrs G Curley

RUSSELL BOWL

Presented by Mrs D Russell in memory of her mother, Mrs R T Phipps. Medal strokeplay over 18 holes, Handicap 21 and over.

Winners

1980 Mrs D Roe
1981 Mrs E K Williams
1982 Mrs A Turner
1983 Mrs R B Catlow

1984 Mrs R A Haig
1985 Mrs L Goode
1986 Mrs I Green
1987 Mrs M Stevenson
1988 Mrs M Douglas
1989 Mrs J Bernstein
1990 Mrs J L Harrison
1991 Mrs D Arrowsmith
1992 Mrs A A Palmer
1993 Mrs S Goodings
1994 Mrs R D Waller
1995 Mrs K Billson
1996 Mrs M Tough
1997 Mrs M Tinson
1998 Mrs S Cooper
1999 Mrs S J Sumpton
2000 Dr D Platt
2001 Mrs S K Jones
2002 Mrs P Oliver
2003 Mrs P Letten
2004 Mrs E Brooks
2005 Mrs M McLain
2006 Mrs E Brooks
2007 Mrs J Matthews
2008 Mrs R Corby

CLUB CHAMPIONSHIP CUP

Presented by Mrs J M Gubbins. 36 holes singles scratch strokeplay. Handicap limited to 18.

Winners

1980 Mrs J Wild
1981 Mrs J Wild
1982 Mrs R G Halliday
1983 Mrs J Wild
1984 Mrs R G Halliday
1985 Mrs M D Duck
1986 Mrs M D Duck
1987 Mrs M D Duck
1988 Mrs M D Duck
1989 Mrs M D Duck
1990 Mrs M D Duck
1991 Mrs M D Duck

1992 Mrs M D Duck
1993 Mrs M D Duck
1994 Mrs M D Duck
1995 Mrs M D Duck
1996 Mrs M D Duck
1997 Mrs M D Duck
1998 Mrs M D Duck
1999 Mrs M D Duck
2000 Mrs M D Duck
2001 Mrs M D Duck
2002 Miss E Parr
2003 Miss E Parr
2004 Miss S L Carter
2005 Mrs K Jennings
2006 Mrs K Jennings
2007 Miss K Hanwell
2008 Mrs K Jennings

HOLLINGSWORTH CUP

Presented by Mrs M Hollingsworth. Medal qualifying round. Best eight play off matchplay. Handicap limited to 26 and over.

Winners

1981 Mrs J L Harrison
1982 Mrs L M Hudson
1983 Mrs R B Catlow
1984 Mrs L M Hudson
1985 Mrs S Cooper
1986 Mrs J L Harrison
1987 Mrs K Sturgess
1988 Mrs H M Mobbs
1989 Mrs S Ashley
1990 Mrs B Smith
1991 Mrs C E Gower
1992 Mrs K V Needham
1993 Mrs M O'Connell
1994 Mrs D Deane
1995 Mrs B C Forrest
1996 Mrs J Bernstein
1997 Mrs D Amos
1998 Mrs B C Forrest
1999 Mrs M O'Connell

2000 Mrs M O'Connell
2001 Mrs M Peel
2002 Mrs J Matthews
2003 Mrs K Kennedy
2004 Mrs B Smith
2005 Mrs E Brooks
2006 Mrs J Bradley
2007 Mrs L Steedman
2008 Mrs J Slinn

SWANNELL TROPHY

Presented by Mrs W T Swannell. Knock-out played in sections. 18 holes singles matchplay off handicap. Played for in the winter.

Winner

1986 Mrs E K Williams
1987 Mrs E K Williams
1988 Mrs H M Mobbs
1989 Mrs J Wild
1990 Mrs M Brown
1991 Mrs J Barlow
1992 Mrs M D Duck
1993 Mrs M D Duck
1994 Mrs M Brown
1995 Mrs A Minor
1996 Mrs A Minor
1997 Mrs E K Williams
1998 Mrs E K Williams
1999 Mrs J Wild
2000 Mrs M D Duck
2001 Mrs G Curley
2002 Mrs S Barrick
2003 Mrs M C Edmonds
2004 Miss A Shine
2005 Mrs L Harte
2006 Mrs G Curley
2007 Mrs D Groves

WILLIAMS ROSE BOWL

Presented by Mrs E K Williams as a memento of her year as captain. 18 holes stroke play among winners of monthly and extra medals.

Winners

1986 Mrs A Minor
1987 Mrs D Arrowsmith
1988 Mrs R H Benbow
1989 Mrs M D Duck
1990 Mrs D Lett
1991 Mrs M D Duck
1992 Mrs M A Savage
1993 Mrs J Bradley
1994 Mrs G Austin
1995 Mrs L M Hudson
1996 Mrs M D Duck
1997 Mrs P M Warrington
1998 Mrs M D Duck
1999 Miss A Shine
2000 Miss R L Smith
2001 Miss R L Smith
2002 Mrs E Brooks
2003 Mrs M McDougall
2004 Mrs H Wain
2005 Mrs S A Lane
2006 Mrs E K Williams
2007 Mrs M McDougall
2008 Mrs J Matthews

DOROTHY COOCH SALVER

Presented by Mr P Cooch and Mrs E Turnbull in memory of their mother, Mrs J H Cooch, 2004.

2004 Mrs K Jennings
2005 Miss S L Carter
2006 Miss K Hanwell
2007 Miss K Hanwell
2008 Mrs K Jennings

Multiple Cup Winners

Mrs M D Duck 50
Mrs E K Williams 22
Mrs W T Swannell 21
Mrs R G Halliday 19
Mrs J Wild 18
Mrs R T Phipps 16

Golden girls: Angela Duck (left) and Glenys Wild

CHAPTER IX

The Club Trophies (1910-2008)

"Golf is a game in which you yell Fore, score six, and write down five"
Paul Harvey

This chapter is just full of statistics but the only other records of past winners of our competitions are inscribed on Honours Boards around the Clubhouse. Should the Clubhouse suffer a fire there would be no other records available.

BOSTOCK TROPHY & CLUB CHAMPIONSHIP

This Cup was given by Mr Fred Bostock for the Club Championship over 36 holes Scratch Stroke Play. It was originally played for at the Spring Meeting until 1969, after which the date was moved to mid-summer. The scores from 1970 probably reflect the difference in playing conditions between the two dates.

Winners

Year	Winner	Score
1937	H P Passmore	149
1938	C S Catlow	153
1939-1946	Not played	
1947	F C Roe	157
1948	C S Catlow	156
1949	J W Taylor	154
1950	R A Larratt	151
1951	G F Clarke	153
1952	R L Mobbs	153
1953	G F Clarke	155
1954	A J Harrison	155
1955	G F Clarke	151
1956	A J Harrison	154
1957	G E Mobbs	156
1958	G E Mobbs	159
1959	G F Clarke	155
1960	I Crawford	152
1961	G F Clarke	154
1962	R G Aitken	155
1963	J H Humphries	160
1964	R G Aitken	155
1965	K Holland	150
1966	R B Catlow	153
1967	A D Bishop	151
1968	M Pounds	154
1969	A N Soutar	153
1970	M Pounds	148
1971	R S Biggin	148
1972	C R Cieslewicz	141
1973	C R Cieslewicz	146
1974	C R Cieslewicz	146
1975	T J Giles	140
1976	L A Johnson	151
1977	R G Aitken	148
1978	R G Aitken	143
1979	R G Aitken	142
1980	R G Halliday	149
1981	R G Aitken	149
1982	R G Aitken	151
1983	R A Haig	155
1984	R G Aitken	149
1985	A J Mc Cleary	151
1986	A D Bishop	150
1987	R G Aitken	144
1988	C R Cieslewicz	147
1989	A J Wilson	147
1990	A M S Lord	148
1991	A C Sinclair	148
1992	M A Lynch	144
1993	A Print	144
1994	A C Sinclair	140
1995	R M Duck	140

1996	A R P Lynch	145
1997	A R P Lynch	144
1998	A M S Lord	146
1999	N Soto	144
2000	N J West	142
2001	T M Duck	147
2002	R J Green	144
2003	C H Green	151
	B J O'Connell	151
2004	R J Green	142
2005	A M S Lord	138
2006	A Print	148
2007	A J Myers	143
2008	S J Ashwood	145

BURN CUP

This Cup was presented by Mr F H Burn a founder member of the Club and is a Summer Knockout Competition off handicap.

Winners

1910	A N Mobbs
1911	C A Cooper
1912	H C Boycott
1913	W A S Talbot
1914	H C Boycott
1915-1918	Not played
1919	L Bostock
1920	L Bostock
1921	W A S Talbot
1922	T E Manning
1923	J F Stops
1924	A Jones
1925	G P M Skae
1926	A S Garrard
1927	H G Jelley
1928	L P Brown
1929	G L Meacham
1930	P G Elliott
1931	C G Mobbs
1932	W S Kennedy
1933	H P Passmore
1934	E C L Nichols
1935	H P Passmore

1936	W W E Tyrrell
1937	W S Kennedy
1938	S F Kennedy
1939	S F Kennedy
1940	J K Arthur
1941	L M Allison
1942-1946	Not played
1947	C S Catlow
1948	R A Palmer
1949	T Askew
1950	C S Catlow
1951	C A Spencer
1952	Dr J F Mitchell
1953	M Worley
1954	G F Clarke
1955	G W Marriott
1956	K Grierson
1957	P Arnold
1958	D J B Lewis
1959	F G D Wilkinson
1960	J W Punch
1961	F J Williams
1962	P Arnold
1963	G F Clarke
1964	R B Catlow
1965	A N Soutar
1966	D R Shelton
1967	K Grierson
1968	H M Denton
1969	J W Punch
1970	R J Patterson
1971	L A Johnson
1972	H R Beirne
1973	R J Minor
1974	R G Halliday
1975	L A Johnson
1976	A W Taylor
1977	J J Parker
1978	A P Bickley
1979	R G Halliday
1980	A W Moseley
1981	R G Aitken
1982	R G Aitken
1983	K G S Nokes
1984	R S Biggin

1985	S C Kelly	1937	E Y Stuckey
1986	L A Johnson	1938	Major N S Regnart
1987	G R Cottrell	1939	F Brawn
1988	A J Wilson	1940	D J Jones
1989	R F Patterson	1941	C S I Margetts
1990	R G Aitken	1942-46	Not played
1991	G R Cottrell	1947	D J Jones
1992	R C West	1948	J H Martin
1993	M Jelley	1949	R L Mobbs
1994	K Watson	1950	J H Mobbs
1995	G R Cottrell	1951	P C Amberg
1996	G R Cottrell	1952	P G Jones
1997	G R Cottrell	1953	R J Patterson
1998	L R M Smith	1954	A J Garrard
1999	G R Cottrell	1955	P Hutton
2000	G R Cottrell	1956	R C Partington
2001	G R Cottrell	1957	R B Catlow
2002	N D Beal	1958	J M Warrington
2003	N Pyne	1959	J E Burnett
2004	A C Sinclair	1960	J P Hall
2005	I Morris	1961	R B Catlow
2006	D W Sleath	1962	L J Belson
2007	D Smith	1963	D R Corbett
2008	J D Winfield	1964	R B Catlow
		1965	E J Baker

BOSTOCK CUP

Presented by Mr Lance Bostock a past Captain. A Competition for the aggregate of the best three Medal rounds in the Saturday Monthly Medals. Owing to later lack of interest, it became in 1967 the Club Scratch Matchplay Knockout Competition.

Winners

1926	V G Whitelaw	1966	J F N Bell
1927	Rev J B Dollar	1967	A D Bishop
1928	W Lees	1968	Dr J L McDougall
1929	P G Jones	1969	M Pounds
1930	W Lees	1970	Dr J L McDougall
1931	S Cooper	1971	R S Larratt
1932	V Corbett	1972	R S Larratt
1933	R T Mason	1973	R S Larratt
1934	D Wardrop (Junior)	1974	A D Bishop
1935	P Butler Henderson	1975	M D Duck
1936	J H Mobbs	1976	R G Aitken
		1977	R G Aitken
		1978	R G Aitken
		1979	R G Aitken
		1980	R G Aitken
		1981	C R Cieslewicz
		1982	R G Aitken
		1983	R G Halliday
		1984	K G S Noakes

1985	A D Bishop
1986	G Gilchrist
1987	C R Cieslewicz
1988	A J Wilson
1989	G Gilchrist
1990	A C Sinclair
1991	A Print
1992	A J Wilson
1993	A M S Lord
1994	M A Lynch
1995	M A Lynch
1996	A M S Lord
1997	A M S Lord
1998	A Print
1999	T M Duck
2000	T M Duck
2001	A M S Lord
2002	A M S Lord
2003	R J Green
2004	A M S Lord
2005	A C Sinclair
2006	A N Myers
2007	N A Connolly
2008	A N Myers

WALLIS CUP

This Cup was given Mr Owen Clarke Wallis JP a founder member of the Club and 1994 President for many years. A 36 hole Medal Competition played for at the Spring Meeting.

Winners

1912	E H Lankester
1913	N F Bostock
1914-1918	Not played
1919	D Elder Walker
1920	G P M Skae
1921	F L Larsen
1922	C A Quinn
1923	S J Davis
1924	W Parker
1925	H Courtney
1926	A S Garrard
1927	O J Hargrave

1928	L F Brown
1929	D S Talbot
1030	G W Baldwin
1931	P G Jones
1932	V Corbett
1933	S H G Humfrey
1934	H Deterding
1935	F F Parsons
1936	P G Jones
1937	H P Passmore
1938	H G Attenborough
1939	L M Allison
1940	F F Parsons
1941	W A B Vann
1942-1946	Not played
1947	R A Palmer
1948	J H Martin
1949	G J W Wareing
1950	J Harrison
1951	J H Mobbs
1952	R L Mobbs
1953	G F Clarke
1954	A J Harrison
1955	H A Lees
1956	G H Emmott
1957	G E Mobbs
1958	G E Mobbs
1959	G F Clarke
1960	J P Hall
1961	P Arnold
1962	D G Roberts
1963	R P Bird
1964	R F Watkins
1965	S Stewart
1966	M J Curwen
1967	A D Bishop
1968	Dr J F Donald
1969	R J Minor
1970	M Pounds
1971	R S Larratt
1972	Dr R Sladden
1973	R J Minor
1974	H E Bradshaw
1975	A L Wells
1976	D Wright

1977	K C Hunter	1987	G Gilchrist
1978	J R Duffy	1988	R G Halliday
1979	N R B Godden	1989	M Pounds
1980	L A Johnson	1990	C R Cieslewicz
1981	C R Cieslewicz	1991	A C Sinclair
1982	L M Leno	1992	A Print
1983	R Brown	1993	A Print
1984	M G Watkins	1994	A J Wilson
1985	R A Haig	1995	A Print
1986	R E Butlin	1996	A R P Lynch
1987	G Gilchrist	1997	A C Sinclair
1988	K Turner	1998	N J West
1989	M Pounds	1999	A J Wilson
1990	P W Godden	2000	B J O'Connell
1991	A C Sinclair	2001	N D Beal
1992	G R Cottrell	2002	B J O'Connell
1993	S J Bickley	2003	M D Bird
1994	M Jelley	2004	B J O'Connell
1995	J McPhee	2005	M D Bird
1996	G R Cottrell	2006	M D Bird
1997	L R M Smith	2007	A J Myers
1998	I Morris	2008	A J Myers
1999	L R M Smith		
2000	C N Green		
2001	N D Beal		
2002	B J O'Connell		
2003	A C Brown		
2004	R E Mason		
2005	M D Bird		
2006	M D Bird		
2007	T Cowley		
2008	S B Reynolds		

SPRING VASE

Presented by Mr E V Corps a past Captain. A 36 Hole Scratch Competition played for at the Annual Spring Meeting.

Winners

1980	A M S Lord
1981	C R Cieslewicz
1982	A D Bishop
1983	A J Wilson
1984	J B Scholey
1985	R A Haig
1986	R G Aitken

GEORGE MOBBS TROPHY

Presented by Mr George Mobbs. A 36 Hole Medal Competition for the Best Nett Score at the Club Championship.

Winners

1993	D J Jeyes
1994	G R Cottrell
1995	N Soto
1996	J J Parker
1997	J B Scholey
1998	A R Nicholson
1999	G R Cottrell
2000	N J West
2001	T M Duck
2002	R J Green
2003	J Kendrick
2004	R J Green
2005	A M S Lord
2006	N D Beal
2007	A M Hanrahan
2008	D S Nicholson

REGIMENTAL CUP

The Club used to play matches against the Northamptonshire Regiment based in Northampton. When the Regimental Barracks closed the Officers gave a Cup (originally for Boxing) to be known as the Regimental Cup and was for the best net 36 hole Medal score at the Annual Autumn Meeting.

Winners

1962	W C Gledhill
1963	A N Soutar
1964	R F Watkins
1965	C W H Lyon-Brown
1966	K R Martin
1967	S A Banks
1968	F J Richmond
1969	M A Rowe
1970	T J Giles
1971	Dr R A Sladden
1972	P Arnold
1973	S J Thornton
1974	R G Halliday
1975	S K Haig
1976	J D F Davies
1977	R V Rawlins
1978	J A Kelly
1979	R G Halliday
1980	K Watson
1981	G C Andrews
1982	D G Bartlett
1983	L A Johnson
1984	A M Rudkin
1985	L M Leno
1986	J Doyle
1987	M Pounds
1988	L A Wilson
1989	R B Aitken
1990	A C Sinclair
1991	R I Statham
1992	G R Cottrell
1993	A R Nicholson
1994	C N Hanley
1995	M Jelley
1996	A C Sinclair
1997	M Jelley
1998	A R Nicholson
1999	R E Mason
2000	R J Green
2001	A C Sinclair
2002	B J O'Connell
2003	S J Ashwood
2004	J Draper
2005	R W Nickson
2006	M R Smith
2007	R G Halliday
2008	A W Hopkinson

COUNTY CUP

This is a Cup for the best 36 Hole Scratch Score at the Annual Autumn Meeting. It is called perversely the Handicap Cup and the original donor is so far undiscovered.

Winners

1965	R G Halliday
1966	K Holland
1967	R G Aitken
1968	R G Aitken
1969	R F Patterson
1970	J H Humphries
1971	C C Back
1972	P Arnold
1973	A D Bishop
1974	R G Halliday
1975	S K Haig
1976	R G Halliday
1977	M D Duck
1978	C W H Lyon-Brown
1979	R G Halliday
1980	A J Wilson
1981	C R Cieslewicz
1982	J B Scholey
1983	L A Johnson
1984	J B Scholey
1985	A M S Lord
1986	R A Haig
1987	M Pounds
1988	C R Cieslewicz

1989	R A Haig
1990	A C Sinclair
1991	R I Statham
1992	A M S Lord
1993	A M S Lord
1994	A C Sinclair
1995	A J Wilson
1996	R M Duck
1997	A J Wilson
1998	N Soto
1999	N Soto
2000	A M S Lord
2001	A C Sinclair
2002	B J O'Connell
2003	S J Ashwood
2004	R J Green
2005	A M S Lord
2006	S J Ashwood
2007	A J Myers
2008	S Reynolds

DUKE OF YORK CUP

This Cup was presented by the Duke of York following his year of Captaincy. From an 18 hole Medal Competition played at an Autumn Meeting the best 16 qualifiers play a Knockout Competition during October and November off handicap.

Winners

1932	R A Palmer
1933	P G Jones
1934	Lt Col P F Bowden Smith
1935	F K Allin
1936	H P Passmore
1937	R A Palmer
1938	S F Kennedy
1939	R B Douglas
1940	R B Douglas
1941-46	Not played
1947	F F Parsons
1948	J Cullen
1949	T Askew
1950	J H Mobbs
1951	C R D Tuckey

1952	R J Patterson
1953	G H Emmott
1954	A J Harrison
1955	J M H Green
1956	C S Catlow
1957	D J Barber
1958	C R D Tuckey
1959	F G D Wilkinson
1960	W H Abbott
1961	F C Roe
1962	A N Soutar
1963	W H Abbott
1964	C Dunn
1965	E G Freeman
1966	G E Mobbs
1967	M A Rowe
1968	R B Catlow
1969	J W Howkins
1970	G A Meynell
1971	E McCarthy
1972	Dr J F Mitchell
1973	P E St Quinton
1974	A Carline
1975	W J Barron
1976	J Pendry
1977	R G Aitken
1978	R J Minor
1979	M D Duck
1980	M J Atkinson
1981	C H Howkins
1982	C H Howkins
1983	R F Patterson
1984	A J Preston-Jones
1985	M G Watkins
1986	E C Dicks
1987	R C Butlin
1988	M Swain
1989	I Burrage
1990	R L Jones
1991	G R Cottrell
1992	R A Haig
1993	B J O'Connell
1994	A R P Lynch
1995	M Jelley
1996	I Morris

114

1997	I Morris	1967	R R Garratt & J R Garratt
1998	J D Winfield	1968	E R Parr & J Waters
1999	N Pyne	1969	J W Punch & M R T Punch
2000	R W Garrett	1970	B W Scott & F A York
2001	B J O'Connell	1971	W G Palmer & C H Howkins
2002	B J O'Connell	1972	H M Fox & R R Mobbs
2003	J D Winfield	1973	M D Duck & M T Higgott
2004	A C Sinclair	1974	R A Flowers & F J Richmond
2005	A C Sinclair	1975	M D Duck & M T Higgott
2006	S V Bevan	1976	C S Catlow & J C J Legge
2007	H W Larkins	1977	G C Andrews & D J Wilkins
2008	R G Halliday	1978	E G Freeman & C E Clubb
		1979	G C Andrews & D J Wilkins

LEES CUP

This Cup was presented by Mr William Lees, a Past Captain of the Club. It is a Fourball Better Ball against Bogey.

Winners

1938	Major N S Regnart & J Cullen	1980	J E Burnett & S W Drown
1939	G E Mobbs & P G Jones	1981	G C Andrews & D J Wilkins
1940	R B Douglas & W Evans	1982	K A Kelly & S C Kelly
1941	R B Douglas & W Evans	1983	J K Mason & B N Jones
1942-1945	Not played	1984	H E Weavers & C E Clubb
1946	J Cooch & R Garratt	1985	N Glew & M Lowden
1947	S M Souter & R E Hammond	1986	G Gilchrist & J Gilchrist
1948	J M Martin & R L Mobbs	1987	A J Preston-Jones
1949	H A Lees & A S Baxter		E D Barltrop
1950	G F Clarke & Dr J M Mitchell	1988	J E Draper & J E Draper
1951	R E G Gubbins & P C Amberg	1989	R A Hamlyn & M O Thomas
1952	R A Larratt & C A Spencer	1990	J M Mahood & R J Spokes
1953	H A Lees & F F Parsons	1991	J A Kelly & S C Kelly
1954	D Chamberlain & A J Harrison	1992	D R Green & M A Lynch
1955	J B Ashley & S McMillan	1993	G R Cottrell & M Jelly
1956	J B Ashley & S McMillan	1994	R J Street & N A White
1957	G F Clarke & M Worley	1995	D Savage & M S T Essery
1958	R A Palmer & S F Kennedy	1996	R J Draper & I C Wilson
1959	A N Harris & J W Milne	1997	R J Draper & I C Wilson
1960	R G Halliday & R B Catlow	1998	T Ward & H B Wilson
1961	L T Heggs & R R Garratt	1999	A S Guthrie & F Malon
1962	Dr D J Jones & A E Limehouse	2000	M Kirwan & T W Ward
1963	C N Bushwell & K C Hunter	2001	J Goodrham & C L Marriott
1964	C S Catlow & R B Catlow	2002	D R Green & R J Green
1965	C J M Watts & R E Rushton	2003	S V Bevan & L R M Smith
1966	J B Ashley & P Rushton	2004	R Martyniak & N Barltrop
		2005	R A Hamlyn & J C Smith
		2006	R K Goodman & J K Evans
		2007	B R Garrett & R W Garrett
		2008	P Starcevic & M D Rickards

CHAMBERLAIN CUP

Presented by Mr Don Chamberlain a past Captain. A Foursomes Matchplay Knockout Competition played off Handicap.

Winners

1938	C S Catlow & R W Kilsby
1939	C S Catlow & R W Kilsby
1940	R G Keays & W W E Tyrrell
1941	A S Baxter & V G Whitelaw
1942-1946	Not played
1947	J S Parker & F F Parsons
1948	C S Catlow & F C Roe
1950	C S Catlow & F C Roe
1951	R M Hall & S McMillan
1952	G F Clarke & F C Roe
1953	G F Clarke & F C Roe
1954	Dr R N Hall & C E G Mumby
1955	G Adams & R E Osborne Smith
1956	C S Catlow & R A Palmer
1957	W H Abbott & H A Lees
1958	W H Abbott & H A Lees
1959	E Brocklebank F G D Wilkinson
1960	Dr J M Mitchell C R D Tuckey
1961	K Grierson & G H Emmott
1962	Dr J L McDougall & J W Punch
1963	C Dunn & K Abel
1964	J H Humphries & R J Patterson
1965	G E Mobbs & A N Soutar
1966	G E Mobbs & A N Soutar
1967	Dr J L McDougall & J W Punch
1968	Dr J L McDougall & J W Punch
1969	J D Haig & R A Haig
1970	J D Haig & R A Haig
1971	R G Halliday & A D Bishop
1972	R G Halliday & A D Bishop
1973	R G Halliday & A D Bishop
1974	J H Mobbs & M Williamson
1975	Dr R C West & L A Wilson
1976	B W Scott & F A York
1977	E C Kottler & P E St Quinton
1978	G C Andrews & A W Taylor
1979	L A Johnson & J Wild
1980	R J Ruffell & J P Hayley
1981	E C Kottler & P E St Quinton
1982	R A Haig & W M McColl
1983	R G Halliday & A D Bishop
1984	A S Guthrie & J Brown
1985	R A Haig & A C Sinclair
1986	R A Haig & A C Sinclair
1987	J K Mason & B N Jones
1988	C R Cieslewicz & A M Rudkin
1989	G Gilchrist & R I Statham
1990	A M S Lord & L J Cantrell
1991	A M S Lord & L J Cantrell
1992	D R Green & M A Lynch
1993	R A Haig & A C Sinclair
1994	A J McCleary & D J Wilson
1995	B J O'Connell & J B Scholey
1996	M A Lynch & A R P Lynch
1997	B R Hardman & J Delves
1998	T M Duck & N J West
1999	G R Cottrell & A J Linney
2000	R G Halliday & A D Bishop
2001	G R Cottrell & A J Linney
2002	P G Lock & J B Scholey
2003	R A Haig & A C Sinclair
2004	N D Beal & B J O'Connell
2005	S B Reynolds & J C Rowley
2006	G Stran & R J Morrell
2007	R Francis & A P C James
2008	A J McCleary & N Pyne

CHURCH CUP

Presented by Mr Ross N. Church for a mixed foursome Knock Out competition off handicap to be played during the summer.

Winners

1938	Dr & Mrs S H G Humfrey
1939	H Lees & Mrs J Cooch
1940	D J Jones & Mrs Jones
1941	R B Douglas & Mrs Kennedy
1942-1945	Not played
1946	G E Mobbs & Mrs R T Phipps
1947	G F Harris & Mrs D Phipps

1948	R A Palmer & Mrs R T Phipps
1949	R A Palmer & Mrs R T Phipps
1950	Mr & Mrs F Roe
1951	S McMillan & Mrs Collins
1952	R M Hall & Mrs K N Loake
1953	C S Catlow & Mrs Phipps
1954	H A Lees & Mrs S Marbrook
1955	R M Hall & Mrs Morton
1956	W S Kennedy & Mrs M Jones
1957	G E Adams & Mrs D Roe
1958	Mr & Mrs P Rushton
1959	Mr & Mrs J F Bryden
1960	Mr & Mrs C S Catlow
1961	S Drown & Mrs Dickens
1962	Mr & Mrs J H Mobbs
1963	Mr & Mrs L J Belson
1964	G F Clarke & Mrs K Swannell
1965	G Scott & Mrs J Green
1966	Dr & Mrs MacDougall
1967	Mr & Mrs J G Sugden
1968	Mr & Mrs R F Watkins
1969	S Stewart & Mrs M E Tennent
1970	Mr & Mrs R G Halliday
1971	Mr P J Cooch & Mrs J H Cooch
1972	Mr & Mrs M Duck
1973	Mr & Mrs M Duck
1974	Mr & Mrs A N Soutar
1975	Mr & Mrs R J W Gubbins
1976	L C Smith & Mrs B Hurley
1977	Mr & Mrs R A Haig
1978	Mr & Mrs G B Hudson
1979	Mr & Mrs G B Hudson
1980	Mr & Mrs G E Mobbs
1981	Mr & Mrs G E Mobbs
1982	Mr & Mrs R A Haig
1983	Mr & Mrs G E Mobbs
1984	Mr & Mrs R G Aitken
1985	Mr & Mrs R G Aitken
1986	L A Wilson
	Mrs D Arrowsmith
1987	M Pounds & Mrs M Bland
1988	Mr & Mrs G Austin
1989	M Pounds & Mrs M Bland
1990	Mr & Mrs R G Aitken

1991	Mr & Mrs R G Halliday
1992	J K Mason & Mrs M Logan
1993	Mr & Mrs R G Halliday
1994	Mr & Mrs M Duck
1995	Mrs S Barrick & R L Jones
1996	Mr & Mrs R G Aitken
1997	Mr & Mrs B J O'Connell
1998	Mr & Mrs R G Aitken
1999	Mr & Mrs R A Haig
2000	Mr & Mrs R G Aitken
2001	Miss A Shine & R A Hamlyn
2002	Mr & Mrs R A Lobb
2003	Mr & Mrs R A Lobb
2004	Mr & Mrs R A Haig
2005	Mr & Mrs R A Haig
2006	Mrs B Forrest & R F Patterson
2007	Mr & Mrs J M Mahood
2008	Mr D Green & Miss K Hanwell

MARSHALL CUP

The Marshall Cup was presented by A G Seward in memory of C C Marshall who died in Oct 1934. It was to be an 18 hole Medal Competition for Members over 50 years of age (subsequently increased to 55) to be played for in the Summer. Charles Cecil Marshall was Manager of the Hunsbury Hill Furnaces Co. He was an original member of the Northamptonshire County Golf Club, the Northampton Golf Club and the Northampton Lawn Tennis Club. He also played cricket for the Northamptonshire County Cricket Club as an amateur from 1886 to 1897 and often captained the X1. He was described as a brilliant bat and a good fielder.

Winners

1935	L C Baillon
1936	V G Whitelaw
1937	B Cheney
1938	B Cheney
1939	Major J J Dunlop

1940	S Cooper
1941	S J Davis
1942-43	Not played
1944	P G Jones
1945	F F Parsons
1946	A G Seward
1947	P G Jones
1948	R G Browne
1949	W Lees
1950	H M Draper
1951	N G Durham
1952	V H C Amberg
1953	A S Baxter
1954	W H Knight
1955	J T P Woolston
1956	H M Draper
1957	J A Turner
1958	A N Harris
1959	M Jones
1960	W A F Hearne
1961	L J Belson
1962	E V Corps
1963	D J Jones
1964	R Gough
1965	K C Hunter
1966	F W Gibson
1967	R G Riddick
1968	S H G Humfrey
1970	R R Garratt
1971	D Laverick
1972	C H Howkins
1973	E C Dicks
1974	S Drown
1975	R A Palmer
1976	C S Catlow
1977	D C Moore
1978	D Laverick
1979	J J Smith
1980	S Teckman
1981	F A Goode
1982	R V Rawlins
1983	C H Howkins
1984	C R D Tuckey
1985	G E Mobbs
1986	P J Bennett

1987	P E St Quinton
1988	R J Minor
1989	J G Downing
1990	C R D Tuckey
1991	E J Shurvington
1992	P Mc Nally
1993	J H Humphries
1994	G H Gee
1995	J L Fearn
1996	N A White
1997	I Burrage
1998	N Morris
1999	D F R Lord
2000	R J Ruffell
2001	J P P Roberts
2002	P E St Quinton
2003	J Beynon
2004	I Burrage
2005	B H Ball
2006	R J H Pearman
2007	J E Draper
2008	D E Goodrham

ST BOTOLPHS SALVER

Presented by the St. Botolph Golfing Society. An 18 hole Stableford competition for club members over 55 years of age.

Winners

1994	A D Bishop
1995	M Williamson
1996	G J Hasler
1997	R F Watkins
1998	D Curtis
1999	T W Ward
2000	R A Parker
2001	A S Guthrie
2002	R J Spokes
2003	R A Parker
2004	D J Hayhurst
2005	M Evans
2006	T L Butcher
2007	J M Mahood
2008	M Pounds

HIGH HANDICAP BOWL

This Cup was presented by the solicitors Mr Faulkner and Mr Browne to be played in early Spring. It is an 18 hole Medal Competition originally for handicaps 13 to 21, but this has been extended to 19 to 28.

Winners

1934	L M Allison
1935	T T West
1936	T T West
1937	Capt P W Cripps
1938	L M Allison
1939	Capt P W Cripps
1940	A C R Walton
1941	L P Dorman
1942-1945	Not played
1946	W Eyton-Jones
1947	W Eyton-Jones
1948	H A Thorne
1949	H M Draper
1950	R R Garratt
1951	R R Garratt
1952	Dr C M Smith
1953	J Milne
1954	G S Groome
1955	A N Harris
1956	R C Partington
1957	R C Partington
1958	Dr T Tennent
1959	W E Eyton-Jones
1960	J W Mc Lure
1961	R P Bird
1962	E V Corps
1963	D R Corbett
1964	P G Jones
1965	K C Hunter
1966	J L Harrison
1967	F G Riddick
1968	D R Corbett
1969	E R Devereux
1970	P G Jones
1971	J R B Liell
1972	A J Wright
1973	G G Linnell
1974	M T Higgott
1975	A R Banham
1976	P Rudkin
1977	P Boseley
1978	E S Needham
1979	E C Dicks
1980	K C J Whall
1981	B H Ball
1982	L J Belson
1983	M P Thomas
1984	J F Romose
1985	A J Cairns
1986	B M Mitchell
1987	P J Bennett
1988	J B Duffy
1989	A Hanley
1990	R Pountney
1991	J D M Gammans
1992	J D M Gammans
1993	G W Short
1994	D J Littlestone
1995	P J Salt
1996	R Leslie
1997	N D Barltrop
1998	E Dinesen
1999	E J Chater
2000	G A Bushell
2001	R P Fletcher
2002	B Godsiff
2003	J A T Lord
2004	P Starcevic
2005	M B Stiles
2006	M G Fairey
2007	G Hoffman
2008	A W Ferguson

WILSON SALVER

Presented by Mr L A Wilson for Handicaps 13-18. An 18 hole Medal Competition to be played for at the same time as the High Handicap Bowl.

Winners

1989	L A Wilson
1990	G N Underwood

1991	D W G Deane	1955	J H M Green
1992	H H Gowen	1956	H M Draper
1993	R F Watkins	1957	F C Roe
1994	T G Tennent	1958	P Arnold
1995	R F Watkins	1959	A R Banham
1996	J L Hannah	1960	J M Warrington
1997	A Amos	1961	R Bird
1998	S Read	1962	A N Soutar
1999	H B Wilson	1963	A N Soutar
2000	P K Thompson	1964	K R Martin
2001	N Morris	1965	A N Soutar
2002	D K Brooks	1966	C J M Watts
2003	P D Bedwell	1967	M Pounds
2004	W B Nickson	1968	F Wesstrom
2005	M G Cousins	1969	F J Richmond
2006	G E Charlwood	1970	F C Roe
2007	T L Butcher	1971	M R Sleath
2008	D J Commins	1972	E S Needham

BAXTER CUP

Presented by Mr Arthur Baxter a past Captain. Originally a fourball Matchplay Competition off Handicap, but from 1954 became an 18 hole Medal Competition between the Winners of the Saturday Monthly Medals, played on the same day as the Duke of York Cup.

Winners

1939	D Chamberlain & S F Kennedy	1973	E D Sleath
1940	R Catt & W A B Vann	1974	L A Johnson
1941	R Catt & W A B Vann	1975	J S Honess
1942-45	Not played	1976	J Pendry
1946	D Chamberlain	1977	R G Aitken
	C R D Tuckey	1978	D F R Lord
1947	D Chamberlain	1979	M D Duck
	C R D Tuckey	1980	B J F Gross
1948	R Catt & T Askew	1981	H E Weavers
1949	D Chamberlain	1982	T Robertson
	C R D Tuckey	1983	J B Duffy
1950	J H Mobbs & R G Hammond	1984	R E True
1951	R M Hall & R A Larratt	1985	M G Watkins
1952	W H Abbott & S R Lovell	1986	S C Kelly
1953	W H Abbott & S R Lovell	1987	L A Wilson
1954	D Laverick	1988	H H Gowen
		1989	P A Smith
		1990	M C Costin
		1991	J C Archbold
		1992	D W Houghton
		1993	J Beynon
		1994	A R P Lynch
		1995	R W Garrett
		1996	S Read
		1997	N Soto
		1998	B J O'Connell
		1999	B J O'Connell

2000	B J O'Connell	
2001	B J O'Connell	
2002	J B Scholey	
2003	N R B Godden	
2004	M G Watkins	
2005	J C Clarke	
2006	J W Jacobs	
2007	R M Cook	
2008	D J Commins	

COUNTY CUP (OPEN)

Presented by Mr H M Draper, a past Captain, as an open 36 hole Medal Competition played in the Summer. The Cup was originally called the Newnham Bowl after the village where Mr Draper lived, but the name was changed to try and attract a wider selection of Competitors.

Winners

1962	J H Mitchell	143
1963	G F Clarke	151
1964	G E Mobbs	153
1965	Not played	
1966	A Forrester	147
1967	A Forrester	144
1968	J M Pettigrew	138
1969	R A Durrant	146
1970	D Butler	141
1971	P Elson	138
1972	G A L Colman	140
1973	H G Hiatt	142
1974	P McEvoy	139
1975	M James	141
1976	K R Waters	144
1977	P M Harris	144
1978	T Leigh	138
1979	P Downes	138
1980	I Mackenzie	139
1981	J E Ambridge	142
1982	N L Roche	143
1983	G R Krause	145
1984	Not played	
1985	J Vaughan	145
1986	Not played	
1987	P N Wharton	146

1988	A S King	143
1989	N Williamson	141
1990	P N Wharton	138
1991	S J Jarman	138
1992	G Waller	140
1993	N A Nicholson	141
1994	J Frankum	142
1995	A M S Lord	143
1996	A Print	134
1997	R M Duck	135
1998	N J West	136
1999	O Wilson	136
2000	A M S Lord	143
2001	S Dunn	137
2002	G S Boyd	141
2003	G Wolstenholme	137
2004	P Maddy	135
2005	A J Myers	135
2006	R Brown	136
2007	B Stafford	141
2008	M D Bird	144

JACK HUMPHRIES TROPHY

Presented by Mrs Joan Humphries in memory of her husband. An 18 hole Foursomes Medal Competition off handicap to be played in the Spring on the original hole layout of the Course.

Winners

1995	R G Aitken & J J Parker
1996	D Blore & P K Thompson
1997	R Mason & J McPhee
1998	A Amos & W A Stephenson
1999	R E Mason & J McPhee
2000	S Howard & M D Yates
2001	A Pearse & R G Beasley
2002	P G McNally & S Morton
2003	H H Gowen & J B Johnson
2004	J K Archbold & W B Nickson
2005	B R Hardman & J E Delves
2006	P D Bedwell & M P Thomas
2007	M R Kappler & J J Parker
2008	G R Cottrell & P K Thompson

BOYCOTT TROPHY

Presented by Mrs H Boycott in memory of her husband Lieut Harold Boycott who was killed in France on 21st March 1918. The Trophy is a pair of Silver Candlesticks.The Competition was originally 36 Holes off Handicap against Bogey. This was reduced to 18 Holes in 1943. The eligible Competitors must have served overseas in one of the Armed Forces in a Theatre of War.

Because of diminishing numbers the competition is now open to all Club members who have served in any of H.M. Forces.

Winners

Year	Winner
1919	J Faulkner Stops
1920	L C Bostock
1921	J Faulkner Stops
1922	L H Church
1923	L C Bostock
1924	R J Phipps
1925	N F Bostock
1926	T E Manning
1927	L C Bostock
1928	R P Swannell
1929	J Faulkner Stops
1930	C Dawson
1931	N F Bostock
1932	L C Bostock
1933	L C Baillon
1934	W J Watkins
1935	T E Manning
1936	L C Baillon
1937	L H Church
1938	R T Phipps
1939	R P Swannell
1940	H St J Browne
1941	A J Fraser
1942	T E Manning
1943	L H Church
1944	W J Watkins
1945	T E Manning
1946	T E Manning
1947	L H Church
1948	L C Baillon
1949	L C Baillon
1950	T E Manning
1951	T E Manning
1952	T E Manning
1953	G E Bellville
1954	L H Church
1955	T E Manning
1956	L C Baillon
1957	T E Manning
1958	T E Manning
1959	T E Manning
1960	T E Manning
1961	No one fit to play (members from World War II now admitted)
1962	R O Baillon
1963	R O Baillon
1964	E de L Cazenove
1965	C N Buswell
1966	T Baker
1967	E C Harley
1968	J H Mobbs
1969	G E Mobbs
1970	G E Mobbs
1971	J S Kirk
1972	G E Mobbs
1973	J F N Bell
1974	R A Palmer
1975	R A Palmer
1976	A N Soutar
1977	D Laverick
1978	E Coker
1979	R L Mobbs
1980	R F Watkins
1981	J F N Bell
1982	F A York
1983	G E Mobbs
1984	R O Baillon
1985	E C Dicks
1986	G E Mobbs
1987	G B Hudson
1988	J F N Bell
1989	G E Mobbs
1990	J A Barlow
1991	E D Barltrop
1992	G C Andrews
1993	J Parker
1994	W Parker
1995	P E St Quinton

1996	R A Grigg
1997	M E Wadley
1998	M Williamson
1999	A P Goddard
2000	P E St Quinton
2001	N R B Godden
2002	N R B Godden
2003	N R B Godden
2004	E K Williams
2005	P E St Quinton
2006	J J Parker
2007	N R B Godden
2008	M Pounds

Minutes have been kept throughout the competition held by the secretary of the time. A luncheon is held for all competitors in the Clubhouse on the day of the competition, and the previous year's winner is expected to provide port for all the members following the lunch.

COKER CUP

Presented by Mr E Coker a past Captain. An 18 hole Medal Competition competed for by the Thursday Medal Winners.

Winners

1971	D H Clarke
1974	D C Partridge
1975	M D Duck
1976	A W Taylor
1977	E Coker
1978	H Cooper
1979	E R Devereux
1980	J W Punch
1981	E Roberts
1982	L T Hadden
1983	A P Bickley
1984	A J McCleary
1985	K Turner
1986	G Gardner
1987	T R Burwell
1988	D J Sturgess
1989	J Beynon
1990	C B Hanley
1991	Dr R A Sladden

1992	R G Kendrick
1993	J C Clarke
1994	I Morris
1995	N Soto
1996	G J Hasler
1997	N Soto
1998	A R Nicholson
1999	N Soto
2000	R G Halliday
2001	J D Winfield
2002	J M Mahood
2003	R M Sharpe
2004	D C Wade
2005	A P Bickley
2006	J Doyle
2007	A R L Kitchener
2008	R J Peters

CLAYTON ROSE BOWL

Presented by Mr Bruce Clayton. The 12 winners of the Running Monthly Medal competition play 18 hole medal round at the completion of the season.

Winners

1989	R S Biggin
1990	R S Biggin
1991	R A Lobb
1992	R M Duck
1993	B J O'Connell
1994	N Soto
1995	B J O'Connell
1996	A McDougall
1997	I R Wetherall
1998	A J McCleary
1999	T M Garrett
2000	B J O'Connell
2001	P G Lock
2002	J D Winfield
2003	G R Cottrell
2004	G R Cottrell
2005	P G Lock
2006	N J Page
2007	A J McCleary
2008	K Stroud

CORRIN CUP

Following his captaincy in 1978 Jack Corrin gave a cup to be played for by past captains annually in September. A supper is held after the golf and minutes of the meetings are maintained.

MILLENNIUM TROPHY

The trophy is a silver tankard and played for every year within the Club seniors' major competition (the St Botolph Salver) catering especially for those seniors over the age of 70. It was donated by subscription at the instigation of Donald Lamb who was the seniors' organiser at the time and for quite a few years.

2000   P McNally
2001   A S Guthrie
2002   J D Pritchard
2003   C E Clubb
2004   H G Tough
2005   J C Clarke
2006   M J Marriott
2007   H G Tough
2008   M Pounds

COLIN GREEN TROPHY

Presented by David and Anne Green. An 18 hole Open Medal Competition, usually played end of August.

This trophy, born in tragic circumstances, is a memorial to Colin Green, one of twin boys of David and Anne Green, our Centenary Captain.

Colin was a fine low handicap golfer and a university student when the tragedy happened. He was representing our Club in a Scratch League match at Kingsthorpe Golf Club as one of our young promising players. Without warning a thunderstorm occurred and a bolt of lightning struck Colin and injured two other members of the foursome. Sadly Colin died.

The day before Colin had tied with Brian O'Connell for the Club Championship which should have led to a play off. The consequence was that the play off never took place. Both names are on the Honours Board.

2004   N Pyne
2005   S W Russell
2006   D Smith
2007   G R Cottrell
2008   L Holder

Multiple Cup Winners (1910-1994)

R G Aitken	31
R G Halliday	22
G R Cottrell	20
G E Mobbs	20
B J O'Connell	20
R A Haig	19
A C Sinclair	18
C S Catlow	15
G F Clarke	15
A M S Lord	15
T E Manning	14
	(13 Boycott Trophy wins)
A D Bishop	14
M Pounds	14
C R Cieslewicz	12
R A Palmer	11
A N Soutar	11
F C Roe	9
N Soto	9
R B Catlow	8
P G Jones	8
A Print	8
C R D Tuckey	8

CHAPTER X

Flora and Fauna of the Course

"Golf is a good walk spoiled"

Mark Twain

Three members of the Club have each contributed an article on the Flora and Fauna of the Course. Mr Eric Roberts, a professional journalist and contributor for over 43 years of the Country Diary in the Chronicle and Echo, Mrs Kath Swannell, a nature lover and outstanding Lady golfer, and Mr Bruce Clayton, an arboreal enthusiast, who together with Mr E Parr wrote a paper for the Committee on the trees on the course. Their observations, which follow, give a vivid insight into the beauties that surround us as we play our round of golf.

Eric Roberts writes:

It would be hard to say whether Northamptonshire County Golf Course looks its best in spring or in autumn.

The course has always been renowned for its spectacular display of gorse and broom which transforms the whole area into a vista of yellow early in the year (although as yellow in recent years has tended to be associated more with fields of oil seed rape, it might be better to describe the scene as golden).

However, a dramatic and devastating change was wrought following the prolonged and bitter winter of 1981/82, which killed off most of these normally hardy shrubs with the result that the spring-time appearance of the course was changed almost literally overnight. Following this catastrophe steps were taken to replace the shrubs that had been lost in the hope of restoring the course to its former glory, but what nature can inflict in a matter of days takes us mortals years to put right. Nevertheless steady progress has been maintained so that the gorse and broom is becoming re-established at an encouraging rate.

So what about autumn? Anyone visiting Church Brampton at any time of year could be forgiven for thinking that the course had originally been constructed around an arboretum so well endowed is it with trees. Oak, ash, elder, sycamore, silver birch, larch, hawthorn, alder - the list is endless. It is not surprising therefore that such rich variety should result in so glorious a panoply of colour in October and November rendering the course at its most spectacular towards the end of the year rather than the beginning.

Autumns do vary, of course, but the autumn of 1994 turned out to be one of the best of all time. Never had the course looked more magnificent. In that year at least I doubt if any member would disagree that autumn had won by a mile.

From time to time other trees have been introduced to add more colour either through their leaves or their berries, or, in some cases, both. Two that catch the eye (not to mention the badly hooked second shot at the 11th) are the rowans and the whitebeams that stand between the 11th and 12th fairways.

Particularly noticeable, too, are the half-dozen amelanchiers that make a splendid show, more particularly in summer, behind the 6th green. There are some who feel that the introduction of what could be termed park or even garden trees to a golf course is a form of sacrilege, but I don't subscribe to that view. Extra colour, provided it is well chosen, can only add to the variety and interest of any golf course, however well endowed it may be with trees more generally associated with the open countryside.

Which brings me to the host of silver birches that feature on one side or the other of so many of the fairways. It is also worth noting that because fly agaric with its scarlet or orange cap decorated with white blotches flourishes particularly well beneath these trees, one can always expect to find this colourful fungus very much in evidence as summer gives way to autumn.

With the pine woods of Harlestone Firs bordering the course on the far side of the railway, it comes as no surprise to find Scotland's native tree featuring so predominantly in many parts of the course. Two fine, albeit smallish plantations, stand sentinel the length of a drive away from the 18th tee separating the fairways on the last hole and the first.

An assortment of fir trees of different species accompany the pines in other parts of the course or stand on their own to add their individual shades of green to the general scene. Finally, special mention should perhaps be made of particular trees with which the high handicap golfer tends to become all too intimately acquainted. I am thinking especially of the ash that catches many a wayward drive at the fourth, and the oak tree does similar disservice at the sixth.

In late spring or early summer, there is no doubt that the outstanding feature of the course is the mass of hawthorn blossom that predominates on both sides of the railway. I need hardly say that the golfer can be made painfully aware of the presence of hawthorn at any time of the year when backing into a bush to chip an errant golf ball back on to the fairway, but it is in late May or more generally early June that one is made to realise to what extent hawthorn covers so much of the course.

A more modest display of colour is provided by an assortment of wildflowers which bloom at their own specific times of year. I always look for the patch of lady's smock that appears in late April or early May in the boggy hollow some 50 yards in front of the ninth tee. A badly fluffed drive may give the golfer all too good an opportunity to study the lilac-colour flowers from close quarters as he (or, indeed, she) contemplates the second shot from what is almost bound to be a shocking lie.

The pungent scent of meadowsweet usually assails the nostrils even before the tall, creamy-coloured heads of the flowers reveal themselves on the railway side of the path to the 15th tee, while odd patches of lesser celandine (which the uninitiated have been known to mistake for early buttercups) may be seen almost anywhere but more especially in the damper parts of the course. What simply cannot be missed are the clumps or individual specimens of that pestilential weed, ragwort, both the common and the shorter Oxford variety, whose yellow daisy-like heads show up unmistakably in the rough.

The same can be said, only more so, of rosebay willowherb, a wildflower that was classed as a rarity less than 100 years ago, but which today, and more especially since the Second World War, can claim the dubious distinction of being one of the commonest, if not the commonest, weed in Britain. Its tapering spikes of pinkish-purple flowers often reach a height of 5 feet or more, showing up defiantly in the rough to remind us that the fluffy

126

seed heads that will appear later in the year will be blown all over the course to enable it to become ever further established almost anywhere it chooses.

Wild flowers are there by nature's design, of course, but in keeping with the character of the course, a large bed of heathers has been planted ahead and to the left of the 13th tee to make an eye-catching display especially when in flower.

Of the small mammals that have made the course their home rabbits, moles and grey squirrels are the most obvious. Indeed, moles and rabbits are in such numbers that steps have to be taken to keep them in check.

Rarely does one play a round of golf in winter or summer without encountering several grey squirrels busying themselves about the course. Not that anyone minds these provided they don't take a fancy to the odd golf ball and remove it. This doesn't appear to happen very often, if at all, at Church Brampton but the removal of golf balls by squirrels has been known to be a considerable nuisance on some other courses.

Foxes and hedgehogs prefer to inspect the course at night although evidence of their visits is not difficult to spot. The same could apply to badgers, but one mammal renowned for its secretive nature but which does show itself from time to time is the muntjac deer. I have seen this barking deer, as it is also called, on several occasions and once actually had to delay playing my tee shot at the 2nd to allow a muntjac to amble across the fairway as if it had all the time in the world.

There is no doubt that there are rather more of these deer on the course than may be generally realised, but for the most part they prefer to spend their time skulking in the more heavily wooded areas.

Eric Roberts: nature writer for over 40 years (picture: Chronicle & Echo)

A more unusual resident on the course is a mink which frequents the area around the brook at the 15th. Not many members will have seen it, but one who has was startled to find the ferocious creature gazing straight at him as he crossed the wooden footbridge on his way to the green. Another member informed me with barely concealed excitement that he had seen an otter in the water, but I'm sure this was a case of mistaken identity, and this was really our resident mink which is also, of course, an excellent swimmer.

A startling announcement once appeared on the Club Noticeboard warning golfers to "BEWARE OF ADDERS!" But again, I am convinced this was another case of mistaken identity as adders do not inhabit this part of Northamptonshire although they have occasionally been seen in the northern extremity of the county in the Oundle area. Any snakes encountered on the course can safely be assumed to be grass snakes which are quite harmless.

The commonest insect at Church Brampton must surely be the wood ant whose population must amount to millions. These ants are confined to the Harlestone Firs side of the course and, in fact, originated in Harlestone Firs itself, having been introduced, so we are told, by Earl Spencer many years ago for the benefit of his Lordship's pheasants.

The huge dome-shaped nests of these ants can be seen in the vicinity of the 13th hole and although they are not really a problem, it is as well to give any nest a wide berth as these ants do have quite powerful jaws. A few up one's trouser leg could play havoc with one's concentration.

Mining bees are also plentiful all over the course, although more especially on the 8th fairway, where their tell-tale holes can be seen from about March onwards. These bees drill burrows to a depth of anything up to 2 feet wherein to lay their eggs, the excavated soil clearly visible in a tiny mound with a hole in the middle looking like a mini volcano.

Most of the insects we see on the course will have been there for a very long time. Some species were no doubt there long before the course was built, but one that most certainly was not is the gall wasp responsible for a growth on oak trees known as a knopper gall.

I noticed knopper galls on the course in the early 1980s and realised that this gall wasp, whose appearance in this country was first recorded in 1962, had now found its way on to our own oak trees, laying its eggs in late May and early June in the incipient acorns. When the larvae hatch from these eggs they stimulate the growth of bright green, sticky tissue from the acorn cup which later congeals into a hard brown substance. The sum total of all this is that the acorn ends up looking as if someone had removed it from its cup, chewed it, and put it back again.

Perhaps one of the more surprising insects to encounter on the golf course is the dragonfly. It wouldn't be considered unusual to catch sight of the odd specimen darting hither and thither, but on one or two occasions as many as half-a-dozen or more hawker dragonflies have been seen displaying their flying skills around the 12th tee. Golfers fascinated by these unrivalled aviators claim to have been distracted to the point of failing to make the green on this short hole (at least, that was their excuse!) but as this part of the course is about as far from the brook as it can possibly be, it may seem strange that any dragonflies should be there at all let alone in such numbers.

However, it is a mistake to think that dragonflies never venture far from water. They quite often do, especially soon after their transformation into mature insects when they are more vulnerable to predators as their bodies have not yet had time to harden.

Butterflies, on the other hand, would surely be expected to take full advantage of a habitat offering such a rich variety of vegetation.

But this doesn't appear to be so. I see very few butterflies on my way round the course even at the height of summer, although I do remember catching sight of several orange tips one year within a day or two of someone having written to ask me what had happened to this species as he hadn't seen one for a very long time!

Of course, the inevitable cabbage white puts in an appearance on fairly frequent occasions, and one may catch a glimpse of other common species from time to time. It has to be said, too, that the buddleia colloquially known as the butterfly bush, will be visited by an assortment of tortoiseshells, brimstones, peacocks, and, provided they have succeeded in making their way here from the Mediterranean in reasonable numbers, red admirals and even painted ladies.

It all depends on how good a butterfly year it happens to be. Butterflies have been diminishing in numbers for some time now, but 1994 will be remembered as one of the worst years so far. Several members commented on not having seen a single butterfly on the buddleia near the first tee during all the time it was in flower.

It is therefore unlikely that any of our golfers will be heard complaining of having missed a putt through being disturbed by "the uproar of the butterflies in an adjacent meadow" a misfortune that befell one of P.G. Wodehouse's characters. However, not the same can be said of the birds!

There was the occasion when one of our lady members found herself in trouble on the greens through the extraordinary coincidence of a pheasant giving its raucous cry every time she shaped up to putt, putting her off completely.

As she and her partner came up the 16th one of these birds could be seen perched on top of the bunker on the right hand side of the fairway, so, as she prepared to play her shot to the green, and in view of the way she had been disturbed all the way round, her partner muttered "Kill it!"

A crisp 5 iron sent the ball flying through the air, and seconds later , to the astonishment of both ladies, the pheasant was seen to jerk its head back, open its wings, and keel over, stunned by the most accurate shot the lady golfer had ever played in her life. Never in a million years could she have hit that bird however hard she tried.

To the relief of both players, the pheasant was already showing signs of recovery by the time they reached it, and it soon flew off apparently none the worse for the experience although possibly suffering from a very sore head.

Cock and hen pheasants frequently traverse the fairways (although normally in complete safety.) Magpies are much in evidence, too. Even when they can't be seen they can be heard "chattering" in the trees.

Two other birds that are more often heard than seen are the two woodpeckers, the green and the great spotted, the former greeting golfers with its unmistakable yaffle, a laughing cry that is supposed to predict rain, and the latter with its loud drumming produced by rapid hammering on a hollow tree trunk or branch.

It is on the golf course, too, that almost invariably I hear my first cuckoo and also the spring song of the chaffinch which with uncanny consistency is rendered every year within a day or two of March 1st.

Yellowhammers seem to favour the undergrowth near the 4th tee. I have also on occasions caught a brief glimpse of a flock of longtailed tits making their purposeful way from one group of trees to another while every now and then a kingfisher will pass like a sapphire streak along the brook near the railway. Pied wagtails are not infrequent visitors, sometimes turning up on the 15th green or even nearer the Club House well within sight of the veranda windows.

The conifers on the course along with those in Harlestone Firs will at times attract that canary-like bird, the siskin, while predatory species such as kestrels and sparrowhawks are never far away, the former being easily identified because of its superb hovering ability.

One bird I have never seen although I was assured by one of our more elderly members that it did put in a surprise appearance one year is the golden oriole. This is a bird that winters in tropical Africa and which does make rare visits to this country. But it is certainly not a bird one need keep an eye open for as the likelihood of its ever coming to Church Brampton again is remote in the extreme.

If a pheasant once proved a distraction to one of our lady members quite the opposite could be said of a crow that was clearly bent on rendering a service to one of our senior gentlemen. Having played his tee shot at the 6th and noting with some satisfaction not to say surprise that it had just about made the green, he and the rest of the fourball were a trifle concerned when they noticed a crow circling above the ball and alighting beside it. These large birds have been known to pick up golf balls and make off with them, but this crow appeared to have the golfer's interests at heart because it proceeded to nudge the ball nearer the hole with its beak.

It would make a nice end to the story to be able to say that the bird finished the job off by pushing the ball all the way there, thus enabling the golfer to claim a somewhat dubious hole-in-one.

But as the fourball neared the green, the crow abandoned its efforts leaving the ball that much nearer the hole but not near enough, alas, for the astonished golfer to sink the putt and claim a birdie of a most unusual kind.

Kath Swannell writes:

My brief visits to Brampton during times of conflict were a great delight. At all times of the year this privileged piece of country was a dream of peace and a haven for wild creatures: foxes, badgers, pheasants, partridge on the adjacent fields, woodpeckers, jays, owls, hawks; kingfishers and herons fished in the brook.

The fairways were lined by gorse and broom, and the greens, which were tended by hand, were like velvet. The age of the motor mower had not yet arrived. The backdrop was Harlestone Firs and from the near side of the Club House the view across the railway line was spectacular - predominately firs and larches, but just visible the beech avenue leading from the boundary of the course, (10th tee), up to the Harlestone Road. On a hot summer's day the perfume of scented poplar would waft over the 11th green. Down by the brook the alders attracted the lesser kingfishers who nested in the bank of the stream by the 5th tee. In those days red, white and pink may trees, wild cherry, crab apples and even a wild pear, were scattered over the course. An avenue of Spanish chestnuts flourished in the firs from the farm gate between the 17th green and the 7th tee. It was interesting to find a small oak tree in the broom on the boundary of the course running the length of the second hole it was an exotic looking little specimen, much smaller in every way from the English oak, and bearing acorns which had hairy cups. Carrick, the Head Greenkeeper, called it a Turkey Oak. I had never seen one before.

In early Spring before World War II, there was an enchanting stretch of crocuses between the 17th green and the 18th tee, followed by daffodils in great profusion, flourishing wild in the long grass. After the war they had completely disappeared, but several years later I was amazed to see one clump of daffodils blooming in the middle of a bramble bush close to the boundary, the sole survivor of many hundreds!

Membership was small in those early years, and the wild flowers bloomed undisturbed. Bluebells invaded the firs where the trees had been felled, and flowed on to the course in a great deep blue tide. Honeysuckle flourished on the boundary fences. The railway banks offered sanctuary to sheets of moon daisies, and in early Spring cowslips, nurtured by the soot from steam-driven engines, established themselves on the grassy slopes.

On a summer's day it was near to paradise, and in the autumn it was extravagantly beautiful as the dead leaves were stripped from the trees by the wild, west wind – "yellow and black, and pale and hectic red", (Shelley, Ode to the West Wind). The silver birches revealed in silhouette the almost incandescent perfection of their trunks and branches against the darkness of the firs. The russet bracken and dead heather went into a winter sleep, and the country took on a stark beauty.

On Boxing Day it was quite usual for the Pytchley Hunt to meet at Harlestone. It often happened that the fox would lead the hunt towards the course. I have seen a resourceful animal cross the railway between the tunnels while the frustrated huntsmen were forced to stream through the most adjacent tunnel. It was quite common to find golf balls in the rough destroyed by teeth marks, sometimes coverless. The greenkeeper told me that he had frequently seen a litter of fox cubs play with these relics at dusk or in the early morning! The darker side of nature was the endless war between stoats and rabbits. If, particularly in the spring, you heard the scream of a rabbit, you knew it was the climax of a life and death struggle, and that the blood of another rabbit was being drained away in the relentless jaws of a stoat.

Bruce Clayton writes:

Northamptonshire County Golf Club was traditionally laid out as a classic heathland course by virtue of the nature of the terrain and the fact that part of the course was Brampton Heath. Heathland occurs where traditional forest and woodland are cleared. It is a natural phenomenon that once light is let in where a canopy of trees previously stood, dormant seeds of all kinds of flora including heather, broom and gorse will generate themselves and assert themselves in a vigorous way. Harpole Heath, Harlestone Heath and Brampton Heath must have done so when woodland was cleared, probably for sheep grazing.

Historically, Northamptonshire was a heavily wooded County and was cleared during the great period of wool prosperity in late medieval times running through to the middle of the 18th century.

Our own course flourished for some years, but it became obvious that the heathland character was diminishing. For instance, a thick belt of gorse and broom stretched across the 9th fairway before the 1939-45 War. This presented the golfer of the day with a serious dilemma. He could either drive short and then hopefully clear the gorse and the stream with his second shot, or he could bravely attempt to clear the gorse with his drive. All in all, it would have been a much more difficult hole than today. By the end of the war years and into the 1950s virtually all that belt of gorse had disappeared. A small pocket remains next to the copse behind the 15th green and part of that has had to be re-planted.

In 1977 over 500 trees were planted on the course, many of which were donated by members. It was at a time when we rapidly lost several hundred mature trees succumbing to Dutch Elm disease. In particular we lost the magnificent specimen of a Wych Elm behind the 13th green which acted as a marker. That tree has now been replaced by a Wellingtonia Gigantea which will eventually mature into a specimen tree over 100 feet in height and fastigiate in form. It was intended as a marker to the golfer playing his second shot to the green as did the Wych Elm before.

Also included in this planting was a thin line of trees dividing the 11th and 12th fairways. Previously this was an open area and it was felt that the tree line would enhance the course. Up to 1963 there was a marvellous plantation in front of the 4th teeing grounds, presenting a psychological problem if not a physical one to the golfer driving off on that particular hole. The especially savage winter of 1963 decimated this area. Both gorse and broom are none too hardy and much of it died as a result of the prolonged period of cold and frost.

In the years that followed it was hoped that it might regenerate itself naturally, but this was not the case. Matters were made worse by the golfer who topped his or her drive off the tee and who tramped through the now dead pockets of broom and gorse looking for it, thus preventing much chance of natural regrowth.

Joe Carrick, the Head Greenkeeper of the day, was conscious of the losing battle and tried himself to transplant some of the gorse which he took from certain areas of the rough and re-planted where he thought it might be better placed and re-grow, but he had little success. Even his small plantations of seed scarcely flourished and this was largely due to the fact that there is a special technique required to tackle the problem.

Following information from the President of Ganton Golf Club who had had similar problems, it was agreed that we should recruit the services of a part time forester whose job it would be to promote and regenerate wherever he could. In some instances it was necessary to remove certain "weed" trees such as self sown scrub Oak, Elderberry and Sycamore which had begun to assert themselves. If this particular problem had not been tackled, then all the areas of the rough on the course would have reverted to woodland and we should have eventually lost all traces of the heathland character.

Over the last 11 years, we have worked slowly and systematically to promote growth. Mr John Gubbins has given a vast amount of time, energy and expertise to producing plants of gorse from seed taken from the course and growing them on in containers to a reasonable planting size, enabling us to to plant whole areas with success. We have also endeavoured to maintain that whatever tree planting has taken place in the past, future species of tree planted should be those indigenous to a heathland type golf course. Thus, we have planted Rowan, Scotch Pine, Larch and Birch trees and have tried to avoid change of character from heathland to parkland.

CHAPTER XI

The Juniors

"The advantage of learning to play golf at a young age is that
you do not realise it is a difficult game"

Anon

The junior members of Brampton have always been recognised as being the breeding ground for the future, but it was not until Ken Hunter, headmaster of Spratton Hall Preparatory School, and his deputy and successor, Piers Bickley, really took an interest that they began to receive serious recognition and training. Ken Hunter officially founded the Junior Section of the Club, and a number of junior members have passed through his school.

In 1987 Michael and Angela Duck took over from Piers Bickley, and have worked extremely hard for many years in producing a thriving number of boys and girls, who are competent and, in some cases, high class golfers.

Matches are arranged during the year against the Club committee followed by a supper, against Stowe School, home and way, and monthly medals are held regularly. Cups have been presented by members for the Annual Gross and Net scores in the junior Club championship.

Junior group coaching with the Club's professionals takes place on a Saturday morning. The Annual Junior Open and the Daily Telegraph qualifying competition both attract entries from all over the country. Boys outnumber girls but Kelly Hanwell (5 handicap) and Laura Peach (11 handicap) both feature well in national girls events.

Outstanding among the boys, who have come through the system, are Adam Print (handicap +1), past Northamptonshire County champion and winner of the Leicestershire Fox in 1994. Robert Duck (also handicap +1) won the Carris Trophy at Brampton in 1994, and both he and Andrew Lynch were picked to play for England and Ireland respectively in the Boys International at Woodhall Spa in 1995.

It is unprecedented for the Club to boast two members with handicaps of +1 and must bode extremely well for our success in future county competitions.

ALLITT CUP
Presented by Mr S Allitt for the best gross score in the junior championship.

Winners

1976 D L Evans	76
1977 B J Dickes	79
1978 N K Adams	78
1979 A J Wilson	78
1980 A M Lord	73
1981 A M Lord	76
1982 J B Scholey	77
1983 J B Scholey	78
1984 J A Barker	80
1985 D K Jones	73
1986 G Gilchrist	73
1987 D Kelly	73
1988 A Print	80
1989 C J Underwood	78
1990 C Lane	70
1991 R M Duck	73
1992 R M Duck	72
1993 R M Duck	70
1994 R M Duck	68
1995 R M Duck	75
1996 T Duck	70
1997 T Duck	76
1998 B R Garrett	80
1999 R J Green	75
2000 R J Green	70
2001 R J Green	71
2002 K Cullum	72
2003 M Bird	73
2004 J A G Smith	70
2005 A J Myers	66
2006 A J Myers	71
2007 A J Myers	68
2008 A J Myers	72

JONES CUP
Presented by Mr Percy Jones for the best net score in the junior championship.

Winners

1969 R R Mobbs
1970 M R Sleath
1971 P T Barnes
1972 P R Patterson
1973 T J Giles
1974 S R Parr
1975 N K Adams
1976 P E Learoyd
1977 A D Learoyd
1978 N K Adams
1979 J B Scholey
1980 E M Allan
1981 C H Shine
1982 J B Scholey
1983 S J Bickley
1984 R M Duck
1985 G Gilchrist
1986 T Lord
1987 R M Duck
1988 C J Underwood
1989 R M Duck
1990 R M Duck
1991 C J Underwood
1992 A Ellis
1993 D T Allitt
1994 N Soto
1995 J Kendrick
1996 T J Howell
1997 R J Green
1998 C N Green
1999 L Zielinski
2000 R Whiting
2001 Miss L Rouse
2002 A J Myers
2003 Miss L Rouse
2004 J A G Smith
2005 D Patton
2006 J Cox
2007 J P Larkins
2008 M J Myers

Above: some of the juniors

*Right: Adam Print (left)
and Chris Lane*

CHAPTER XII

Professionals, Secretaries and Greenkeepers

"The right way to play golf is to go up and hit the bloody thing"
George Duncan

THE PROFESSIONALS
1910-24

Len Holland, the first Club professional, was certainly the most prestigious golfer to hold the post. He came from Sheringham GC in 1910 and stayed with Brampton until 1924. In 1914 he won the Matchplay Foursomes Championship with J. B. Batley but he was unfit for military service and was employed by British Chrome Tanning Co. in Grafton Street.

After the War he rejoined Brampton and had notable success in the Open Championship, being fifth in 1920 at Deal, 16th in 1921 at St. Andrews, 13th in 1922 at St. Georges Sandwich and sixth in 1924 at Hoylake. He was runner-up in 1923 and 1924 in the Daily Mail Tournament and reached the semi-final of the News of the World Tournament in 1920 and 1925. He won the Leeds 1000 Guineas Tournament in 1925 after he had joined Gerrards Cross GC.

He was a superb iron player and used to play exhibition shots from the left of the 10th tee UNDER the railway arch on to the 15th green!

He was featured among the 30 Prominent Golfers on Churchman Cigarette cards first published in 1931.

1924-39

In 1924 W G (Bill) Saunders came as professional from Brocton Hall GC. He had previously been an assistant to Len Holland at Sheringham GC. Bill was a good teacher and a popular member of the staff. He played in a professional tournament in France and accompanied the Duke of York (later King George VI) on a golfing holiday in Scotland prior to playing in the Open Championship. He made golf clubs under his own name.

1940-47

Saunders stayed on at the beginning of the War but there was little for him to do and he soon left. After the war Len Holland's nephew, Jim Holland, who had been at Gorleston GC, came to the club but only for a short period. Otherwise, no professional was employed until 1947 with the arrival of Geoffrey Gledhill.

1947-52

Geoffrey Gledhill joined the PGA in 1945 and came to Brampton two years later. He is chiefly remembered as a strict time keeper, and if the clock struck to end your lesson at the top of the back swing, Gledhill would have disappeared by the time you had completed the stroke.

1953-66

William H. (Billy) Cann came from Bideford in Devon and had 13 years at Brampton. He was no particular golfer but he was of cheerful disposition and was a forceful salesman from his well-stocked shop. If you had lost anything on the golf course, it was likely to turn up for sale in his shop. His wife ran an antiques shop in Northampton.

1966-72

Stuart William Thomas Murray probably never intended to become a professional, but was classified as one in 1963 as he was making his living from selling golf equipment.

As an amateur Stuart played for Scotland (1959-63) and for Great Britain from 1958-62, and played in the Walker Cup in 1963. He won the Scottish Amateur Championship in 1962 and won many other titles during this successful period.

As a professional he won the Midlands Championship in 1964, 67 and 68 and finished 12th in the PGA Order of Merit in 1964. He came to Brampton in 1966 and went on to the Far East Tour in 1967. He was third in the Indian Open, seventh in the Hong Kong Open and broke the Hong Kong course record with a 64.

Stuart was a very popular member of the staff at Brampton, where he was a good teacher and excellent player. He had seven holes in one in his career, the first being the 15th at Brampton.

1973-74

Eric Overend qualified with the PGA in 1968 and came to Brampton following the departure of Stuart Murray to Hendon GC. Although joining with excellent credentials, he was not a success at Brampton and stayed only for one year.

1974-82

Robin Day joined the PGA in 1962 so was well established as a club professional when he joined Brampton. He was a useful player without any notable success, but was a competent teacher, and was responsible for turning George Mobbs from a right to left to a left to right player, thereby saving George a few lost golf balls.

1982-91

Stuart David Brown joined the PGA in 1965 and had a distinguished career as player, coach and administrator. He was Sir Henry Cotton's Rookie of the Year as a young professional, having been All England Assistants champion. He was captain of the South West, North Hants and Midlands PGA. Prior to coming to Brampton he had been professional at Tewkesbury GC and on the professional circuit he had won the Dunlop Open in Africa, the Zambian Open, the Lomas Open in Argentina and the Tryall Open in Jamaica. He was PGA champion of the South West and the Midlands and was European Club Professional Champion.

Stuart has had 26 holes in one in his career, including two in one day at the same hole with the same club and the same ball. This feat was captured on TV and is unique in golf history. He was a teaching panelist for six years to Golf World and PGA Sky Television video instructor. He left Brampton in 1991 to become Golf Director at Slaley Hall Golf and Country Club.

1991 - the present

Timothy Rouse, born in Grimsby, was accepted as a member of the PGA in 1979. He was professional at Coventry Hearsall, and had been captain and chairman of Warwickshire PGA from 1986-90 prior to coming to Brampton.

As a coach Tim has had appointments with the English Ladies Golf Association, and the Greek Golf Federation, coaching the Greek national team.

Although never very high in the Midlands Order of Merit, he has held course records at Boldmere, Coventry Hearsall, Nuneaton and Glen Gorse, and has won the Warwickshire and Northamptonshire professional championships.

In 1987 he qualified for the Open championship. Tim still lives in Coventry with his wife and two daughters. In the Millennium Tim has coached Gary Boyd, one of his very talented pupils, who qualified for the 2008 Open.

CLUB SECRETARIES

1909	H. Boycott Rev. Eddows	Joint Honorary
1911	L. H. Gray	Salaried
1914	B. Cheney	Honorary
1918	W. A. S. Talbot	Salaried
1919	Miss A. G. Hughes	Salaried
1926	B. Cheney	Part Salaried
1930	Col. Bourne	Salaried
1931	Ralph Langley	Salaried
1934	Col. Dening	Salaried
1939	R. G. Browne	Salaried
1953	N. Durham	Honorary
1958	R. G. W. Gubbins	Honorary
1964	R. F. Watkins	Honorary
1966	G. E. Mobbs	Salaried
1981	G. G. Morley	Salaried (pictured above)
1992	M. E. Wadley	Salaried (pictured below)

(M E Wadley died tragically on the ski slopes. An inter-regnum period followed during which Richard Halliday the Club Captain officiated.)

| 2002 | P. Walsh | Salaried |

THE GREENKEEPERS

The fact that in its 85 year history, the club has only had five greenkeepers speaks volumes for the quality of the men who have held the post and their relationship with the different chairmen of greens committees with whom they have worked.

William Berridge served the club from its inauguration in 1910 until his death in 1939, and had all the responsibility of the opening years and the problems of the War years (1914-18). He saw the transition from horses to mechanical transport, from hickory to steel shafted clubs, and a doubling of membership in his lifetime.

R. G. (Bob) Browne was appointed both secretary and greenkeeper in 1939, and played a major role through the war years of keeping the club and the course in such condition that both could be resurrected after the war without major upheavals.

Between the resignation of Bob Browne in 1953 and the appointment of Joe Carrick from the Portmarnock Club in Ireland in 1956, Frank Roe, the chairman of the greens committee, acted as head greenkeeper, overseeing the work of the staff.

'Gentleman' Joe had started work on the green staff at Portmarnock at the age of 13. He worked a 12-hour day, which included a round as caddy. He had an official handicap of four but usually played below it.

Joe continued as greenkeeper at Brampton until 1981, when he officially retired owing to failing eyesight, but stayed on a part-time basis, imparting his wealth of experience to the young members of the green staff.

Joe was succeeded by his deputy Michael Lake, who Joe trained and who held the post until 1988. He was succeeded by David Low, who holds the post today.

CHAPTER XIII

Sporting Personalities who have been Members

"The mark of a champion is the ability to make the most of good luck and the best of bad"

Anon

The Mobbs and the Bostocks

The family name that is indelibly linked with the County Golf Club throughout its history is the Mobbs, and as Herbert Mobbs, father of Humphrey, George and Roger married Norah Bostock, the two families have an astonishing record as trophy winners from 1910 to 1988, collecting 69 cups between them. Frederick, Lance and Neville Bostock have all been club captains, Norah and Rosemary Mobbs have been captains of the Ladies Section, and George Mobbs has been auditor, secretary and honorary life member of the club.

George Mobbs has been the winner of 20 club trophies, including twice as club champion, an honour also achieved by Roger Mobbs. In George's opinion, Eric Bostock, second son of Frederick, was the best golfer of both families, although he was sadly killed in the 1914-18 War. Sir Noel Mobbs, chairman of Slough Estates, was the first winner of the Burn Cup in 1910, and Graily Mobbs, both brothers of Herbert Mobbs, won the same cup in 1931.

On the distaff side, Norah Mobbs won eight cups, Humphrey's wife Rosemary won six and George's wife Helen has won five, including three times winner of the Church Cup, playing with husband George.

The Bostocks were directors and major shareholders of Lotus Shoes. Herbert Mobbs was a motor engineer and owned the Henry Oliver Garage in Northampton. Both George and Humphrey spent some time at Lotus, but eventually Humphrey went to run the garage,

Neville Bostock

Lance Bostock

Frederick Bostock

and George rejoined Coopers & Lybrand, to whom as A. C. Palmer, he had originally been articled as an accountant.

The Catlows and the Aitkens

The other two families with multiple success among the club's trophies are the Catlows and the Aitkens, the connection being that Richard Aitken married Charles Catlow's daughter, Sue.

Charles Catlow was without doubt the finest golfer in the county before and immediately after World War II. His early golf was played at Royal Lytham St. Annes. He then went to Haileybury College, where he excelled at cricket, rugby and fives, and played cricket as an amateur for the county and hockey for Wales.

He was a member at Rushden GC, Northampton GC and Clapham GC before coming to Brampton in 1932. By 1936 he was a scratch golfer at Brampton and won the county championship 11 times between 1934 and 1960, and twice played in the English Amateur championship, and one occasion reached the last 16. He once won the county championship, going round on a bicycle to protect a damaged leg!

Charles was especially interested in course architecture and was very friendly with C K Cotton, the professional golf architect and assisted him on several courses. He also designed the 14th and 15th holes at Thorpeness GC, where he was made an honorary life member. He reconstructed several holes at Rushden GC and was responsible for the 'bumps' at the eighth hole and re-designed the 17th hole at Brampton, where he was greens chairman for many years. He and Frank Roe, another scratch golfer who was also greens chairman for many years, were a formidable foursomes pair for the county. Charles's son, Richard, was a county golfer, and has won a number of club trophies at Brampton. He is a skilled bridge and chess player, and is much in demand as an after dinner speaker.

Charles Catlow's son-in-law Richard Aitken carried on the family tradition and has been,

Charles Catlow, watched by Don Chamberlain and Bill Hollingsworth

without doubt, the outstanding golfer at Brampton from 1960 until the present day.

Richard was born in Edinburgh and learned his early golf at Prestonfield GC. He reached the last eight of the British Boys championship aged 15, represented Scottish Universities from 1957-60, the last year winning the British Universities championship. On coming to Northampton he joined Northampton GC for a few years before being elected to Brampton. He has played countless times for the county, has won the county championship eight times, has had seven holes in one, and played on 280 different courses. His successes at Brampton are chronicled in the chapter on club trophies, and the combined total of cups of the two families and their wives is a formidable 61.

Charles Catlow was a director of leather merchants, BB Vos & Son, Richard Catlow is a solicitor, and Richard Aitken a consultant clinical biochemist with Kettering hospital.

Above: Richard Aitken
Right: Jack Humphries

John Henry 'Jack' Humphries

Jack Humphries, apart from being a high class amateur golfer, held important posts in the administration of the game.

Born in 1923, Jack joined the Royal Navy as a young man and served in the last war as a lieutenant in command of a tank landing craft during the Normandy landings.

After the war he trained at Jordan Hill in Physical Education, and taught PE at Roade School. He enjoyed all sport and in his youth was a professional footballer, but his main love was always golf. He played countless times for Northamptonshire and captained the County team in 1968 and 1969. He was County Seniors champion in 1980 and captain of Brampton in 1986. He was president of the Northamptonshire Golf Union in 1984, president of the Midlands Golf Union in 1987 and chairman in 1989. At the English Golf Union he was a member of the executive committee in 1988 and of the EGU greens committee in 1990.

Apart from golf, Jack who later became Staff Liaison Officer at Pianoforte Supplies, was a star performer and teacher of Scottish Exhibition dancing, had a wide knowledge of Robert Burns poetry, and was a talented painter of china, which he fired himself.

In the hot summer of 1976, Jack went to Peterborough Milton GC to play in the county competition for the Higgs Bowl, a trophy he had previously won. Owing to the weather, he came to the 1st tee dressed in smart shorts and stockings. The club captain refused to allow him to compete, saying he was not dressed according to club dress rules. Needless to say Jack was not amused - and probably said so.

Rugby Football

Many club members have played for the Saints and East Midlands over the years, but special mention should be made of Ronnie Knapp who scored four tries for Cambridge in the University match against Oxford and as a result received an invitation to play for Wales. Owing to the war this was his only cap.

R B (Bob) Taylor, however, apart from representing the Saints, Hampshire, Midlands and Barbarians, played for England from 1966 to 1970 (captaining the side once in France) and was in the British Lions squad that toured South

Bob Taylor

Africa in 1968. He continued to play for the Saints until 1978. Recently retired from school teaching, he is a justice of the Peace on the Northampton bench.

Tennis

There have not been many members who have shone at tennis. Spriggs Baillon captained the county side for many years but the international tennis star among our members is C R D (Raymond) Tuckey.

He was at Queens College Cambridge and represented the university in 1931 and 1932 in doubles and singles. On leaving university, he joined the Royal Engineers as a regular and won the Army Lawn tennis championships singles in 1932, 33 and 34, and won the doubles in 1934 and 37.

He won the British Hard Court championship doubles in 1936 with G P Hughes, and in the same year won the Wimbledon men's doubles title with the same partner. He was in the Great Britain Davis Cup team, again with G P Hughes in the 1935 and 36 competitions, both of which Britain won. He partnered F H D Wilde in the doubles in the 1937 Davis Cup competition in which Great Britain were defeated. On leaving the Army in 1937 Raymond joined British Timken, in which company he ultimately became Sales Director. He was a Justice of the Peace on the South Northamptonshire Bench, and lives in Church Stowe still playing golf at least twice a week.

Bob Taylor has been honoured with the presidency of the English Rugby Football Union, probably the highest honour the game can bestow on any of its former players.

In the sport of Rugby Union, Matthew Dawson joined Brampton whilst playing for the Saints but when he left to join Wasps, he resigned as one of our members. Paul Grayson, Saints and England, who played stand off half outside Dawson for quite some years is also one of our members, as is Nick Beal, a former Saints and England full-back and a highly talented golfer. Rodney Webb, another ex-Coventry and England wing three-quarter, is a member. Webb ran the company called Gilberts which manufactures rugby footballs.

Above: G P Hughes and Raymond Tuckey
Right: Laurie Johnson (second right) in his cricket benefit year with ex-county team mates Mike Warrington, Peter Arnold, John Wild and Keith Andrew

Cricket

Club members who have played for Northamptonshire include Charles Marshall, Harold Boycott, T E M Manning, Stuart Humphrey, Charles Catlow, Peter Arnold (who also played first class cricket in New Zealand), Laurie Johnson, Lewis McGibbon, Mike Warrington and John Wild. Although we cannot boast any internationals among our members, Laurie Johnson deserves mention in that as wicket-keeper, he twice dismissed all 10 batsmen in an innings. Ten Sussex batsmen were caught in 1963 and two years later, Laurie caught eight and stumped two Warwickshire batsmen.

Soccer

David Lloyd Bowen a previous Club member was born near Maesteg and moved to Northampton when his father took over the Roadmender Club. He began his football career with the Cobblers, and then spent 10 years with Arsenal as a wing half, eventually taking over the position from Joe Mercer.

He won 20 caps for Wales, and the highlight of his career was to captain Wales in the World Cup competition in Sweden in 1958, where they were put out by Brazil, the eventual winners of the cup, to an own goal in the quarter finals. Dave marked an 18-year-old forward called Pele.

In 1959 he took over as manager of the Cobblers and took them on the meteoric rise from the Fourth to the First Division. After relegation from the First

Chilly work – Dave Bowen on the training ground with the Cobblers

Division, Dave became secretary of the club. Despite offers from some of the biggest clubs, he preferred to remain in Northampton and retired from football in the mid Eighties.

Hockey

Two of our Lady members have played for England at hockey. They are Mrs Janet Gubbins, who died in the spring of 2007 and who was a Lady member of Brampton for many years, a fine golfer, a past Captain and Lady President. The other is Mrs Karen Lobb who is one of our current Lady members and who has also represented her country.

Since Neil Soutar wrote the original text Raymond Tuckey died in the year 2005 (see obituary under Familiar Faces). Lewis McGibbon, Peter Arnold and Laurie Johnson are all ex-Northants County Cricket Club players. Robin Matthews joined Brampton. Of tall stature he played county cricket in his younger days for Leicestershire. Allan Lamb, born in South Africa and a fine batsman for Northamptonshire County Cricket Club and England on many occasions is a Club member. Greg Thomas, also a member, played cricket for England, Glamorgan and Northamptonshire (1989-91) as a right-arm fast bowler.

CHAPTER XIV

A Hundred Years of the Ruling Passion

"It ran a hundred years to a day".

Homer

Profiles of our Centenary Captains and Chairman

David Green

David is by birth a Dubliner, the eldest of four children educated at Mountjoy School where he represented the school at hockey, rugby and athletics. During his teenage years he was a prolific swimmer and represented Leinster at schoolboy level. David was the Irish Schools' breaststroke champion in 1968.

After leaving school, David took articles in the accountancy profession with the firm then known as Cooper Brothers, later to become Coopers and Lybrand, large international chartered accountants. David qualified in the mid-1970's and became a Fellow of the Institute of Chartered Accountants in Ireland some 10 years later.

In 1986 David moved to Northampton with his family to take up the appointment as Financial Director of Target Furniture Limited of Northampton. David was obliged to become a temporary member of the Club for a year because of the large waiting list for new members and finally became a full member in 1990. He has

David Green

served on the Management Committee since 1999 and has been our Honorary Treasurer since the year 2002, succeeding Keith Archbold.

With his partner, David has won the Lees Cup twice and the Chamberlain Cup once and was runner up in the Burn Cup in 2002, losing at the thirty-sixth hole.

David's twin sons Roger and Colin were brought up and encouraged to become fine golfers. Roger plays off a handicap of one. Sadly, Colin was lost to David and Anne his wife and his twin brother when he was accidentally killed on Kingsthorpe Golf Course whilst playing a match, a cross few of us have had to bear but which David has overcome with great fortitude.

Centenary Ladies' Captain - Susan Aitken

Sue Aitken (née Catlow) joined the Club as a junior member in 1957 but only took up the

Susan Aitken

game seriously in the late 1960's. Her sporting background was promising - the daughter of a former Welsh ladies' hockey international and a father who was 11 times Northamptonshire golf champion. Her mother, father, husband and sister-in-law have all been Captains of the Club.

Sue was educated at Hawnes School in Bedfordshire where her sporting interests included tennis, lacrosse and, in particular, hockey. On leaving school she embarked on a secretarial course at St Godric's College in London and secured her first employment in Cambridge. Seeking further advancement, she applied for and was appointed to the position of secretary to a senior executive at the Royal Automobile Club in Pall Mall.

By 1978, Sue was running a home and bringing up two children but her handicap improved dramatically. She became a regular on the scene at Brampton, was elected to the Committee, played a prominent part in Cecil Leitch matches and ultimately became Captain in 1990.

Not surprisingly, her efforts caught the eye of the county Ladies and after a spell in the second team she won her Northamptonshire Ladies' County Golf Association colours in the season 1997-98. This experience was to lead to further honours as in 1999 she was appointed County Vice-Captain (to the former Curtis Cup International, Carol Gibbs) and ultimately Captain in 2001-02. Her leadership at this time was in no small way responsible for a resurgence in Northamptonshire ladies' golf.

Sue's qualifications for centenary captaincy are impressive. She is well known at club and county level. She has won the Deterding Cup with her partner on four occasions, the Church Cup six times and has her name on several other Club trophies.

Centenary Club Chairman –
Christopher Thompson

Chris, as he is popularly known to his friends and family, was born at Washington in Tyne and Wear, Northumberland, a town with common linkage with Northamptonshire. Thinking of its Washington family connections, another branch of the family of George Washington, first President of the United States of America, was domiciled in the North East.

Once Northumberland was a separate kingdom and after the Norman Conquest, Durham with its hugely impressive cathedral and ancient university

Christopher Thompson

perched on high ground in a dominating position over the river Wear was always a principality and stronghold of the Kings of England.

Christopher's father was a banker with Lloyd's Bank and served in the RAF during World War II. He was a dedicated sportsman, which included golf at Ravensworth Golf Club, County Durham, where he served as its Club Captain. Chris learned his golf there as a 13 year-old schoolboy but his enthusiasm was inevitably subjugated to other team sports in his boyhood and early manhood. Educated at Durham school, Chris became head boy, captain of rowing and played for both the first XV at Rugby and the first XI at cricket.

Chris went into banking as a career joining Lloyd's Bank as a junior clerk straight from school and was obliged to pass the examinations of the Banker's Institute. Thus began a peripatetic number of experience-improving jobs ranging from Brigg in Lincolnshire to both the regional head office in Nottingham, covering the Midlands, and the bank's head office at Threadneedle Street in London and finally moving to more senior positions in the south. Jane, his devoted wife, has helped me paint this broad canvas covering Chris's curriculum vitae. Chris and Jane have known each other since childhood when Jane's brother was a school friend of Chris's and a fellow rugby player. Two boys make up their family, both of whom also went to Durham School. Simon, the elder, is now a chartered accountant and a merchant banker. He played Rugby for England as a schoolboy international and won a Rugby Blue at Oxford where he also rowed. Nigel, the younger son, was captain of rowing at Durham School and is now a chartered surveyor in London.

Chris played first class Rugby football and also maintained during those years an eminently respectable handicap at golf. He first arrived in Northamptonshire in 1981 and has resided at Collingtree since then. After early retirement from Lloyd's Bank, Chris has been able to give much of his time and experience to Northamptonshire County Golf Club, serving on the Management Committee, becoming Club Treasurer, later Captain and is now the second Club Chairman, succeeding Michael Bairstow.

Chris who is noted for his easygoing charm and firm, but friendly, conduct at meetings, has the gift of diplomacy and many other talents, for which we are all beneficiaries.

CHAPTER XV

More Brampton Golfing Families

"Rooks in families homeward go".

Thomas Hardy

The Gubbins/Haig Families

John Gubbins was an outstanding member of our golfing fraternity and certainly helped to keep the Club afloat during the "difficult" years of the late 1940's and early 1950's

John Gubbins

when our membership was numerically low, with consequentially low subscription income, and diminished interest in the game. John was elected as Honorary Secretary then.

John was a character with a curious amalgam of utter integrity and aloof and dispassionate judgement on most issues, and who was the epitome of fairness.

Having gone off to war after his schooldays, John became a pilot in the RAF flying Halifax four-engined bombers. With demobilisation he had to settle down to a job in "Civvy Street" and became a chartered secretary. Study for professional examinations was hard graft to fellows who had just returned from the hyper-excitement and dangers of war time. But succeed John did, in joining his uncle Alfred Johnson, who was a distinguished London based financier residing at a fine house – The Grange at Flore, a property later occupied by Brigadier Ted Taunton, of the Northamptonshire Regiment, Trevor Dangerfield a Brampton Club member killed in the Paris Rugby football air disaster and later Roger Buswell, referred to elsewhere in this book.

John commuted every day to London in his early years after the War and thus his services to the Golf Club at that time were all the more estimable. Later in his career he ran the family leather business at Earls Barton with his bachelor brother, Bob, who was also a keen member of Brampton (handicap 8) and had been a Royal Naval officer serving on torpedo boats. John served as Captain, Vice-President and a Trustee of Brampton Golf Club and was finally honoured with honorary membership.

John duly met the young Janet Hawtin, daughter of Leonard Hawtin of the building contracting family firm of that name. Janet had two brothers, Douglas and Roger, the latter a life member of our Golf Club, a member of Royal West Norfolk at Brancaster and a county hockey player.

Janet followed typically in the Hawtin family tradition. They were all sporting fanatics. Her father and uncles were the last of the gentleman cricketing and soccer players in the Corinthian tradition. Born in 1928 and five years younger than John, she was educated at Malvern Girls' College and trained as a physiotherapist at Guy's Hospital in London. Janet excelled at hockey, playing at county level and later for England in 1950. Her early golf was at Kingsthorpe with her mother Florence (Queenie) Hawtin who was a Ladies' Captain there. Janet developed as a gifted golfer with a handicap of 9, played for Northamptonshire county Ladies and was the Ladies' Captain at Church Brampton in 1970 and its Lady President in the millennium year, 2000.

The issue of this happy marriage was Charles, now a chartered accountant by profession who is a long-standing Brampton member and who resides in Cambridge and Annie, wife of Rodney Haig. Annie also went to Malvern and as a young girl was a keen lacrosse and hockey player like her mother, but soon took up golf aged 12 at Brampton where she later was to meet the young Rodney. They have three grown up daughters. Rodney is a solicitor and Deputy Coroner in Northampton. He is also a fine golfer, assiduous and always attentive to practice. Annie tells me that they met playing the Church Cup as a duo, which is a trophy they have won five times over the years. Annie herself has been Ladies' Captain. Turning to the Haig family, Lieutenant Commander Jim Haig and his wife Eileen, settled in Wollaston after Jim's long career in the Royal Navy had ended. He was an ex-Dartmouth graduate and this lean, wiry, pipe-smoking figure would be seen often on our course with a slightly bow-legged stance. In 1978, Eileen became Ladies' Captain. Rodney's lowest handicap is three and he still plays off four and has represented Northamptonshire county and the Midland Seniors. Rodney's brother, Simon, and younger sister, Nicola, were both young members of Brampton and they still both play golf elsewhere in the country where they reside. Additionally, Rodney and Annie's children Ellie and Rebecca (known as Boo) have also taken up golf, creating a further generation.

The whole Gubbins clan as far as I can make out have been members of Frinton Golf Club for holiday golf over very many years. As a family they follow in the fine tradition, which has been a feature of Brampton since the Club was founded, of golfing families invariably forming the very core and backbone of the Club.

It was the Haig family who donated the weather-vane which bids us welcome so encouragingly and hangs on the Clubhouse gable.

The Myers Family

All five members of the Myers family have made a significant impact on the golfing scene amidst the Church Brampton ranks and one senses that much more is yet to come.

Neil and Mary Myers joined our Club soon after the millennium. Together they have produced three fine sport-loving sons, who were encouraged by their parents to attend lessons on Saturday mornings, given by our various assistant professionals. All the boys took to the game, and responded well to the tuition they received.

Andrew, the oldest son, is now nearly 19, and at the time of writing this piece, is at Bournemouth

Adam Myers

University reading Sports Management. He is of tall and strong stature with a current golf handicap of scratch. He has been a member of the EGU regional squad and has already played at county level for Northamptonshire and captained the under 18 county side.

The middle son, Adam, is 17, with a current handicap of plus 2. He won the under sixteen English stroke play championship and County Cup aged 14 and has represented England in international junior matches on many occasions. He was the 2007 Club champion and named county men's and county junior player of that year. Adam has also represented the Midland men's team and is the 2008 county junior captain, following in his elder brother's footsteps.

Matthew, the youngest son at 10, is also an enthusiastic golfer with a handicap of 21, with every indication of emulating his elder brothers.

Father, Neil, is a middle-ranking golfer and his wife took the game up to keep up with the men in her family fairly late on. Mary says, with some justifiable pride, that this great game has given all her boys a degree of confidence, both on the course and in the Clubhouse, which they probably would never have derived elsewhere. They are able to hold their own socially in any company and communicate well with their peers and elders. This says much for the boys and for the sport of golf. It is a refreshing change to meet young people who are not gauche and are at ease with all age groups over the whole social spectrum.

The Church Family

Since the Golf Club began there has inevitably been a Church presence amongst the membership. If you speak to a native of the town of Northampton and put to him the name of Church, he is likely to reply "Which of the three – Church's Shoes, Church's China or Bob Church, the famous and successful fisherman?".

Church & Co was founded as a partnership in 1873 by Messrs Thomas, Alfred and William Church. A multi-storey factory was built in Duke Street, Northampton, where the company flourished for many years before moving to the present building on St James Road. Alfred Church resided in a fine house which is now the Cheyne Walk Club in Northampton near the General Hospital.

The company has enjoyed an outstanding reputation for the production of fine shoes, both men's and ladies, of a quality equivalent to those handmade. It became a public company many

Leslie Church

years ago and fairly recently was taken over by Prada, the Italian company.

Leslie Church was a longstanding member living in the village of Church Brampton and was Captain of the Club in 1936. Ross Church presented the Church Cup as a mixed foursomes knockout trophy which remains so popular today. Dudley Church, Chairman of True-Form and later a non-executive Director of Church's was also a member.

Many other members of this family have been enthusiastic members of the Club including

Leslie's daughter, Mrs Sheila Bradshaw and her first husband, Colonel Jack Ashley and her stepson, John Ashley. Also the late Stewart Kennedy (former Chairman), his son-in-law, Anthony Gledhill, Iain Kennedy (formerly Managing Director) and John Church (former Chairman) and other key executives working for the company. They have provided loyal support to this Club over the entire century of our existence.

The Lord Family
The Lords are another thoroughly interesting golfing family who have made a serious impact on our Golf Club. Their involvement with Brampton began in 1965 when David Lord, the father, first became a member. He had arrived in the Midlands some years earlier and had been a playing member at both Rothley Park and Lutterworth Golf Clubs in Leicestershire. Marrying in 1962, he and his delightful wife, Tricia, bought a home in Welford and soon after David, with the help of two of Tricia's friends, was duly proposed and joined the Club.

David Lord learned his golf at Willingdon in Sussex where he was born. His father had returned from India where he had spent most of World War II, and found that he could not hunt over the Sussex Downs and took up golf again after some years and encouraged his son, David, to play. David loved all sport and team games, particularly cricket, but his hip coming out of joint curtailed these activities. David was educated at Marlborough followed by St John's College, Oxford, and later began his working career in the industrial diamond trade in the Midlands.

David spent many happy golfing years with his great friend Alan Meynell as his regular partner. Alan was a delightful companion and keen Club member. David managed to retain a single figure handicap for some time winning the Baxter and later the Marshall Cup.

However, David confides that he was overshadowed in due course by his sons, with whom one of his proudest achievements was reaching the final of the Father and Son Foursomes Tournament at West Hill Golf Club in 2002, partnered by Tony Lord.

There are three sons of the marriage and Tony and Tim, who is two years younger than his elder brother, became junior members at the same time. As most parents testify, this is wonderful value for youngsters and soon they were spending whole days at the Club under the watchful eye of George Mobbs and with tuition and coaching from Robin Day, Mark Dewdney et al.

During the school summer holidays, 36 holes a day was de rigueur and quite often extra holes were played when mother or father were late in collecting for the transportation home! Lasting friendships were forged then.

Both boys went to their grandfather's preparatory school in Eastbourne where they were in the first XIs for all team games. In those days the Daily Telegraph had started its interest in junior golf, providing great value in their competition, with free green fees and a prize for the best net and gross scores.

The family summer holidays had to be carefully planned. Their debut in this particular competition, rather against their father's wishes as he thought they were too young, was at Sidmouth in which Tony shot a gross 88, net 52 and Tim grossed 93, net 57. Considerable adjustments to handicaps soon followed and father was proved completely wrong on this occasion!

Tony Lord became Junior County Champion and later the Northamptonshire county First Team Captain twice – 1992-94 and 2000-02. Tony has won the Northamptonshire county scratch foursomes four times, the Northamptonshire county Championship in 1995, the Northamptonshire county Match Play Championship in 1996. On two occasions he has won the Northants county Cup, the Club Championship three times and the Bostock Cup six times.

Outside the county, Tony won the South East England Colleges' Championship in 1984 and the Midland Mid Amateur Championship in 2005, which brought his handicap down to plus 1. Tony is currently Midland Golf Union Captain, the first Northamptonshire player to be so honoured.

Tim played junior county golf with Tony. He captained Wellington College in the Gerald Micklem Trophy for two years and played for Nottingham University for three years. Working in France and marrying a French girl, Tim is now a member of Royal Mid-Surrey Golf Club where he plays off a handicap of 6. Tim plays corporate golf and on alternate years in the Father and Son Tournament at West Hill, having many adventurous rounds with the "old man"! Above all, Tim is the family's "swing doctor", particularly helping his father and Jamie.

Jamie, the youngest member of the Lord family and seven years younger than Tony, became a junior member following in his older brothers' footsteps. Golf was not the same obsession as for his brothers and consequently he does not have their same grooved swings. Jamie's father says that maybe it is because he decided to become left-handed and was hence not able to take up any golf clubs discarded by his brothers, though this became much more of a problem for his parents who had to buy completely new clubs for him!

Schooling at Maplewell Hall brought Jamie a Duke of Edinburgh Award and a spirit of adventure which has led to many different jobs, including working on a kibbutz in Israel. Jamie remains the family's most popular choice as a fourball partner. His handicap which is high, as he does not practise too much, does not reflect those occasional purple patches which come and go and which infuriate opponents. One such purple patch occurred when he won the High Handicap Bowl back in 1998.

David Lord omitted any reference to his own personal current golfing attributes since retirement. From all accounts he too is a highly desirable partner with an exceedingly helpful handicap! The Lords are another family who have enriched Brampton Golf Club collectively and individually.

CHAPTER XVI

Club Characters, Downright Eccentrics and a few Pen Portraits

"Thanks for the Memory".

Leo Robin and Ralph Granger

I have endeavoured to compile a miscellany of interesting Club members who I have encountered as an ordinary member of the Club over these past forty years. Some older members will recollect them as clearly as I do myself. Some may have even known them more intimately. Sadly some of those from times past have faded into obscurity, although in this context George Mobbs has been enormously helpful and remembers many who would also have been forgotten.

To new members these names may become the stuff of legend or perhaps just a name proclaiming itself on an honours board years hence. I have made a modest attempt to ensure they will not be forgotten.

It is left to the readers to decide under which classification they fall according to their own perceptions, bearing in mind the heading of this chapter.

Dick Stevens

Dick was a remarkable man whose life developed in a way he did not envisage, could not

Dick Stevens

necessarily control and would not have chosen in some ways maybe. Dick was the youngest of three sons of a prosperous shoe manufacturer, who made boots and shoes in the very early days of this trade when it ceased to be a "cottage industry" and became factory organised. His factory was in St Andrew's Street, Northampton. Dick told me that his father purchased either the second or third motor car owned by any private individual in the town of Northampton in the early years of the 20th century, having built up a good business, doubtless aided and enhanced during the 1914-18 War when government contracts for the manufacture of army boots ensured that all the order books were permanently full. Indeed, so prosperous did old Mr Stevens become that he retired altogether in 1925 with none of his three boys wishing to succeed him in the business.

The Stevens family home was on the Wellingborough Road with the front aspect overlooking Abington Park and the County Cricket Ground to the rear. All three sons were educated at Oundle. The eldest son became a doctor and the middle son a solicitor, practising in Bedford and Peterborough and later becoming Under Sheriff of Bedfordshire. Dick wished to become an horticulturist and plantsman and his father sent him to Hilliers of Winchester, the finest firm of its kind in the country, to become an apprentice and learn the trade. Old Mr Stevens had the foresight and wisdom to be amongst the first of his kind to acquire retail freehold shops intended to sell exclusively his own company's merchandise. When he died, Dick's father left about twenty-five shops in the environs of London, along the Edgware Road for example, and I remember Dick telling me that in later years they would all eventually fall vacant by which time they had become extremely valuable.

Dick became an horticulturist and was all set to be set up in business by his father who acquired exactly the right type of holding extending to just under thirty acres near Leighton Buzzard with precisely the correct light sandy subsoil and a small dwelling for residential purposes and suitable outbuildings. No sooner had this taken place than the 1939-45 War broke out and within months the government of the day issued an edict that all such smallholdings must be devoted to the war effort. So it was that Dick Stevens was never actually able to work as he was trained and found himself obliged to grow whatever the Ministry of Agriculture ordered him to do. In effect he became a small farmer. Dick was a bachelor and was obliged to accommodate evacuees including a lady whose husband was away at the war. We used to tease Dick and ask him if this particular lady was "A little on the lonely side?". Dick's riposte was "She had her mother there at the time as well"!

Even when the war ended the same dictum prevailed because of food shortages in Britain and so it was that Dick continued to run his smallholding as a farmstead and was never able to use his knowledge as an horticulturist, as he would have liked. However, Dick came into his own on our golf course where his deep knowledge, understanding and expertise were called on in the matter of tree planting, conservation, planning etc.

Dick retired in his late forties to look after his aged mother who, by this time, was widowed and he continued to keep an eye on her for some years until her death. A wealthy man, he lived in a small flat in Bedford Mansions in Derngate, Northampton, which he rented, until he purchased a flat at Phippsville Court, opposite St Matthew's Church. The flat was always tastefully furnished with charming antique pieces of furniture inherited from the family home .

Dick became a very keen golfer and it was his wont to play several times during the week but always on Saturdays and Sundays. A regular participant in the monthly medals, Dick made himself available on Sunday mornings on a freelance basis whereby he would partner others in an ad hoc and friendly way. He was always very well dressed and his silver hair invariably well groomed. He was to be seen in the Clubhouse wearing a green Bliss tweed sports jacket.

In those days boy caddies frequently turned up and would pull trolleys for the elderly golfers. One such callow youth was called Arthur and he was a fairly regular puller of Dick's trolley. Dick was known to be irascible and grumpy at times. On the thirteenth tee on one occasion he struck a ball with an errant fade and it was last seen heading for Harlestone Firs. "Did you see where that one went, Arthur?" said Dick. "No sir, I didn't" replied the youth with honest candour. "No, of course you didn't" said Dick "because you weren't bl.......dy well looking"!

Dick was a regular member of both the St Botolph and the Agaric Golfing Societies. He was never known to refuse an invitation to play if it was humanly possible, with one exception when the late Dudley Hughes asked him if he would make up a four on Thursday, on one occasion. Dick hesitated and pondered for a while. "Well no, I'm sorry, I can't. My stockbroker usually rings on Thursdays and I have to go to the supermarket!". This was the only occasion when he was ever known to decline such an invitation.

Dick was addicted to the use of strong language which could be extremely earthy but it was never used in the presence or earshot of a lady. He was always heard to berate himself, his luck and providence if his ball should suffer some misadventure on the course. I can recall playing with the Agaric Golfing Society at Royal Porthcawl when Dick was partnering the late Geoffrey Diamond. Both drove off well from a tee, as they thought, not realising that there was a sand bunker strategically placed to catch anything on the particular line they had chosen. As they approached their golf balls which were quite clearly near to each other, they became aware of the bunker concealed from their view on the tee. One ball was in the bunker gleaming brazenly in the sand, the other just short of the hazard. This brought a voluble stream of protestations to the Almighty and to his playing partner a string of adjectives describing his bad fortune. Geoffrey looked at the ball short of the bunker and said "This must be yours, I'm playing a Slazenger". Sure enough the Slazenger was there in the bunker. "Oh, well that's alright then" said Dick with a smile on his face, with not a hint of commiseration for his playing partner's bad luck.

Clive Blackburn tells me that he played on another occasion in a popular Tuesday evening social greensome Stableford competition. Dick persisted in using a Commando golf ball (which was a cheap and particularly hard ball) and his playing partner, Jack Bell, was complaining bitterly that Dick never played with a decent ball. By the time the foursome reached the short twelfth hole, Clive Blackburn and his partner had joined in sympathy with Jack and so they all prevailed upon Dick to play another type of golf ball. Dick produced a rather grubby Dunlop and promptly hit it over the back of the twelfth green. Dick turned to the other three and very grumpily said "There you are, if I had played the Commando it would have been on the green".

When I relinquished office as Club Captain, a great deal of tree planting was going on and I donated the Wellingtonia which now stands to the rear of the thirteenth green. This was intended to replace the most magnificent wych-elm which towered close to this point and acted as a good marker for the second shot to the thirteenth green. Sadly it succumbed, in about 1979, to Dutch Elm Disease, despite having been injected for three years consecutively with some recommended antidote which was hoped to kill the moth which caused the fungus leading to destruction of the tree. At this time this disease killed thousands of trees in England, decimating the elm, which had prevailed in England since the seventeenth century. Sadly the preventative measures taken failed and the tree died and had to be cut down. My tree was intended to replace it, tall and fastigiate in habit and which would eventually achieve a height of between 80 and 100 feet and take up little room by its spread and would encourage wildlife because of its soft bark. This particular tree is from the Sequoia Gigantia species of trees. I procured a good specimen and it was duly planted and stood about eight feet high then, as a sapling. Within two months shortly before Christmas of that year, a trespasser and thief entered the course and decapitated the tree by removing the top four feet. I suppose he took it as a kind of Christmas tree, although only a moron could have mistaken the type of tree for a Norwegian Spruce. Dick spotted the tree and instantly did something about it. He tidied up the wound where it had been savagely cut off and sealed it with Stockholm tar. He then took a side shoot and bound it on a cane splint so that the side shoot projected upwards. The tree now stands as a permanent memorial to Dick, in a sense, because he saved it. The tree once showed a slight kink in its main trunk at the height of about four feet, but this is now barely discernible. The tree stands about 20 feet or more in height and is a good specimen again. In a few years it will serve the purpose for which it was planted.

Bob Taylor JP
Article in The County – Winter 2004
Those who attend Rugby club dinners know the form. The atmosphere is boisterous but genial. Home club speakers are cheered and heckled in equal measure. Visitors get the

Bob Taylor

respect they deserve provided they know when to sit down. But there is one, rare, category whose members are assured of a relatively hushed and reverential silence, who may speak for as long as they like, and whose jokes will be applauded irrespective of their quality. This is the category reserved for players who have "done it all". Their pronouncements carry the weight of authority, their accounts of epic contests are never thought boastful, when everyone knows that nobody of their generation played the game better.

Bob Taylor is in that category. He won sixteen caps for England and four for the British Lions in their 1968 tour of South Africa. As a back row forward with the advantages of natural strength and speed allied to superb ball handling skills, his reputation measures with those of the great Rugby footballers who have represented the Saints and their countries with so much distinction over the years.

Born in Northampton in 1942, the son of a police inspector, Bob was educated at Northampton Grammar School, that great breeding ground of Rugby talent, where he was part of XVs in all age groups. When he left to take his teachers' training course at St Alfred's College, Winchester, he was already recognised as an outstanding talent. Soon he was playing for Hampshire, and before long won a place in the Southern Counties' team which lost only 9-6 to Wilson Whineray's unbeaten All Blacks of the 1962-63 season.

Bob returned to Northampton to take a teaching post and has remained in the area ever since. He joined a Saints' side which included such giants of the game as Jeff Butterfield, Ron Jacobs and John Hyde. There was also the fleet-footed Bob Leslie with whom he now plays golf regularly. He gives back a great deal to the sport at which he excelled. He is secretary of the Saints' Members' Club and represents the East Midlands on the Rugby Union Council. He also serves on their disciplinary panel, a task for which he is well qualified from his long service as a local magistrate.

Bob was 45 when he took up golf, encouraged by his rugby playing friends Ronnie Knapp and Bob Leslie. He borrowed a heavyweight set of clubs from them but now prefers a lighter set. For 15 years he made do with irons but has now graduated to woods – perhaps not surprisingly these have added a new dimension to his game. He plays off a respectable handicap of 9. He is a long hitter and a powerful recovery player: now and then he has a tendency to inconsistency, perhaps brought on by a swing which deviates slightly from classic principles of golfing orthodoxy. However, like many powerful men he enjoys putting and displays a deft touch on the greens.

Bob Taylor has excelled at rugby and played many other sports to a high standard. As a golfer he has yet to establish living legend status, but maybe this is only a matter of time. Meanwhile, if he chooses to speak to a golfing audience, he is assured – if not of a hushed and reverential silence – at least of the kindly attention due to an outstanding sportsman and Northamptonian.

R A "Peter" Palmer OBE JP FCA

Bob Taylor wrote a pen portrait of the Senior past Captain in The County - Summer 2005
To be greeted by a dog barking loudly does tend to put visitors to any household on their guard. Thus was my announcement at the home of Richard Augustus Palmer but the subsequent welcome was incredibly friendly from both Rory, the dog and the man I had gone to see.

His names are straight from his parents, though to everyone he is known as Peter Palmer. At a very early age a cousin referred to him as Peter after a pet cat and he has answered to Peter ever since. Born and brought up in Church Brampton, Peter received a seemingly normal education, an education funded he told me, entirely by his mother's family money, earned by Mannings Brewery. His father, being a chartered accountant, had no such funds to call on. Prep School, Uppingham School and then Jesus College, Cambridge, where he reckons he had three of the happiest years of his life. He became a member of the Hawks Club, without actually achieving a university Blue, as a result of his all-round sporting activities at rugby, hockey, golf and cricket.

His parents were founder members of Northamptonshire County Golf Club, so it is no surprise to find that he received tuition from the Club professional, Len Holland, at the age of eight when he joined the Club in 1920, nor to be told that he went on to achieve a handicap of 4. Peter was modest about being selected for the county Golf Team, claiming that "It was usually because somebody couldn't play". A survey of the honours boards in the Clubhouse will show the many competitions he won and particularly pleasing to Peter is that he was the first Duke of York Cup winner in 1932 and again in 1937!

Peter was elected Captain of the Club in 1947 at a time when there were very few members and absolutely no money available for development, with only two greenstaff. Following a meeting of members in the Grand Hotel which he chaired, a unanimous vote agreed to the removal of thirty bunkers by a bulldozer, purely to cut costs. He was persuaded to do a second year as Captain because the Committee thought "He had done a good job". He had no Vice-Captain and the Trustees refused him a Club dinner though he persuaded his successor to have one.

Since this article was written and published, Bob Taylor has been honoured with the Presidency of the Rugby Football Union, the highest honour that the game can bestow on any of its members. This brings great distinction to Bob himself who thoroughly deserves the honour but some reflected glory in a way to his own Golf Club where he continues to play regularly with his friends.

Peter was keen to point out that at that time all prospective new members were made to play a round of golf as part of their interview and this enabled the Club to maintain high standards both on and off the golf course.

He became President of the county Golf Union in 1952 and in 1965 he started the Captains' Society which celebrated forty years in 2005 with a dinner at the Club. He organised the Boycott Trophy and managed to win it twice despite the very social aspect of the competition which he insists must continue i.e. you have to have lunch with plenty of liquid refreshments in the Clubhouse before you play.

Peter has difficulty in walking nowadays but always carried his bag on the golf course until he retired from playing some ten or twelve years ago. He was a Trustee for many years and the Club's Honorary Auditor with his father's firm of accountants.

Peter has led a very full life away from the golfing scene. In 1930 at 18 years of age he played for the Saints at fly-half and went on to be selected for the East Midlands in the season they won the County Championship. He was forced to withdraw from an England trial through a pulled hamstring, an injury that was to return throughout his Rugby career. He became President of the East Midlands in season 1954-55 and spent thirteen years representing the East Midlands on the Rugby Football Union until 1971. He was President of the Saints in 1966-67 where he is now an Honorary Life Member. He watches games now from the comfort of his armchair with the view that "Nothing stays the same", doubting players find as much fun in the game as he had. Nowadays his view is that "Rugby players have got to win" whereas in his day the game was very amateur.

Also in 1930 Peter joined the Territorial Army and stayed with them throughout the Second World War when he was posted to work in searchlight regiments all over England. This was not considered to be very exciting by Peter and at the end of the war he retrained as an infantryman and was sent to Norway to supervise prisoners of war and their repatriation.

For over sixty years Peter has enjoyed being a Freemason, where he spent thirteen years as the Provincial Grand Master. He has caught a lot of trout from the river Test in Hampshire where he thoroughly enjoyed fly fishing whilst he had the right to a beat each week. I know from personal experience of his work as a local Justice of the Peace where he became the Chairman of the Advisory Committee in assessing prospective new magistrates. Given an OBE for this work he was also appointed Deputy Lieutenant of the County in 1972.

Peter admitted to me that he has had lots of surgery, and now uses two hearing aids. Until recently he regularly played bridge and to this day he sometimes attends Sunday worship at St Botolph's in Church Brampton.

He married his first wife Nancy in 1937 and she died in 1985. They had a daughter Primrose who has produced two granddaughters and three great grandchildren, all of whom clearly give Peter much pleasure. I am pleased to report that Peter has remarried to Agnes and continues to enjoy a very happy second marriage.

"At my age I find I can call anybody by their Christian name." For Peter this may not be surprising but at 93 years of age he has a remarkable amount of life left in him. As much as I wanted to inquire about his activities he was equally keen to hear about what is happening now. It is his opinion that progress in all matters is inevitable.

Peter is still going strong and aged 96. He is seen occasionally on a personal electrically driven scooter.

159

Michael Costin
A pen portrait by Michael Bairstow – The County - Autumn 2006

"You're lucky to catch me in", was Mike Costin's first response to my phone call about meeting up. "Can't do next week as I'm in a gliding competition. How about Tuesday week when I return from taking my daughter to Luton airport?". I grabbed at the chance, but shouldn't this man be leading a quieter life? After all he's now retired from the world of motor racing that was his all consuming work for nearly forty years.

Brought up by good parents as a reasonable sort of bloke (his own description) his engineering education began when he joined the de Havilland aeronautical technical school as one of about 1,000 apprentices. On returning to de Havilland after a period of National Service, he was given a job in the drawing office where he became a designer of test equipment for a variety of planes including such famous names as the Comet, Mosquito and Vampire.

Like many other impecunious young men, having married Rhoda in 1951, he bought his first car, an Austin 7, for £20. This was to open the door to an outstanding life as an engineer, for after joining the 750 club for Austin 7 owners he was to meet and eventually work for Colin Chapman, the founder and architect of Lotus Engineering. This was the start of a ten year period of high activity at Lotus where Mike was to become Colin Chapman's right-hand man and a director of the company.

After building kits for the first eight Lotus Mark 6 models there was enough money available to finance the ninth in which Mike was to demonstrate his skills as a racing driver, appearing at all the major UK circuits and winning more often than not. When asked to explain why he didn't become a full time driver, Mike's answer was that the top professionals know they will get out of their car alive whereas he wasn't quite so sure. This meant that he chose to defer to the likes of Jim Clark, Graham Hill and Jackie Stewart. Although work and racing was now dominating his life, Mike still found time for flying and skiing and on several occasions was to fly off to the ski slopes with fellow Golf Club members Alan Goddard, Mike Leno and Geoff Ekins.

With the arrival at Lotus of another new recruit in 1957, Mike was to add an additional challenging role to his already busy life, taking on the task of mentor to the remarkable Keith Duckworth.

Within a year of joining Lotus, Duckworth was to leave to form a new company, which he did together with Mike Costin. Cosworth Engineering was a combination of part of their two surnames but at the outset Costin still had to serve the remaining period of a three year contract with Lotus, which meant the start of an eighteen hour working day.

By the time Mike was able to move full time to Cosworth in 1962, the company was completely focused on the manufacture of engines. This meant that the 18 hour working day was to continue with the company's obsessive commitment to research, design, development and manufacture. The Cosworth engine was to become a famous name in the racing industry with 155 victories in world championship Formula One races, a dozen wins in the Indianapolis and several in the Le Mans 24 hour race. Although the company employed close on 1,000 people worldwide and was hugely successful, Mike Costin considers that one of their most important achievements was to provide good stable employment for up to 400 people in the Northampton area.

While Mike remains modest about his own achievements, describing Keith Duckworth as a genius, it is the opinion of others that Mike himself is an incredibly gifted engineer. Respect for these two and Benny Rood, the third member of the top management team, stemmed from the fact that their employees knew that whatever job they were asked to do, one of the bosses could do it just as well, whether it be design, casting, forging, machining or any other aspect of the manufacturing process.

It is impossible in a brief article to do full justice to the work of this most able, friendly and charming man, but for those who would like to know more, books are available describing in fascinating detail the history of both Lotus and Cosworth.

I almost forgot to mention that Mike can often be seen on the Golf Course with his early bird group of golfers. He volunteers that if he'd flown or raced as he plays golf, he'd be dead. Happily he is still able to drive straight from time to time, cope with a few bends and avoid most of the hazards that come his way.

John Bowes "Jack" Corrin OBE

I first met Jack Corrin in 1950 and was introduced to him by a chance encounter in Northampton whilst walking in the centre of the town with an office colleague. "Do you know Jack Corrin?" I was asked. "No, we've never met" I replied. Seconds later an immaculately dressed, slim figure approached wearing a bowler hat and carrying a briefcase. I was duly introduced and thus began an enduring friendship, which lasted until Jack's untimely death in 1994 one Sunday morning, just as he was preparing to dress for early morning golf.

After the war only four men in the borough of Northampton wore formal headgear, so the Chronicle & Echo reported, although at that time most men wore trilby hats of all shapes and types from the "pork pie" style hat to the black homburg named after Sir Anthony Eden. "A J" Pat Darnell, solicitor and Borough Coroner and legendary eccentric, continued to wear the full rig of top hat and frock-coat right up to his death in his nineties during the 1960's. It is said that he always dressed in this way when he practised in the law courts at the back end of the nineteenth century right through until the date of his death. Three other gentlemen were noted for their bowlers - Ossie Swan (proprietor of Swans gentlemen's outfitters and tailors of Gold Street), J C J Legge of this Golf Club and Jack Corrin.

Jack's family hailed from the Isle of Man and the name is still well known there. Years ago the Isle of Man was the only place in Europe where the birching of young criminals remained and was used and the Tynwald came under fire to force that early Parliament to abolish this practice, by edict from the EEC. They protested vigorously at the time and perhaps it is a pity that they should have acquiesced. However, a BBC television crew interviewed the then Attorney General of the island who was announced as Mr Jack Corrin. Not only did he bear the same name as ours, but both looked like him and spoke like him. They obviously shared the same genes!

Jack qualified as a chartered accountant as a young man during the war years when he was articled to Mr Felden Baker. The firm was then Baker and Co, later to become Thornton Baker and, later still and by now a very large firm of international accountants, Grant Thornton. Old Mr Baker commuted in reverse, choosing to live in London and practise accountancy in Northampton, so could be seen arriving at Castle Station every morning and departing every evening.

During his boyhood at Berkhamsted School, Jack endured poor health with his lungs in a dangerous state, in the days long prior to antibiotics as a form of treatment, but eventually and after many tribulations, he overcame this disability. Jack always said that his long public service as a politician, Mayor of Northampton and member of the Borough Council, of which he was leader, were his contribution to society for not having gone to the war as most of his contemporaries had done, owing to poor health.

Jack's parents thought that golf would be both therapeutic and health giving and Jack played at Kettering Road before joining Northamptonshire County Golf Club where he was Captain in 1978. He was a very useful player off a handicap of 8 at one time. His swing seemed to go to pieces after personal tuition from John Jacobs, the eminent professional. However, he continued enjoying playing the game for many years well into his retirement, invariably smiling and good-tempered, whatever fate held for him.

Richard Bradfield Catlow

Son of Charles Stanley Catlow and Mrs Anne Catlow, both fine golfers and part of the Catlow family golfing dynasty, Richard is the eldest of three children. He has two sisters, the younger being married to Richard Aitken, himself a county golfer of immense golfing prowess and stature.

Richard Bradfield Catlow

Richard was born in 1935 and was educated at Miss Marriott's primary school in Weston Favell like many other Northampton boys of his generation, and then Haileybury. As one would expect, Richard was introduced to golf by his parents at a tender age and quickly became both enthusiastic and proficient. Many of his father's skills were passed on, doubtless in the genes.

From Haileybury, Richard went on to fulfil national service and after basic training found himself at the War Office Selection Board and on to Eaton Hall Officer Cadet School occupying a large Victorian Gothic ancestral home belonging to the Dukes of Westminster, near Chester. Eaton Hall was generally full of vitally fit and strong young men, anxious to prove their suitability as infantry officers with bull macho physiques and the agility of apes. The officer training course was meant to develop and bring out many talents and initiatives in the cadets in order to produce combatant officers, many of whom saw service in Kenya, Korea, Malaya, Cyprus, Egypt and Aden. It was an action packed and fairly frantic course from the moment of arrival to final commissioning, if you lasted the course. Some, disillusioned, were RTU'd (returned to unit).

During that time various tests of physical fitness had to be completed to the satisfaction of the exacting physical training instructors. At the same time there pervaded throughout the squads an "esprit de corps" where the cadets looked after each other in every sense, and were expected to, just as they would be expected to look after the welfare of their soldiers. When the day finally came for Richard, by far the least fit of the candidates, to endure these physical tests, just as the cross-country run began and the squad departed through the gates of the park of Eaton Hall, so the squad seemed to bunch together. The kit on Richard's back was suddenly removed, as if by magic, and shared out by his colleagues as well as their own to ease his burden. It was later returned to him in similar manner as they approached the gates on the home run. The officers in charge would have probably known what had happened but, admiring the squad spirit, turned "a blind eye".

After national service Richard went up to Pembroke College, Cambridge, where he read law. After he came down he joined the international law firm of Herbert Smith in the City of London to be articled as a solicitor and after qualifying he remained with that firm for some years. Later he returned to the town of his birth and joined the legal practice of Dennis, Faulkner and Alsop, soon becoming a partner and specialising in, amongst other things, planning law, where his advocacy skills were in constant demand.

Richard played for the Northamptonshire county golf team for many years, often partnering Richard Aitken who later became his brother-in-law. In the fullness of time he captained the side, then served as Secretary for five years, and was later elected County President. He has been our Club Champion, and has won the County Scratch foursomes twice, which he attributes to the quality of his partners, Richard Aitken and Richard Halliday respectively. He contributed, he claims only marginally, to Northamptonshire's first success in the Anglian League in 1972. He is an Honorary Life Member of four golf clubs, including ours, and was elected the first Honorary Member of the NGU. Richard served as our Club's Honorary Solicitor for many years, following Lionel Harrison in this role, and is currently Editor of the Golf Club newsletter. His wife, Judith, is also a golfer, a past Captain and current Ladies' President of Brampton.

As an after dinner speaker Richard is much in demand, and has spoken at the dinners of over a third of the English counties. As a conversationalist, Richard is both profound and sharp! As the poet John Betjeman said "Broad of church and broad of mind, broad before and broad behind". One might think this couplet to be particularly apposite.

What is not commonly known in the Clubhouse is that at the age of 17, Richard was sent off with his sister for ballroom dancing lessons. His parents fully understood the importance and necessity of such social graces, however reluctant their son may have appeared. His instructress at the Phyllis James Academy of Dancing was none other than one of our own lady members, Mrs Deidre Groome, who invested him with the skill and lightness of foot to rival even that of the great Victor Silvester. She comments that it was something of a challenge! He says it was mission impossible.

Laurence "Laurie" Johnson
Laurie Johnson is not only one of the Club's well known characters but a highly popular member and has been since he first joined the Club. He is known affectionately as an excellent raconteur.

Modestly Laurie recalls how in 1953 he sat beside Jack Hobbs (one of England's greatest opening batsmen) as England won the Ashes at the Oval at the final Test Match of that season. It had taken almost two decades to regain the Ashes and there was much celebration at the time.

The son of a Sussex ladies' cricketer, Laurie joined the playing staff of Surrey County

Cricket Club (one of the most successful in the land) as their third wicketkeeper where he stayed for three years. Inevitably, during that time, Laurie became acquainted with the Bedser twins, Jim Laker and Tony Lock (two of the finest spin bowlers of their generation) and Peter May, former England Captain, amongst many others. This was prior to going off to do his national service.

Laurie then came to Northamptonshire as the number two wicketkeeper, understudying Keith Andrew who was also a member for many years of Northamptonshire County Golf Club. This gave Laurie time and opportunity to take up golf and sure enough within two or three years he was playing county golf and later became their playing captain. From the mid 1960's until 1972, when Laurie finally retired from cricket, he was in the Northamptonshire County Cricket Club's first XI, during which time he held the world record for 10 catches in a match twice.

In 1960, Laurie went with the Cricket XI, captained by F R "Freddie" Brown to East Africa and two years later he returned as part of an eclectic XI made up of various international cricketers under the captaincy of M J K Smith.

Laurie has won the Club Championship once and was the first player to win the Burn Cup three times. He remarks that fifty years ago he first met fellow cricketers Peter Arnold, Lewis McGibbon and John Wild whilst playing cricket and they still remain good friends and members of our Golf Club today.

Laurie's pet saying about our Golf Club is that "It is good to go somewhere where everybody knows my name".

CHAPTER XVII

Ladies Of Distinction

"Furnished and burnished by Church Brampton sun".

Apologies to John Betjeman

As Neil Soutar has mentioned, Margery Troup, daughter of Mal Troup the solicitor in the firm of Phipps and Troup, frequently partnered Mrs Kathleen Swannell and they teamed up together as quite a good foursome and won many prizes. Mrs Jill Phipps was another good performer as was her daughter Diana. Before the War Mrs Betty Humfrey, wife of Stuart Humfrey, the eye surgeon, was a member of the Ladies' county team. She was a very long hitter and could carry the corner of the dog-leg fourth hole (now the eighth) which was remarkable for a lady at that time and would be still to this day for most. Her physique, as I am informed, was a bit like today's professional Laura Davies also known for her long driving.

Mrs Winifred Deterding played at high speed, more often than not with her husband, and they would reckon to complete a round in one and three-quarter hours. The length of course was different then, rather shorter than now, especially the distances from greens to tees. In any case, the general practice was to "get on with it" and most people played much quicker then. Generally speaking, one took only one practice swing on the first tee and then commenced to strike the ball. One glance at the line of a putt, hole out and clear the green quickly. The influence of television and today's professionals has definitely slowed up the game.

The Misses Hughes
Roger Mobbs also informs me that before World War II the secretarial work required to be done at our Club was carried out by two spinster sisters. The ladies, the Misses Hughes, lived at the Old House at Lower Harlestone which is the house with two sundials on the corner, so that Earl Spencer could see the time when carriage driving to and from Northampton. This house has been occupied in recent years by Ebbe Dinesen, one of our members. The two lady secretaries, cycled to the Golf Club on sit up and beg type bicycles. Mr Clarke was then the Secretary and he and his wife on Sundays walked to the fifteenth green watching the fourballs. He would bet his wife that more tee shots would miss the green than those that were on it and he usually won.

Jane Margaret Harley
Popularly known as Janie, she was one of a long line of distinguished, hard working and highly effective lady Secretaries who ran the Ladies' Section in a gentle and firm way, as some of her predecessors did and several successors in this capacity. She was a tower of support always to the various Ladies' Captains who came and went during her regime and certainly held her own when dealing with the Club Secretary and/or General Committee. Born in Scotland at Gatehouse-of-Fleet, she was the daughter of a farmer who later moved

to Warwickshire to farm during the 1930's and Janie was educated at Leamington. Her father was killed in a motor accident which then brought the family to Preston Deanery. Thus began her association with the county of Northamptonshire.

As a youngster Janie was a keen and capable sportswoman, excelling at tennis, hockey and later golf. She played first at Northampton Golf Club, Kettering Road, and later at Church Brampton (a well-trodden path through which many of our members have passed over the years).

It was through golf that Janie met Tim (E G Harley), also a keen playing member of Kettering Road, whom she was destined to marry in 1948. Tim was back from the war having served as an officer in the Royal Artillery with a mountain regiment during the Italian campaign for quite some time. He had joined a local legal practice and one got to know him as a highly competent solicitor as well as a keen and better than average golfer. Two girls were born to Janie who were to become very useful tennis players under their mother's influence, guidance and tutorage. Janie played golf to a respectable handicap in her teens and always looked good, slim and fit.

Holidays and golf were frequently taken at Royal Dornoch in Scotland. Janie always ensured a strict and disciplined approach to dress and course etiquette amongst the Lady members and was missed by a wide section of friends as well as her nearest and dearest, after her untimely death at the young age of 68. She always set a fine example to others.

Norah Goodman Mobbs

Norah was the daughter of Fred Bostock and sister of the three bachelor Bostock sons, Eric (killed in action in World War I), Neville and Lance.

The Bostocks founded Lotus shoes, which traded originally under the name of Fred Bostock Limited, with factories at Stone in Staffordshire and Northampton.

Fred Bostock, son of the founder of Lotus, and bearing the same name as his father, thus came to Northampton and lived in a fine house at Cliftonville, later to build Pitsford House into which he moved in 1923-24. He was a founder member of our Golf Club. George Mobbs tells me that his grandfather "Was no great shakes as a golfer and played as a left-hander, never addressing the ball in conventional manner, always striking it on the move, if not on the run!".

By this time Norah had met Herbert (Bertie) Mobbs and married him in 1913. She learned her golf as a youngster and played to a single figure handicap, representing Northamptonshire in the Ladies' county side. She gave to the world and to Brampton four children: Rachel, Humphrey, George and Roger, the three young men all becoming fine golfers.

Bertie Mobbs ran the Pytchley Autocar Company and Henry Oliver Ltd, who were appointed as the first main Ford dealers in the county.

Norah's marital home built in 1913 was Green Close in Adlands Lane, (now Golf Lane) Church Brampton, close to our Clubhouse (and until recently occupied by Lewis and Pauline McGibbon) where she resided until she died. Arthritis caused her to give up playing golf but she continued non-playing membership.

Dorothy Cooch MBE

Dorothy was a much respected member of one of the Brampton golfing families of distinction. Her father was William Lees, whose business was in the wholesaling of

166

Dorothy Cooch

tobacco, a highly lucrative trade for most of the twentieth century, if not nowadays, who lived in some style at a fine house in Cliftonville, Northampton. William Lees was at first a member of Kingsthorpe Golf Club, later joining Church Brampton in the fairly early days, becoming Captain in 1934. Both of his children became keen golfers. Dorothy was educated at Queen Ethelburga's College at Harrogate and at the unusually early age of 26 became Ladies' Captain. This was in 1935, more or less at the same time as her father's captaincy.

In 1938, Dorothy married John Cooch and soon afterwards found herself driving a public service vehicle (a canteen lorry) from the outbreak of war and took this to Coventry the morning after the horrendous Coventry Blitz. This was essential war work which led to Dorothy being honoured later with an MBE. Two children were born, Peter in 1943 and Esther in 1945.

Dorothy's brother, Harry Lees, was Captain in 1952. She won the Church Cup with him in 1939, an achievement repeated 32 years later when partnering her son Peter.

In her young days, Dorothy always played to a very respectable handicap of around 10/11 and represented Northamptonshire county. It was whilst playing matches at Aldeburgh that she developed a love for both the course and the area and the Cooch family were thus tempted to acquire a second home there.

John Cooch (a quiet and charming man), Dorothy's late husband, was also a Club Captain in 1955, completing the quartet of family members so honoured by our Club, so far.

Dorothy's playing days phased out in the early 1970's. She lived a large part of her married life at Great Brington overlooking the Althorp estate and is remembered with great affection by many of us.

Angela Duck

Angela tells me that it was encouragement by both her parents which led her into a love for the great game of golf, her father playing off a handicap of 4 and her mother 17 but it was not until Angela was 14 years old that she took to the game in earnest.

Richard Catlow writes:

Within the confines of the Ladies' Lounge there is an honours board, unique of its kind within our Club. It records the names of the runners up in the Ladies' Club Championship. There can be no criticism of this. The runner-up in this event, having proved herself to be the second best player in the Club's premier event is arguably entitled to the recognition of posterity. This is all the more so since the topmost perch was for so long occupied by Angela Duck, the dominant player of her generation. Indeed Angela's achievement of winning our Ladies' Club Championship for seventeen years in succession would be remarkable anywhere, but especially at Northants County where she has been up against so many strong and ambitious opponents.

Angela is a native of Staffordshire, a countrywoman by upbringing and preference. She soon learned to ride, and remains a fine horsewoman. However, her parents were both keen golfers at Beau Desert Golf Club, a challenging heathland course on Cannock Chase, and it was there at the age of 14 that Angela took up golf. Four years later her handicap was down to 5. Her form attracted the attention of the England selectors and later that year she played for her country in the England Girls' Home Internationals at Wollaton Park.

Her golfing career blossomed. She represented Staffordshire regularly, won both the County Championship and the Midland Championship twice and also the Spanish Ladies' Open in 1969 and the Swiss Championship in 1972. She was a semifinalist in the German Championship in 1962 and 1963 and runner-up in 1964.

Angela moved to Northamptonshire in 1963, played for Northamptonshire and won the County Championship in 1972, 1984, 1985 and 1988. She was our Club Champion between 1985 and 2001. More recently she played twice for the England Senior Society team against the rest of Europe.

Angela and Michael Duck, himself a successful and versatile sportsman, married in 1970. Their two sons, Robert and Thomas, have emulated their parents in the pursuit of golfing excellence. Robert Duck won the Carris Trophy, played for England as a full international, and holds our amateur course record of 65.

Angela has just completed five years as an England selector and she and Michael were our Club's Junior Golf Delegates to the NGU for ten years. They continue to support junior golf in all its aspects.

Meanwhile, Angela, despite her golf and the demands of a busy home life, is active on behalf of Hope and Homes, a charity seeking to provide homes for children in need following disasters. She has also taken to bridge, an activity which she pursues with the enthusiasm, but not as yet with quite the technique she has for so long demonstrated on the golf course. Now that would be an achievement indeed!

* * * * *

Northants County Golf Club can be deeply grateful to Angela and husband Michael for the enormous part they played in the encouragement of youngsters at our Club. We now have a number of their former pupils playing county golf with ambitions of greater things to come. Of her sons, Robert who won the British Youth Championship in 1995, went to university in the USA and is now involved in golf management and Tom has a golf handicap of 2. Robert and Angela live near Welford in a country dwelling and are able to enjoy the countryside which is one of Angela's principal delights in life.

Margery Hollingsworth

Margery was a native of Leicestershire, born at Ashby-de-la-Zouch, where she grew up with her elder sisters Dorothy and Kathleen. Dorothy and Margery became keen young golfers in their formative years at Willesley Park Golf Club at Ashby-de-la-Zouch.

As a young girl, Margery was trained as a nurse at the Derby Infirmary and there met a young surgeon in the gynaecological department, Dr Geoffrey Hollingsworth. A courtship followed and they married, as did so many other young couples, as soon as war broke out, realising that their lives would inevitably suffer a huge upheaval.

In 1942 a daughter was born who caddied for her mother later at the Northampton Golf Club, Kettering Road, and who is now Professor Helen Ap Simon, residing in Surrey.

Dr Geoff Hollingsworth became diabetic and was advised to change his medical speciality and had to retrain in London. He became a radiologist and moved to the Northampton General Hospital in 1947 where he headed the radiography department. Geoffrey Hollingsworth was a conscript to golf under the mandate of his wife and both were playing members of Kettering Road and their home was at Overstone. Geoffrey's golfing prowess was no match for that of Margery, who excelled. She became Ladies' Captain at Northampton Golf Club and later at Brampton in 1975. She played for the Northamptonshire county Ladies' side on a number of occasions and represented the Ladies' Midland counties.

Geoffrey retired from golf and developed a large garden in which both of them slaved and of which they were immensely proud. Margery continued to play until she was into her seventies and died in 1999 aged 83.

The Marchioness Of Northampton

Lady Virginia was a fine golfer and an enthusiastic member of Northamptonshire County Golf Club. I am advised by Lord Northampton, the present Marquess, that she took up the sport in the early 1950's and became well and truly hooked on the game, as so many of us become, to the point of being fanatical about golf. The catalyst which triggered off this profound love for the game was a holiday in Bermuda, after which she converted the lawns around Castle Ashby House into golf greens.

Castle Ashby had its own golf course in the park, and I knew several friends who were members there before the 1939-45 War. During the war years I believe that it was put to other uses but it was revived as a golf course once the hostilities were over and things began to get back to normal. I recall that one could become a member or just as easily pay a green fee for the occasional round which was delightful. Lady Virginia would hone her driving skills with practice in the park and the young Lord Spencer Compton, then aged 7, and his brother and sister were paid sixpence for every 100 balls they retrieved on her behalf.

Born Virginia Lucy, the youngest daughter of David R Heaton DSO, she married the Marquess of Northampton in 1942. She produced two sons and two daughters, thus protecting the lineage, and the four children were born over a four year span. I remember Lady Virginia as a fine looking

The Marchioness of Northampton

lady of beautiful countenance, tall stature and possessor of a well-groomed swing.

Lady Virginia's golfing triumphs on the course include winning the Guthrie Cup in 1954, the Fitzroy Cup in 1953 and 1954 and the Deterding Cup in 1956, partnered then by Mrs W T Swannell, another excellent Lady golfer. She was well liked and greatly admired by the Lady membership and caused many a gentleman player to pause in his swing if she was sighted on or off the course. I am advised that she hit the ball with exceedingly good timing, distances more redolent of a man than a Lady player.

After leaving the county, Lady Virginia went to live in London and subsequently became a member of Royal Wimbledon Golf Club, becoming Ladies' Captain later on. Her playing days continued into her sixties until arthritis took its toll. She died in 1997 and her ashes were interred by the family in the gardens of Compton Wynyates, the glorious Tudor country house of the Marquess.

Meg Tennent

Meg was a very popular Lady member and later Ladies' Captain of strikingly good looking appearance and full of grace and charm. Brought up in Esher, one of a family of nine, Meg trained as a physiotherapist and worked at King's College Hospital in London where she met her husband Dr Thomas Tennent, who was then working across the road at the Maudsley Hospital. They were married in 1931 and there were three children, two girls and a boy.

In 1939 Tom Tennent was appointed as the Medical Superintendent at St Andrew's Hospital. They moved to Northampton and lived in the grounds of the hospital until just before Tom's death in 1962 (at the time of his sudden and unexpected death he was Vice-Captain of Northamptonshire County Golf Club) when they moved to Church Brampton.

Always a keen sportswoman, Meg played hockey to a high club level and only took up golf in her mid-forties, as so many ladies do, having a family to raise. Never a long hitter, Meg worked hard to get her handicap down to 16. Slow play was something she could not abide (nor could and would Tom tolerate it) and a foursome definitely could not and should not ever exceed two and a half hours as far as they were concerned. Meg was well known for steaming down the eighteenth, yards ahead of her playing companions, even in her later years. She loved her golf and particularly after Tom's death was especially fond of Brampton Golf Course and the fellowship of its members who were very supportive of her.

Meg Tennent

Always willing to help out and arranging flowers for the Club was one of her great pleasures. Bridge and amateur theatricals (the Brampton Players) were her other great interests. Whatever Meg took on, she did with great enthusiasm and commitment, carrying others along in her wake. Although in her late years Meg had back problems, she never complained or turned down requests to help others and the red flowering may tree stands by the footbridge near to the fifth tee as a memorial to her.

Janet Dicks

When Janet Dicks died in 2007 aged 92, a thought occurred to me that some reference ought to be made in this history concerning her rewarding life.

Janet was one of three daughters of the late Harold Bassett-Lowke who was a friend of George Bernard Shaw, the Irish playwright. Her younger sister, Vivienne, was a fine swimmer who was chosen to swim for England at the Berlin Olympic Games in 1936.

Janet was also an excellent swimmer and devoted a great deal of her life in coaching the young in this particular sport. She became the mentor of the young Elizabeth Church (now Mrs Elizabeth Still residing and farming in Harpole), who swam for England in the 1948 Olympic Games in London. In her younger days, Janet was handy at a number of sports and, in the fullness of time, became a member at Brampton Golf Club with her husband, the late Edgar Dicks.

Perhaps Janet's highest point in golf was when she won, together with her daughter Jane, the prestigious Mothers and Daughters' Golfing Trophy in the 1970's.

In her old age, Janet was the authoress of a biography of her uncle, W Bassett-Lowke, the model maker and sometime owner of 78 Derngate, Northampton, which is now a place of pilgrimage to the myriad followers of Charles Rennie Mackintosh.

CHAPTER XVIII

The Course and its Changes

"And splendour, splendour everywhere".

John Betjeman

Heath-land

"The characteristics of heath-type courses are in the soil (sandy), the vegetation (gorse, heather, bracken and birch), and the relative flatness. They are probably closest to links courses in style, turf and hazard".

A Lovely "Parkland" Circuit
Extract from Golf Illustrated by Tom Scott - circa 1950

The Northamptonshire County Club's course combines beauty and charm with testing golf.

When we think of Midlands' courses our thoughts almost immediately go to the several fine courses to be found in Warwickshire or Staffordshire. In allowing that, we are forgetting that the Midlands is indeed a vast area which stretches roughly from Buxton in the north to Northampton in the south and from Cromer in the east to Stourbridge in the west.

It is to be expected, therefore, that in such a large area there will be found golf courses of every type. Great seaside courses like Hunstanton and Seacroft, magnificent heatherlike courses, such as Woodhall Spa, and lovely parkland circuits like Little Aston and Northampton.

I do not propose to go into the merits of Midlands' courses in general, for the purpose of this article is to say something about the Northamptonshire County Golf Club whose home is at Church Brampton. The club is perhaps a couple of miles out of Northampton town, if my geography is correct, on the way to Kettering and the north.

I am being perfectly frank when I write that until about a year ago I had not made the acquaintance of the Northamptonshire Club's course, but once I had sampled its beauty, charm and testing golf it was not long before I paid it a return visit.

You get your first glimpse of the course as you drive out of Northampton. It lies away to the left on a lovely part of undulating ground surrounded by trees. In the bright sunshine, as it was when I first set eyes on it, the course made a pretty picture. It is picturesque, pleasant and restful.

And when you drive up the little lane towards the pretty Clubhouse which harmonises beautifully with its surroundings, the feeling that you are miles from anywhere is immediately experienced. Many of us, by reason of circumstances, are doomed to play our golf on courses closely ringed by houses or factories. But there are few who would not spend their leisure golfing hours in a more rural setting if that were possible. In that respect the members of the Northamptonshire Golf Club, and the visitors, too, are well-favoured. This fine club is now some forty years old, having been first mooted in 1909 when a few enthusiasts including the late Lord Annaly, the Hon E A Fitzroy, for so long Speaker of the House of Commons, Lord Lilford, Mr Guthrie, Mr Wallis, Mr Monckton, Mr Bostock, Mr Millington and Mr Boycott, held a meeting along with some others whose names, according to the early minutes "Were not to hand".

These forthright and enterprising men of Northampton wasted no time, but there and then decided to form a Golf Club. Without further delay they set about the first task, that of finding a suitable piece of ground. Their choice fell on a piece of farmland which was part of the estate of the Earl Spencer. It was land farmed partly by the Messrs Drage and part by a Mr Deacon. After inspection, the part cultivated mainly by Mr Deacon was chosen, and with the wholehearted support of the Earl Spencer the work of laying out a golf course was put in hand on a site which, according to the local paper of the day, was four miles in circumference and which covered 200 acres.

Next thing was to have the ground cleared to some extent, and for this job one Frank Elliott was engaged at a salary of 25 shillings a week for four weeks, which clearly shows that the pioneers were not to waste their money. When Elliott had completed his job and pocketed his well-earned money, H S Colt came along and began to lay out the course with the assistance of a heavy roller borrowed from Lord Annaly.

This was a shrewd bit of business, the borrowing of a roller, and so delighted were the officials with it that they went off to the local market and purchased a horse and harness for a price which the minutes do not divulge.

With the construction of the course under way, the next step was the obtaining of the necessary capital, and in this they seem to have been singularly successful, for not only did they raise enough to defray the cost of the course, but they built a Clubhouse costing £2,400 - quite a substantial sum in those days.

Nowadays, when a new golf course is planned - and there are precious few of them - from the early planning to the opening ceremony is a matter of years. In these spacious, Edwardian days, either man's productivity was higher or they weren't so pernickety about the finished article. In any case, the Northamptonshire course was ready for play rather less than a year after the first meeting on the subject had taken place. A fine achievement. The opening day – 7 April 1910 - was a real gala day and golfers from far and near came in their new-fangled petrol automobiles to see John Ball, J H Taylor, James Braid and Ben Sayers engage in an Exhibition Match. What a game it must have been. I cannot now recall, what the pairings were, but almost certainly, I should think, it would have had an international flavour which would mean that the wee man from North Berwick and the long man from Earlsferry would be partners. I can just picture James Braid, loping along with his free, easy gait and wee Ben almost running to keep up with him.

James Braid has always had a keen interest in the course, of which I have heard he has a good opinion. As recently as 1947 he visited it in order to make one or two suggestions as to how improvements could be made. The Club Committee listened carefully to the words of the great man and, as a result, several alterations were put in hand. These included the making of a new eighteenth green. Another alteration was at the sixteenth hole (now the seventh) and takes the shape of one of the most diabolical bunkers James Braid ever thought of.

I say that after having been in it on practically every round I've ever played at Church Brampton, and the first time I played there was in the company of my friend Charles Catlow, who has won the Northamptonshire Amateur Championship goodness knows how many times. Now he says he is getting old for big time golf, but his game immediately disproves that. Although the course is forty years old it is very much the same as it was. In a circuit so good, so sporting, it is difficult to pick out one or two particular holes, but there are several, which, to my mind, are outstanding. There is the fifth (now our ninth), for instance, a grand old-fashioned hole, with a stream to cross for the second shot. This is one to delight the heart of any old Scottish golfer. No hole this for the faint-hearted.

The seventh (now our eleventh) is another of my favourites. It is played alongside the railway to a green cunningly sited in the corner of the course. Here the hand of Colt is clearly in evidence, and it is one of the best holes he ever designed on an inland course.

The downhill tenth (now our fourteenth) is another teaser which has a profound number of bunkers. I have been able to get past them or over them, but usually with more luck than good guidance. This is a hole for a well-placed tee shot. Indeed, nothing else will do.

Under the railway after that, to play the short eleventh (now our fifteenth), a wonderful short hole which has a stream running across the fairway. Near the green the stream turns round alongside the green on the right-hand side, so from that you will be able to deduce that there is little margin for error. It is on record that not so long ago when the stream was dredged at this point three dozen and eleven golf balls were found. That tells a tale for itself.

The fifteenth (now our sixth) is another exceptionally fine short hole in the grand manner. Plenty of trouble in front, which means that only a brave shot will do. That to my mind is what a good short hole should be.

I have said that the last hole has been recently reconstructed. Now it is a stiff right-hand dogleg played to a new heavily bunkered green just in front of the Clubhouse. It is not a hole at which many can be confident of getting back a stroke from bogey (old redundant word meaning par).

And mention of the Clubhouse reminds me that this is the self-same Clubhouse built forty years ago. A very good one it is, too, with every amenity, including a comfortable bar lounge, and a most beautifully furnished mixed sitting-room. There is also, of course, a dining room and changing rooms.

Church Brampton, as the Club is widely called, is a Club with tradition but it is not stuffy and, speaking for myself - and I am sure it has been the same with every visitor - there is always a warm welcome waiting from Secretary Browne or one of the members. Yes, if you want a pleasant day's golf you cannot do better than have 36 holes at Church Brampton, and 36 holes won't tire you either !

As one would expect from a course of such charm and quality Church Brampton has played its full part in housing county golf events. We find, for instance, that it was the venue of the Ladies' County Championship from its inception in 1932 until 1947. It has also housed the county Amateur Championship seven times. When the Northamptonshire Professional Championship was first played in 1947 it was on Church Brampton that the professionals' choice fell. And writing of professionals, the club has a

This article was written by Tom Scott, a distinguished journalist and broadcaster in the late 1940's. He refers to golf holes as to the "old lay-out", thus the fifth, we now know as the ninth and so I have clarified his narrative.
Mr Scott's idea of geography is somewhat lacking and his distant glimpse of the course was understandable then, long before so many houses were built on the Welford Road.
Mr Harry Colt, the golf course architect, was a graduate of Clare College, Cambridge. He also designed Royal Madrid and many other great courses.
Tom Scott once spoke as our principal guest at the Gentlemen's Annual Dinner, as I recall, roundabout 1966.

fine young one in the person of G. Gledhill, who if my memory is correct was an assistant with the late Jimmy Ockenden at North Middlesex.

Irrigation System Reservoir

Michael Wadley, Club Secretary of the day, reported in the summer of 1999 as to the completion of the new irrigation system reservoir:

"The construction of the irrigation system water storage reservoir was completed in February. Once the work started, there were numerous queries and enquiries about it, and the following paragraphs hopefully gave the members some background information to the project, its purpose and progress after the builders left.

The period of drought conditions from 1993-97 emphasised the need for adequate irrigation to maintain a modern golf course in good condition; it dramatically highlighted the gross deficiencies of the existing provision. The Club Committee decided to install, in stages, a new course irrigation system which would cover not only the greens and summer tees, but also the winter tees, approaches and fairways.

Water in the Northampton area, even in dry years, is normally freely available without restriction but, at roughly 65p per cubic metre, was expensive; an Environment Agency licence to draw up to 15,000 cubic metres of water annually from the Brampton brook would cost less than £40. Clearly, where large amounts of water were required and a cheap source of supply was on hand, the capital investment cost of constructing the Club's own storage facility would quickly be recovered. The Club Committee's planning went forward on this basis. Several sites on the Club's property were surveyed, trial borings taken, but at the end of the day the only satisfactory location found was in the scrub and woodland area between the seventeenth fairway and the fertiliser sheds. Unfortunately, this was on relatively high ground and it would have to be excavated out of porous sandstone, so a waterproof liner would be necessary; the liner and associated geotextile protective membrane would nearly double the costs of the project. Tenders were invited from seven construction companies with experience of this type of reservoir, and the Miles Group of Bury St. Edmunds was selected.

Clearance of the site began in the October and the project continued throughout the winter. During the excavation, the very wet conditions and high level of the watertable in the sandstone made the working conditions difficult, and at the end of the day the capacity of the reservoir became slightly larger than the planned 14,500 cubic metres (3.2 million gallons). Linked to the reservoir construction was the installation of a water transfer system from the brook to the reservoir, and from the reservoir up to the irrigation storage tank by the greenkeepers' sheds. Water was to be extracted from the stream by the old pumphouse not far from the fifth tee and a submersible pump was installed within the reservoir. In the first year, the reservoir was filled to only about 60% of its capacity to allow grass to grow above the surface water level and to consolidate the soil covering on the liner and protective membrane on the upper banks of the reservoir.

Our Environment Agency licence allows us to draw water from January to March. The pumping system fills the reservoir in approximately forty-five days. This amount of water is sufficient to provide irrigation in a "normal summer" for greens, tees and approaches, and with the occasional watering of the fairways - obviously, overwatering of the fairways would turn our course into an undesirable parkland! It is likely that in a lengthy summer drought we would have to turn to the public supply to supplement our own water resources. The whole system is managed by a computerised control unit located in the Head Greenkeeper's office, and the 520-odd sprinklers can be turned on in batches within their irrigation zones to ensure that the water is distributed as and when needed.

The construction costs of the reservoir were in line with the figures approved at the Club General Meeting in April 1998; however, at a later date a number of additional, originally unforeseen expenses occurred, such as those for the safety signs and equipment, the fencing, the landscaping and the archaeological survey, the latter two items being necessary requirements of the planning application. There are also maintenance and other running costs, but these are insignificant when put against the water bill saving".

Bunkers

Naturally, all the original bunkers on the course were classic Colt bunkers with the steep slope furthest away from the green, the face grassed all the way up. As has been noted elsewhere in this narrative, many bunkers had to be abandoned in the post-war years on the grounds of economy and labour saving.

With the constant evolution of the game, the design and construction of clubs and the materials used have also altered radically over the years. The earliest clubs that I have ever personally handled were made in years earlier than 1835 by the famous Scottish club maker, Philp, and were made from a solid piece of apple wood with no joint between the club head and the shaft. Philp must have found a suitable piece of well-seasoned timber and shaped it roughly to size, carved the club head which approximated to the shape of a driver, brassie or spoon (I have forgotten which) and he must have turned the handle so that it gradually narrowed from the grip to the point at which it disappeared into the club head. As to the grip, this was bound loosely with a piece of suede type leather tacked on. Just as a matter of general interest, the four clubs in which I was involved were sold at auction in 1989 for £5,000 to a dealer to be restored and resold on the American, Japanese or German markets. Few such clubs materialise these days. Such finds are akin to "barn discoveries as to veteran and vintage motor cars".

In our lifetimes we have seen such a club as I have described give way to hickory shafts then on to steel shafts through the 1930's and after the war years and the advent of graphite and the modern materials and vast club heads one sees today. This has, of course, had an enormous impact on distance. So has the improvement of the distance which golf balls fly now as compared with yesteryear.

There has been constant change with the replacement of sand bunkers on our course. Some have been done away with completely in recent years such as the bunker on an original driving length for some of us on the thirteenth hole and others have been altered

---

The whole system has been up-and-running now for the last eight or nine years. The installation of an aeration unit in the centre of the reservoir (to oxygenate the water) and the building of a permanent weir and sump at the water extraction point completed the work since the beginning of the project. The reservoir with time and the further maturing of the landscape has blended well into the setting and has become an attractive feature on the course. The Club has been able to draw on the financial and also the environmental benefits and will continue to do so for many years to come.

In order to fund this project, the Club were the recipients of an interest-free loan from the R & A, thus relieving the membership of any direct contribution.

By the year 2007 Michael Wadley's words have been seen to be prophetic. We are constantly warned of a changing climate and global warming which seem to indicate the future value of our own reservoir. As one stands on the seventh tee, the embankment standing about 20 feet high and supporting the northern and western sides is covered in trees and shrubs, most self-generated, especially broom, which is so pleasing to the eye in springtime. This is now the new championship tee for the seventh hole.

in shape and design. More latterly, new bunkers have been put on the course to catch the "young lions" who are capable of driving such enormous distances these days.

At the time of writing in 2007, two new bunkers have been placed on the fifth hole, and the layout of bunkers has been changed on the first, second, sixth, eighth, ninth, tenth, thirteenth and fourteenth holes.

Quite apart from this, I recall what to me was an extraordinary change in the topography of the third hole. Just before Joe Carrick, our Head Greenkeeper, handed over to Michael Lake quite some years ago, he observed to Spriggs Baillon, our long-standing Greens' Chairman, that the height of the mound on the right-hand bunker, looking at the third hole from the tee, had changed dramatically over the years. It had gradually got higher. Thus it had completely altered the design by Harry Colt, the original course architect.

Charles Catlow was consulted and the conclusion of the matter was that there was a constant dusting of sand onto this area every time a player splashed out of the bunker trying to get their ball near to the flag. If one stops to think about it, a handful of sand is virtually thrown out on a comparatively small square yardage of green or apron and over a period of sixty years it was reckoned that the height of this particular mound had increased by something like 2 feet.

In order to return it to its original design as near as one could, the turf was removed and the level was reduced by about 2 feet. The dome shape of the bunker was retained, the turf was replaced and precious few people today would remember that it had changed considerably. Most would say that the bunker shot is difficult enough as it now is!

The Course As It Is Now

In recent years it became obvious that our course lacked length. The development of the latest technology and its rapid assimilation into the manufacture of golf clubs and golf balls meant that a generation of young and strong golfers, gifted with the all important element of perfect timing, have emerged. Such players are capable of striking the ball huge distances and at the same time imparting back spin whilst striking iron shots to the green, sufficient to bring back the ball after impact, a shot seldom seen other than from top professionals in earlier times.

Moreover, these highly developed clubs approved the world over have become available to all. In my lifetime, I have seen and experienced the transition from hickory to steel and to graphite, the one overlapping the other over the years. Now we are into even more exotic materials. Comment has been made by even the mighty Jack Nicklaus that courses cannot and should not be forever elongated. Perhaps stricter control should be legislated upon as to our clubs and the balls in use to restrict distance.

Whatever views one may have on this philosophy, our own course, whilst never diminishing in subtlety around and on the greens in the context of modern golf, badly lacked distance, which in turn rendered the location of some bunkers irrelevant.

In the 1950's it was a rare phenomenon to see anyone drive the fourth green. When Charles Catlow once drove the eleventh green it was sensational although in his usual inimitable and modest way he played down this feat by saying – "Well, I was off a shorter tee, the turf was more downy, it was high summer and the wind was behind". It was practically unheard of for anyone to drive from the ninth tee and clear the brook.

Then in the early 1980's during Stuart Brown's tenure as the club professional, he amazed his three other playing companions by driving the seventh hole. They were even more shocked when he drove the ninth green. The occasion was when Jack Bell was Captain, the most taciturn of men, who said "It was astonishing because we were playing off the white tees and the wind, although behind, was not all that helpful".

So we have reached a new era when youngsters of sixteen can smash the ball huge distances and replicate Stuart Brown's achievements and maybe far exceed them.

The wisest and most experienced golfers in our Club under the leadership of Chris Thompson, our Chairman, led the way. Cameron Sinclair drew up a clever scheme by which certain holes were lengthened within the constraints of the terrain. New bunkers were strategically placed more relevant to the modern game. Further hazards by way of new plantations of gorse and broom further tighten the course against the wayward shot. Whilst all this was mooted and plans of the proposed alterations were displayed for the rank and file membership to consider, inevitably and understandably there was a good deal of comment from the rather more elderly members, both male and female, that the course was quite difficult for them as it was! The constructional work, mostly undertaken during the winter months by our own greens staff with help on occasion from hired bull-dozers, was expensive and it was thus that some reservation both as to cost and necessity were freely expressed.

The Management Committee sensibly presented the entire background and case to the membership by way of an Extraordinary General Meeting and good sense prevailed. The work has been accomplished quietly and efficiently without too much inconvenience to our members over two winters. The costs have been within budget. The project and design has been imaginative and new challenges test the skills of our best golfers in particular, but all of us in general.

This background led to my inclusion of the graphics showing the course as it now is, as against Neil Soutar's course plan, hole by hole, which illustrates both Harry Colt's original design, and various alterations as advised by various course architects or experts over the years until 1995.

Since the publication of Neil Soutar's book three new holes have been added to our original eighteen hole layout. A project was conceived and discussed at the height of the great golfing explosion of the 1960's and 1970's. This was to acquire 30 to 40 acres of freehold land immediately next to our course in the ownership of Mr Brian Rice who had moved his core farming enterprise to Draughton and his place of residence. This would have provided an opportunity for us to build an additional nine holes which would have provided a very useful facility and relieve pressure on the main course by those wishing to play only nine holes. This idea was vetoed sadly, practically at birth. Brampton Heath now stands on this land.

Many more potential and new enthusiastic would-be golfers emerged on the scene to face a paucity of golf courses. Most of the long established courses in Northamptonshire were full with a waiting list, including Northampton Golf Club, Kingsthorpe Golf Club and in our own case one that extended five years for full membership.

New courses were constructed at this time at Farthingstone and Cold Ashby out of farmland and a new eighteen hole Municipal Course on the parkland of Delapre Abbey on the southern outskirts of Northampton. This complex also provided a Clubhouse with bar and catering facilities, and a small team of teaching professionals with a covered practice area led, initially, by the famous golf professional John Jacobs and later by John Corby, now one of our own members. Delapre can also boast two nine hole courses.

Another development of a similar nature was pursued which would have involved the outright purchase of freehold land from the Earl Spencer which included Fox Covert, woodland adjacent to our eighteenth hole and other land. A great deal of praiseworthy work and effort was put into this possible acquisition but a caucus of members took against the project and it was subsequently aborted.

However, with hindsight many think that such opposition was ill-conceived because three new holes have since been built through Fox Covert, now leased from the Spencer Estate. These are a joy to play and behold in all seasons, full of bluebells and other wild flowers and profuse with broom which asserted itself as soon as the trees were cleared to build the fairways. Once again Cameron Sinclair excelled himself by designing three delightful holes. Thus it is now possible to play nine holes conveniently and obviating the need to "cut in" at the seventeenth hole, a necessary requirement that had prevailed for over ninety years. One plays the first six holes in a conventional manner and can now enter Fox Covert from a point adjacent to our seventh tee.

The "new holes" comprise a par four of 360 yards, a par three of 171 yards and a par five of 487 yards, bringing one back to the Clubhouse via the original practice ground. The new holes are private and enchanting and virtually out of sight of the old course. When playing them one might well be on a beautiful Scottish course like Rosemount Blairgowrie in Perthshire or the Boat of Garten in the Highlands just south of Inverness. They provide a wonderful amenity and have enabled us to create a new category of nine-hole membership, a boon to some of our membership, both Lady Members and Gentlemen. Such a pity that the opportunity was lost to acquire the freehold by outright purchase, as our wise forebears did by buying the main course from the Spencer Estate. Depictions of the three new holes are also shown graphically.

Colt Course

Finally, and at the time of writing this chapter (March 2008), a new "Academy Course" is being constructed on the old practice ground using approximately two-thirds of the six acre practice field, also leased from the Spencer Estate with effect from around 1950. Hithertofore our only practice opportunity was a chip and run and putt on the original eighteenth green.

The Academy Course was considered to be a highly desirable additional facility by Tim Rouse our professional and others, as a teaching aid to encourage the young and as an additional facility for all-comers, young and old alike. The Committee backed this idea with enthusiasm and sought and obtained encouragement and help from Golf Mark (English Golf Union) and above all financial grant aid from Sport England. This is the division of The National Lottery Fund which deals with all lottery grants appertaining to sport in all its many forms. Barclays also provided funding.

At the time of writing only fifty five courses in the UK have received the backing of Golf Mark. So during the winter months of 2007-08 our ground staff set about the construction of six par three golf holes ranging from 85 yards in length to 125 yards. The greens have been constructed using "state of the art" techniques with soft self-draining membranes laid beneath the astro turf to prevent penetration by deep rooted pernicious weeds and to create a softer recipient green to hold the high pitched shot even in high summer dry conditions. There are no sand bunkers but broom and gorse will be planted in due course to add both character and a touch of hazard. This is a highly creditable enterprise.

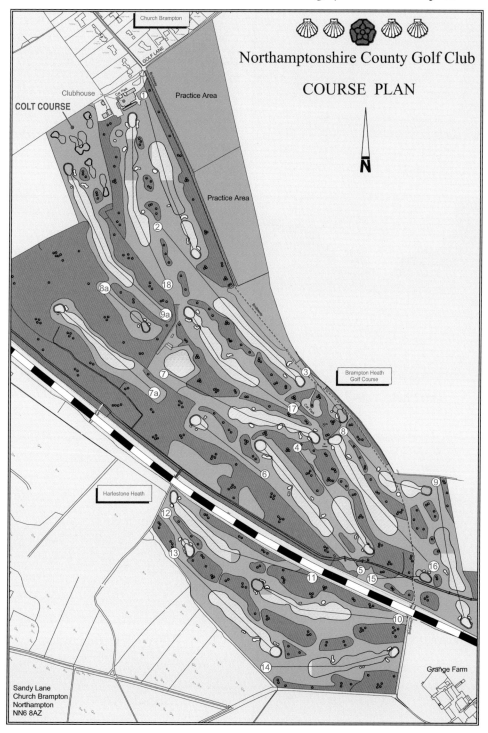

A Colt Course green

Third hole – view from tee

Third green

View from 4th tee over the gorse

Approach to 4th green

5th hole from the teeing ground

7th green

9th hole view from the tee

12th green

13th hole looking back towards the tee

13th green

14th hole from the tee

The brook 15th hole

15th hole from tee – "one of the finest short holes in England"

16th green

18th green view from clubhouse

THREE NEW HOLES

7A Approach to the green

8A The tee

8A Green

9A Hole

184

A miscellany of photographs depicting the course as it is. The inspirational and artistic glimpses have been carefully selected at various times during the four seasons by Brian Ball, a long standing club member to whom I am deeply grateful. They may be a happy reminder to us all as to how privileged we are to enjoy such a pleasing, scenic and beautiful course.

10th Hole

8th Hole – Gorse and Green

13th Hole – Approach to Green

18th hole – Green, Clubhouse – Winter

Reservoir – Winter

Brook – 5th hole – Pumphouse – Winter

*7th Green / Ladies 4th
Tee – Gorse*

15th Green – Babbling Brook

13th Green – Looking Back to
Teeing Ground

7a Hole – Springtime

7a Hole – Green – Bluebell Time

1st Hole – Frosty Sunrise

6th Hole – From Tee to Green

3rd Hole – Light and Shadow

10th Hole – Springtime

*13th Hole – Tee – Wild
Woodbine*

CHAPTER XIX

Familiar Faces, Past and Present

"From quiet homes and first beginnings
Out to the undiscovered ends
There's nothing worth the wear of winning
But laughter and the love of friends".

Hilaire Belloc

Tony Palfreyman

Born into a Leicester shoemaking family, Tony was educated at Shrewsbury and during national service was commissioned into the Leicestershire Regiment. As there was no vacancy for him in the family firm, Tony joined W W Chamberlain and Co at Higham Ferrers. After suitable management training, Tony went to their factory in King's Heath, Northampton, eventually succeeding the late Harry Holmes to run that particular section of the company. Tony was invited to join the board of directors in the much enlarged group of Chamberlain Phipps and survived all the vicissitudes of take-overs (the only director who did) only to succumb to a terminal illness just as he was about to take over as Captain of our Golf Club.

Short in stature but fit and determined, Tony was a keen and brisk walker who always carried his bag and possessed a sunny nature and good sense of humour. A fanatically keen golfer and member of both the St Botolph and Agaric Golf Societies and supporter of the leather trade's National Golfing Society, Tony died tragically in his early sixties, when Vice-Captain of the Club and thus was denied taking his rightful place as Captain. Knowing precisely the prognosis of his illness, he saw all his friends by sending for them in orderly fashion to say adieu and planned his own memorial service.

John Waters

John Waters died in 2005 in his early eighties, continuing to play golf until six weeks before this happened. As a youngster he attended Cambridge and County High School and like so many of his generation was effectively awaiting call-up from his matriculation onwards. John spent a year or so at the office of a quantity surveyor before joining the RAF. Rejected from the pilot's course because of colour blindness, John became a navigator and his aircrew training was in Canada and the USA.

Returning to the United Kingdom John flew as part of the crew of two in the de Haviland Mosquito, a wonderful aircraft, the airframe of which was built of balsa wood and the power of which came from twin Rolls-Royce Merlin engines. Thus this aircraft became a fast and very formidable fighter bomber. John and his pilot with whom he remained in contact for life, joined a squadron engaged in coastal marauding and the destruction of enemy airfields.

John became a member of the Royal Institution of Chartered Surveyors and after working in the practice of E J and R S Ashby he joined the late F P Phelan in the firm of Phelan and Agutter where he remained until retirement.

A very keen and useful golfer, John played as a member of the Incorporated Auctioneers Golf Society, won a number of trophies and also became a much respected member of the St Botolph Golfing Society.

Donald Barltrop

Donald Barltrop is Chairman of R E Tricker Limited, the oldest firm of shoe manufacturers in the county and one of the few old-established firms which are still producing fine handmade shoes, despite all the chances and changes in this industry. The youngest child, Donald was suddenly pitchforked into running the factory unexpectedly when his elder brother, Ray, died prematurely and young when Donald was then barely 30 years old.

Donald joined the Royal Navy from school and served on the lower deck on destroyers and minesweepers in the Mediterranean until sent for officer training in the UK. After commissioning, Donald became second in command of a motor gunboat operating in the Irish Sea against U-boat and E-boat penetration.

On the golf course, Donald's "banditry" is legendary, the only thing lacking being a Mexican style wide-brimmed hat. Donald came to Church Brampton in the early 1960's from Kettering Road and was a co-founder with Alfred York of the St Botolph Golfing Society. Donald gave lessons on how to play liar dice, a sport in which he became world-class.

Sidney Stewart

In the war years Sidney trained as a pilot in aircrew and arrived in Northampton in the early 1960's when he was transferred into the local branch of the North British Mercantile Insurance Company. Sidney was passionate about golf and soon after joining our Club he became heavily involved in its affairs for some years on the Committee and became a founder member of the St Botolph Golfing Society.

After some years, Sidney's career took him to London at which point he became a member of Beaconsfield Golf Club. He was later moved overseas, first to the Far East and then to the West Indies. After retirement, Sidney bought a house overlooking the tenth tee at East Devon Golf Club, Budleigh Salterton.

Alan Westley

Alan was formerly Chairman of Airflow Streamlines, a company which he founded during the war years with his elder brother George. In those dark days, by government edict, they manufactured aircraft parts as part of the general war effort. The transition from the protected world of contract work for H M Government to peacetime manufacture in the motor trade, fraught with post-war austerity and shortages and many other frustrations, must have seemed like an insuperable hurdle. However, under clever leadership, the company flourished and eventually became a public company quoted on the Stock Exchange.

Alan played his early golf at Kettering Road eventually becoming Captain there but became a member of Church Brampton as well. Alan was a man of infinite charm and an agreeable golfing companion and amongst other things, a benefactor to the course. He donated a colonnade of small Japanese maples as a backdrop behind the sixth hole.

Herbert Norman

Son of the late Alderman George Norman JP, Herbert was born in Northampton in 1868 and became a distinguished architect practising in Northampton at 4 Wood Hill and residing at 61 Billing Road.

Herbert was educated at Northampton Grammar School. After leaving school he was articled to Matthew H Holding ARIBA, an eminent architect of his day who designed a number of public buildings including St Paul's Church in Semilong and the first extension to Northampton Town Hall, Godwin having designed the original part and Maurice Walton in more recent times the final phase.

After considerable experience in the Midlands, Herbert Norman commenced practice at Northampton in 1896, chiefly in domestic

Herbert Norman

work. However, in due course he became responsible for and designed several important buildings both in the public and private domain in Northampton and in the county.

In competition he was successful in securing the new Carnegie Public Library in Abington Street with its fine façade. He was also the architect to the Northampton Town and County Grammar School (as it was then) on the Billing Road, Northampton.

It is said his recreations were skating, golf and gardening. More importantly, as far as Northamptonshire County Golf Club is concerned, he was the architect chosen to design the original Clubhouse which has, of course, over the years been much extended and altered. Nevertheless, the original design possesses many features of the Arts and Crafts movement including the inglenook fireplace in the original men's bar and open sun loggia facing south-east, as was the fashion in 1910, later enclosed by virtue of the generous benefaction of Don Chamberlain and Alan Timpson. The latter was doubled in size under the design and supervision in more recent years of Peter Haddon, another member and architect by profession and past Captain, and the extended Clubhouse, latterly by Rex Bryan and Pennock.

The wall clock over the honours board listing past Captains in the inglenook is a fine example of an Arts and Crafts movement timepiece and should be carefully looked after for posterity as it may well become an antique of the future, if not already. (See page 25). Herbert Norman submitted a watercolour drawing of the front elevation of his newly designed Clubhouse with ladies in the foreground depicted in the contemporary dress of the Edwardian era, to the Royal Academy in 1910 with justifiable pride. Many architects submit such pictures to the Royal Academy and several architects have become its President, the last being Sir Hugh Casson. The watercolour was accepted and duly hung. The drawing remained "lost" in an old tin trunk where it had been discarded and forgotten at the home of Herbert's daughter, Mary Norman, until "rediscovered" by the author of this update in the late 1970's. The executor of the estate of Miss Norman, Humphrey Mobbs, was persuaded to donate the watercolour to our Clubhouse, which he generously did and it now hangs in the dining room.

Turkey Baillon

"L C" Turkey Baillon was a founder member of our Golf Club and Managing Director of the Northampton Brewery Company. I believe that the Baillon family came from the

Falkland Islands. The various members of that family seemed to attract nicknames. R O Baillon, our former Club President, was always known as "Spriggs". His brother the brewery architect was always known as "Brabs", and their father "Turkey". Two other brothers were killed in the war years in the RAF serving as aircrew.

Alan Goddard

Alan Goddard is a man whose career was spectacularly successful in a trade that was already in decline in Britain after the war years. Alan followed his father who had spent a lifetime

Alan Goddard

in the business of importing leather from India, where he was highly respected, and a Director of B B Vos in London.

In 1942, Alan went from school into his father's company as a trainee but was soon called up, joining the 11th Hussars (the Cherry Pickers). The regiment was engaged in the infamous Charge of the Light Brigade under Lord Cardigan (who lent his name to that form of woollen garment) during the Crimean War. Originally a cavalry regiment, by the middle of the Second World War years horses had long since given way to armoured cars. Thus this regiment's role was to probe ahead of both infantry and armour in reconnaissance. Alan landed in Normandy on D-Day plus four,

their regiment held up, unbelievably, by a wartime strike by dockers at Tilbury where the regiment eventually loaded its own equipment aboard their U S Liberty ship and set sail. From the Normandy beachhead, the regiment fought their way through France, Belgium and Holland and into the Fatherland until the unconditional surrender of Germany.

Demobilisation took Alan back into the trade and ultimately, after various vicissitudes, to the purchase of an old and all but redundant company. Alan breathed new life into this company, based in Northampton, which prospered. Alan is a skilled and very shrewd collector and appreciator of fine art. He played golf all over the British Isles with the Shoe Leather and Allied Trades Golfing Society and his Captaincy led to a number of reforms at our Club. Alan was the donor of our fine display cabinet in the dining room.

Michael Bairstow

Michael was Club Captain in 1998 and our first Club Chairman and did the job extremely well. There were no guidelines or precedents for him to follow. It was a completely new office as far as the Club was concerned and the reality, which soon became obvious, was that the Club Chairman who officiated at all the Management Committee meetings and dealt with the affairs of the running of the Club on a daily basis, of necessity, had to work in complete harmony with the Captain of the day, elected for one year only. The Club Chairman was elected for a period of three years and if the membership so wished could be re-elected for a further three years which was the case as far as Michael Bairstow was concerned.

Michael retired as Club Chairman in 2005 and at that time I wrote the following tribute in The County.

"I always think that I can hear the county of Yorkshire in Michael's voice, but his "alma mater" is Eltham College in North Kent where he was educated.

Michael, like others of his generation, was called to do national service with the Royal Air Force. A keen Rugby footballer who played for his old boys' side, graduating to the Kent County 2nd XV, left him with a few physical reminders of those happy days! At the end of his playing career he took up refereeing, mainly in Leicestershire, which may explain his leaning towards and support for the Leicester Tigers.

Michael enjoyed a long career starting in 1959 with the paper merchant Robert Horne, when the company had only 20 employees, long before the company moved its headquarters from London to Northampton in 1975. At this time Michael was Joint Managing Director, a position he held until 1990 when he succeeded the late Kenneth Horne as Chairman and Chief Executive. The gift of salesmanship and a determination to succeed was the route through which his career developed.

Golf came as relaxation when his rugby days were over and he joined Church Brampton. He was head-hunted some years back by a past Captain talent spotter who was convinced that some reforms were necessary in order to achieve successful continuity in our Golf Club's affairs. Michael was chosen to lead a "think-tank" which led to his ultimate appointment as the first Club Chairman. Six years of outstanding leadership in his capacity as Chairman followed. During that time much has been achieved as is evidenced by the three additional golf holes, more and better practice facilities and a vastly improved Clubhouse. His handling of Annual and Extraordinary General Meetings invariably displayed masterly, but firm, diplomacy when dealing with an often critical and enquiring body of members.

Good communication with the entire membership was seen as a vital necessity. We were all kept informed. His battles with planners and those critical of the proposals were handled with a measure of firmness and fair-mindedness - an example to us all. Whatever administrative problems beset any Club Captain in his year of office were soon over and done with. It is vastly different when one is charged to undertake the handling of the Club's affairs for three years, followed by a further similar term.

Michael has set a high standard to follow - a hallmark of excellence.

Alfred York

Alfred York was a tall, dark-haired, and good looking man of quiet and gentle demeanour. After leaving Northampton Grammar School, Alfred's first job was in the Northampton County Treasurer's Department, under the tutelage of Bert Cheney who features in these pages as a considerable force for good in our Golf Club during the darkest days of World War II and earlier. As I mentioned, Bert Cheney was the County Treasurer who doubtless "rated us all highly", as they all do, but then not so much as now! Soon off to enlist with the Royal Naval Fleet Air Arm, Alfred was taught to fly in the USA and joined the fleet in the Far East flying Grumman fighter bombers aboard an aircraft carrier.

After the war, Alfred joined the family firm of York Brothers who, for many years, ran the eastern route bus service from Northampton to Cogenhoe, Whiston, Castle Ashby, Grendon etc. The company branched out into the coach hire business, each coach named after a Royal Navy ship and later Alfred advanced the company into the full scale travel business when, just as he retired, the company was bought out.

Alfred was popular, likeable to all with whom he came into contact. He played Rugby football as a young man once for the Saints and for other Rugby football clubs and later learned his golf at Northampton Golf Club, Kettering Road. In the early 1960's Alfred, together with his long-standing golf partner, the late Bernard Scott, joined Church Brampton. He had a single figure handicap and founded the St Botolph Golfing Society, about which more detail is given in this book. Alfred died on the course, as he might have wished, playing with his friends.

H R "Ray " Beirne

Ray, an Ulsterman and pharmacist by profession, was a good golfer and a regular early Sunday morning player. Quite a gathering of us would form up and we would organise ourselves into suitable four balls. Ray was a devout Roman Catholic. He became Jack Corrin's regular golf partner when the late Ken Rutherford was prevented from continuing his habit of playing on Sundays. They were a formidable duo. It is difficult to say with certainty, who was the most effective of the two, in the great psychological part of the game. On balance, I would find in favour of Ray whose "talk" and antics outgunned most others. One Sunday morning just as we were putting on the second hole Jack Corrin told Ray that four of us were off to Rome for a holiday. "Would you like to meet the Pope?" asked Ray. Silence followed. I said rather hesitantly "Yes, I would" but secretly felt that such a proposition was unlikely.
Several weeks later, Ray quietly announced, once again on the putting green, "You will not be able to have an audience with the Pope as he will be in Brazil the week you are in Rome, so I have fixed for you to go to visit the English College just outside the Vatican. You must be there at 12.30 pm for Sunday luncheon followed by being shown round". It was a wonderfully memorable occasion. Ray was a man of some influence, quite plainly.

K A "Ken" Rutherford

Ken was Deputy General Manager of the former Anglia Building Society and always full of fun and good stories. He was a charming sportsman, former Saints' and East Midlands' Rugby footballer, a competent tennis player and a late entrant to the science of golf. Ken is the only player in my experience who, as a beginner, was given a lesson by the professional at Kettering Road (who later emigrated to New Zealand) who told Ken to give up the game, as it were, before he had really got started.
During the war, Ken served with the Northamptonshire Yeomanry and was present at the Battle of the Falaise Gap when the regiment fought in the strategic and vital tank battle to break out near Caen in Normandy some weeks after the D-Day landings. He was immensely proud of his regiment in which he rose to the rank of Warrant Officer, First Class, declining commissioned rank when persuaded to take it by his CO, Lieutenant Colonel Lowther DSO, because it meant transferring to another regiment.

Ray Minor

Ray was a tall, slim golfer, and a heavy smoker who became a very useful player in his forties. He was a man of quiet and good-natured disposition. After retirement, Ray fell victim to emphysema which curtailed his ability to continue to play golf in retirement. Ray's wife, Annette, is a Lady member of our Club.

Sir Murray Fox

Sir Murray was Lord Mayor of London and a wealthy and distinguished member of the estate profession - a chartered surveyor and senior partner of Chesterton's. He practised in London and was for a great number of years a member of Hendon Golf Club in north London but he bought a country home at Bradden near Towcester and joined Northamptonshire County Golf Club in the mid 1970's.

Sir Murray was a very keen golfer and was never happier than playing in Club competitions as an ordinary member, entering the Saturday monthly medals whenever time permitted. On one occasion he forgot his medal entry and failed to turn up on the day. This brought instant summary justice in the form of a severe ticking off and banning from monthly medals for the following three months by way of retribution. This was all accepted with good grace. Later that year he was invited by Roy Banham, the Club Captain, to speak at his annual gentlemen's dinner, which he did, making humorous mention of his lapse of memory and "punishment" by George Mobbs. In his speech, Sir Murray said "This is a good Club. It protects its members from casualness and lack of manners by others" - quite a self indictment.

Andrew Roy Banham

A general surgeon at Northampton General Hospital, Roy was slim and small in stature and serious in his demeanour. When he retired as a surgeon from the Northampton General Hospital he undertook work as a locum for various GPs in the district and happened to be on call on the night that the Eighth Earl Spencer suffered his stroke. Roy made an instant and correct diagnosis of the problem and probably, by so doing, was instrumental in saving the Earl's life, although the Earl was sent off to the London Clinic, all of which is written elsewhere.

One of the quirks in Roy Banham's nature was his Achilles' heel concerning anyone standing behind him when he took his shot on the course. Once when playing a Burn Cup match with Roy, I stood some 50 yards away from him and well to his rear as he was taking a practice swing prior to hitting his second shot on the tenth hole. He was aware, and so was I, that something was not quite right. He ceased practising and turned round and walked over to me and said "Would you mind not standing behind me?". I apologised at once and asked where he would like me to stand. "In front of me, over here" replied Roy. So I walked the long trail to the approved position and our match recommenced. Others, likewise were reprimanded if they stood in the "incorrect spot".

John Leonard Bernstein

John was born in Middlesbrough in 1931 whence his mother came. John's parents later lived immediately opposite Northampton Grammar School on the Billing Road where John became a pupil as a youngster, later moving to Oakham School.

As a schoolboy, I remember John as full of "joie de vivre", which schoolmasters often took for "cheek", with plenty of personality and the gift to speak without inhibition, a facility which John has always retained to this day. Some say that "He could talk for England" if needed.

During national service John was commissioned in the Royal Army Service Corps and served in Egypt and then for the succeeding five years in the Territorial Army (RASC). Afterwards John was trained in fashion design and prepared for the time when he was to return to Northampton and run the family business - E & J Bernstein (Sylvan) Ltd, light clothing manufacturers.

John has served as leader of the local Jewish community. He was a keen hockey player for the Northampton Hockey Club and has been a keen golfer most of his life, as was his late father. John served for some years on the Management Committee and was honoured with the Captaincy in 2001.

John plays with his wife, Joyce, a Lady member, in the mixed foursomes and they are both members of the Golf Society of Great Britain.

Richard Aitken

Richard Aitken has been the outstanding amateur golfer of his generation for both Club and county. Born in Edinburgh in May 1938 he learned his golf at Prestonfield, a parkland

Richard Aitken

course within a short iron shot of his family home, and at Kingussie, a Vardon-designed course with wonderful views of the Cairngorm Mountains across the River Spey.

Educated at George Heriot's School, he went on to study biochemistry at Edinburgh University where he captained the golf team, winning the British Universities' Championship in 1960. By then Richard had become a qualified biochemist and in 1960 he came south like many an ambitious young Scotsman, to take up a post at Northampton General Hospital.

In 1974 Richard left to become Consultant Clinical Biochemist at Kettering General Hospital. There he gained the higher qualifications of FRSC and FRC Path, remaining at Kettering until his retirement in 1998.

Richard made an immediate impact on the Northamponshire golf scene, firstly as a member of Northampton GC at Kettering Road, and then at Northants County GC. Here we could offer a warm welcome to a genuine scratch man, an established champion, and a successful contender in the cutthroat competition of the Lothians. Although a powerful and determined competitor, he was soon found to be an agreeable opponent, always quick to put longer handicap players at ease.

It did not take Richard long to make his mark, winning the Northamptonshire Championship and our Club Championship in 1962. His record speaks for itself, County Champion eight times, County Seniors' Champion three times, Club Champion nine times, with ten further successes in county events, and no fewer than thirty-one at Club level. He is one of the few Northamptonshire golfers to represent the Midland Golf Union and compete in the Open Championship in 1961. He has enjoyed a remarkable record of success in match play, including a massive contribution to Northamponshire's first success in the Anglian League, and dominating golf for the Club in the Scratch League, Hollingsworth Trophy, Social, Senior, and mixed matches.

Richard's game has been based on consistent and accurate striking, the product of an orthodox repeating swing honed by practice and long experience. He can be a devastatingly effective putter, particularly on fast greens, on which his judgement of line and length is an object lesson to all who watch him. He has had nine holes in one, including all four short holes at Brampton. His NCGC lifetime eclectic score here is 39, (out 331221223: in 331321322), which will take some beating!

Richard has held all the high offices, including the Presidencies of the County Union and the Society of Northamptonshire Golf Captains. Here he has served the Club as Captain in 1984, and also as Vice-President and Trustee, devoting a significant proportion of his free time over the course of nearly half a century to Committee work on behalf of the Club.

In 1968 Richard married Susan Catlow, a daughter of the only man to win the County Championship more often than he himself, and herself a future Ladies' Captain of Club and county. They have two children, a son and a daughter, both of whom are keen sportspeople in their chosen activities.

Richard and Susan are both keen bridge players, which they enjoy without quite demonstrating the same accuracy and success they have achieved on the golf course. They also participate vigorously in Scottish activities including Burns' Night festivities and Scottish country dancing - their prowess at which, mere Englishmen, are best advised to resist any temptation to pronounce upon!

Richard Halliday

Only a very select few stand comparison with Richard Halliday for achievement on the golf course and service to the game off it. Indeed, over the course of seven decades he has arguably held for Club and county every post worth holding, and won every event worth winning.

Born in Northampton in November 1935, Richard enjoyed a variety of sports at school, and performed as a useful goalkeeper for Elmhurst Rangers in the Town League for a time. He joined the RAF as a national serviceman, served for three years, and not long afterwards began a career with Lloyds Bank, where he remained until his retirement as an Assistant Manager in 1992. Richards parents were keen golfers living within a drive and a pitch from the old Northampton Golf Club in Kettering Road.

Richard Halliday

In 1947 he became a junior member and soon demonstrated a precocious talent for the game, winning the best net prize in the county Junior championship with a 59. His handicap was more closely monitored after that; soon he was in single figures, and then down to 1; at the age of 71 he plays off 5; for fifty years it has never been higher than 6. His swing is perhaps a little shorter than it once was, but all the old accuracy through the green remains and his short game is as tight as ever. He is still a formidable match player.

Richard's career took off with his win in the County Championship at Kettering in 1959 after a play-off against John Kingdon, a redoubtable opponent whom he outplayed on the day. He has continued to play in the event for six decades. He won the county Scratch Foursomes in 1967 playing with Richard Catlow. The highlight of a successful county playing career, lasting from 1959 until 1986, was his Captaincy in 1972 of the first Northamptonshire team to win the Anglian League when, as a player, he led from the front with an excellent personal record, and every decision he made as Captain turned out triumphantly.

Richard became a member of the NCGC in 1958. Not surprisingly for such an accomplished player his name features prominently on the honours boards. He was Club Champion in 1980, Match Play Champion in 1983, won the Burn Cup in 1974 and 1979, the Chamberlain Cup with Tony Bishop in 1971, 1972, 1973, 1983 and 2000, and the Church Cup in tandem with his wife Janet, herself an excellent player, in 1970, 1991, and 1993. There have been many other successes. As a senior he has won the County Seniors' Championship twice and the Club Seniors' Championship three times.

Away from the course his achievements have been no less remarkable. He has devoted much of his free time and drawn unstintingly on his wide experience for the benefit of Club and county alike. Here at Brampton he served four terms on the Committee, enjoyed a successful year as Captain in 2002, and stepped in as Acting Secretary during the interregnum following the untimely death of Michael Wadley. He was elected an Honorary Member in 2006.

For the county Union Richard served as President for two years from 1986, and then as Secretary for no fewer than thirteen years. This was a period of unusual expansion for the Union as many new clubs were seeking affiliation. Inevitably there were increased demands on the expertise, and often on the tact, of the Secretary, but Richard was equal to them all. In 2001 he was elected an Honorary Member of the NGU - one of only two to have been so honoured by both Club and county.

Despite his eminence as a golfer and his experience as an administrator, Richard remains the same as always, a generous and agreeable opponent, happy to play in any company. Back in the Clubhouse he is no less in demand, and often called upon to rule on the most abstruse of points. Here he is in his element, modesty and authority personified, and, quite uniquely among Brampton members, he is always right, and nobody argues!

Malcolm Peel
Richard Catlow writes in The County, Spring 2005

Malcolm Peel was born in Harrow, son of a Scottish mother and a Cumbrian father. He was educated locally, before gaining admission to Worcester College, Oxford. University was preceded by national service. He first reported to Fort George – a bleak Highland Brigade Training Centre on the Moray Firth. Basic Training was followed by sixteen weeks officer training at Eaton Hall. He was commissioned into the Seaforth Highlanders, soldiering with the 1st Battalion in Germany. Service with the Territorial Army followed, for which Malcolm was transferred to the 8th Battalion of the Argyll and Sutherland Highlanders.

Whilst at school, rugby and cricket were predominant but by 1946 Malcolm's interest in golf reached the point where he took up junior memberships, first at Hartsbourne Manor, then at Pinner Hill, and finally at Moor Park where there were more juniors of his own age.

Apart from the academic side of university life, golf featured strongly, with all the benefits of weekend matches against major clubs in the south and the Midlands. Malcolm read physiology at Worcester College, Oxford, and upon arrival there had a handicap of 2 which improved during his time at Oxford to 1.

Malcolm gained four successive Blues for Oxford in university matches against Cambridge, winning five of his own matches and losing three.

After university, Malcolm joined the Inveresk Paper Group. Following an initial period in London on sales, he reverted to the production side, training at the New Northfleet Paper Mill in Kent.

In 1960 he and Marion were married. They would hardly have guessed that forty-four years later they would be Captain and Ladies' Secretary respectively of the Northamptonshire County Golf Club!

In 1961 the couple went north when Malcolm was transferred to the Donside Paper Company in Aberdeen. However, 1969 heralded a new job in London as a result of which Malcolm, Marion and their young family moved to Northampton. They have lived here ever since.

In 1971 Malcolm joined Clarke and Sherwell, the local printers, but in 1979 he left to start his own company. His career in printing lasted until his retirement in 1998. Once Malcolm and Marion had started their own company, neither had too much time to enjoy golf and both travelled extensively all over Europe.

Malcolm joined Northamptonshire County Golf Club, initially as a temporary member for two years (a category existing at that time), taking out full membership in 1971, playing regularly until 1976, then less frequently due to his family and business commitments.

In the course of his golfing career, Malcolm has been a member of nine golf clubs: he played internationally for England Boys, has distinguished himself in the English and Amateur Championships and for a time played off a handicap of 1. He is an active member of five golf societies and a member of the Royal and Ancient Golf Club, whose Spring and Autumn Meetings he attends every year. Malcolm endeavours to participate in the President's Putter at Rye every January. So far he has played forty-five times.

Alexander Cameron Sinclair

Cameron is a Scotsman with golf indelibly stamped in his personality and lifestyle. He was born at Coatbridge in 1958 and read landscape architecture at Heriot Watt University, Edinburgh. This led to his becoming a golf course architect and moving to Rugby in 1980 having taken up a position with distinguished international golf course architects, Cotton, Pennink, Steel and Partners. He joined Northamptonshire County Golf Club in the early 1980s and has played county golf for Northamptonshire. He is a past winner of the County Foursome Championship with R A Haig. He is four times winner of the Chamberlain Cup, again partnering Rodney Haig, twice winner of the Club Championship, twice winner of the Club Match Play Championship, winner of the Burn Cup, and twice winner of the Duke of York Cup.

As his career has developed and between 1987 and 1990, Cameron worked as a golf course architect for Graham Marsh in Australia. In 1990 he set up his own practice and has designed courses locally, including Whittlebury Park, Rutland County, Bedfordshire Golf Club and our own three new holes which are such a delight. Cameron is a member of the Royal and Ancient Golf Club as was his late father, Sandy Sinclair, who was also a past Captain.

T E "Tem" Manning

Popularly known to all Club members and friends as "Tem" both nickname and monogram, this great sportsman was a founder member of Brampton and served as its Captain twice, first in 1926 and again in 1944 during the Second World War.

Tem served in the First World War as an ex-Territorial Army Officer in the Northamptonshire Yeomanry which was part of the British Expeditionary Force sent to France in 1914, complete with horses, but soon found themselves in the trenches after the retreat from Mons.

Tem is the uncle of "the young Peter Palmer" who was later adopted as his protégé. His own son, Tom Manning, was an exact contemporary of Peter and they were great friends. Peter went to Uppingham School whilst his cousin Tom went to Harrow. Both went up to Jesus College, Cambridge, simultaneously.

Tom, however, decided to travel the whole world after two years at university and went first off to Russia and then on to Ottowa, Canada. Canada became his land of adoption and he remained there for the rest of his life achieving great distinction as an explorer of the frozen north, cartographer and naturalist. His whole life was spent in this field, apart from service during war time with the Royal Canadian Navy. His fieldwork led to his being granted the Order of Canada, a great distinction.

Tem Manning was by profession a brewer, a noble calling, and he ran the family firm of Mannings Brewery which stood almost opposite Northampton Castle Station. The company later merged with Phipps Brewery of which he became a Director and remained so until retirement. He lived at Shrublands, Dallington, and apart from golf, hunted the fox with the Pytchley. Tem was Captain of the Northamptonshire County Cricket side in 1908 and later became part of the Committee for many years.

However, Tem's golfing achievements were outstanding. He ran the Boycott Trophy from its inception to the year 1960 when no one remained alive from the 1914-18 War who could manage to get round the course. At this time his nephew, Peter Palmer, was deputed to take over and those who served in the Second World War overseas and in a theatre of war were permitted to play. Tem Manning won the trophy 13 times personally.

Dick Manning, Tem's brother, was a local solicitor, the grandfather of Iain Kennedy, one of our current members and erstwhile Managing Director of Church and Co, Shoemakers. Tem Manning was an immense character and lover of the game of golf and of Church Brampton in particular.

Michael Wadley

An article from The County – Summer 2002

"The news on 5 March 2002 of Mike Wadley's fatal heart attack on the ski slopes of France cast an air of gloom over the Club and made for one of the saddest days in the Club's history. There were no signs of the impending tragedy as Mike and Janet prepared to join up with their children for a family holiday to which they had all been looking forward with eager anticipation. Just time for one more game of golf with David Goodrham, Michael carrying his bag as usual, and then off to pack. The family were only to enjoy two happy days together.

Mike Wadley served as Secretary for eleven years and proved to be a true professional. He stamped his personality on the Club as an efficient and friendly servant and ambassador. His knowledge of golf quickly blended with a profound grasp of all matters associated with the County Golf Club.

He coped brilliantly with a myriad of daily problems and with the help of his logical thinking, developed while serving as a wing commander in the RAF, he could always make a valuable contribution when discussing the more complex issues or new initiatives. Perhaps his only weakness was his desire to please all our members all of the time.

During his tenure of office as Club Secretary, my wife and I had the pleasure of entertaining Michael and Janet Wadley, together with others at a dinner party staged at our own home. During the course of the evening's conversation, Michael mentioned that at one stage he had been posted to a squadron in Norfolk and had played as a rugby player for the Norfolk county side. Intuitively I asked him where his boys had been educated. He said that they both went to Norwich school. It so happened that my own brother was Head of the English Department and Assistant Head at Norwich school, set under the shadow of Norwich cathedral and which, amongst many other distinguished old boys, can claim Admiral Lord Nelson.

At hearing this news I said to Michael that my brother must have taught the twin boys (now both doctors) whereupon Michael immediately confirmed the fact, suddenly realising that the Peter Clayton he knew as a schoolmaster was a relation of mine. He then astounded me further by saying "As a matter of fact, your brother taught me and my own twin brother (who died young, like Michael, but during Michael's term of office as Club Secretary) at Westcliff High School. This was indeed the case. My brother's first job after coming down from Cambridge was at Westcliff High School, moving on to various other schools until he finally settled at Norwich. There can be not too many occasions when one schoolmaster teaches two sets of twins within the same family in two successive generations at different schools.

Sidney Willmott Drown
An article by Bruce Clayton from The County – Autumn 2004

"Will you take four kings and a queen?" I asked, and hoped that his gimlet eye and penetrative gaze might not be at that moment X-raying my soul. He replied "I'd like to, but I think not" and what a shrewd measure that was! It took place one evening at the Berystede Hotel at Ascot where we had gone down to play the Wentworth Course and got sidetracked into liar dice in the evening.

I first met Sidney Drown in the early 1960's. He was a snappy dresser, who loved a fag and wore his trilby at a jaunty angle. He moved like a Cambridge man - he didn't give a damn who owned the place. His shoes were often suede but he always observed what others were wearing, being a true professional of his trade.

Sidney had always been a fine and successful sportsman. Hockey at county level was hard to give up so he kept goal at the age of forty when he found (to his amazement) that he couldn't run quite as fast as those half his age. Therefore, it never occurred to him that golf might be difficult, as it is for most of us.

He played to a single-figure handicap for many years with a generous spirit worthy of the gentlemanliness deeply ingrained in his persona. On arrival at the Clubhouse after work for an evening match, he would remove his jacket, don a navy blue cardigan, change his shoes, and step out on to the tee. Nothing else was necessary. No fancy gear or anything like it. In all his dealings, whether in business or otherwise, he was resolute, full of integrity, and utterly reliable. How I enjoyed our golf outings all those years ago. He enjoyed a gamble, played bridge, golf or dice with flair and skill. He always talked sense and was profoundly and serenely aware of the blessing of Jean, his wife, a Lady member of our Club.

R O "Spriggs" Baillon

Spriggs was our first President elected from the membership of our Club after the resignation of Earl Spencer. He took on this task with a great deal of modesty and reluctance saying, when asked, that he was not only too old but not capable any more of speaking publicly and suchlike.

Spriggs had more than his share of disaster in his life having lost two brothers in the war years and his only son from an horrendous car accident when he was aged around 30 and just about to marry. Spriggs and his wife Vera had great difficulty in coming to terms with this huge loss in their lives. Nevertheless Spriggs, if nothing else, had colossal fortitude and strength of character.

Turkey Baillon, Spriggs father, was a founder member of Brampton and the Baillon family has been closely associated with the Club ever since. Father and son have each been Chairman of the Greens' Committee for long periods and the Baillon influence on the heathland style of our course has been substantial. Indeed, Spriggs encouraged the use of gorse and broom by growing substantial quantities at home and transplanting them on the course with suitably "green fingers". So when you are next stuck in the gorse off the fourth tee, before you curse, give a thought to the efforts made by Spriggs in producing the course that we all love playing today.

In his earlier life, Spriggs was a very keen and fine sportsman. He played Rugby for the Saints and East Midlands and became a very fine tennis player at county level. In later years he became President of the Northamptonshire County Tennis Association.

Of the original four sons of Turkey Baillon, two were killed in World War II as part of RAF aircrew, as I have mentioned, and his brother, Brabs Baillon also a colourful character, was an architect by profession. Spriggs himself served in the war years in the British Army and returned after the war as did his brother, Brabs, to join the family business which was the Northampton Brewery Company of which his father, Turkey, was sometime Chairman.

Quietly spoken and with a shy air about him, Spriggs was quickly recognised by everyone as a very charming person. On the golf course he was very competitive but a joy to play with. Spriggs always used a putter of the croquet mallet type, taking a stance on the putting green and swinging the putter facing forwards as one would handle a croquet mallet. In the late 1960's these were outlawed by the R & A for some reason. However, Spriggs continued to use the putter but this time with a side stance instead of putting astride. He is the only player I ever saw putting in this fashion, although I later learned that, as Prime Minister, Sir Harold Wilson, putted in this way. Spriggs was not amused when told so!

When one looks back on men like Spriggs Baillon one realises that one's life was very much enriched by getting to know them.

Raymond Tuckey JP

Raymond died aged 95 in October 2005. Important obituaries were written in both The Times and the Daily Telegraph. They disclose that Raymond was one of the finest British doubles players before the Second World War when the doubles game was taken much more seriously by the leading exponents of tennis.

In 1935 and 1936, Tuckey and his partner Pat Hughes were part of the British teams which won the Davis Cup (Britain has never won it since). In the latter year they also became the Wimbledon champions for which each was rewarded with a ten guinea voucher for the Army and Navy Store. Additionally, Tuckey still holds a record established in 1931 and 1932 for being the only player to enter the mixed doubles at Wimbledon with his own mother.

Although Tuckey and Hughes had been playing together for only a few weeks before the Davis Cup challenge round in July 1935, they proved a partnership with ample reserves of stamina. Hughes, who was the elder, provided unobtrusive generalship, looking for their opponents' weaknesses and slowing down the game by lob and slice, whilst Tuckey delighted spectators with his combination of fireworks and hard driving shots. The Americans were the strong favourites. The non-playing British Captain, Roper Barrett, had been offered a bet of 40-1 against his players on the morning of their match against the United States – an offer which he refused. The crowd was all the more astonished when the 1929 and 1930 doubles champions Wilmer Allison and John van Ryn went down to the British pair 6-2, 1-6, 6-8, 6-3, 6-3. The next year in the Davis Cup, Tuckey and Hughes lost their match against the Australians, Jack Crawford and Adrian Quist, although the British team triumphed by three matches to two.

Charles Raymond Davys Tuckey was born on 15 June 1910 into a tennis-loving family who had their own grass court at Charterhouse. Raymond's father taught mathematics at the school and he played into his seventies with his wife who, as Agnes Daniell, had won the Wimbledon mixed doubles in 1909 and 1913. Raymond's sister, Kay, played in the Wightman Cup between 1949 and 1951. Raymond distinguished himself by winning the public school title at Charterhouse before going on to Cambridge to read engineering at Queen's College where he won a Blue.

After graduation he was commissioned into the Royal Engineers and this fair-haired 21 year old Second Lieutenant attracted attention on court by showing what was regarded as military aggression, hitting considerably harder than either of his parents had done. He won the Army Singles' Championship, then defeated the more experienced navy champion, Commander P F Glover, followed by the RAF champion, Wing Commander H J F Hunter.

At the same time Raymond attracted further interest by entering Wimbledon with his mother who, aged 54 years and 11 months in 1932, became the oldest ever competitor. The pairing attracted the interest of the press and Raymond's father was not pleased when photographers arrived at their home to take pictures of mother and son rolling their own court, since this was a task which he normally performed.

In their first attempt Raymond and his mother lost in the third round and in the following year they went out in the opening round. It was not long before the young Tuckey was being talked of as one of the finest emerging British players, along with Bunny Austin and Fred Perry.

Raymond did not defend his army titles in 1935 because he was practising for the Davis Cup. He and Hughes beat the British pair Charles Hair and Frank Wilde in the men's doubles final at Wimbledon the following year.

In 1937 Tuckey and Hughes lost 0-6, 4-6, 8-6, 1-6 in the Wimbledon final to Donald Budge and Gene Mako. But Hughes then had to withdraw from the practice match at Eastbourne for the Davis Cup because of illness and Tuckey played instead with Wilde. After some moderate play in the first two sets, they made a brilliant recovery only to lose in four sets to Budge and Mako after Tuckey's serve was broken in the twenty first game. If Hughes had been in his accustomed place, the chances that went begging might well have been taken.

In the same year, Tuckey decided to retire from competitive tennis and left the army, in which promotion was slow during peacetime, to join British Timken as a salesman. This was a company which made tapered roller bearings for tanks and so Raymond was refused permission to rejoin the colours on the outbreak of war but remained with the company until his retirement by which time he had been Sales Director for many years.

Tuckey settled down in Northamptonshire with his wife Muriel Godfrey, the widow of a brother officer, Colonel AST Godfrey, the arctic explorer who had been killed on active service. For some years he was Chairman of the Daventry Magistrates.

CHAPTER XX

Charivaria

"And Dick the shepherd, blows his nail".

William Shakespeare

A Winter's Tale

The following article appeared in The County, our Club quarterly bulletin. It recorded the horrendous winter of 1946-47 soon after World War II had ended. Privation and austerity still prevailed. Not only did food rationing remain but also coal and fuel rationing, so that it really was a bleak time. George Mobbs recalled it as follows:

Snow

Nobody who lived through the winter of 1947 will easily forget it. Although there had been some snow soon after Christmas it was not until mid-January that the weather materially worsened. A bitter wind from Siberia brought frequent snowfalls.

The whole of February was marked by sullen cloudy grey skies and the sun rarely put in an appearance, so on many days the temperature by day failed even to reach freezing point. With frequent power cuts, shortage of coal, and with the roads and railways blocked by snowdrifts, it was a problem keeping warm or getting about.

I was living in the family home, a big house in Adlands Lane (later renamed Golf Lane) which ran from the Golf Club to Church Brampton village and which was about half a mile from the Clubhouse.

With little traffic, or snow ploughs available, the A50 (now the A5199) Welford Road soon became blocked, and it became impossible to drive further out of town than the Boughton railway level crossing. So I often had to walk to Kingsthorpe and catch a town bus to get to the office in the centre of Northampton.

One day I ran out of tobacco so I resolved to try to get along to the Clubhouse through snow, often waist high, which I managed after a struggle.

The house staff consisted of two ladies who had been evacuated from the East End of London as the result of German bombing. They greeted me with open arms and told me I was their first cash customer for the last six weeks!

They also told me that the butcher, the baker, the milkman etc (there were no supermarkets in those days) had to leave their supplies at the junction of Golf Lane and Sandy Lane because they were unable to get down to the Clubhouse - the goods were picked up by a member of the greenstaff mounted on the Club tractor.

Committee meetings were held in the Northampton and County Club in George Row Northampton, because of the impossibility of members getting to the Golf Club.

The weather finally relented in mid-March, which brought a lot of flooding, so competitive golf often became impossible as the fifth, eleventh, and fourteenth holes (now holes 9, 15 and 5) were frequently under water. The snowdrifts in the hedgerows did not finally disappear until the end of March.

The winters of 1962-63 and 1978-79 brought weather equally as bad as 1946-47, but by then roads could be cleared of snow and there were no such shortages as in 1946-47, when the country was only just beginning to recover from World War II.

The only noticeable effect the winter of 1962-63 had upon the golf course was that the weight of snow on the broom bushes caused their branches to break off.

For the next few years thereafter it was possible to have a clear view of the fourth (originally the thirteenth) fairway and green from the tee.

Let us hope that global warming will prevent us having to endure again such harsh winters as those I have described.

The winter of 1947 is indelibly seared in my own memory. The aftermath of war brought privation and misery and everything was scarce - food, petrol, coal, sweets, clothing, indeed everything was rationed. Many believe that it need not have been so. The Attlee government imposed a "Soviet style" administration on us.

Following that awful winter came one of the loveliest summers of the twentieth century and London and indeed the whole nation was cheered up by those two marvellous West End blockbuster musical shows Oklahoma and Annie Get Your Gun. Apart from everything else, 1947 produced a magnificent long-lived vintage port, comparable with any of the best of the twentieth century.

* * * * *

Following his recollection, one worthy editor saw fit to record some of the following achievements by the Mobbs family, followed by a poem written by George's great aunt, Susan. The brothers George, Roger and the late Humphrey Mobbs have been distinguished members of our Club for the greater part of its existence. They were all successful players: Roger won the Club Championship in 1952 and the County Championship two years later: George won the Club Championship in 1955 and 1956 before going on to become our Club Secretary in 1966.

They are descended from Frederick Bostock (1812-90), the founder of the Lotus Shoe Company, whose son, also named Frederick, was one of the founder members of our Club. This Frederick had one daughter, Norah, and three sons: Eric, who was killed in the Great War; Neville who was Captain in 1919 and Lance who was Captain in 1929 and again in 1935. Both Neville and Lance were good players, with handicaps of scratch and 2 respectively. Their name is perpetuated in the cups awarded for the Club Championship and Match Play Championship.

Since the Mobbs brothers are the sons of Frederick's daughter Norah, it is evident that golfing prowess has been an ubiquitous family characteristic. However poetry is another case.

George Mobbs writes descriptively about snow, but these lines of verse were composed by his great aunt, Susan Bostock (1860-1948) a daughter of the first Frederick. and a well respected local poet. Susan, who never married, lived in Knight's Lane, Kingsthorpe, taking a close interest in literature, local history, and the arts. George, given the opportunity to compose some lines of verse of his own for The County, modestly responds that the poetical muse is restricted to the female side of his family.

"Snow" by Susan Bostock

"Hark! Not a footfall
Sounds upon its whiteness
Shroud-like over all
With an airy lightness
Steals the silent snow.
Like a muted string
Held almost to dumbness
Like a hunted thing
Stupefied to numbness
By a cruel blow".

Winter 1962-63

I would also mention the harsh winter of 1962-63 which I recall so well. It is probably the worst experienced in the United Kingdom since 1946-47. The first serious snowfall in this county was on New Year's Eve. As it so happened, we were invited to a party and took with us in the boot of our car, both shovel and a doormat, in case we got stuck returning home late.

In the ensuing days of January very heavy snowfalls followed. Our golf course was enveloped with snow with some drifts several feet deep. Intensely cold frosts followed and persisted with precious little relief during February and March.

The pavements in Northampton were swept clear of snow but four feet heaps stood at the roadsides and remained testament to this bitter cold winter with traces of ice still there and remaining until Eastertide.

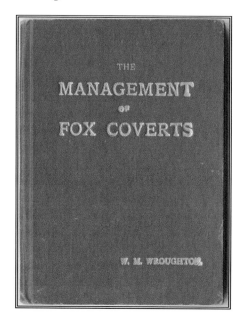

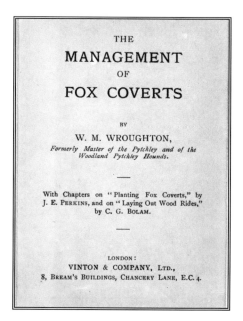

THE

MANAGEMENT

OF

FOX COVERTS

BY

W. M. WROUGHTON,

Formerly Master of the Pytchley and of the Woodland Pytchley Hounds.

———

With Chapters on "Planting Fox Coverts," by J. E. PERKINS, and on "Laying Out Wood Rides," by C. G. BOLAM.

———

LONDON:
VINTON & COMPANY, LTD.,
8, BREAM'S BUILDINGS, CHANCERY LANE, E.C. 4.

A

LATER NOTES ON RESUSCITATING A GORSE COVERT.

BY W. M. WROUGHTON.

Since I wrote this booklet on the management of fox coverts I have gained further experience in re-suscitating a gorse covert which has been neglected for many years ; a most difficult job, but it can be done by intelligent and continuous work.

The gorse covert in question had become a mass of weeds and long grass, and the old gorse stems were dead.

The work should commence on April 1st—the ground with grass

vi

and weeds should be chopped up with "straight-faced" hoes to a depth of five or six inches ; it should be forked over to separate the soil from the grass and weeds, as you go on from day to day when the weather is favourable ; the grass and weeds should be collected into heaps and burnt. The ashes should be scattered over the ground.

On the 1st of May the work of chopping up the ground with straight-faced hoes to the depth of five or six inches should be commenced again. Great care must be taken to ensure the loosening of every bit of soil to that depth. It must be forked over again and the grass and weeds collected into heaps and burnt, and the ashes scattered as before.

The gorse seeds which have been lying dormant in the ground

vii

will germinate when the sun shines and the seedlings will soon show themselves coming up all over the ground.

Weeds and grass will also grow much more quickly. The young gorse must be "set out" in rows six inches wide with spaces or troughs 12 or 14 inches wide between the rows, in which troughs the weeds and grass can be hoed up with small five-inch blade hoes, and the weeds and grass in the rows of gorse seed-lings must be picked up by hand with great care. This work must be done over again every fortnight, or more often if necessary, until the middle of September.

Wire netting eight inches in the ground and three feet four inches above must be put round the covert to exclude rabbits and hares.

viii

In the following Spring, early in April, the weeds and grass between the rows of gorse should be hoed up and carried away, and the weeds and grass amongst the gorse should be picked out with care ; and probably no further work will be necessary and the wire netting can be re-moved in September.

Straight-faced hoes can be made by any blacksmith. They should be seven inches wide and seven inches deep, fastened on to socket by three rivets ; the blades are usually made out of the steel shell-board of an old plough which is solid steel.

As to the golf course, it remained firmly closed, just impossible to play, with consequential loss of income in the Clubhouse and in green fees. Nowadays one may think that the course tends to be overplayed all year round, with scarcely any winter closure. One can only speculate that there were perhaps benefits to the course by the enforced, prolonged closure but at the same time, consequential damage to the economy of the Club.

However, it was that winter which played such havoc on the gorse and broom on the course, especially in front of the fourth tee. Gorse is a tender plant and could not tolerate the phenomenally low temperatures. Large tracts lay open in this area and derelict, with dead plants and maybe there were those within the Club who did not mind this at all, as they drove off the fourth tee.

But in the 1980's we learned the secret of gorse and broom regeneration, and the rest is history as far as our golf course is concerned. Huge efforts have been made for the regeneration of both and once more our course displays its natural characteristics of heathland, which we all like to see.

Golf courses may have taken long to learn the lessons and methodology of regeneration but the masters of the Pytchley Hunt knew all about the problem, in so far as the maintenance of fox coverts were concerned. I set out an extract from The Management of Fox Coverts by W M Wroughton circa early 1900s.

The Old Thatch Barn

I wonder how many of our members recall the old thatch barn which once stood in the valley on our seventh hole, until it was finally demolished in the early 1970's.

Probably built in the early nineteenth century, it was of stout timber construction and thatched with a pitched roof with what I recall as bundles of faggots made up of thin birch wood prunings. It is the only building that I have seen in Great Britain roofed in such a manner. Once it must have served the working farm there, which preceded our Golf Club but was not of any particular use to our greenkeeping staff in later years.

It was located short of the bunker on the left of the seventh hole as one drives off the tee, and down in the dip between the seventh and seventeenth holes.

On one occasion David Barber, then a keen member, an accountant by profession and a useful golfer, was playing a Chamberlain Cup match and to his consternation saw that his partner's wayward drive to the left off the seventh tee had landed on the barn roof and appeared to stay there. Indeed, when they reached the barn they could see the ball glistening in the evening sunlight, amidst the twigs of the thatching.

Thereupon, David Barber climbed up the wall of the barn, with some difficulty. His playing partner passed him a club, and he took a precarious stance and swung, dislodging the ball once more to the earth, thence to be played by his partner.

The German professional golfer, Bernhard Langer, did something similar once whilst playing in a professional tournament. His ball lodged in the branches of a tree, which he ascended and chipped back to the fairway in order to complete the hole without penalty. I recall seeing this incident on television.

Sadly the barn was badly storm-damaged and the insurers were loath to pay for its re-erection. A sweet chestnut tree was planted on its site in the hope that it will flourish and become sizeable and it stands there as a reminder to us of a distant memory.

The Span Golf Bag Circa 1935
By Roger and Edgar Mobbs

The Span golf bag was designed and manufactured by a founder member of the Club, Herbert (Bertie) Mobbs.

During the 1930's the Northamptonshire County Golf Club employed a caddie master – and most days there were caddies available.

The concept of the Span golf bag was to ease the burden of carrying one's own clubs by making it very lightweight and easy to pick up from the ground after each shot.   It was constructed of canvas and strengthened with leather at the seams and pressure points. The carrying strap had a thin ribbon of steel sewn into the sleeve which prevented it collapsing into the ground.   Attached to the bag's collar, a small horseshoe-shaped bracket was fixed opposite to the carrying strap, so that when the bag was put down, the bracket held the club heads clear of the ground and the strap under its own tension remained upright to about knee height. This enabled the bag to be returned to the shoulder without having to bend down. Both bracket and strap were hinged, so as to be flush for storage. There was a small pocket for carrying golf balls

Bertie Mobbs

and the size and balance of the bag were suitable for carrying seven to eleven clubs. Bertie Mobbs designed the Span bag and was awarded a patent and had a small team making the bags on his own business premises, the Pytchley Auto-Car Company, a garage in Bradshaw Street, Northampton, which became the site eventually of the Northampton Fish Market. Several bags were made, rather than thousands, because the outbreak of World War II put an end to this enterprise.

Alwoodley Yorkshire
The reader may wonder why I refer to this delightful course in a book which is recording the history of Church Brampton. To quote Donald Steel:
"Alwoodley is a course of unsuspected beauty. It lies a shortish bus ride from the centre of Leeds which suggests a setting within sight and sound of urban outline and bustle, but those familiar with the glorious dale country to the north will know how quickly it can be reached, and that the Club's attractive name is remarkably descriptive and apt.
For much of its existence, Alwoodley has been one of the most private clubs in the country, where a round for a visitor was very much a privilege. There was no wish or need for the Club to seek attention and nobody could blame them for that. In 1965 the Club acted as host to the Yorkshire Amateur Championship for what, according to the Golfer's Handbook, was the first time. Since then, many championships have been staged there.
Golf at Alwoodley, on part of Lord Harewood's estate, had often been described to me in enthusiastic tones, but I must honestly confess surprise at finding what must surely rank as one of the finest inland courses in Britain. It's admirers, to my mind, had not done it justice".

* * * * *

In 1984 I organised the annual trip of the Agaric Golfing Society from Church Brampton and we decided to head north to Yorkshire, staying in Scarborough, and playing there as well as at the great Ganton Golf Club.

It was during this visit to Ganton that I discovered the clue to the regeneration of gorse and broom. That was because Ganton was heavily involved in resuscitating their own at that time. Their Club President was a farmer whom I contacted after first having a chat with the Secretary and it was the President who provided us with the know-how as to what should be done. But that is another matter.

We decided to travel on the Sunday and en route northwards to play at Alwoodley or somewhere else in Leeds. I had the temerity to write to the Secretary of Alwoodley Golf Club and propose that we should be permitted to play on the Sunday but indicated a willingness to co-operate fully as to the time, fitting in precisely with whatever their membership needs dictated. Normally and in most golf clubs this would have evoked a straight "no". However, to my pleasant surprise a week or two later, I received a letter from the Secretary saying that the Committee had decided, notwithstanding their normal rule on the matter, that we would be allowed to play provided that it was after three o'clock. It was June and the hours of daylight permitted this easily and it fitted in with our plans extremely well.

So it was that we duly turned up at about half past two, paid our dues, changed for golf and assembled on the tee soon after three o'clock. The party comprised twelve and I can recall that the course was serenely beautiful, enhanced by the fact that it was such a lovely day. I was in the first fourball and as we approached the eighteenth green, over which the Clubhouse has a vista, I saw a large man in a blazer standing with his arms folded on the Clubhouse steps and it seemed to signal that he was awaiting our arrival. The rest of the Golf Club was virtually deserted, everyone else having gone home.

We holed out and as I walked in the direction of the Clubhouse in order to put my clubs away in the car this man smiled and then said in a cultivated Yorkshire accent "Are you gentlemen the party from Northamptonshire?" to which I replied "Yes we are". I then added that we were deeply grateful for being permitted to play and being suitably accommodated on a Sunday. The man smiled and in a rather inscrutable fashion said "Well, you can thank me for that", which I promptly did. In fact, my gratitude was rather fulsome but I did add afterwards that he seemed to know about Northamptonshire County Golf Club. He smiled again and said "Oh yes, I know your course well and I spent a chunk of my boyhood in Northamptonshire and I have played your course many times". In actual fact he had been a pupil at Oundle and was a fine schoolboy golfer and had remained so and was now serving on the Alwoodley Committee. Thus it was quite clear that the fact that we were all Church Brampton members had rung a bell for him and it was his intervention on our behalf that effected the consent against all the odds at the time. It was a very pleasant meeting and he had quite clearly stayed on or turned up to make our acquaintance. He asked quite a few questions about the state of our Club then and we parted as good friends.

* * * * *

It so happens, as I am informed by Peter Cooch, that Alwoodley is one of those courses where the members had a paranoia about our four-legged friends - namely dogs. The rule was very severe. No members' dogs were permitted on the course at any time for exercise or to accompany members playing, nor were outsiders' dogs allowed near the course. Before World War II, two elderly members were having a very friendly evening match when they saw a gentleman quite casually dressed, within the boundaries of the course, exercising two dogs. The members became very bothered by this sighting and went over to remonstrate. The members were extremely rude and rather abusive to the man, telling him in no uncertain terms to remove himself and the dogs from their course forthwith, in peremptory fashion.

The next week the Secretary received a letter from the Earl of Harewood on whose estate the course then bounded. Indeed, part of the course is actually on the Harewood estate. The letter began, "I must write and protest at the abusive and ungentlemanly behaviour of two of your members one evening last week, to one of my house guests. Normally I would not bother to write about such an event but on this occasion feel I must do so as my guest was His Majesty, King George VI". One wonders how such a situation was dealt with by the Club Secretary and the Committee!

Trees

I thought I ought to put on record something of the tree planting that has gone on over the last fifty years. To begin with, quite a number of trees on the course were not planted by human design nor by human hand. Many are as a result of the freakish and capricious hand of nature. For example, a number of trees emerge by the scattering of seeds through bird and animal life and by sheer accident. Others are as a result of acorns and other nuts being planted by squirrels or jays.

To illustrate this point, the colonnade of oak trees bordering the left hand side of the third hole where it adjoins Brampton Heath Golf Club, were never planted by the Club members and all came about by accident. About seven or eight remain forming a colonnade but there were many more which had to be grubbed out when we made a concerted effort to regenerate the broom which once flourished in this particular spot. Gone is the broom, more to the pity, but the oaks do serve some purpose in providing a measure of privacy in summertime from the course next door, preventing errant golf shots from our side occasionally going out of bounds and vice versa.

A colossal number of weed trees have also invaded the course such as sycamore which are really neither useful nor ornamental. Organised tree planting has, of course, also taken place and has produced some very good results. The copse of pine trees behind the fifteenth green and the two on the right of the eighteenth, between the eighteenth fairway and the first fairway, have added a great deal of beauty to both holes. They were thinned out some years ago but further thinning is now taking place and replanting so that all the copses are carefully farmed to ensure that they are never bereft of trees at any time and that, in effect, they are progressively replaced. Similarly, Lionel Harrison gave a large number of Norwegian spruce trees which came from his home at Overstone and were planted in various places on the course, especially in the area between the fourth and fifth, not far from the fifth teeing ground.

I have made mention of the sweet chestnut which is meant to commemorate the old thatch barn on the seventh hole. Nearby there is a large ash tree between the sixth green and the seventh fairway. About twenty-five years ago this started to look far from healthy and the Committee considered the matter carefully and decided to plant a replacement ash just in case the old tree succumbed, which it very much looked like doing. In actual fact it has recovered to an extent and now both continue to flourish.

Similarly, trees which form part of the original course layout have been replaced from time to time. There is a lone may tree on the second hole about 100 yards from the green which was planted a few years back to replace a very old tree which had become bedraggled and was at the end of its lifetime. In much the same way, trees were replanted on the eleventh hole to the right on a driving length in order to replicate what had been there for very many years and were now dying off.

From the beginning of the Club there were a few large elms standing in the hollow to the left of the eleventh gentlemen's back tee and to the right of the tenth hole as one approaches the green. All these very tall elm trees, some quite 80 feet high, were devastated by Dutch Elm disease in the 1970's. We employed a woodsman to cut them down to stop the contamination spreading further. When I invited him to do the work I thought we might have a dozen or so trees. Later he reported that he had cut down a total of eighty trees of varying sizes.

Within a few years, suckers from the old elms started to reappear which was an encouraging sign. Alas, they too having reached heights of about 15 to 20 feet have succumbed to the same disease.

I have also made mention of the huge wych-elm which stood as a sentinel on the thirteenth hole, forming a marker for one's second shot to the green and is now replaced by the Wellingtonia.

During my own year of Captaincy the "Dawn Patrol wood" was planted in spare land between the second green and forward of the seventeenth tee. This has formed a useful copse and comprises birch, rowan and wild cherry – all indigenous species.

The late Alan Westley donated a small colonnade of Japanese maple with light green foliage and these were planted behind the sixth green. Soon after the old Bloxhamist Golfing Society donated some amelanchier flowering shrubs which were interspaced between the Japanese maples. The amelanchiers, which look a glorious sight when they flower in spring and assume a very pleasant coppery coloured foliage in the autumn, have become more predominant in this particular location.

Another large tract of land, left of the ninth green, was frequently boglike in character and had never in effect been cultivated since the course was built in the first place. It was used as a dumping ground for the spoil removed which was stinking and fetid when the ninth green was first dug up and reconstructed on the direction of Charles Catlow and Spriggs Baillon.

Charles Catlow was at pains to ensure that the former contours of that green should be replicated by the new one and this was done faithfully and accurately. It was not altogether a success and further complete reconstruction occurred, this time under the design and guidance of Cameron Sinclair, which seems vastly better. The green itself is better shaped and adapted to modern golf and presents a better test than before. Returning to my theme, the spoil was dumped on this spare land.

Once the fact became known that there was to be a north-western bypass around Northampton the Committee, in their wisdom, felt that an acre or so of woodland should be planted at that particular point there and then. This would form a sizeable wood and give a good deal of protection from the sight of any flyover or dual carriageway bypass and at the same time afford some protection against noise. It was to be a mixed wood comprising Scots pine, rowan, silver birch, may trees and larch. The trees were purchased and planted by our own staff and have had about ten years to take root and flourish undisturbed. They have been suitably pruned on occasion and are already forming an attractive woodland feature which will come into its own doubtless in years to come and have made good use of what, in effect, was an eyesore.

Although the north-western bypass did not take place quite so soon as was anticipated, further rumblings are going on at the time of writing and there is little doubt that it will become an entity at some stage in the future when our woodland is most needed, notwithstanding having provided us with a pleasant vista over the years.

I would also make mention of one or two individual trees on the course which are commemorative of certain people.

My own tree behind the thirteenth had a purpose behind it and for better or worse I hope that it will one day achieve its aim and object.

There is a fastigiate cedar tree on the right-hand side of the fourth fairway which commemorates the late Jack Corrin. This will soon become a handsome tree and the site for this particular planting was on the premise that Jack invariably struck his ball there or thereabouts on occasion even borrowing the fifth fairway and always had to pitch onto the fourth green from that direction.

A Scots pine commemorates J C J Legge as a single entity between the eighteenth and first fairways and a hawthorn tree is planted close to the footbridge leading to the summer fifth tee to commemorate the late Mrs Meg Tennent.

Finally I would add that a very positive policy towards tree planting has now been adopted by the Club which lays down guidelines for the future. Haphazard tree planting is not encouraged. Indigenous-type heathland trees are encouraged and are planted when and where needed and many such trees have been planted in recent years, particularly to the left of several of the gentlemen's winter teeing grounds. Weed trees are to be discouraged and we are doubtless making continuous effort to maintain the beauty of our gorse and broom, regenerating this whenever needed.

The long hot summer of 1976

The long hot summer of 1976 proved to be the hottest and driest since weather and temperature details were first recorded.

Through June, July and August, the sun beat down unmercifully and any rain that fell was negligible. The country side became parched and brown, and many rivers and reservoirs fell to their lowest levels. On many days the temperature rose above 90 degrees Fahrenheit.

The government created a new post- the Minister for Drought – but he did not appear to be equipped with any supernatural powers for controlling the weather.

It was the media that dubbed 1976 "The Year of the Ladybird" as swarms of hitherto friendly ladybirds took to attacking human flesh in search of moisture that was otherwise unobtainable elsewhere.

In July the Club hosted the Midland Counties 36 hole Team Championship. So great was the heat that by lunchtime the competitors staged a mutiny, led by Michael Lunt (an English Amateur Golf Champion), complaining that it was too hot to play the second round of holes. So with the good old English talent of compromise it was agreed that they need only play 9 holes for the second round.

The golf course became so parched that it became impossible to replace divots as they just crumbled into dust, so in order to minimise damage to the course, a local rule was imposed that, for friendly golf, tee-pegs must be used on all teeing grounds and any ball finishing on the fairway must be moved sideways with the next stroke to be played from the nearest semi-rough.

On a Monday morning in late August the telephone rang in the Secretary`s office and a voice announced `This is the Northampton Evening Telegraph and we are doing a series of articles on how the hot summer is affecting local sport – may I ask how it is affecting your golf club? `Yes you may` I replied, `it has just set the b****y place on fire!`. And I slammed the phone down as I had just seen clouds of billowing smoke rising above the trees in the vicinity of the 18th tee. At that moment Joe Carrick the Head Greenkeeper appeared and we raced down to the 18th tee as fast as our ancient vehicle could carry us. We were far too late to do anything as flames were already ripping through Fox Covert in the area now occupied by holes 7A, 8A and 9A. Miraculously a fire engine appeared, soon followed by others. They started to lay their hoses towards Brampton Brook (the stream alongside the railway), so I explained to them that the stream now consisted of little more than a series of stagnant muddy pools, and that they needed to lay their hoses back to the main water supply at the clubhouse.

The poor weary fire fighters were nearly out on their feet from fighting so many fires, and their reaction to my helpful advice was `Who is this b****y civilian telling us what to do!` It wasn`t until a senior fire fighter appeared that commonsense prevailed.

Fox Covert trees stood amongst years of accumulated pine needles and fir cones, and, throughout the week, fires kept breaking out from underground, and one at a time we had a maximum of 17 (seventeen!) fire appliances fighting the fire.

By Saturday all the fire had been snuffed out and the Fire Officer said to me `I will leave one fire engine here until 2200 hours and if no further fires break out it will be none`.

My wife and I visited relatives that Saturday evening and returning from Coventry towards midnight, coming through Lower Harlestone, to my horror we saw flames once more in the area of Fox Covert.

By the time we had reached the 18th hole there was a fire engine present, called out by someone from Harlestone, and the fire was extinguished.

On August Bank Holiday Monday the heavens opened and the consequent deluge brought the long hot summer of 1976 to its final conclusion. Could the summer of 1976 be a foretaste of what is to come from global warming?

The old original timber built stables, in which golfers who rode to the course, or arrived by carriage, would stable their mount, and in which working horses on the course were housed.

CHAPTER XXI

Other Golfing Societies

"In solemn troops, and sweet societies".

John Milton

The "Whisky Macs"

This soubriquet has come into common parlance in the Clubhouse in recent years to describe perfectly the small coterie of golfers who tend to play together, as do the St Botolph golfers, on Tuesday afternoons in the summer time and on Wednesday mornings during the shorter days of winter. They tend to turn up on the day and divide themselves into suitable groups of four, depending on numbers present. Away games at Tadmarton Heath and Frilford Heath, together with a three-club Christmas competition (followed by a festive lunch!) are also included in the annual programme.

The original "eight" were Bill Stephenson (past Club Captain and Treasurer), David Deane (past Club Captain), his close business partner and friend, Tony Amos, Dr Hugh Ferguson (formerly a Senior Medical Officer in the British Army, retiring at the rank of Brigadier), Dr Gavin Tennent (formerly Chief Medical Officer at St Andrew's Hospital and the son of the highly popular and charming past Ladies' Captain, Mrs Meg Tennent), John Shurvinton (former Saints' rugby player and their Club President 2007-09), Brian Stoneman and Jack Barker who sadly died in May 2006. Others who have joined this elite band are Malcolm Row, Malcolm Lowdon, Nigel Glew and Peter Haddon.

The name "The Whisky Macs" dates back to a particularly cold round of golf in the early 1990's when, as usual, the first member into the bar, Bill Stephenson, decided to dispense with normal cold beer and ordered eight Whisky Macs. Despite the confusion behind the bar and with Bill's expert guidance, eight drinks were produced, consumed and reordered! It naturally followed that in order to combat the chill of further winter games on the course, fully charged flasks of the sublime mixture of whisky and ginger wine became mandatory. The tenth tee is invariably the main refreshment point, but not surprisingly over the years a number of other "pit stops" have been introduced. Furthermore it is not surprising that the group identity was established.

Dr Gavin Tennent's parents were both keen members of the Golf Club and his mother, Mrs Meg Tennent, was a popular and charming past Ladies' Captain whose memory is commemorated by the planting of a red may tree close to the bridge leading to the fifth teeing ground.

The "Whisky Macs" always play their golf together in the finest spirit of the game and, on the death of their close friend and fellow member, Jack Barker, donated a bench seat which is positioned at the back of the twelfth tee. Take comfort there and remember the "Whisky Macs" (2 measures of whisky to one of ginger wine!).

Jack Barker who was a keen Whisky Mac, and his brother Ted (also a Golf Club member) were both sons of the late Stanley Barker JP and perhaps the most famous and successful of all the Pytchley huntsmen. Stanley's portrait was painted by Sir Alfred Munnings, several times, as well as by Lionel Edwards. On one occasion Jack accompanied his father to Sir Alfred's studio in Dedham, Suffolk.

The County Cricket Golf Society

Lewis McGibbon is a longstanding and much respected member of our Club. He is a chartered accountant by profession and began his career at Newcastle-upon-Tyne. Lewis had a dazzlingly successful career later with a number of non-executive directorships with a number of companies in disparate lines of business activity, which took him all over the world until retirement.

Lewis originally came from Northumberland where he learnt his cricket. Finishing his accountancy training before national service in the RAF, he married Pauline and they moved to Northampton. This was to play cricket for Northamptonshire County Cricket Club. He was then young, slim and an extremely useful medium to quick bowler, cleverly using the seam. Lewis played for the county side, first under the captaincy of Dennis Brookes and then Raman Subba Row, before the accountancy profession and career took precedence over the game which he loved.

After leaving the county side he played for the Saints' Cricket Club along with many fellow Golf Club members and soon took to golf. The sport of cricket threw him into contact with many fine players from all the counties playing for the county championship, many of them test match players.

The County Cricket Golfing Society was formed in 1935 soon after the infamous body line series in Australia. Nowadays it has an annual fixture list of about thirty matches, played all over the UK, from Ganton to Rye, for example. Lewis ran the match for quite a few years when it was hosted at Church Brampton against a Brampton side. Over the years came Freddie Brown, D B Carr, Brian Close, C A Milton, Mike Gatting, Peter Parfitt, Reg Simpson, A C Smith, M J K Smith and Fred Titmus, all test cricketers and five of whom captained England.

Frank "Typhoon" Tyson, one of England's greatest fast bowlers, also played our course many times, when staying with Lewis on many of his trips to the UK back from Australia. It all goes without saying that numerous other Northamptonshire County Cricket Club players have played our course, some as members, and others, including great names like George Tribe, Jack Manning, Keith Andrew, Laurie Johnson, Peter Arnold, Roger Prideaux, Geoff Cook, John Wild, Allan Lamb and Neil Mallender to mention but a few.

The Northamptonshire Golf Circus

No mention of one of our oldest Golf Societies was made in Neil Soutar's book. He may have felt that any such reference might be injurious to his good name or the health and well-being of the membership of the Club as a whole. After all, it's name was only ever mentioned in a whisper, covertly and never committed to paper until now.

So it is that I have prevailed upon Michael Learoyd, who is of sound mind and both articulate and literate, to recount something of the fifty years of "Circus" history, recently celebrated suitably at Church Brampton. Mike has responded well to what must have been an enormous challenge. To have cajoled the Circus members into providing him with their recollections within the disciplined time frame imposed by me, was a miraculous achievement. I publish it in it's almost unexpurgated form and instantly wash my hands of any culpability or liability and hope that some of you will recognise the characters who form this great society and enjoy reading something of their exploits.

The Circus - Fifty Years and Rising
Michael Learoyd writes:
From the outset I wish to make it clear that I accept no responsibility for what follows, particularly as to its accuracy, despite being present at much of that which is related here and that it may not form the basis of any claims against either me or my successors. My fellow Circus members are a sharp lot and I wish to avoid a welter of writs simply because of an occasional economy with the truth.
It is nevertheless a supportable fact that we are just emerging from our 50th anniversary and it is neat and timely therefore that a record of events, successes, mishaps and highlights be committed to paper together with an introduction to some of our Circus members.

The Birth of the Circus
Keith Durham, Archivist to the Northamptonshire Golf Circus writes:
"In the fifties "Brampton" needed to encourage new younger members. Sunday morning was the preserve of the senior gentlemen members, so as the course was deserted in the afternoon, an idea was put forward to the younger element in the Club by Arthur Baxter and Don Chamberlain, two prominent senior members, that they might like to play for a cup, which Messrs Baxter and Chamberlain would present. So was formed the Northamptonshire Golf Circus in 1957 who, from that day to this, have annually played for the said cup which was christened the Oozlum Bird Cup.
These young members decided on a pink elephant, holding a golf club, sitting on a golf ball as their emblem. They played regularly on Sunday afternoons under very relaxed rules, often allowing five or sixball matches. Their game was followed up with boiled eggs and soldiers in the Clubhouse, produced by the then Steward and his wife Mr and Mrs Parsons. After tea something a little stronger was consumed. From 1966 the Oozlum Bird Cup has been contested at Aldeburgh Golf Club on the annual autumn visit.
The Circus still consider "Brampton" their heritage home, so when the new three holes were made they decided to mark the 50th anniversary of the formation of The Circus (a little early) by donating a bench which will be found by the tee on 9a and was presented to the then Captain of the Club, Keith Archbold, and the President, Bruce Clayton, in December 2003."

Some notes regarding the Archivist's account:
The Society's Archivist was elected at an AGM in the 1980's. His election was unanimous and unopposed.
There are some slightly differing accounts of the birth and one such reads:
"In the 1950's the members used to play on Sunday afternoons and as no one else was on the course, were able to go round together, regardless of numbers. Seeing seven players coming down the eighteenth, the late Arthur Baxter remarked "They look like a ...... circus" and so the Society was born".
Arthur Baxter was of course father of Derek, another early member of the Circus and an all-round sportsman of considerable gusto. I was playing with him one day when he was on song and a model of accuracy. We were playing the sixteenth - it is now the seventh I believe - and it had a thatched tractor shed at the bottom of the dip with an open side. Derek drove through the open (or missing) door and his ball came to rest in the corner

furthest from the opening. Nothing daunted he played a sidewall boast (squash or fives' players will be familiar with the term), the ball flew off the front wall, over his shoulder and back in play and he carried on as before. We tried to interest Bill Cann, Brampton's professional, in developing this shot but he could see little use for it.

I surmise that most of our readers will be aware of the Oozlum Bird and its unique ability. In common golfing parlance an oozlum is a score of three (or better) on a par three hole. We see few enough of these unusual birds in the Circus although the "real" definition of an oozlum almost split the Society asunder at one stage - the debate raged at successive AGM's as to whether the drive had to land on the green or not. The purists (those who insisted that the drive had to finish on the green) were led vociferously by John Merry. The pragmatists i.e. opposed to this, consisted of everyone else. A compromise was reached - we decided not to bother.

Membership

Membership of the Circus has been drawn largely but not exclusively from the Northamptonshire County Golf Club and the association has been very strong over the past five decades i.e. throughout the life of the Circus. Currently out of the seventeen playing members (few frequent, some occasional and one annual) fourteen are or have been members of Brampton at one time or another and twelve are still paid up playing members. None however is a "leech" (as commonly defined) although we boast very few who are currently in work, indeed very few who are employable. I estimate the average age of the Circus membership as over 73 years but under 78, but will not be drawn further on the issue.

A profile of some of our members follows:

Roger Buswell - Despite having taken his golfing skills down to the south-west, Roger remains an active Circus member. We take the Circus to Somerset each year and Roger joins us in Aldeburgh each August. A long-term Brampton member along with other Buswells.

Tony Cooper - A Northamptonshire all-round sportsman of distinction, only part of which was earned on the golf course. Has been a Circus member for only three decades but a Brampton member for longer.

Keith Durham - Another age-old member as was his father before him. An early member of Brampton's Social Committee (50 years before iPods), his organisational skills are invaluable and his handicap a tremendous asset in foursomes.

Mark Eyton-Jones - A Circus and Brampton member for many years, he was one of our few "real" golfers in that he seemed to know where the ball was going before he hit it. It took some time to bring him down to our level.

Bomber Harris - A Brampton member for many years, a Circus member for even longer and one of the only Circus members still in gainful employment. The wielder of a long putter but only because he let it grow.

Peter Merrikin - A Wellingborough Golf Club member, he was invited to the second Circus trip to Aldeburgh in the early 1960's and has been prominent in our midst ever since. A cavalier spirit to golf and life, he is a worthy President of the Skiing Division.

John (Jacko) Merry - Another original Circus member, as well as a paid-up Brampton member, he putts with a three iron as Joe Carr used to do. There the resemblance ends as Jacko is left-handed and putts with one hand (and one eye). He was first a Brampton member in 1937.

Pat Patrick - An early guest player with the Circus, he plied his trade in Kent and the north, before returning to North Bedfordshire and Circus golf. The erstwhile Commodore of the Sailing Division, this has become a frustrating appointment without water or a boat.

Bob Poole - One of the game's great theorists and enthusiasts, he will go wherever a game of golf is to be had. I have been lucky enough to play with Bob in many different countries and they have not caught up with us yet.

Peter Rushton - At last we have come to a genuine golfer. A Brampton member since 1950 and a Circus member from the start, he could probably play to his age if you gave him a few putts.

Mike Savage - The "sine qua non" ("without which, nothing", a note to assist non-classicists) of Circus golf, long time Secretary and currently President, where would we be without him? Also a long time Brampton member and supporter of social events.

Arthur Wright - Has probably been a Circus member for little over 20 years but has shot to the top. At under 75, age is on his side but he has golfing ability as well.

Despite all this, the Circus is not concerned with the cult of the individual. I received a pleasant note from the most recent product of our youth policy, a one time Committee member of Brampton and, I believe, an exterminator of many of our rabbits. He wrote: "The members of the Circus are friends of long and lasting standing. They have no preconceived ideas concerning their skills as golfers but, make no mistake, they play the game with as much enthusiasm and as competitively as any I know. Some are members of other Golf Clubs but most are members of Brampton .... I have no hesitation in saying that Church Brampton, in every respect, is their favourite venue".

There are, however, additional criteria to be followed, that good fellowship and an atmosphere of the highest degree of comradeship should at all times be maintained. Members have no problems with this.

I could not have expressed it better myself ... so I have not tried. The Circus likes to see itself as an unscripted part of Northamptonshire County Golf Club.

The Circus - Some Habits

This section is not intended to be either embarrassing or even a confessional but simply how we behave in relation to golf.

Structure - we have a President, a Secretary and then rank and file members (this is not to ignore the Archivist). The President is normally in place for two years but as the Society is just passing its 50th birthday and we have twenty members it follows that some have been in office twice (for those who cannot follow this, please give me a call). The Secretary is our bedrock and here we have struck lucky. Mike Savage has been the Society's permanent Secretary for forty (or is it more?) years but more importantly has been efficient, charming and firm. What the Circus has done to deserve him I do not know but it must have something to do with prayer.

Membership Selection - the route in (to membership) is an arcane mystery but you know you have arrived if you are brought into the discussion concerning possible new members. There are no elections, no blackballing, no counts and recounts and no release of white smoke, just a consensus. Perhaps there is something for the democratic process to learn here.

Back in the old days new members received a conditional invitation and were asked to undergo two years of probation at Aldeburgh, the annual fest. Do not for a moment assume that this probation involved any test of golfing ability - rather the reverse. But if you lost about six balls a round and got to bed after 2 am you stood a fair chance of getting in.

Handicapping - handicaps are peculiar to the Circus and Circus events. They reflect to some extent a member's Club handicap but depend rather more so on the Handicap Committee's firsthand experience of a member's golfing prowess and, even more so, whether the member has won in recent Circus events or lost. On one occasion at Aldeburgh one player enjoyed a handicap of zero and another of 48. I believe the par player still won but I am not sure. The Handicap Committee is Peter Rushton.

Air Shots - the Society's attitude to air shots is quite relaxed: they do not count provided the member is either the current or a past President of the Circus. As almost all members have held this high office at some time or other over the last fifty years, it is a largely inclusive benefit. It would be better if this were not brought to the attention of the R & A.

Circus Meetings and Tours - we meet as a Society fortnightly for seven months of the year, once per month for a further three months and wrap up warm and sleep in January and February. The meetings are mostly at Church Brampton whilst our Bedfordshire wing

Top Row Middle: A.J. Merry
Middle Row: 2nd from left: A.E. Wright
3rd from left: M. P. Learoyd
Bottom Row: 1st on left: M. J. Savage

invite us to Colmworth (aka North Bedfordshire Golf Club) from time to time, an ideal Circus course in the east (the near east rather than the middle or far).

We frequently play as many as 18 holes although there is no disgrace in playing 9 or less. Accurate scoring is a "must" particularly for those who understand the Stableford system and I notice an unnecessary but growing insistence on the holing of putts.

The Circus is almost nomadic in its programme of out-of-county tours. Quite apart from the Aldeburgh trip which merits a section to itself, we also visit the Lincolnshire coast (to catch up with the Circus' Lincolnshire representative who is sadly no longer with us) and the south-west to check on the progress of one of our founder members, Roger Buswell. We humbled Saunton Sands in 2007 after bringing Tiverton and other fine courses to their knees in previous years. The tour to "Buswell Country" includes a fiercely contested skittles match against a team of local farmers, bank managers and other local cheats. We have yet to worry them let alone win and, rather prudishly, they insist that air shots count.

Golfing Successes

It should not be imagined that, because our attitude to the great game appears superficial or even frivolous, our members have been without significant successes. Amongst many triumphs, both at Brampton and elsewhere, we would list:

Peter Rushton - During the 1950's winners of the Church Cup with Mrs Rushton senior (Peter's mother). The win is certain, the date uncertain as the relevant board has now been removed from display in the Clubhouse.

1966 Lees cup winner with John Ashley. This is set in stone or similar in the Clubhouse.

John Merry - 1954 runner up in the Burn Cup. The circumstances concerning this personal triumph are related elsewhere in this volume.

1972 winner North Nigeria Left-Handers Championship (John had the only set of left-handed clubs and refused to lend them).

Flemming Rathsach - 2007 Ram Trophy winner.

It is interesting to note that there have been over 50 years between the earliest and latest of these successes.

Aldeburgh Tour

The Circus has had an annual tour to Aldeburgh since its foundation. This was normally the high point of the Society's year although not necessarily because of the quality of golf played. For many years we went down to the east coast on a Friday in August and returned on the Sunday night. However, since members now have mostly retired from gainful employment, the Aldeburgh trip starts on a Sunday night and finishes in a leisurely fashion on Wednesday. We invariably play Thorpeness and Aldeburgh itself and from time to time Woodbridge as well. There is a multiplicity of incidents and myths arising from these tours over the better part of fifty years. Amongst those I may mention the following:

Peter Merrikin. "Members quite obviously displayed a very, very high standard of golf in the early days at Aldeburgh. I remember on one occasion when we played the Circus Cup at Thorpeness that my partner and I won the cup with 19 points and during the round I lost eight balls and broke my seven iron".

There was another occasion at Woodbridge where one of our members had returned from a business trip to Thailand with several exploding golf balls. He slipped these to his playing partners and others at varying times and the result was a minor version of a battalion military exercise. Woodbridge members found little humour in this and you have to sympathise with them. Happily now after thirty years we are welcome there once again. The Circus tried out all the hotels in and around Aldeburgh at one time or another. The partings were generally by mutual agreement and we are now returning to hotels from which we parted several years ago. In particular the Uplands Hotel was our venue for several years as it was owned and run in those days by an ex-Northamptonian, Tim Forge and his wife. Tim was a tolerant and understanding landlord and would actually go to bed with the bar and its contents left available to Circus members.

There have always been strong connections between the Circus and the Saints' Rugby Club. Indeed, out of a random list of twenty Circus members taken in the early 1980's no less than ten had appeared for the Saints (or Wanderers or Crusaders) at some time or another. The list includes David Coley, a long time member of Brampton, the Circus and the Saints, Jack Parry and Peter Arnold both Circus members in earlier days and notable members of Brampton, and Derek Baxter and Peter Rushton, founder members of the Circus and Captain and Secretary respectively of the Crusaders in their time.

These two took a Crusaders' side to the Bournemouth Festival in 1955 and returned undefeated. Peter Rushton was reported in the Green 'Un of Saturday 16 April 1955 as follows: "In addition to the rugger, several players indulged in golf at which they were far less successful. Although an invitation to attend the festival next year has been received, other accommodation may have to be found".

We have faced similar problems at Aldeburgh.

Society Silverware

The Circus competes annually for several cups, indeed we are reaching a point where there are almost as many silver cups as playing members. The individual cups are:

The Buswell Beaker: competed for at Thorpeness Golf Club.

The Cooper Chalice: competed for at Woodbridge Golf Club.

The Arthur and Anita Wright Challenge: a mixed foursomes competition played at Church Brampton in August and organised by Keith and Janet Durham. This competition was originally introduced to dispel the slur of male chauvinism which has been levelled at Circus members. Wives and WAGS are invited provided they are back at the sink in the evening.

The Oozlum Cup: this is effectively the Victor Ludorum award of the Circus year and has been competed for at Aldeburgh Golf Club in its present format i.e. men's foursomes, for over 45 years. The Secretary and members at Aldeburgh have been very welcoming and patient with us over this long time and, provided they will continue to have us, we will continue to make our annual pilgrimage there.

The programme follows a well-established pattern. The teams of two are selected at dinner on the evening before the big day. The pairings and the handicaps are determined by the Handicap Committee, Peter Rushton, and are then announced to a hushed audience concealing their nervousness behind a mask of indifference. A book (of odds) is then drawn up by the only one of us who understands that sort of thing, Jacko Merry. Players do not usually back their own team as such behaviour is seen to smack of self-indulgence but each team will usually attract at least one bet even if it is only out of pity.

As the great day dawns, the contestants gradually muster for a "full English" trying to remember what they are meant to be doing that day and eventually get together on the first tee. Golf being golf, we are required to fire off a few shots and about two hours later we meet again in (or outside) the Aldeburgh Clubhouse for lunch of soup, sandwiches, Adnams out of silver tankards and Kümmel (a traditional Roger Buswell gift). We return to the course for the back nine without obvious enthusiasm and scoring now is higher than on the front nine. A year or two ago one couple had scored 17 Stableford points on the front nine and finished with 19 overall. Golf and temperance are brothers.

What of the Circus Bookmaker, you may want to know? It seems unlikely that over the years John Merry has enjoyed any declarable income from this source to be of interest to HM Inspector of Taxes. One year he lured Peter Rushton into becoming a partner with the attraction of splitting a "lucrative pot". Challenged by the two of them to be "Men and not Mice" with their wagers, He that Shall not be Named and other members duly obliged. The result was that the "pot" became a lot less lucrative than the dynamic duo had envisaged. With a deficit of over £800 the swift demise of the partnership was inevitable. Peter Rushton's bookmaking career finished as quickly as it had begun.

Divisions and Sub-divisions
With such a wealth of multifaceted talent available it is no surprise that Circus members have joined together in successful pursuit of other sports and pastimes. Particularly worth noting are the activities of the Cruising Division and the Skiing Division whilst the recently formed Television Quiz Division has had its moments. The Circus also enjoys the occasional Race Day put together by Honest Jacko and will accept challenges to compete at snooker, bowls, croquet and 5's and 3's, provided that the challengers are prepared to spoof for dinner afterwards.

Television Quiz Division
Only recently formed and then without formal recognition, a Circus team of five was conscripted by John Merry to challenge the resident BBC team of superbrains, the Eggheads, in a programme of that name (BBC2, weekdays 6 pm) in the autumn of 2007. The team consisted of John Merry, Flemming Rathsach, Arthur Wright, the author and Flemming's son-in-law, David, our own superbrain. We are prevented contractually from disclosing the result at the time of writing but the team has not ordered Lamborghinis yet. (Editor's note – they lost!)
The Circus Television Quiz Division has been suspended sine die.

Conclusion
All current Circus members have contributed to this account of their Society in some shape or form. This includes our three latest recruits, Rob Blomfeld affectionately known to us as the Hanging Judge who has been a member for several years now, and the products of our youth policy, Jim Chater and Flemming Rathsach.
By way of preparation for this piece, we asked some members to voice their views on such weighty matters as our youth policy, handicapping as an art form and the possible appointment of a non-member as President of the Circus. One or two were stunned into silence on receiving the questionnaire (and the dictaphone accompanying it). Most were

very helpful and replied to the profound questions quite earnestly. I particularly liked:

The advice from one member who felt that we should look for more experience in exercising our youth policy.

Tony Cooper's reaction to the handicapping system which had denied him a win on Ladies' Day (Ed note: due to a sad accident affecting his hand, Tony could only putt on that day).

Mark Eyton-Jones's claim that Keith Durham, when driving off the first, hit the ball over Cann's hut (where the new entrance to the Club now stands).

Bob Poole's fine hole in one at the second at Kilworth Springs: he says that he closed his eyes as always when playing a shot and, on opening them, he was being mobbed.

The general response to my question "There is a move afoot to invite a non-member to become Life Patron. Who would you like to see in this role and why?" I had expected inventive responses such as Nelson Mandela or Freddie Flintoff or Groucho Marx but I was to be disappointed. For those who gave a name at all rather than personal abuse, everyone chose Keith Durham. For someone who had been a member since the start of the Circus, it was curious to choose Keith given that the appointment was restricted to non-members.

Finally the birth and death of the Circus Dining Club: the second meeting was arranged by Derek Norton, again one of the originals. It was as ever a male-only occasion with selected guests and the boat was pushed out as you can see from the copy of the original invoice (see right):

Cigars were ordered at 10/6 a throw which equates to about £14 at today's values and the whole amounted to £11.10.6d each, roughly £290 today. Derek did the sums and posted off accounts to each of the diners. Cut to Mr and Mrs Merry Senior's breakfast table two days later. John's father was also J Merry, the post had arrived and had received father's attention. John joins mother and father at the breakfast table but receives little rejoinder to his cheerful greeting. Instead Mr Merry Senior drops Derek's opened envelope onto John's cereal plate with the dry observation "If you can live like that your mother and I can't". John had just under £4.10.0d in the bank at the time.

The final words come from Pip (I am using an old nickname to conceal an old member):

"I am proud of my membership of the Circus and very grateful for the

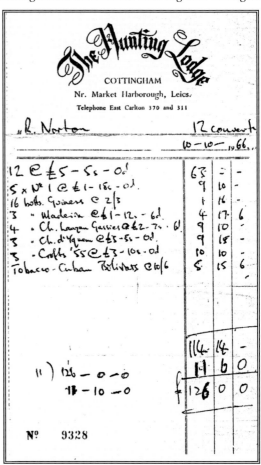

Hunting Lodge Receipt

hospitality shown to us by the Northamptonshire County Golf Club and also to those senior members in the 1950's, who conceived the idea which has brought together a group of friends whose comradeship and sheer enjoyment of being together means so much."

The Golden Oldies

A very small coterie of friends, all of whom are not in their first prime of youth, have for some years met on an ad hoc basis two or three times every week to chat and to play nine holes of golf, the former when the weather is inclement, doubtful and wintry.

Many served in HM Forces during the war years. Many nurse arthritic joints or have had them replaced. Invariably they ride in buggies and take advantage of the brown tees which were created especially for them.

This particular brotherhood has existed for quite some years and perforce because of age occasionally a chair falls vacant without much warning, redolent of a Royal Air Force mess in wartime.

I think of Eric Roberts, a long-standing, professional journalist and broadcaster who played until recently, well into his nineties and has now had to retire and of Eric Douglas, another father figure in the Club, who died in 2006 aged 97.

John Ashley, an urbane and amusing soul, Don Barltrop, George Short, Eric Sleath, Philip Blacklee and Roger Mobbs … continue the tradition when others have long since abandoned their set of golf clubs to the attic. It is a joy to be admitted into this distinguished fraternity. Long may this group, also known as the Toffs, flourish!

The Dawn Patrol

The society was formed in 1965 by Peter Bennett, Tony Hood and John Pendry. Peter Bennett was a wavy-haired, cigar-smoking figure who had joined Brampton from Kingsthorpe Golf Club where he had been a member for a number of years. He had headed an American company trading in the UK at a factory in Round Spinney in Northampton known as Bostrom. Peter was an easygoing and agreeable man, playing off a handicap of about 15. John Pendry came to Northampton from away and was a co-founder of the Society with Tony Hood. Since then, many Club members have thrown their lot in with the Dawn Patrol and thus there have been new members and those who have died or who have left the area. The premise on which they play is that they should forgather prior to 7.30 am or first light in the dead of winter. Whosoever is there is eligible to participate in the draw so that they form themselves into fourballs. No one is excluded from the draw even if they are complete strangers and if there is an odd two or three ball, so be it, that is how the arrangement works.

The Dawn Patrol has always been very well supported by stalwarts of the Club including Keith Archbold, Robin Patterson, Michael Swain and Iain Burrage, Brian Mitchell, Michael Thomas, Jim Smith, Michael Bairstow, Ron Hamlyn, to name but a few.

It is said that George Mobbs coined the name of "Dawn Patrol" when he was Club Secretary because of their early morning start. The Dawn Patrol continues to this day in that same spirit whereby fourballs go off, largely before other members arrive and provide players with the opportunity to participate without the rigid necessity of fixing up by prior arrangement. This system has been especially helpful to new members who are gradually endeavouring to meet the established members of the Club. Peter Bennett has always been the guiding light throughout the years and has thus become the titular head as membership numbers increased. Frail health and advancing years has made it impossible for Peter to play with the gusto of former years. Over the years this Society has provided several Captains and hard working Committee men. The Society arranges its own golfing weekends away, various annual competitions are played for trophies, a visit to a course elsewhere, a snooker league and a variety of social events.

Now forty-two years on, their numbers have grown progressively. No one is turned away. One recently joined new member of our Club said to me with obvious pride "I have taken to playing with the Dawn Patrol several times a week. I have been made most welcome and it has led me to the acquisition of an immediate entrée into a new group of golfing friends. I have found no cliquishness and no fuss. Everyone who turns up is guaranteed a game. No one is left behind but you must turn up before 7.30 am". Thus the concept of dear Peter Bennett lives on.

As some of the founders have now retired from their working lives, the midweek early sessions have started, quite apart from those on Saturdays and Sundays. Once a year there is an organised shotgun start followed by a full English breakfast in the Clubhouse. There is also an annual match against the Ladies' section.

A snooker competition has also become part of the Dawn Patrol's curriculum, the trophy matches played away from our Golf Club. So far, the Dawn Patrol has produced three Brampton Golf Club Captains, namely Mike Bairstow, Keith Archbold and Robin Patterson. Many utterly friendly men have joined its ranks and left the area including John Pendry and some have sadly died, probably in a state of grace, thinking of our course and holing a long putt.

Over the years, the Dawn Patrol has always embraced within its ranks, dedicated members of our Club, who are invariably quick to volunteer themselves ready to render excellent service when a general "three line whip" or call for helpers goes out, such as ball spotting, bunker raking, starter duties and such like, whenever big competitions are staged.

Ron Hamlyn has served on the General Management Committee and Iain Burrage and Leslie Worthington are the official Club hosts to outside golfing societies. Jim Smith is the computer guru who has set up and maintains our Club website.

The Red Cat Golfing Society
Peter Arnold writes: "The Red Cat Golfing Society are due to celebrate their half century in the year 2009. The Red Cat Society began in 1959 and took its name from the Red Cat Hotel at North Wootton, near Kings Lynn, where they had previously stayed whilst playing in a cricket benefit match.

The first group comprised Peter Arnold, Jack Parry, Jack Belson, Ron Bird and Dick Hopkinson and were very soon after joined by Mike Warrington, George Scott, Dick Wells, Jack Bell, George Clarke, John Patterson and Lewis McGibbon,

Invariably invitation to join the party was left to the organiser, Peter Arnold, who appointed Mike Warrington as his Secretary (later followed by the late Roger Toseland) and Lewis McGibbon as his Treasurer. In later years many others, mainly drawn from the Church Brampton Golf Club membership, including several former Captains, were invited. Some found the trips too hectic and fell by the wayside.

The trips were always organised prior to the start of the cricket season. The weather was inevitably unpredictable and occasionally snow and wind predominated, which was not altogether surprising as the matches were always played in north Norfolk at the Royal West Norfolk Golf Club, Brancaster. It is at this Club where the Society compete for a trophy annually.

Other trips which have been organised over the years include visiting Woodhall Spa Golf Club and Cromer. The most frequent winner has been Laurie Johnson.

For many years a week's golfing tour was organised on the west coast of Ireland and the wearing of green sweaters and driving green Range Rovers caused eyebrows, on occasion, to rise. Only once whilst staying in Ireland was the party requested to leave a public house and that was at Ballina. In those times Golf Clubs of the ilk of Killarney and Ballybunion were all magnificent courses with reasonably priced green fees.

At the time of the last trip in 2002, such courses had become "Americanised" in quite a big way and green fees were considerably higher. We did, however, manage to find a number of exacting courses with modest green fees. We have also enjoyed trips to St Andrews where Alistair Ferrier and Tony Wright now reside having moved to Scotland some years ago.

On one occasion Lynn Wilson discovered a band playing in a village pub. Lynn persuaded the band to go with him to the hotel where the party was staying and it became one of the highlights of not only that trip but our collective memories.

Our two resident comedians, Mick Dent and Laurie Johnson, have kept us entertained through the years and many of the jokes have become apocryphal with constant repetition. The only time when we have been cautioned as to our noisy behaviour at a Golf Club was at our own, at Church Brampton, one Sunday lunchtime during our annual one club competition. The club professional, Stuart Murray, was with us at the time but not the actual culprit who caused the row, who has since departed.

From 1970 onwards we have kept a very careful record of every trip or get together and after all these years it makes fascinating reading for those involved.

So it is that next year we shall celebrate our half centenary at a time when our favourite Golf Club has just celebrated its own hundred years of existence."

The Agaric and St Botolph Golfing Societies
Since 1995 and the publication of Neil Soutar's book, these Societies have changed perforce by the loss of so many of the original members, through death and old age. A most expedient solution was found by merging the remaining Agarics with the remaining Botolphians.

After the passing of Alfred York, Chris Thompson took over as leader and organiser and we now play on Wednesdays in the winter months and on Tuesday afternoons, after the ladies in the summer season.

Happily, stalwart and charming replacements have bolstered the ranks and these include Dr Tom Ormerod, Ron Smith, Joe Pyke, Peter Darby, Richard Aitken, Peter St Quinton, Dennis Pritchard, Jorgen Romose and Ebbe Dinesen (a Dane whose family is related to the famous Danish authoress of Out of Africa, which was made into a box office record-breaking film). Others include John Devereux, Richard Marshall, Jerry Doyle and Jim Chater. A few are obliged to use motorised buggies. Some almost need a mobile Stannah chair lift to get in and out of the buggy! The fun and friendship and spirit of competitiveness remains.

One of the most interesting outings was to Killarney in 2001. Whilst one of our fourballs was holing out on the eighteenth green of that wonderfully beautiful golf course, an unknown gentleman walked over to us and told us of a fearful drama unfolding in the USA. By the time we had changed and entered the bar, a TV set with a very large screen was revealing the destruction of the World Trade Centre with the twin towers, live and as it actually occurred. All of those present then can say for certain what they were doing at that precise world shattering moment in their lives.

Annual visits to France continue, indulging our taste for good food and bolstering the sales of wine from this vinous land across the Channel.

St. Botolphs GS

CHAPTER XXII

Golfing Trophies And Events

"And be among her cloudy trophies hung".

Keats

The County Cup
Keith Mason writes about the origin and history of the County Cup:
Originally called the Newnham Cup, it was presented to the Club in 1962 by Harry Draper, our Captain in 1960 and named after the village where he lived. It was to be played for over 36 holes at the summer meeting, strictly for members only. In 1966 the competition changed its format to an Open event and the name changed to the County Cup. This was done to attract some of the better players in the Midlands' area (see narrative under George Mobbs).

In 1964 whilst still being played for as the Newnham Cup, George Mobbs won it by a single stroke, having taken a 12 at the tenth (now the fourteenth). In the greenside bunker for two, George slashed out over the hedge (in those days the wire strand fence was not out of bounds) and landed in some hoof marks on the bridle path. Heavy rain made a real quagmire of the lie and seven shots later he arrived back on the course! A chip onto the green and a single putt made up the 12 strokes. Six threes on the next seven holes got him back on track. Lesson learnt, never give up.

In the first year as an Open Competition, the cup was won by Andrew Forrester, a Worcestershire county player. Another early winner was Bob Durrant, county champion of Bedfordshire and an England international player. In preparation he came up to practise; while waiting to commence play he noticed an elderly gentleman of 80'ish on the putting green and offered to play nine holes putting for a shilling (for the younger members that's 5p.) The elderly gentleman pocketed the shilling having won three and two. Now the elderly man, as far as I know and verified by George Mobbs, our Secretary at the time, was and is to this day, the only "Putting Only" member for which he paid an annual sub of £10. 1971 saw the first teenage golfer who was established on the amateur circuit to win the Cup and that was Pip Elson, a member of Coventry Golf Club (Finham). His knowledge of the course must have been useful to him since he also won the British Youth Amateur Championship when it was played at Brampton later that year. Pip went on to become an accomplished professional.

Gary Coleman of Nottingham won in 1972. He owned a dance hall in Nottingham and this had to be open and ready for the Saturday night swingers. Having tied with – of all people – Peter McEvoy, he could not hang about while other players were completing their rounds. The organisers sent Gary and Peter down the first where Gary holed a big putt for a three to win. Luckily for the organisers, Conrad Cieslewicz, the one person in contention out on the course, lost a number of shots on the back nine to fade out of the running. Peter returned several times and in 1974 won the event. As we know he went on to become the British Amateur Champion twice, a member of the Walker Cup team on several occasions, then Captain of that team and finally a Walker Cup selector. On being presented with the County Cup he stated "Any top amateur who aspires to be in the top echelon of amateur golf in the United Kingdom should play on this fine course in this competition".

The following year saw another winner in Mark James who went on to win the English Amateur Championship before becoming a professional of the highest calibre and later Captain of the Ryder Cup team.

The winner in 1979 was an English international at schoolboy, youth and senior level who hailed again from a local club, Coventry. This was Paul Downes, easily recognised by his shock of bright red hair. In 1984 and 1986 the Cup was not played for due to lack of organisers in the Club, but Jack Humphries, who was then a member of the English Golf Union, resurrected the event and from then it has gone on to become one of the major events in the Midlands' area.

I took over the running of the event in 1989 when I first became a member of the General Committee and was given a position as assistant to Conrad Cieslewicz on the Golf and Competitions' Committee.

In the latter part of the 1990's we started to attract some of the golfers who were in the England elite squad and other notable amateur players. Oliver Wilson from Coxmoor Golf Club won in 1999 and went on to represent Great Britain and Ireland in the Walker Cup, playing in his first Ryder Cup in 2008. In 2003 the winner was Gary Wolstenholme, probably the best known amateur of our day and, like Peter McEvoy, twice a winner of the Amateur Championship. Last year's winner was Paul Maddy from Gog Magog Cambridge with two wonderful rounds of 67 and 68 for a cup winning 135.

The lowest winning score is 134, an outstanding achievement by home club member Adam Print.

We continue our support for this event by contacting as many of the top amateurs as possible in the run-up to the competition. Peter Walsh has given of his time most generously in support of this event since arriving as Secretary, as has one of our past Captains, Malcolm Peel.

May we, with the members' support, turn this into a top amateur event that will rival the likes of The Berkhamsted Trophy, The Berkshire and The Lytham Trophy?

The Corrin Cup
By W A (Bill) Stephenson
An extract from the Corrin Cup Minute Book:
"This trophy was the gift of John Bowes Corrin, Esq, OBE, FCA to commemorate his happy year of office as Captain of Northamptonshire County Golf Club. It is his wish that an annual competition of one round be played on the basis of Stableford points scoring, to which exclusively all past Captains will be invited. The immediate past Captain of the day shall organise the event as to invitations, catering and prizes. All participants shall contribute to the cost equally. Those past Captains who do not feel fit enough to compete are to be encouraged to attend the dinner which follows the competition. No other guest shall be invited.

Minutes shall be written to record faithfully the weather and features of the course and standard of play and any items of interest and amusement.

Those minutes relating to the previous year and for the 10 years earlier shall be read".

Thereby in these "tablets of stone" were laid down the fundamental rules and regulations of the Corrin Cup Competition and indeed its exclusiveness.

The inaugural meeting of course was the year following Jack Corrin's Captaincy and this took place on 28 September 1979. Ten past Captains took part and the event was won by Spriggs Baillon with 35 points playing off a handicap of 18 and his is the first name on the trophy.

It was incumbent on Jack to organise the event and, as you would expect from an accountant, the costs were particularly detailed and recorded. Nine past Captains dined at a cost of £5.50 each, including wine – Merlot at £2.90 a bottle – and the prizes were golf balls, as it is to the present day. Strangely enough the accounts show a

Corrin Cup

surplus of 5p but there is no record of this balance being carried forward at the following year's event!

The restriction on eligibility is very strictly enforced and whilst some might say that it would be courteous to invite the current Captain he must wait until his title carries the "past" prefix and is able to wear the past Captain's tie. This tie is in itself part of the proceedings with fines being threatened if one is not worn.

In accordance with Jack's wishes, the minutes of the previous year's meeting and those of ten years earlier are religiously read by the immediate past Captain often to great hilarity, for it was his further wish that the event was to be a happy light-hearted occasion. The event has now been played some twenty-eight times and time has moved on. The past Captains have decided, in order to expand Jack's intent, to read additionally the minutes of even earlier meetings. This further cements Jack Corrin's wish for the event, in it's own way, to form part of the history of the Club and be brought to the fore.

Jack Corrin was a very well respected Captain of the Club and in donating the trophy he has left his own legacy. Past Captains take great pleasure in taking part in the event, even though it might only be for attendance at the post-match dinner, but the greatest endeavour is to have their name engraved on the trophy for posterity.

Events at Northamptonshire County Golf Club
English Ladies' Close Amateur Championship 18-22 May 2004

An extract from The County – Autumn 2004

The production team had convened, the stage had been set, and finally practice day arrived and seventy-three ladies arrived to test their skills against our challenging course. The course had actually been lengthened to a distance of 6117 yards; an increase of 274 yards with three par 5's becoming par 4's. The highlight of this practice day was undoubtedly a hole-in-one for Fame More from Chesterfield and a Curtis Cup player, when she holed out with an 8 iron on the third hole.

Round one 18 May started really well for Danielle Masters and Emma Duggleby, Curtis Cup team members, who showed us all how golf should be played when they both eagled the fifth. Is this really the same game that "normal" Club members play?

So it was too, on the following day, when Emma was still in the lead having birdied the second, sixth, ninth, twelfth and sixteenth holes - one bogey on the thirteenth! Her play on the ninth had to be seen to be believed. Having driven into the trees way out right near the fifteenth green she played out of the trees through a gap to the front of the green and sank a 20ft putt for a birdie. The stuff that dreams are made of.

The highlight of the day was the play-off for one place between five players and this was won by Katie Dobson on the third extra hole - really nail-biting stuff.

The 20 May gave us two match play rounds and we were treated to consistently awesome demonstrations of how golf can be played, and I know I was not alone in thinking "If only I had started playing this game at an early age; if only I had practised more" - the whole day was a delight to behold.

The quarter and semifinals were played out in fine style and our finalists emerged - Kerry Smith from Waterlooville and Shelley McKevitt from Reading.

Saturday was a bright, clear, chilly day and our Club members once again earned much praise for the way in which the Club rose to the challenge of hosting such a prestigious event in the ELGA calendar.

Although it would have been more encouraging to have had more members just turning up as spectators, those who did venture out were well rewarded with an excellent final under superb conditions with Kerry Smith emerging as the winner after nine attempts in this championship.

Praise must go to Ele Brooks who was a co-opted member of ELGA for this event and who represented our Club efficiently and who well deserved the thanks and praise given to her by the ELGA officials at the presentation.

Thanks too to those Club members who willingly acted as ball spotters and caddies, those who acted as cloakroom monitors and to those who hosted the players over the days of the competition - on and off the course - you all played your part in making this event such a success.

And praise too for our own dedicated ladies who helped to organise this event.

The Atlantic Cup

Peter Lock advises - In 2003, our Vice-Captain Peter Lock, was chatting in the professional's shop with Tim Rouse who asked if he had given any thought to a venue for his 'away trip' during his Captain's year of office. Although Tim himself regarded it as perhaps a little ambitious, he suggested that it might be worth considering a match based on the Ryder Cup format, against an American club with a similar name to ours.

Having established a degree of interest with some of the members, Peter then investigated the idea further and found that there were at least two clubs in the USA incorporating the name 'Northampton'. Peter decided to contact Northampton Country Club in Pennsylvania because of its relatively close proximity to New York. Thus a letter was sent in September 2003 to ask if they would consider such an event and with hindsight, Peter thinks that the key sentence in his letter was "although we regard golf as serious fun, we would also look upon this proposal as a social event at which we would also hope to establish new friendships." The response from Pierre Bohemond, the club's General Manager, was positive and was followed by a lengthy exchange of e-mails between Pierre and Peter to finalise the details. As 2004 was a Ryder Cup year, it was agreed that the matches would be played during the same week. Also, during this exchange of correspondence, it was suggested by Tom Plath, the American Captain, that the clubs should play for a trophy which subsequently became known as 'The Atlantic Cup.'

A notice was posted in the club inviting members to form a team of 12 players but ultimately the list became over-subscribed and the two clubs agreed that each side should comprise 16 players. Those participating covered a wide range of ages and handicaps and it was therefore proposed that the matches consist of eight greensomes, eight fourballs and 16 singles. Thirty-six holes a day and the inclusion of foursomes were both unanimously considered as "undesirable"! Another school of thought might have said "What a pity!".

Although Peter and his American counterpart arranged the logisitics of the event. participation by the team members in the organisation of the trip gathered momentum and several ideas were forthcoming. For example, sponsorship for the team strip was secured and gift packs for the American team were collated.

On Wednesday 15th September 2004, the team flew from Heathrow to JFK airport, New York and travelled onward by coach to their hotel in Easton, Pennsylvania. Other than the fact that they were keen golfers, our own club members knew little about the people they were about to meet. To quote one member, "We were all somewhat reticent and apprehensive of what might await us." From the warm welcome we received at the hotel a feeling of general camaraderie rapidly developed and any such concerns were quickly forgotten. It was instantly apparent that we had fallen into the company of a party of very likeminded individuals.

The Americans play their golf in buggies and when the team arrived at the course on Thursday morning for lunch and an official practice round, 16 buggies - each labelled with the players names and loaded with their clubs (which had been collected earlier from the hotel) - were lined up like a squadron of tanks in readiness.

In the evening the whole team was completely overwhelmed by an official opening ceremony when, standing beneath the Union Flag and the Stars and Stripes, both teams stood in awe as a band of pipers suitably attired in traditional Scottish dress marched towards them down the 18th fairway. One of the team, Dick Zielinski recalls "There were probably about 150 people present and it sent a chill down my spine and a lump in my throat as I gazed round and began to wonder what we might have started."

Speeches followed during which Peter was presented with a proclamation from the equivalent of our local mayor. Both teams enjoyed a welcoming dinner in the sumptuous club house and the conversation turned towards Friday's opening matches.

All attired in the team strip, generously sponsored by Barclaycard, the NCGC team was defeated in the first day's greensomes but worse was to follow later that evening. A tropical storm suddenly struck and flooded the course which inevitably cancelled the second round of matches. As a result our American hosts hastily arranged for the following day's singles matches to be played on another course as it was clear that their own course would be unplayable for several days. The end result was a narrow victory for the home side but needless to say the NCGC team were convinced that things might have been different had all the matches been played!

On Sunday evening following the presentation ceremony during which our captain was presented with the American flag duly signed by each member of the US team and folded triangularly in traditional American military fashion, the teams enjoyed a celebration dinner. The festivities continued into the early hours.

The following morning the team departed and enjoyed a few days further holiday in New York City before flying home.

It was originally proposed that a return match would be played in the UK in 2006 but the American team were anxious to visit us earlier. The next match was therefore arranged for 2005. Fifteen of the original sixteen NCGC participants took part and on this occasion, captained by Malcolm Peel, the home side was triumphant reflecting the significance of local knowledge. This factor was further endorsed by the Americans who achieved another resounding victory on their home soil in 2007.

It has now been decided that, subject to the ongoing agreement of both clubs, the matches will be contested on a biennial basis with the Americans due to come to Church Brampton in this our centenary year.

Atlantic Cup Team
Back row left to right: Steve Russell, Les Cantrell, Bob Andrews, Michael Bairstow
Dick Zielinski, Peter Topping, John Raphael, Tony Hewitt
Front Row left to right: Chris Hanley, Jeff Jacobs, Ashley Major, Andrew Nicholson
Peter Lock (Captain), David Green, Brian O`Connell, Godfrey Hammon

CHAPTER XXIII

The Passing Show

"Where my caravan has rested,
Flowers I leave you on the grass".

Edward Teschemacher

Artists
Christopher Thompson, our Club Chairman, recently showed me a copy of the history of Bamburgh Castle Golf Club in Northumberland. This is a lovely seaside course within sight of Bamburgh Castle. It is a links course, always made difficult by the cold winds blowing in from the North Sea, so it seems to the occasional visitor. However, the locals love it and thrive on it, as do the Scots.

Sir William Russell Flint RA PRWS, perhaps one of the most distinguished water-colourists of the twentieth century and a painter whose brilliance enabled him to depict naked or semi-naked ladies in the best possible and most modest and subtle way, was a visitor to this Golf Club after World War I.
During World War I, Russell Flint had flown in an airship over the course whilst serving in the Royal Naval Air Service. He spotted the glorious near-white sands of a large deserted beach and vowed to return and paint it, once the war was over. This he did, embracing the view from the course over this lovely beach to Holy Island. The picture now has pride of place in their Clubhouse.
Sir William spent many of his later years in the Mediterranean both in the south of France and Spain - the scenario for many of his most famous pictures. These have been reproduced and grace many a study wall or even some drawing-rooms and are highly popular. The originals at the time of writing generally realise somewhere between £35,000 and £85,000 in the London auction rooms. I simply mention this because it shows the desirability and value which collectors put on them.
This led me to thinking of artists who have known our own course. G H B Holland, one of Northampton's most distinguished artistic sons who achieved considerable distinction as a portrait painter, was born and bred in Northampton and trained at the Leicester School of Art before moving to Chelsea where he took a studio near to the great Augustus John.

George Holland was commissioned by me to paint an oil scene from the fourteenth tee looking back over the thirteenth hole towards the tenth and this is now to be seen in the dining room of the Club. Simultaneously he did several other oil paintings of various other golf holes and I know that two of them were purchased by the late E G (Tim) Harley. One of these gave a glimpse of the third hole from tee to green. It was painted on a bright sunny afternoon in May. On the left of the bridle road, large tracts of broom in full flower were prevalent then all the way to the hole. One could almost smell the perfume of the broom and hear the melodic cries of the birds in one's mind's eye. George Holland caught the beauty of the scene as with careless rapture. Tim Harley saw it being painted as he passed and expressed the wish to buy it, there and then. Alas, the broom has now gone being superseded by a colonnade of oak trees, all self sown or the work of squirrels.

Roger Corfe, a retired dental surgeon and also an enthusiastic and gifted amateur artist was commissioned by Rodney Haig to do a number of Golf Club drawings and watercolours.

The late **E J (Ted) Dolby** was also a gifted amateur artist. He was the General Manager and Director of the old Northampton Town and County Building Society, which later became known as the Anglia Building Society, and had a very good personal art collection. He had painted continuously from his school days and there is an oil painting by him of the seventeenth green in the Clubhouse, a gift from the artist, when he was a member.

Clifford Ellison, for some time a member but now retired and living in Wiltshire, was an art restoration expert. He held the Royal Warrant as a restorer of Her Majesty the Queen's pictures and dealt with many that are in the Queen's Gallery at Buckingham Palace including a number of Canalettos. He is a most interesting person who started life at the Chelsea School of Art and was an artist in his own right until he took up restoration of Old Master paintings after the war.

One of our members, **Brian Ball**, had artistic training and spent his working life as a commercial artist for Clarke and Sherwell and is much talented and I know he has been extremely helpful to Richard Catlow in the production of the Club Newsletter.
Are there any other budding artists amongst us?

Lost Formats
In the annals of pre-war golf, mention is made of four ball eightsomes taking place on our course. Until reading the latter I was quite unaware that such things have in the past and do, even now, take place. I know that three ball sixsomes were played some years ago at Aldeburgh Golf Club in Suffolk. They were always played on a Sunday and were mixed, as I understand it, and were very sociable indeed. I imagine that four ball eightsomes would be similar social affairs, eminently suitable for bank holiday golf one might think. The course would accommodate a great many golfers on such an occasion and it might remind those who served in her majesty's forces of an infantry platoon out on patrol!

Hoylake
One of our members, Dr Tom Ormerod, owns a copy of Golf at Hoylake - a book published in 1990, reviewing 120 years of the history of the Royal Liverpool Golf Club.
Within a medley of gossipy anecdotes about members past and present, it refers to a ticklish moment which occurred in the 1930's there, concerning a member of some standing (reputedly a retired colonel), who was discovered in his motorcar in a compromising situation with a female member of staff just near to the seventh green.
An emergency Council Meeting was called during which someone who knew the gentleman concerned very well, explained that he had planned to bequeath a large some of money for the benefit of the Club in his will. Thus it was that this caused more than a measure of

controversy inasmuch as one faction of the Council was adamant that he should be thrown out of the Club in disgrace, whilst the remainder wished to be rather more pragmatic in the sure and certain hope of clinging to the eventual inheritance for the Club.

After agonising about the matter for quite some time, a compromise was found whereby the gentleman in question was deemed to be "out of bounds" at the time and thus not on the course. In this way the Club rules could be deemed not to apply.

The car park at Hoylake used to be a bowling green until the late 1950's and has been the scene of one or two incidents over the years.

An old lady in a scruffy raincoat was walking out of the car park just after the war to the bus stop near by. A newish member stopped and politely asked her if he could give her a lift. The lady was suitably grateful and as she got into the car he asked "How long have you been working here?". In a firm and rather cultivated voice she said without any undue fuss "Oh, I'm a member". The new member became even more embarrassed when he discovered later that she was a past Ladies' Captain and the sister of Hoylake's senior past Captain.

* * * * *

A tale concerns one of our own members who claimed to have visited our course late one summer evening with his secretary and took advantage of the car park close to the third hole. It was a mild, balmy evening, the remains of a beautiful day. The couple walked several holes in the moonlight and enjoyed the serenity of the course with scarcely a breath of breeze. Whatever followed, it is a fact that our own member was certainly within bounds, although no gossip reached the ears of the elder statesmen and mandarins of power at Brampton.

* * * * *

I am also reminded that there was a tricky situation concerning a female member of our own staff whereby one of our quite elderly members, a good player and who was in the leather industry, made something of a fool of himself by becoming involved in a dalliance with this particular lady. It certainly endangered his marriage and in his case he faced the full fury of the Club Committee members at the time who told him in no uncertain terms that he could do what he liked elsewhere but should avoid any imbroglio with a lady member of staff. Good staff were hard to get and certainly should not be upset by members in this way with a risk of causing them to leave. This earned the offending member the soubriquet which was given to him by the late Alan Thorne of "The Canteen Romeo".

Frank Roe later relating the tale to someone else got the details rather muddled and referred to the offender as the "Larder Lover" which brought a good deal of merriment to our ears for a short time!

"Timken Golfers"

Mr Stephen Bennett succeeded the late Sir John Pascoe as Chairman of British Timken, a large company based at Duston on the western edge of Northampton. British Timken was the British arm of American Timken, a very large and powerful international company. The factories manufactured high grade roller and tapered bearings which were so essential for the war effort and the post-war economic recovery of industry. The company was established in the UK before the war at Aston in Birmingham but came to Northampton as a wise precaution when the threat of the Blitz was at its height and the Midlands were under the attack of the Luftwaffe with heavy air raids on Coventry, Birmingham etc. British Timken moved to Duston and acquired a large site which was gradually expanded over the years until the firm became Northampton's largest employer and that was the situation by the end of the war and in the immediate post-war years. Sadly the buildings are no longer extant and the site is in the process of redevelopment.

Sir John Pascoe dominated the company and it was his company's philanthropy and sponsorship which led to the revival of the fortunes of Northamptonshire County Cricket Club in the desperate post-war era. At that time Northamptonshire regularly propped up the bottom of the County Championship table and because of his own personal enthusiasm and his company's help, the process of the recruitment of fine cricketers was initiated. They included George Tribe, an Australian all-rounder and former test player under Sir Donald Bradman, Jack Manning, Jock Livingstone, Peter Arnold, Albert Nutter, Reg Partridge, Gordon Garlick and a host of others. All of them were persuaded to play for Northamptonshire and were guaranteed a winter job at British Timken.

Perhaps the greatest coup of all was the enlistment of the amateur F R "Freddie" Brown as skipper of the side. Freddie had last played for England in the famous bodyline series in Australia under the captaincy of Douglas Jardine, having then only just left Cambridge and was thought to be a very promising all-rounder. He certainly was a fine leader and aggressive batsman but by 1945-46 many thought Freddie's playing days were virtually over as he had been taken prisoner of war and had been denied the playing of cricket for quite some years. However, this was not to be. Freddie was enticed into becoming the Captain of Northamptonshire, which he did to such effect that their fortunes were turned and they became a fine county side under his leadership, and following that, by Dennis Brookes. In 1953 Freddie also had a huge impact on the MCC side and finally wrested back the Ashes from the Australians in 1953 after so many years.

Stephen Bennett who succeeded Sir John Pascoe as Company Chairman was a bespectacled, highly civilised gentleman, who looked more of an academic than a captain of industry. Perhaps that is really what he was because he had a Cambridge background and his wife, Valerie, who lived in the village of Church Brampton for quite some years after the death of Stephen, was a former ballerina and a great beauty.

A fanatically keen golfer, Stephen Bennett gathered round himself a coterie of his staff and employees on Saturday and Sunday mornings. They were a closed society within the Club and these included Ronnie Knapp, Stan Jakeman, Ted Canning, Richard Ruffell and others as well as Stephen Bennett's own son, William, first as a schoolboy, then undergraduate. They were regarded in a friendly way as a club within the Club.

The late Raymond Tuckey, although a Director of British Timken, was not part of this particular society. He played quite independently and is referred to elsewhere in the narrative of this book.

Later Avon Cosmetics, another American manufacturing company, set up a factory in Northampton in the late 1950's. This company which flourished for about forty years, eventually moved most of its UK operation to Poland. A number of its top executives became members of our Club and enjoyed its amenities.

Seven out of Ten
Northamptonshire have won the Anglian Counties Golf League twice in thirty-five years under the captaincy of Richard Halliday in 1972 and again under the late Dick Biggin in 1991: both were members of the County Club and Dick has a seat in his memory on the course at the eighth.
In March 1972 the county first team selection committee met for the first and last time. The players judged to be the best eight in the county plus two reserves were picked for the season. The theory was that players good enough to be selected in the first place were also good enough to play themselves into form for the matches.
The county team, drawn throughout from those ten players, enjoyed a perfect record: played five, won five. Over the course of the season none of the ten scored worse than 50% in either singles or foursomes.
Seven members of that team were Brampton members. They have since produced one President of the Midland Golf Union, four Presidents of the Northamptonshire Golf Union, three County Champions, thirteen times between them and five winners of the County Scratch Foursomes. The seven have served the Club in various ways. They have provided Committee men, Trustees, Vice-Presidents and various other officers of the Club. Three of them have been Captain. Their names feature prominently on the honours boards. Some still play effective golf among the seniors. Others stay in hiding, only venturing out anonymously when the course is empty. Each of the seven has won our Club Championship at least once.

President's Putter
Currently Malcolm Peel enters this event every year, which shows both fortitude and resilience, bearing in mind his age. A number of other distinguished golfers also make a point of being there each January and face the fiercely cold winds and, on occasion, snow. As there are so many younger entrants, winning the putter may be "a bridge too far" but it is the continued participation that is so important.
The following headline and short report appeared in The County, Spring 2007.
"Stalwart Peel remains happily defiant in Rye defeat"
Richard Catlow writes:
Past Captain Malcolm Peel hit the headlines in the national dailies on 3 January by reason of his considerable feat of participating at Rye in the Oxford and Cambridge Golfing Society's President's Putter for the 45th time. Since the tournament continues in any weather except thick snow, only the most intrepid "stalwart" succeeds in building up such a record. Having survived the rigours of Rye for more than two hours "windswept and ruddy-faced" Malcolm with wife Marion, who has recently retired as our Ladies' Secretary, will next undertake an exploration of Chile and Patagonia. There Malcolm will surely remain as cheerful as always, but, fortified by the experience of Rye, "happily defiant" even in the face of occasional misfortune.

Golf Club Aviators
Throughout the Club's history we seem to have had several playing members who owned their own aircraft or who flew regularly. These include Jack Jeyes, one of the great

pharmacist family in Northamptonshire, a tall and gentle soul who lived at Holly Lodge at Boughton Green, the family home, in which his grandson still resides. This is a large stone Victorian Gothic house with various Gothic follies associated with and contiguous to it. Its entrance gate has always been ornamented with various gardening tools which have given it a certain distinction.

Jack Jeyes flew with considerable bravery as a pilot in the Royal Flying Corps during World War I and his exploits are written up in the history of the Royal Flying Corps. After that war and in the 1920's, Jack became a shareholder and active member of the flying club at Sywell Aerodrome. By the time World War II broke out he was back in the Royal Air Force but by this time he was in his forties and thus not considered suitable for active service but actually flew various types of aircraft, including the Anson. As an elderly officer, in service terms he was generally consigned to deal with administrative duties. Jack Jeyes was a longstanding member of our Golf Club.

Henry Deterding was just such another who lived in a fine house at Newnham. His wife was Mrs Winnie Deterding and both were not only keen golfers but very supportive members of our Club before World War II, during it and for a time afterwards. Henry Deterding's father was one of the pioneering owners of Shell Petroleum, which, of course, made the family enormously wealthy. Henry's elder brother entered the business and legend has it that Henry was told by his father that he would be provided with an equal amount of capital, to compensate him for not going into what was, in effect, the family firm. Thus, Henry lived as a landowning gentleman of leisure and means. He became

Henry Deterding (third left) in Budapest in 1935

a keen aviator and organised a landing strip, complete with air sock at Newnham, from which he flew his own light aircraft wherever he wanted to go, provided that there was a suitable airfield upon which to land.

Henry would frequently fly to Sywell and get himself conveyed by one means or another from Sywell to the golf course whenever he played at Church Brampton. This has often been pondered by us as something of a mystery. Perhaps it was the thrill of the flying that made him do it because it must have been just as quick to travel by motor car from Newnham to Church Brampton, as his wife used to do. When playing with his wife at Brampton, they broke all records for speed. Their singles match would be completed in one and a half hours. Is this a record?

Mike Costin was co-founder with the late Keith Duckworth of Cosworth Engineering, both of whom have achieved near immortality in their own lifetime as brilliant designers of racing motor car engines (see separate article).

One of Mike's keenest interests is to fly gliders and he has so far clocked up 3,500 hours piloting his glider. Michael built a glider in his own workshop which he flew for many years. Currently Mike owns a quarter share in a four-seater aircraft made by Robin, the French aeronautical company. He also flew the company aircraft of Cosworth Engineering and his log book shows over 2,500 hours flying time in powered aircraft, plus the gliding hours.

John Belson is another aviator - son of Jack Belson – and a former regular RAF Officer and later instructor in flying modern airliners.

I mention but four persons having private flying licences and their own aircraft but of course the Club is and was rich in former wartime pilots in the Royal Air Force and Fleet Air Arm, many of whom are mentioned elsewhere in this narrative.

L T "Pip" Hadden is also a long-standing member of the Golf Club. Born in South Wales his parents moved across the Bristol Channel to Somerset for business reasons and so Pip's formative years were spent in Somerset.

Called up into the RAF during the war, Pip was trained as a pilot in Canada and then brought back to the UK where he was due to be posted to a squadron. Pip must have been good because he was posted to Sywell Aerodrome as a training officer of Free French pilots, those who had escaped from Vichy France or from North Africa (Algeria) etc and wished to assist General de Gaulle's aggression against the Nazi regime. André Baldet, the well known local motor trader and former champion motor cyclist, was among the French who learned to fly at Sywell during those war years.

In 1944 Pip met his wife, Margaret, they were married and thus he settled in Northampton. When hostilities ended he joined Brooklands Aviation at Sywell as a test pilot but his ambition led him to seek and accept a job as a pilot with British Overseas Airways Corporation, first flying the Constellation, the Britannia and then the Comet, VC 10 and Super VC.

Pip tells me that he frequently transported members of the Royal Family all over the globe but was disappointed not to be able to fly Concorde as he was nearing the end of his working lifetime as a Commander. His log book shows about 15,000 hours of flying time and he has visited all the romantic places in the world. Among other things he experienced a wheels-up crash landing once at Karachi in the 1950's having circled the airport for three hours or so to use up the aviation fuel.

The NCGC Requisition Books

There have been three requisition books, each confined within hardbacked covers embossed in gold lettering "NCGC Requisition Book". The first lasted from 1911 until 1995, the second from 1995 until 2003, and the third from 2003 to the present day. At the present rate of progress we will be well into a fourth by the time we reach our centenary. The tabulation shows there have already been eight times as many requisitions in the second fifty years of the Club's existence as there were in the first fifty. Since the length of the requisitions and the Committee's replies are currently running at twice the length of those of our predecessors it might be thought that we of our generation have sixteen times as much chance of unearthing pearls of wisdom than they. It would be unduly critical of our more prolific latter-day requisitioners to suggest otherwise. Moreover the Committee endorses the inflationary trend. As recently as October 2005 the Secretary, in response to a requisition, assured members that "The Committee is happy to encourage greater use of the Requisition Book". With such support as that nobody need fight shy of recording their thoughts upon the open page.

Nevertheless access to "the open page" has not proved entirely straightforward. Over the years there has been an ongoing struggle for control of the right side pages. This continues to the present day. The contest began in 1930 when the Secretary stipulated, "Suggestions to be made on this side only (the left). This side (the right) reserved for the Committee's decision". On the next page, four requisitions later, he forgot his own edict and endorsed his response on the left side page. The membership immediately invaded the right side in force; the Committee riposted by ignoring the next ten requisitions.

Subsequent bids for exclusivity have been made with mixed results. At one point some distinguished signatures in support of a requisition on the left appeared, guerrilla-style, on the opposite page backed by little arrows pointing leftwards. In 2004 a former Captain surged onto the right side with a biblical quotation - unattributed - from Ecclesiastes 1.2, the only time this has happened. The following year as many as twenty-one members' signatures, made in support of a left sided requisition, overflowed onto the right. As a result every page in the book has now been marked "Requisition" or "Committee's Response". Has the membership been banished from the right forever? No doubt the Committee lives in hope.

Decade starting	Number of requisitions	Average words per requisition	Average words per Committee response
1910	21	30	10
1920	19	30	7
1930	8	28	6
1940	0	0	0
1950	8	25	2
1960	21	41	32
1970	50	31	26
1980	105	35	30
1990	139	38	33
2000	95	50	49
Totals	**466**	**308**	**195**

Our links with the past endure. The favourite topics remain constant - the price of tea and beer (excessive), the condition of the course (bad), and the provision of towels (inadequate) and the whereabouts of the Club nail brush (missing). Likewise the style of the suggestions, ranging as they do between proposal, entreaty, demand, and denunciation. And likewise the handwriting. Admittedly now, as in the past, some suggestions are made in a fine copperplate hand or in capital letters, but others are illegible. Some signatures are boldly and clearly inscribed, others are indecipherable. Nothing has changed.

There were no requisitions during either of the world wars, members having more important matters to think about. It puts our present concerns into perspective. However the continuing moratorium between 1945 and 1957 was attributable not so much to concentration on higher things as to the Secretaries of the day keeping the Requisition Book well hidden in their bottom drawer.

On the whole, our Secretaries have been patient with our foibles although seldom reluctant to hit the nail on the head. In June 1937 the Secretary replied to a requisition "Unnecessary as it is governed by common courtesy and the Rules of Golf". That reply would suffice to see off many a requisition. Add in the former Captain's recital of Ecclesiastes 1.2 and we have a design for living worthy of the work of any scratch handicap moral philosopher, and far shorter.

Only now and again do the Committee sound a little tart in their responses. For example, in 1990:

Requisition: "(In other clubs) the portraits of both Men's and Ladies' Captains are displayed in a prominent position so that they can be easily recognised by all members. Is there a prejudice in our club against this?".

Answer: "Yes".

It might have been suggested that it is incumbent on all members to identify the Captain, if only to offer him the courtesy of the course. However insofar as the perceived prejudice reflected a becoming modesty on the part of our past Captains, it should be firmly stated they have always presented a fine and manly appearance. The only possible exceptions are from the distant past when one or two of our Captains may have appeared now and again slightly the worse for wear. It goes without saying, of course, that all our Ladies' Captains have been and are both amiable and photogenic.

Is caution in the use of the Requisition Book recommended? Not really, but potential requisitioners may wish to reflect on the words of Edward FitzGerald:

"The Moving Finger writes; and having writ,
Moves on: nor all thy Piety, nor Wit
Shall lure it back to cancel half a Line,
Nor all thy Tears wash out a Word of it".

Once a member's thoughts are in the requisition book with his signature underneath, they are there for good: they will be mulled over not only by his contemporaries, but also by future generations, including, perhaps, another such as myself, writing for The County about the requisition books in advance of our bi-centenary in 100 years time.

In the meantime write on - but for best results keep to the left.

Dives Durus

CHAPTER XXIV

Our Club Professionals

"An ornament to their profession".

John Bunyan

Bill Cann - Professional 1953-66

Bill was a remarkable man of medium build, with a brick-red coloured face and he was by nature highly talkative. Bill's professional shop had a window directly overlooking the course and stood where the Secretary's office is now located. A wily eye was kept open by Bill for everyone who passed his shop en route to either the Gentlemen's or Ladies' locker room and he never missed an opportunity of trying to interest you in his merchandise and sell you something.

On one summer evening Bill had set up a teaching/practice device called "BIFF-IT". This was a normal type of golf ball attached to a considerable length of quarter inch thick elastic cable. Both ends of the cable were attached to fastening pegs which were driven into the ground. The procedure was to tee up the Biff-It golf ball and strike it with a wooden golf club or perhaps any club as you saw fit. The ball would always return to your feet. Thus practice became easy and quite a lot of members were persuaded to buy this device and set it up on their own lawns at home, including the late Harvey Gawthorne, and indeed it was quite a useful teaching aid, although one was never absolutely certain as to whether the practice drives were moving in precisely the correct direction, fade or draw being virtually undetectable.

I fell prey to Bill's salesmanship when he was using the device himself outside his shop on this particular summer evening. Bill demonstrated it and the ball returned to his feet to an absolute nicety every time he struck it. "Go on sir, you have a try". I did and I fell immediately into the trap of buying the kit.

* * * * *

On another occasion Bill made a wisecrack as I passed by his shop carrying a canvas and leather holdall in which my golfing attire was housed. This holdall had accompanied me throughout my army service days and was much travelled and showed the wear and tear of its years including, I confess, one or two small holes where it had become damaged. As I passed him, Bill eyed me up and down and his gimlet eyes fixed on the bag. "I see you've got a good nine-holer there, sir. I've got some nice new bags in my shop. "Yes, and as far as I'm concerned, they will remain there" said I. "I'm rather attached to this one"!

* * * * *

Dr Tom Ormerod writes:

"Bill Cann was a great character and a master salesman. If a member showed the slightest interest in any golfing equipment, he was after him until a sale had been made.

One day when I arrived at the Club, I found Bill standing in his doorway. Stuck firmly in the centre of the window overlooking the course was a large divot and in the centre of the lawn was the pit from whence it came.

Bill explained that a member had asked about the new Jack Nicklaus matched clubs that had just come onto the market, as this great golfing star began to hit the headlines as a great champion. A member casually mentioned the new Nicklaus clubs in a kind of rhetorical way in passing to Bill Cann one day. Cann scented the possibility of a sale so he went to some personal trouble to order a set and have them in his shop and he then telephoned the member and invited him to come and try them out, which he did. Taking a seven iron out on to the lawn, the member took a few swishes and then tried a proper practice swing . He hit it "fat", and projected the divot onto the window. I asked the professional if the member had bought the set of clubs. "No", said Bill, "He had the cheek to tell me that he always bought his clubs from the Army and Navy Store!".

Bill Cann's salesmanship was never better illustrated than when reject golf balls first went on sale. These were regularly named balls with so called "paint defects" - Pin High, GBDs and Dunlop 65s.

Bill had a tea chest full of reject balls in his shop and he offered them at a bargain price, then about 2 shillings each. Bill hardly sold any of these balls as the members at Brampton were not going to play with rejects! However, two weeks later when I went into the shop the lot had been sold. "How did you do that?" I asked. Bill pointed to a sign he had put over the box which read Undersized balls. These balls can be driven much further than standard balls. Not legal for competitions!".

* * * * *

Clive Blackburn writes:

Bill Cann was the professional when I first joined Northamptonshire County Golf Club in 1960. On fine days many of the items from his stock were displayed on the small lawn. Any member or visitor who entered the shop was at the mercy of Bill's sales patter and it was impossible to escape without at least buying something, even if it was only half a dozen tee pegs.

* * * * *

Mrs Gardiner-Hill was a formidable Lady Golfer who was once playing our course in a Ladies' veterans' match as the visitors' Captain. By her very nature, she was an assertive, masterful and determined character. There was deference and respect wherever she went and graciousness pervaded whenever she played as a guest away from home, so to speak. Lesser mortals quailed before her, both men and women.

On this particular occasion, it was a rather hot and humid day and she knew that our course had a reputation for flies being something of a nuisance on the holes near to Harlestone Firs and she did not wish to be troubled by such pestilence. To her irritation she found that she had not brought a suitable fly repellent with her and she feared that her perfume might well invite visits from these insects.

Mrs Meg Tennent recommended that she should seek help from Mr Bill Cann, the professional, and ask whether he could provide her with an anti-fly spray of some sort.

When Mrs Gardiner-Hill made the inquiry in the shop, Bill Cann was ever ready with an instant response "Yes, madam, I cannot sell you one, but you are welcome to borrow mine". True to form Bill added saucily "but you will find that flies never land on good meat!".

* * * * *

Bill Cann once told me that one of his great pleasures was to be invited to join Dr Tom Tennent as a holiday guest at Llanfairfechan in North Wales. Dr Tennent was the Superintendent at St Andrew's Convalescent Hospital on the Billing Road, an institution which also owned a convalescent hospital in North Wales. Patients would go there for recuperation and rest.

Dr and Mrs Tennent would also go there for a few weeks in the summer. Nothing pleased Bill Cann more than to be taken as a holiday guest there to play golf every day with Dr Tennent. Bill Cann said "Over all the years that I played there, I never once beat Dr Tennent because he always made me play off the teeing ground farthest back while he played off the foremost tee that he could find. I needed a bike to reach mine! I suspect that Bill Cann was too wily a bird to win the matches. Much better to play the customer's game!

Stuart Reynolds
An article by P Walsh, Secretary from The County – October 2005:
It is with a great deal of disappointment and sadness that I have to report that Stuart has decided to leave the world of golf and take up a new and different way of earning a living. Stuart has decided that even with his obvious high level of skill on the course and his highly regarded teaching, he needs a new challenge on the work front.

Those who have purchased a series of lessons will not lose out but need to be aware that the pre-booked lessons should be taken as soon as possible. The likely time-scale when they should be completed by is before the end of the year.

We have been fortunate enough to have had Stuart's services for over ten years and there is no doubt whatsoever that he will be sorely missed. The guidance and encouragement he has given to juniors has been immense and it will be very difficult to fill the gap he leaves behind him.

The Club wish him well in his search for new employment and if anyone can assist in this field I am sure he will be pleased to hear from them.

I would like to thank him for all he has done for the members and as an ambassador for this Club. He has been outstanding on the Midlands' circuit and I am sure no one will ever forget his record-breaking score of 59 achieved at Burton-on-Trent. It is hoped that he will not sever his association with Brampton and we look forward to seeing him back here for many years to come.

In 2008, Stuart has regained his amateur status, already winning best gross and nett amateur prize in the NGU Open in spite of very little time to practise.

Len Holland
Richard Catlow writes:
Len Holland was our pro from 1910 until 1924. Born in Burgess Hill in Sussex, he was an assistant at Sheringham Golf Club, from where he applied for and obtained the post here.

At first he was expected to double up as professional and course supervisor, but he found it impossible to devote enough time to the course and soon gave up that part of the job. He was a fine golfer, setting a professional course record of 64 in September 1924, remarkable scoring with the equipment of the day even over the original course layout. He was a strong all-round player, but the strength of his game was his iron play, his favourite club being the one iron. By the topmost standards his putting was reckoned to be only moderate, nevertheless he won the Midland Professional Foursomes in 1913, 1919, 1920 and 1921, the Yorkshire Evening News Tournament in 1924, the West of England Open in 1930 and many other events. His record in the Open Championship between 1920 and 1924 set out below was a model of consistency, marking him out as a golfer of the highest class.

If 2006 prize money were applied to these placements, Len would have earned over £400,000 over the course of those four tournaments alone. Sadly, however, only slim pickings were available to him in the early 1920s.

Year	Venue	1st Round	2nd Round	3rd Round	4th Round	Total	Placing
1920	Royal Cinque Ports	80	78	71	79	308	5th
1921	St Andrews	78	78	76	74	306	16th
1922	Royal St George's	79	81	74	76	310	13th
1924	Hoylake	74	78	78	78	308	6th

* * * * *

Peter Palmer writes:

My parents were both founder members of the Club and were both playing one day with Len Holland the professional. At the fifth hole (now the ninth) he drove the green, the ball pitching on the teeside of the brook and bouncing in a capricious way on the hard frosty surface of the fairway. It was as if his ball had bounced on a concrete path and it leapt onto the green.

Peter recalls that Len Holland was a wonderful character and in due course was succeeded by W G Saunders.

Tim Rouse

Our current professional joined the staff at Church Brampton in 1991 and quickly established himself as a fine teacher of the game. Born in Grimsby, Lincolnshire, in 1959, Tim first became an assistant at Grimsby Golf Club in 1975, qualifying as a member of the P G A in 1989. He served at various Golf Clubs before becoming Club professional at Hearsall Golf Club, Coventry, in 1982.

Tim has held various distinguished offices which include the Captaincy of Warwickshire P G A in 1986 and Northamptonshire P G A in 2002-03 and chairmanship of Warwickshire county P G A in 1988, 1989 and 1990 and Vice-Chairman of Northamptonshire P G A in 2002-08. In 1992 he was Midland P G A Captain and Chairman in 1988-90 and 2004-08. Tim has coached and been swing instructor to several European tournament professionals, as well as leading amateur players, county teams and beginners of the game, invariably backed-up by competent teaching assistants.

Tim always has a pleasant demeanour and is charming. He runs a good shop, stocking excellent merchandise.

Nick Soto

Nick joined our Club in 1989 as a 13 year-old schoolboy after taking lessons at the Saturday morning junior classes conducted by Andy Jolly (assistant professional to Stuart Brown). Making rapid progress as a gifted young player, Nick soon represented the Club at junior level and then the Club side in the scratch league. He played Northamptonshire county golf from 1997 to 2001 and was picked for the Midlands' team in 1999 and 2000.

Amongst Nick's trophies are the Club Championship in 1999, the County Cup in 1999 and 2001 and the Northamptonshire County Open Championship in 1999.

In 2001 Nick became a professional and is now a fully qualified member of the P G A and returned to Church Brampton as an assistant professional to Tim Rouse in 2006. He has become another smiling, friendly face in the professional shop and also teaches.

Ed Chapman

Ed, the latest assistant professional to join Tim Rouse's staff, started playing golf at the age of 16, after playing cricket, tennis and football. At 19, with a handicap of 3, he started the PGA training programme with the ambition of becoming a full-time coach. Ed has a regular class for aspiring girl golfers most Sundays and the main highlight of his professional career to date has been his course record 65 at Staverton Park, on his way to finishing tied 4th in the NGU Open.

CHAPTER XXV

The Shape Of Things To Come

"The shape of things to come".

H G Wells

e are privileged to have amongst our membership a coterie of talented golfers, both young and experienced who have done a great deal so far for the prestige of Northamptonshire County Golf Club and the county sides and promise much more to come. They are in alphabetical order:

Gillian Curley

Gillian became a golfer following in her father's footsteps, himself a scratch player, on leaving university and joined Ladbrook Park Golf Club in Warwickshire. Later she joined Edgbaston Golf Club where she was Club Champion and represented Warwickshire.

In 1992 Gillian won the Goodyear Challenge Cup, an 18 hole medal competition open to lady golfers of handicap 26 or lower in Northamptonshire, Leicestershire and Warwickshire. Gillian joined our Club in 1999 and played for the county team in the years 2003, 2004 and 2006.

In 2005 Gillian represented Brampton in the final of the Coronation Foursomes with Annie Haig on the Jubilee course at St Andrews, Fife, Scotland.

Gillian won the Midlands' English Ladies' Senior Championship in 2006 and in 2007 she was the Emirates' Ladies' Amateur Champion. She also represents the Club in the scratch league team.

Kelly Hanwell

Kelly started playing golf at the age of nine at Northampton Golf Club and became a junior member at Brampton between 1991 and 1994, later rejoining as a full Lady member in 2005. Kelly has been a member of the county team from 1994 onwards and featured in the county's first ever appearance in the national finals in the year 2005, jointly with Kirstie Jennings, which was played at Brancepeth Castle Golf Club in County Durham. The team was ably led by non-playing Northamptonshire county captain Heather Williams.

Kelly was awarded a golf scholarship to the University of Arkansas where she graduated with a degree in financial management. In 1995, Kelly reached the semi-finals of the English Girls' Championship and represented the England girls in home internationals at Northop Country Park Golf Club in the same year.

Kelly won the English Schools' Championship at Sherwood Forest Golf Club in 1996 and in the same year represented the English Schools' team against Scotland and Wales and was also the girls' team captain.

In 2001 Kelly won the Midland Ladies' Championship and was Northamptonshire county Champion in 2002, 2006 and 2007. Kelly has won many other trophies and her lowest handicap was scratch. At the time of writing her current handicap is three.

Kelly's career has been in the sport of golf and she now works for the English Golf Union and the English Ladies' Golf Association (now known as the English Women's Golf Association) as a Regional Development Officer, where her role is to support clubs and counties with the recruiting and retention of ladies within the game of golf through a number of different initiatives and grants that are available.

Kirstie Jennings

At the age of nine, Kirstie joined her first golf club - North Oxford Golf Club - where she obtained her first handicap of 36, later reducing this to 32 and then to 13 in one year and down to five in the following year. She then joined Frilford Heath Golf Club where she remained as a member until 1994 when she transferred to Tadmarton Heath Golf Club. From the age of 15 Kirstie played for the Oxfordshire county team and won the Oxford County Championship in 1999.

Kirstie has played for Northamptonshire county since 2000 as she has lived in Northamptonshire but only became a member of Brampton in the year 2002, then winning the county Championship in 2003, the Dorothy Cooch Salver in 2004 and the Northamptonshire County Golf Club Championship in 2005 and 2006.

In the year 2000, Kirstie joined the English Ladies Golf Association (ELGA), as the National Girls' Development Officer, responsible for increasing participation of girls in golf in general. Her role at ELGA has changed and since 2005 she is Compliance Officer for the England Golf Partnership, responsible for child protection and equality issues across golf in England.

Karen Lobb

Karen was a Leicester girl who trained as a teacher in physical education and who came to Northamptonshire to work at the comprehensive school at Roade from which she retired early after 28 years of service. Karen was an extremely gifted hockey player, representing Leicestershire, the Midlands and England before taking up golf when her hockey days were over at the age of 35. Her current handicap is 5 and she is playing in various national seniors' events. Karen has won the Spier Trophy at St Andrews and has played for Northamptonshire county and is also a member of Northamptonshire County Golf Club scratch league team.

Emma Parr

Emma is another bright star on the Brampton horizon at the present time. She is the only child of Simon and Anne Parr of Flore and was born in 1987. Emma was educated at the Northampton High School and at sixth form level at the Northampton Town and County School on the Billing Road, Northampton, where she achieved very gratifying and high standard results.

The Parr family are golfers including her grandfather, the late Dickie Parr (the dental surgeon), Sheila Parr, still currently a Lady member and a very keen sportswoman and Emma's father, Simon Parr, who was and is a talented player. There is little doubt in my mind that if Simon had had the time to devote to the game, he would have achieved an extremely low handicap. Dentistry, Simon's profession, has always had first demands on his time but he did join the Agaric Golfing Society on many away visits.

Emma was first taken by her late grandfather to see if she liked the game aged six, but showed no spark of response then. At the age of 12 she took to it immediately with great enthusiasm and made very rapid strides and was much helped by her grandfather who acted as constant chauffeur and devoted endless hours and much patience with her on the practice ground, never dampening her enthusiasm for the game.

As a result of this rapid progress and improvement, Emma was tutored by David Ripley of Coxmoor, the distinguished teacher, golf professional and guru as the national coach when she was 14 years of age. Her progress was remarkable. Starting at 12 her handicap was 45 and by the age of 16 it had reduced to six.

Emma was chosen for the England young elite squad at the age of 15 and was runner up in the English Girls' Championship (under fifteen). She also played for the England under sixteens against Spain. At that time she made a conscious decision not to pursue any kind of career in golf other than as an enthusiastic amateur. This was a pivotal and extreme decision for a youngster to make at the age of 16, but it led to utter devotion to academic study for 'A' levels which gained her entrance into Worcester College, Oxford, where she has almost completed her third year reading mathematics and statistics. Emma captained the successful Oxford University Ladies' golfing side in 2007 and has a current handicap of 3.

Emma has won the Ladies' Club Championship and maybe one can reasonably expect much more of her in years to come.

Rachel Smith

Rachel is another Lady Golfer who began young at the age of 9 and joined Brampton in 1999 as a junior. In 2002, Rachel was Junior Club Captain and county Junior Girls' Captain in 2005.

At the age of 13 Rachel began county coaching with a handicap of 44 and played her first county girls' match that same year. She has represented Northamptonshire at a number of levels – junior girls, Ladies' second team and Ladies' first team, playing in county week in 2004 and 2007.

The highlight of Rachel's golfing career is that she won the Goodyear Challenge Cup three times, first in 2002 and then back to back in 2005 and 2006. It has been won twice by the same person but never in successive years.

Rachel is currently in her final year reading for an LLB at university and will follow a legal career.

Other Club Faces

In recent years much help and encouragement to young golfers has been given by a variety of voluntary helpers, beginning with Michael and Angela Duck. Later Bob Garrett took over the mantle and David Goodrham (who now runs the Hollingsworth Trophy and Scratch League sides). This highly important role has now been taken over by Gary Smith. Many of our most promising juniors have been given enormous help in all aspects of golf, not forgetting the importance of manners and etiquette.

Promising Young Men
I mentioned earlier the three Myers boys and in addition I should also name:

Stuart Ashwood
Stuart started playing golf for Northamptonshire Boys in 2001 in the under sixteen team and was promoted to the under eighteen team the following year. In 2004 he progressed to the N G U second team and has played for the first team since 2006.
In 2002 Stuart joined Church Brampton and the following year he won the Higgs Bowl with a nett 69 and was runner-up in the Boys' Championship where he won the Handicap Trophy. He also played in the winning team in the Irish Association Cup and represented our Club and the N G U in the National Team Championships held at Woodhall Spa.
Aged 16 in 2004, Stuart was the youngest ever winner of the county Championship, won the Parsons Trophy for the best nett score and won the Braid's driver for the leading gross score for an under 22 year-old player. The same year he won the Boys' Championship – the first player to win both the County Championship and Boys' Championship in the same year. That year also saw him as part of the successful England Boys' team versus Wales and Scotland.
Stuart's handicap is scratch and he is at present on a Golf Scholarship in the USA where he plays for the university team and expects to major in finance.

Matthew Bird
Matt first started winning golf competitions in 2001 and in the following year when he was a member of Brampton Heath Golf Club. In 2002, he was the N G U under sixteen champion and in 2003 he was our junior champion and winner of the Spring Vase which he won again in 2005 and 2006. That year he also won the Wallis Cup and in 2005 and 2007 he won the N G U Scratch Foursomes.
Now with a handicap of scratch and aged 21, Matt is reading psychology at the University of Eastern Illinois where he plays regularly for the university team.

* * * * *

Other names include Gary Boyd, now turned professional and Adam Print (handicap plus 1) who has been a member of Brampton for some years. Adam has produced the lowest score in the County Cup of 134 in its annals. Glen Cottrell comes from a good golfing stable and has been a tour de force in our Club ranks for some years and has won the Burn Cup eight times, establishing a kind of personal fiefdom!

CHAPTER XXVI

Tales From The Locker Room

"These foolish things remind me of you".

Eric Maschwitz

George Mobbs

George wrote the following article which appeared in The County in 2004:

In July 1939, at the age of 20, I first played county golf for Northamptonshire and played in a match at Church Brampton. I was allotted a caddie to carry my clubs, named Bill Coulson. On weekdays the caddie swept the streets of Northampton but caddied at the Club at weekends. He had been a regular soldier and at the age of 40 had been recalled to the colours and rejoined the 4th Northamptonshire Territorial Battalion, which I had recently joined myself.

He behaved impeccably as a caddie and it was "Will you have your driver, sir, will you have your niblick, sir" etc, etc.

Next month we both went off to camp in Arundel Park in Sussex. It so happened that at the first mealtime he was mess waiter and he plonked my lunch in front of me and said "Well, 'ow are yer, yer old ******?" I said "You're not going to call me that". He said "Oh, so we're all toffee-nosed now, are we?". I said "It's not a question of that. I'm a corporal and you're a private. You'll stand to attention and call me corporal". So he went off cursing and swearing.

About two hours later he sought me out and said "Sorry about that at lunchtime, me old china". I said "That's OK Bill, forget all about it". From that moment there was not a thing he would not do for me. If I lost any kit I had only to tell him and he would say "Don't worry about that me old china" and in a flash he would pinch somebody else's kit and replace whatever was missing.

Regular soldiers make wonderful friends and appalling enemies! I think that was my first lesson in man management, successfully passed.

Dr Tom Ormerod

Tom Ormerod recounts the following tale. "Thirty years ago four of us, all members of Kettering Golf Club joined Northamptonshire County Golf Club. In those days Kettering was so muddy in the winter and we were keen to play all the year round. Becoming members of Church Brampton gave us the benefit of the use of not only a very fine course but one capable of being played virtually all year round. We played usually at 2pm on Thursday afternoons in the same fourball for the next twenty-five years. As we were all fully active members at Kettering, serving as Committee members and eventually Captains etc, we took no part in the social or administrative activities at Brampton other than playing our regular Thursday golf. One of our four, a young GP and a good golfer, was known to be extremely sensitive as to extraneous noise or distraction when he played, especially when putting. This golfer was not quite as bad as the P G Wodehouse character

254

who could not concentrate owing to the "roar of the butterflies in the adjacent meadow" but he came a close second.

One day standing over a putt on the fifteenth hole a young lady on a horse came along the bridle road and seeing the GP standing over his putt, stopped her horse on the bridge. At the critical moment the horse, unaware of the proper etiquette of such an occasion, broke wind. This was no normal affair. One of the foursome described it later as absolutely monumental and another swore that there was an echo. It was like a "thunderclap" as written by Neville Coghill in his translation of Chaucer. The putter twitched at the ball, missed the hole and he turned to glower at the culprit who had caused the mishap.

"I am so sorry" said the lady rider. The joke about the Queen and the distinguished state visitor accompanying her as they rode down The Mall, had not been related by then where a similar event occurred, so he made no reply, but ever after we warned him whenever there was a horse about!"

Harry Makin Draper

In his notes about past Captains, Neil Soutar referred to an unusual feat accomplished by Harry Makin Draper when Harry distinguished himself by playing a ball off the fifteenth tee and ending up on the green, the ball having passed under the road bridge.

A solicitor by profession and a graduate of Lincoln College, Oxford, Harry Makin Draper was the Northamptonshire County Court Registrar and part of the judiciary for the Northamptonshire County Court.

Harry married Phyllis, a considerable beauty in her day, whose parental nickname was "Fifi". Disliking this pet name (as it might be thought to have risqué connotations), Harry decreed after their engagement that the nickname "Fifi" should be abandoned and that hereinafter he would call her "Judy" by which she was known by us all. In the 1930's, Judy was a young lady who typified the art deco period. She drove a drop-head coupé sports car for years and always served "high octane" dry Martinis to her guests in her home. Both Harry and Judy were members of the Club for many years and both were past Captains. They lived for some years at Legatts, a fine and large stone house in Flore and later just outside Newnham in a Deterding property, on the top of Newnham Hill.

Harry told me that he was playing in the Saturday monthly medal and reached what is now our fifteenth hole. He drove off and played what appeared to him to be a very disappointing and poor shot. The ball was dipping as it flew to the bridge and seemed destined to end up in the stream with an irksome inevitability. Cross with himself, Harry could not bear to look to see what happened. In the next few seconds his playing partner saw the ball strike the supporting brickwork of the bridge over-sailing the stream. It then ricocheted from one wall to the other like balls on a fairground pinball table until it flew out and flopped onto the green in the most unlikely and inexplicable way. Harry could scarcely believe his good fortune but, sure enough, he identified his own ball on the putting green. He concluded this tale by saying to me "I wish I could tell you that I had holed the putt for a score of two. Sadly I did not. I suppose I was still in a state of shock and only just avoided three-putting".

Dr Tom Ormerod was a GP practising in Kettering. Once by a quirk of fate we met by chance on the promenade at Bellagio on Lake Como where we were both holidaying at the time. Tom, together with Ron Smith, a retired dental surgeon also from Kettering, have joined the St Botolph Golfing Society in recent years and added wisdom as well as golfing prowess to our endeavours on the course and humour après golf.

The Famous Brampton Wager

The late Alan Thorne, whose immaculate appearance and well-groomed brilliantined silver hair gave him the appearance of a latter-day Ronald Colman, was another doyen of the leather trade. His smoothed coiffure gave rise to the soubriquet of "Ronuk" after the furniture polish of that brand name. Alan joined Church Brampton in 1938 before going off to the war like countless others of his generation. From 1946 he was a regular player and on Sunday mornings from the 1960's onwards would feature with a foursome involving the late Dick Stevens (of immortal memory), Dudley Hughes, Jack Bell and myself. In later life when his playing days were over, one would see him playing bridge with Dr Jim Mitchell, Bill Percival and Lionel Harrison. Alan was always affable and friendly and one of his oldest friends was the late Norman Barratt of "Walk the Barratt Way" advertisement fame (shoe manufacturer and sometime President of Northamptonshire County Cricket Club). They would meet almost every evening in those days at the Cheyne Walk Club in Northampton, as did many other Golf Club members.

On one occasion Alan was delivering a lecture on how well he had played that afternoon in the Saturday monthly medal. This was an irritant to Norman Barratt who frequently interrupted the painfully long saga with cryptic and sarcastic comments. There was a long-running friendly rivalry and banter between them from youth to old age. Alan ignored all interventions and persisted with his tale until he was finally stung into a heated riposte "You, Shufty, (as Norman Barratt was known to his friends) know nothing of golf. You wouldn't know one end of a club from the other". "Of course I would" came the reply. "The game is not that difficult". This provoked Alan to say in front of the assembled company "I've never heard such balderdash. I challenge you to get round Church Brampton in under 250 shots and I will lay you 100 to 1 in fivers that you don't". "Done" said Shufty Barratt, "But I need to play your course in practice and I need several weeks to get into training for the match".

A date was set about one month ahead. Friends of Norman Barratt took him to the practice ground and later onto the course. Alan Thorne was excluded from these practice sessions but doubtless spies would pass on intelligence as to "form and progress". The monetary side of the bet must be seen in perspective. I am writing of the days of the old white British £5 note. In order to translate the purchasing power of £500 then, compared with today, is a difficult equation to estimate or prove but a factor of times ten is very probable. Thus the equivalent sum at stake would probably be around £5,000 in today's currency. Clearly the bet was taken seriously by both parties.

The appointed day and time eventually came. Norman Barratt was allowed a caddie (Prisoner's friend) who was a Brampton member and he had been coached as to "dos and don'ts". Aware of the layout of the course and danger areas, Norman used irons only, mainly a seven iron from the tee or fairway, never a wood, and a putter (the patina of which indicated its age and might well have been a relic of the nineteenth century). Over the first three holes Norman made steady progress scoring eights or nines, faithfully recorded by a neutral card marker.

Alan Thorne was part of a considerable field of followers, all keenly interested in the wager - Alan for obvious reasons, and who knows, perhaps there were side bets between other members of the party. Alan later confided that he believed that nemesis would surely come at the fifth hole and again at any others involving the brook.

When Norman Barratt arrived at the thirteenth tee he amazed most present by asking his caddie for his putter which he used to tap the ball off the tee to the path and thereafter tapped the ball short distances until he reached the fairway, thereafter resuming use of the seven iron which he played to good effect. He may have expended about fifteen shots in reaching the fairway but he avoided all real trouble.

The challenge continued with wily cunning being employed. Norman never went into a sand bunker. He progressed to the stream with judicious short shots and executed the crossing with a short pitch with a nine iron confounding his challenger's certainty that the ball would inevitably go into the brook.

Norman easily won the wager, his score being well under the prescribed and agreed number. The bet was honoured in the Clubhouse, paid and received graciously. The winner, with utter generosity, immediately gave his winnings to the Roadmender Club in Northampton. This was a youth club founded by Ernest Harrison of Bugbrooke for the benefit of young underprivileged youths.

Later Norman revealed that he was by no means the complete novice assumed by his challenger. His father, the late Richard Barratt, who lived at St David's, Kingsthorpe, (a fine gentleman's property and later a school, sitting in about four acres) laid out a pitch and putt course within the grounds. With his two brothers, Dennis and David, Norman played golf as a youngster at home. Norman told me later "I always knew how to make the club face do the work". He was also overheard to declare "I could have won the bet even if he had given me a ruddy umbrella to play with!". How many other such wagers have ever been staged?

Frank Parsons JP

Frank Parsons was a charming man who lived at Irchester. He was an extremely keen sportsman, as is described earlier by Neil Soutar. He was a member before the war and one of those older men who kept the Club running during the gloomiest days of the war. He was a County Councillor for many years, County Magistrate and a good friend of Peter Palmer who succeeded him as Captain of the Club.

On one occasion Frank Parsons was holidaying in Bournemouth and decided to play golf at Parkstone where Reg Whitcombe (former Open Champion) was the club professional. Frank decided to seek a lesson from this eminent professional golfer and Reg Whitcombe immediately said that he would give him a teaching session.

Reg Whitcombe began the lesson by asking to see Frank's swing and Parsons duly obliged. "Let me see it again" said Whitcombe which Frank did, "And again " said Whitcombe, several times more. Frank Parsons turned to the good professional and said "What do you think?". "Well" said Whitcombe "You've got a b****y good swing for felling trees, that's for sure. Let's forget the lesson and just play a round of golf together", which they duly did.

* * * * *

George Mobbs tells me that at the end of World War II the procurement of any kind of motor vehicle was nigh impossible. All that one could buy at that time because of austerity and shortages, were very old second-hand vehicles, frequently in a pretty decrepit state. The Committee of the day in desperation were asking the various members if they could help out in any way. Frank Parsons said at the time "Well I'm prepared to donate you a van, but only on condition that my handicap is increased". The Committee duly obliged!

Eddie Corps

Eddie Corps was a Northamptonian by birth, whose father played golf at Kettering Road Golf Club. Eddie was very bright and full of amusing tales. Educated at Northampton Grammar School, Eddie later won a scholarship to Cambridge and became a geologist, working for the Burmah Oil Company before the war in oilfield exploration which he continued throughout a long career. Eddie remained in India and Burma and when Burma fell to the Japanese occupation Nancy, his wife, was evacuated to Tibet with the other wives. It was during that time that Nancy became such a fine bridge player, representing Northamptonshire county in later years.

Eddie owned a house with two acres of garden (where two dwellings now stand) in close proximity to the Clubhouse in Church Brampton. Thus, after retirement, Eddie was an ubiquitous figure frequently turning up and seeking a game with his fellow members. On one such occasion Eddie was all set to play but discovered that his shoes were missing. They were always left beneath his locker and in those days were regularly polished by Bill Cann, the professional, or one of his assistants as part of the service provided by the professional shop for a small annual fee. Eddie soon became extremely upset not to trace any sign of the whereabouts of his shoes and so he had to forego his golf match. Not so easily deterred and by patient detective work and endless enquiry of friends and members who gradually filtered into the Clubhouse, Eddie was tipped off that a visitor had arrived earlier to play the course only to discover that he had omitted to bring any shoes. Seeing Eddie's gleaming brogues which happened to fit perfectly well, he was sorely tempted to borrow them.

Once in possession of this vital intelligence, Eddie set off down the course examining the feet of all players as they gradually came in hole by hole. People may have thought such scrutiny just a trifle eccentric. Finally, at the sixteenth tee, Eddie found the culprit sporting his shoes without a care, or so he thought. "Excuse me" said Eddie, "I believe that you have something of mine". Rather embarrassed, the wretched borrower said "Oh really, I don't think so". "Oh yes you have" said Eddie "You are wearing my shoes and I would like them back as I wish to play". "We shall be in shortly, will that do?" replied the felon. "No" said Eddie, "It will not do. I want them now, this minute". Reluctantly they were removed from his feet, warm and humid.

Eddie said later "I didn't actually play, but I wanted to discourage him and others from repeating this offence". Such conduct would be unlikely, as "the villain" had to play the last three holes in his socks!

* * * * *

On another occasion whilst playing in India, Eddie Corps holed in one with the benefit of a stroke on that particular hole. Thus his score was one net nought as far as his medal score or Stableford points were concerned. This fact is recorded in the annals of the R & A.

Roger Buswell

A story concerning Roger Buswell springs to mind when one year he entered the Burn Cup as a high handicapped player and became the giant-killer that summer with many scalps on the way to the quarter or semifinals. Amongst others he was drawn to play Lieutenant Colonel Charles Watts, former Commanding Officer of a battalion of the Northamptonshire Regiment. During the war years Charles Watts had had the misfortune to be a Japanese prisoner of war, with all the callous, uncivilised cruelty that this implies. He was tall, lean, taciturn and rather inscrutable in his manner. For a number of years he was a magistrate and Chairman of the mid-Northamptonshire Bench. He built a house in Harpole Park of modest size, eschewing Harpole Hall, which he also owned and let. Indeed, he owned many properties and acres of land in this village. I now reside in the house which he built, which I acquired after his death.

A match date and time was fixed. Roger, who really did not know his opponent, duly turned up and was waiting by the first tee. The figure of an elderly man of military bearing appeared and they introduced themselves. Roger was a keen sportsman who had played Rugby football in his younger days, including an appearance for The Saints. Likewise, Charles Watts had been a good sportsman, turning out for Hampshire County Cricket Club as an amateur fast bowler, well before the war.

At the time of this match Charles had a golfing handicap of 15 and Roger's was higher in the "bandit" classification. They drove off the first tee and Roger chatted away like a magpie, as was his wont, politely to the good Colonel all the way to the first green and there they holed out. On the second tee Charles Watts said to Roger "Would you mind if we do not constantly talk. I simply cannot concentrate". This was said more or less as a direct order. The game was then played out in near silence, save for the odd "Would you like the flag in or out? Is it your putt or mine? It's your honour" and such like. Roger established a lead and by the sixteenth hole the match was over. Roger had won the game and Colonel Watts smiled sportingly and congratulated him as the winner. As they walked in, the veil of silence was thrown off and they chatted away all the way to the Clubhouse and to the bar. Normal conversation had been resumed.

* * * * *

In another such Burn Cup match, Roger was drawn against a retired county cricketer, a formidable low handicap and wily opponent. His cricketing days provided him with experience enough to deal with the tension of such a head to head contest on the golf course. Nevertheless, Roger was in good form, playing far better than his high handicap suggested. His known association as a founder member of The Circus, one of our longest established societies within the Club, whose principal aim and object has been to treat golf as good fun, rather than anything else, was also known to his playing opponent. The promotion of excellence at golf has never been the raison d'être of The Circus. Probably expecting an easy win, Roger's opponent was obliged to face up to the fact that he was conceding many strokes and was trailing most of the match.

Standing on the sixteenth tee, Roger stood and waited because a train was going by at that particular moment. He was one up in the match, so he just said politely "I thought I would wait for the train". This elicited the reply "You're getting nervous, are yer?". However, Roger got to the green in three. The tractor with the gang mower was there, so the opponent went over to talk to the greenkeeper and this held up play for a few minutes to disconcert Roger further. The hole was halved. On the seventeenth the opponent's bag of clubs fell over with a clatter as Roger was putting. Another halved hole ensued. Roger managed to halve the eighteenth to win the match against all the odds.

Gerald John William Wareing

A gentleman whose appearance as to face and figure could be thought of as a reincarnation of Jorrocks Mr Pickwick and John Bull all in one, Gerry Wareing was a thoroughly well liked man throughout the membership, always smiling and genial. His rubicund complexion resembled a blend of good red Burgundy and old Bordeaux wine with a network of veins adding a touch of blue filigree. His physique was rotund, especially around the middle. He wore a deerstalker hat as part of his golfing attire.

Gerald Wareing (with Clayton and Parr children)

Gerald was a manufacturer of clothing, mainly in leather and sheepskin and his factory still stands to this day, in other ownership I believe, and is in Horseshoe Street, Northampton. As Neil Soutar outlined in his Captain's notes, Gerald lived in the village of Great Houghton in close proximity to a favourite "watering hole" of many people known as The Cherry Tree and he was a "season ticket holder" of this village pub.

As stated, Gerald was at one time churchwarden which led to censure by his three other friends who made up the Sunday morning fourball on one occasion when he turned up rather late. He explained "Well, as churchwarden, I simply had to attend the early morning communion service today and in order to save time I put on my golf shoes before the service. The spikes clattered down the aisle and this led to a row with the vicar and now I'm late with you lot". The foursome often comprised the late Percy Jones, chairman of Crockett and Jones, shoe manufacturers, Faulkner Gammage, partner in the practice of Becke, Green and Stops, Solicitors, (then) and now known as Hewitsons, occasionally Bill Percival also in the leather and finishing trades or Roy Barker, also of Crockett and Jones and/or Lionel Harrison. It varied according to availability. All travelled in petrol-driven buggies. Whatever else transpired, the match always ended before noon so that the quartet ended up with sufficient time to devote to the cocktail hour.

Mrs Percy Jones, it is alleged, firmly believed that her husband was a non-drinker and a stranger to alcohol and said as much to Dr Richard Marshall (a keen golfer and a former consultant anaesthetist at the Northampton General Hospital). Mrs Jones was at pains to ensure that this particular doctor would take extreme care with her husband whilst on the operating table on one occasion, as he was a teetotaller!

If time was running out, the match was suitably truncated. Once I heard "the gin wagon", as it was known, returning at high speed from the lower part of the course as our own Sunday fourball was putting on the seventeenth green. Hymns were being sung with gusto and the buggy containing Gerry Wareing and partner seeking to out sing, at least in volume, the other duo. The Club sales of gin, Angostura Bitters and/or tonic water were assured of a high volume in those days.

It so happened that Gerry Wareing was unable to play one Sunday morning because of gout but faithfully turned up just before noon so as not to miss the companionship of his friends. To this end he procured four largish looking pink-gins from the Club steward, placed carefully on a tray, together with a jug of water.

Michael Savage, my informant, tells me that the most terrible calamity then ensued. Gerry was carefully making his way to the veranda carrying the tray before him which obscured his vision downwards. Sadly he tripped over the step as he emerged from the bar and the tray and all its contents cascaded before him, almost drenching those in the line of fire. Gerry fell in a heap. It was feared that he might be injured. Members picked him up to ensure that he was not badly hurt. Mike Savage, who had seen the entire misadventure, commiserated on the rather obvious calamity and misfortune of losing four pink-gins. "What do you mean four?" came an indignant reply. "I've just lost twelve!".

* * * * *

Gerry was persuaded to go to a test match at Lord's and was seated with a small coterie of his friends watching the game. It was at the time when small transistor-type, battery operated radios had first become available on the market. Gerry had one with him and kept it in his pocket but plugged in the tiny earphone. The radio was tuned in to the continuous ball-by-ball commentary provided by John Arlott, Rex Alston, Jim Swanton et al. As the game progressed during the day, so Gerry was heard to come out with all manner of wise words, as to the drama unfolding on the pitch. He was quoting exactly the verdicts of the experts when a wicket fell or a change of bowling took place or whatever tactics manifested themselves. A stranger sitting two seats away was much impressed by all this "cricket wisdom". The more he heard, the more he came to admire the portly gentleman dispensing such obviously profound cricketing knowledge. After a while he addressed one of Gerry's friends sitting next to him and said "Who's your friend next to you? He must have been a fine cricketer in his time. Who did he play for? It's such a pity he's so deaf and has to wear that deaf aid!".

John Ashley states:

When the Breathalyser test became enacted, its ramifications had a dramatic impact on both Gerry and his neighbour and drinking companion, the late Jack Gurney of Great Houghton. Someone suggested that it might be wise to test each other to see how each of them fared on this particular kind of Richter Scale.

So it was that various Breathalyser kits were procured and each tested the other five times during the course of a typical day in their respective lives. Whatever the time of the testing, however, all proved positive. Gerry was uncertain as to whether this was any kind of record!

Jack Legge JP

J C J Legge was a past Captain and a rather stern character with a permanent lugubrious expression on his face. He was a doyen of the estate profession and could be sometimes intimidating when dealing with his peers and professional colleagues, especially any younger men who needed to negotiate with him. I recall one brash young surveyor whose office telephonist reminded him to ring Mr Legge who had telephoned in his absence. The following conversation took place late in the afternoon, no doubt just as Jack Legge was signing his post. "Ah, Mr Legge, I believe that you wish to speak to me". Like a flash came the husky response "I don't wish to, I am obliged to!". Such irascibility was commonplace.

* * * * *

Soon after he became Captain, Jack Legge, who seldom troubled par, was driving off the first tee in a Saturday morning medal with quite a crowd assembled around the first tee, swishing clubs and awaiting their turn to drive off. "J C J" topped his drive which barely carried fifty yards. His playing partner, out of civilised compassion for his embarrassment, called over sympathetically "Not one of your best Jack". Some wag in the crowd of bystanders called out, "No, but not far off it".

* * * * *

Laurie Johnson and Richard Aitken were playing in a fourball early one Sunday morning. The day previously they had played in the Saturday medal. As they passed under the railway bridge and approached the tenth tee they saw something quite large standing in the bunker on the right. Intrigued, they all drove off. As they neared the bunker, they saw that it was a Ford car standing vertical with its bonnet and front wheels uppermost. Upon reaching the Clubhouse the explanation was given by George Mobbs.

The unfortunate car owner was J C J Legge who had himself played in the Saturday medal quite late on. When he reached the Clubhouse to put away his bag of clubs, he realised that his sand wedge was missing and recalled that he had last used it on the tenth hole. He asked George Mobbs, as Secretary, if he might be permitted to take his car, as he was tired, on the course in order to retrieve the club. This proved to be a ghastly mistake. He found and picked up the club but then attempted to back his car, only to reverse into the bunker and have to extricate himself from this hazardous plight. And there it remained until help could be obtained the next day. "J C J's" face was red for some time and he was not allowed to forget the incident.

Minister For Slow Play

Some time in the early 1970's I was serving on a Committee and reports came in at every meeting of the increasing tendency for the Saturday monthly medals becoming bedevilled by slow play (Thursday medals had not yet come into fruition).

George Mobbs, our "learned" Secretary, suggested that every medal card should bear a strict starting time and an even stricter concluding time, based on his well-experienced estimate of how long each round should take. Competitors went off in threesomes and were made palpably aware that, for every five minutes over their allotted time span, penalty strokes would be added to their cards. The theory was that when held up by the trio ahead, those behind should become assertive and go through. This was all very well in theory but it caused some aggravation when an innocent trio, in effect, were penalised because of delays ahead. The hold-ups tended to ripple across the pond, so to speak.

I recall the late Humphrey Mobbs looking at his watch on the sixteenth tee when playing with me in a medal, together with another long since forgotten participant, and saying "For God's sake chaps, we must get going. We are running two minutes late and we shall be fined extra shots by George if we don't get a move on". There was a seriously worried look in his eye. I said "Well you're the older brother, you must tell George that we've been genuinely delayed". Humphrey said "A fat lot of difference that will make - you'll see that I am right". Sure enough, we were fined two strokes each.

This state of affairs could not go on. One particular entrant to all the competitions was known to be a painfully slow player, going through a well-rehearsed routine of a half dozen practice shot strokes every time before addressing his ball, followed by a lengthy "cockpit drill" as to grip, stance and line. People began to avoid putting their name down against this particular member's name.

It was then agreed that every month when the medal took place, one of the Committee members, detailed by way of roster, prepared by George, should not himself participate. Instead he should walk the course attired suitably as to the weather conditions but perhaps more properly to be seen as a presence on the course, taking note of any recalcitrant golfers who were taking too long. We were told especially to organise our visit to the course at a time when the known chief suspect had started out and to watch carefully to see if he caused any loss of ground.

On one such occasion when it was my turn to undertake this particular duty I was walking the field under the railway bridge and tried hard, on the one hand, not to put anyone off their game and thus keep a low profile, whilst on the other hand, to be seen. It presented quite a dichotomy for those committed to this particular task. As I reached the eleventh hole, the late E G (Tim) Harley called over to me in his inimitable fashion "Are you the Minister for Slow Play today?". "Yes", I said keeping up the banter "and don't let me see you lose a yard on those in front". This produced an unprintable and well-deserved retort. Soon after, this scheme was abandoned. Looking back the problem was then a microcosm of what was to creep into the game later, despite the best endeavours of all our golf mandarins of power.

G A T (Tubby) Vials

Tubby was a solicitor by profession who founded the legal practice with Major Ray which was known as Ray and Vials, for many years located in a period building at 18 Market Square, Northampton, and later relocated at Spencer Parade, at the corner of York Road. Tubby Vials was an articulate lawyer and highly gifted sportsman. Tubby captained Northamptonshire County Cricket Club in the years 1911-12 and became its President years later. Tubby was "an amateur" when there was a huge distinction between amateurs and professionals - a relic of eighteenth and nineteenth century class distinction. Indeed, "gentlemen" and "players" persisted until well after the Second World War. "Gentlemen" emerged at Lord's Cricket Ground from different gates from "players" as they went out to bat. Amateurs traditionally and frequently captained the county sides and England and many were men of great character, hugely influencing the game. The annals of cricket include such names as Dr W G Grace, Captain Wynyard, Douglas Jardine, Lord Hawke, Brian Sellars, F R (Freddie) Brown, Colin Ingleby-McKenzie etc to name but a few. Tubby Vials was of this school.

When his cricketing days were over, it was a natural thing for Tubby to turn to golf and he became a handy player, first at Kettering Road and then at Brampton. Tubby regularly played golf during the war years with a small circle of friends including Arthur Baxter, Alfred Garrard, Ossie Hargreaves and others. They were all good chums of similar age and every match was played in a highly competitive spirit. Sadly, during the war years Tubby lost two sons and his wife too.

During the darkest days of the war, the course was let out to be grazed by cows and sheep in order to save on costs of maintenance. On one occasion Tubby drove off the eighth tee and found, to his utter astonishment and annoyance, that his ball had landed fair and square into a large cow pat. After a minute or two's search, the ball was found and sat shining like a poached egg in a pan. Tubby said to his opponents "Okay, if I take a drop?". They had seen his predicament and Arthur Baxter seized the initiative. "Oh no, that wouldn't do. Play it where it lies. That's the rule, that's what I say!". Of course a moment's thought would have made relief from such a lie quite obvious but they had succeeded in riling Tubby. So nettled was he that Tubby seized a five iron and without more ado played the ball picking it off this extraordinary lie and he propelled it to the green but not without consequential damage. As Arthur Baxter confided "S... flew everywhere". Tubby was splattered with "sweet violets" as the words of the popular song relate. "Nobody would go near him on the course or in the bar afterwards" said Arthur.

Major N S Regnart

Late of the Indian Army and a relic of the days of the British Raj, he was a rather weird and eccentric playing member before the war who had retired and was living in the county. He was known and celebrated for his inordinately long preparation before making his shot. This involved thirteen waggles of the club head - no more, no less. George Mobbs used to play with him on occasion as a schoolboy and was much intrigued to watch him go through this repetitive cockpit drill of thirteen waggles each time he played his shot. In George's case, it wasn't so much that he wanted to play with Major Regnart. George was a schoolboy, often playing the course alone during the school holidays. The major would say "Are you free? Then you may play with me", which was more or less a command!

On one occasion, as they got under the railway bridge and arrived at what is now our tenth tee, a platelayer was working on the railway line just above the tee. The major went through his routine, deep in concentration. The railwayman watched at first with a desultory glance but this turned to utter amazement as the waggles proceeded and continued. After the tenth waggle he could stand it no longer. "For Ch.....t's sake, hit the bl.......y thing". The major stopped in his tracks and did not bat an eyelid, no stranger to being under fire in the military sense, such verbal abuse was but a trifle. The major leered with venom at his critic, recommenced the routine and went through a further thirteen waggles and then swiped his drive off the tee to George's obvious amusement.

Bill Stephenson Writes:

Saturday morning golf was always a pleasure with Fred Matthews and David Welch and every game was keenly contested. Their individual handicaps were generous and almost to the extent that not only did they get a shot in the bar, they got one in the locker room as well! David was a pipe smoker and one wondered if he ever took it out of his mouth other than to kiss his wife or drink his beer and Fred had (and indeed still has) a golf swing that could quite easily be choreographed to a Strauss waltz.

One bright, fine Saturday morning David Deane and Bill Stephenson played against Fred and David for the usual stakes, 50p on the front nine holes, 50p on the second nine and £1 on the game plus 10p for "oozlums" and "birdies" with the winners buying the drinks. On the eighteenth tee, Stephenson and Deane were one up but a net 10p down on the "bits". David and Fred had lived for the day when they would beat us and they were extremely happy at such a close game. Walking down the fairway Messrs Stephenson and Deane realised that if they let their opponents win the hole, the game would be halved and they would have to buy the drinks with 10p. Fred and David did "win" the hole and, of course, we congratulated them handsomely and then handed them 10p each and said that we would both have a gin and tonic!. It did not take many seconds for them to realise that we had "done" them but the drinks went a full round and honour was saved.

Concerning Charles Catlow

A young man, the son of an experienced member, had not played golf for long and was still at the beginner stage. With some trepidation he entered the Burn Cup for the first time. As luck would have it he was drawn in the first round against Charles Catlow, the reigning county Champion. The young man spoke to his father, suggesting that he ought to concede a walkover as he could not imagine that a good player would want to waste his time with a beginner. His father said that this would be entirely the wrong thing to do. Although Charles was the best player in the Club and a formidable match player, he would be an agreeable opponent and one from whom any opponent could learn a great deal. However there was one thing to be wary of. Charles was a good player and good players do not like being told "good shot" every time they hit the ball. No doubt pretty well every shot Charles played would seem like a good shot to a beginner, but a good player might not be satisfied with it. The thing to do was to take everything in one's stride and to say nothing.

The match began. There could be only one result, of course, but Charles quickly put the young man at his ease and searched diligently hole after hole for his opponent's ball in the thick rough. Meanwhile he started with three, three, three, three, three, three (old course layout where hole one was a bogey five), eagle, eagle, par, birdie, birdie, birdie, holing out every time as his opponent was unsure how to go about conceding a hole.

Nobody said anything, although during the sequence Charles played a number of good or very good shots and no bad ones. Charles was not a man to blow his own trumpet and the beginner, mindful of his father's advice, assumed that to a good player this sort of thing was commonplace and that congratulation would be an irritant.

The story did not come out for several months when the beginner, having by then played occasionally with several lower handicap players, had come to realise that a start of six threes in succession was worthy of notice despite the parental advice!

* * * * *

Charles was county Champion eleven times - an English record. He never considered himself accurate enough with his driver to become a top class player, but he had a formidable record playing top for Northamptonshire, a lowest handicap of plus 1 and reached the third and sixth rounds of the English Championship the only times he was able to play in it. He developed his short game during boyhood on the fast greens of Royal Lytham and St Annes. He was seriously accurate with his mashie niblick (seven iron) which he would usually take from the twelfth tee (then the eighth). While playing the eleventh (then the seventh) he made it a practice to walk over to the twelfth green to check on the exact pin position. This must have paid off since he once had seven twos in consecutive rounds there.

* * * * *

The late Frank Roe, a fine golfer, and Chairman of our Greens' Committee for eighteen years unbroken, used to organise, several times a year, outings to fine courses away from home. He would take a party of eight or possibly even twelve golfers and most of the invited felt at the time that it was like "a dub on the shoulder". One felt that "one had arrived" as a member of Brampton Golf Club, if such an invitation was forthcoming. In general terms, only the better golfers found themselves on such trips. However, Frank Roe was himself a generous and extremely kindly person who would always play with anyone, regardless of handicap, generally in monthly medals and such like.

On this particular occasion, the visit was to Hunstanton Golf Club and they set off at the crack of dawn, breakfasted somewhere en route and played 36 holes on this fine seaside course. Charles Catlow was one of the party which numbered eight on this particular occasion. They played as two fourballs. Charles Catlow was in the first fourball with George Mobbs and they came to and played the seventh hole, which is a short par 3 and blind, once the players have left the tee. When driving from the eighth tee they decided that for a joke they would pop one of the four balls into the hole, which had landed on the green within their sight, but not that of their compatriots. They duly drove off the eighth tee and were walking forwards when, to their consternation, they saw that the four players who had just driven the seventh, were not the four other members of their own party but strangers to them.

What had happened was that their own playing comrades had allowed another four playing behind to go through for some reason or other. Naturally this latter four could only see three balls on the green and then discovered one in the hole which brought about exclamations of great joy and thrill. None of the recalcitrant four who had breached all rules of golf and etiquette dared admit to their mischief and they left the four strangers behind convinced that one of their number had holed in one. George Mobbs told me that they simply did not have the temerity to own up to their folly!

Charles Catlow once told me a story concerning James Braid whom he knew very well. James Braid was one of the finest professional golfers and Open Championship winners of the early part of the twentieth century. He also became a notable golf architect and was, of course, professional at Walton Heath Golf Club. Charles Catlow got to know James Braid very well as a golf architect having been frequently involved in alterations to various courses, including our own. Indeed, James Braid was responsible for the recommendation that the bunker on the right of our seventh hole which attracts so many wayward drives, fading to the right, should be put there. Prior to that, there was no bunker in this particular spot. We all know it now as "Braid's Bunker" and I doubt if there are many Club members who have not ended up in it, at some stage or other.

In 1939 the Open Championship held at St Andrews was won by Dick Burton, a British professional, who was a fine champion. Of course, immediately thereafter, the Open ceased to be played for some time because of the war years. The nation was preoccupied with much more important events.

It so happened that Charles Catlow met up with James Braid and they were ruminating about the last Open Championship prior to the outbreak of war when Burton won it.

There was vastly less media coverage of The Open, no TV and comparatively minor radio reporting, but the press said that Burton's driving was long and powerful and led him to win the championship.

Catlow inquired of James Braid as to these reports of the length of the champion's drives. He asked "How would he, Dick Burton, stand compared with yourself?", meaning would he be much longer than James Braid in his heyday. Braid was a modest, softly spoken and, in many ways a shy man, never given to exaggeration, hyperbole or self aggrandizement. He paused for a moment and then said "Well, I doubt if he would be more than 30 yards behind me at my best". This was some claim, pronounced as a statement of fact and as Charles Catlow said to me, "I knew he was right because he was incapable of dissembling or making an assessment which could possibly be wrong given the circumstances".

Brigadier Gage

George Mobbs as a teenage schoolboy spent many hours during the school holidays playing on the course, sometimes alone, and would partner anyone looking for a game. One such partner was Brigadier Gage of West Haddon. They set off on the first hole and George hit two good shots and was then on the green. The hole then ranked as a "bogey five" as opposed to par 4, as it is now. The Brigadier plodded along and ended up on the green having taken about five shots whereupon he said to George "Look here, young man. You needn't think that you have won this hole yet. The way I play is that you get half a point for getting on the green in the least number of strokes and half a point for taking the fewest number of putts!". George stood agog but was too polite a schoolboy to argue. Might this curious system be adopted and are we missing anything?

Bill Percival

Bill Percival was wont to take family holidays in North Devon and play at Saunton Golf Club, who regularly catered for masses of visitors during the summer season and staged suitable competitions for them. Bill told me that he once scored 54 Stableford points with his playing partner who was a stranger and a fellow holiday visitor like Bill, with whom he had been drawn to play. Anyone who has played this classic links course, knows that it is a tough test, especially when the wind is blowing. An average of three points per hole is without doubt remarkable. Some members suggested that this surely could not be so. One member was both indignant and totally dismissive when I mentioned this to him at the time.

When I discussed the matter with George Mobbs, he said "I don't doubt it for one moment. I, too, when playing with my son Robin at Thurlestone Golf Course in Devon, once marked our card which ended up with a total of 51 Stableford points. I have often wondered what is the world record in Stableford points over 18 holes in a better ball fourball competition? Does anyone know?

Turkey Baillon

"L C" Turkey Baillon was a founder member of our Golf Club and Managing Director of the Northampton Brewery Company. I believe that the Baillon family came from the Falkland Islands. The various members of that family seemed to attract nicknames. R O Baillon, our former Club President, was always known as "Spriggs". His brother the brewery architect was always known as "Brabs", and their father "Turkey". Two other brothers were killed in the war years in the RAF serving as aircrew.

Mr And Mrs Turkey Baillon

Mr and Mrs Turkey Baillon lived within a hundred yards or so of the Golf Course along Adlands Lane. Members will recall that later Spriggs, their son, built a house in the orchard which is known as Orchard House, still in the family.

Turkey and his wife invested in an attractive white Scottish terrier who would accompany both on their daily walks along the bridle road through the course. In its early days of puppyhood it was inclined to wander at will, if allowed off the lead. The puppy had a special partiality for chasing rabbits through the thickets of broom and gorse. As a consequence, old Mrs Baillon would go looking for it and my informant, George Mobbs, tells me that gentlemen members were on occasion rudely disturbed when they themselves took to the gorse in preparation for a call of nature long before our smart purpose-built lavatory was built close to the seventh green. Thus, to avoid being taken by surprise upon entering the gorse, it was prudent for members to say in ringing tones "Good Morning Mrs Baillon". This might or might not evoke a response. Occasionally, if Mrs Baillon were present she would respond by saying "Good Morning". One felt if there was no response, that it might be safe to unzip.

* * * * *

George Mobbs advises:

I was aged 20 and as Mr and Mrs Turkey Baillon only lived two doors from us in Adlands Lane, our families became firm friends. Before the war and perhaps still to this day, many Northampton people owned properties in Hunstanton or Brancaster. The Baillons had such a house and I was invited by Turkey Baillon as a 20-year old to join him for a weekend's golf at Hunstanton.

The Baillons were devout Catholics and Turkey indicated that he would not wish to play golf on the Sunday morning but spoke to the Club Secretary and arranged for young George to play with someone else who turned out to be a retired major from the Indian Army who was highly eccentric. He played with the assistance of a caddie but insisted that the caddie should not only carry his clubs but push his bicycle around the course as well, as he feared that the bike might be stolen if left in the Club car park. It became apparent to George that this wretched caddie could not cope with the bike, clubs and hold the flag whilst the twosome putted out. So George then told the caddie to leave the flag to him and thus the caddie stood back supporting both golf clubs and bicycle.

When George related what had happened to Turkey Baillon he became very cross and made a point of admonishing the Club Secretary for palming George off with such a strange playing partner.

* * * * *

During the War years Turkey Baillon and Claude Palmer (father of Peter Palmer) headed the Home Guard for Church and Chapel Brampton. George Mobbs came home on leave and saw Claude Palmer armed to the teeth in his full Home Guard uniform with grenades attached to his belt, looking far more frightening than anything George had seen so far in the army. He had just been with Turkey Baillon on an exercise over the golf course which was used for training purposes.

Members' Dogs

Over the years, members' dogs have become part of the legend of the course. I have mentioned Turkey Baillon's dog. His son, Spriggs, acquired a yellow Labrador called George. Like most puppies of this breed he was big, boisterous, floppy and at first rather wild.

Both Spriggs and his wife Vera would walk their dog down the bridle road and occasionally across the course to keep it well exercised. This happened most days. Sometimes they would undertake the walk together and at other times separately. Many is the time that I have seen Spriggs in a worried and agitated state when he allowed George to go off the lead, only to find that he had disappeared charging after a rabbit, real or imaginary, or encountered some other distraction.

Our own members were always constrained by the stricture laid down by the Committee that our own pet dogs should be kept on a leash and controlled at all times so as not to distract other golfers. Would it be that dogs belonging to the general public walking across the course were under the same compulsion. Alas, they are not and cannot be.

Richard and Judy Catlow often could be heard talking about Montmorency, their Norfolk Terrier.

David Partridge owned a Great Dane, Jason (nicknamed "Jaws" by Ray Minor), and brought it with him golfing, suitably attached by a long lead to his golfing trolley. In size the dog seemed to be as large as a New Forest pony and looked highly dangerous but was, in fact, docile and friendly, at least when with its master. It sat quietly whilst the foursome drove and behaved at all times whilst on the lead. However, once under the railway bridge David would allow Jason to go for a run and one would frequently see huge dog paw prints in the sand bunkers where it had seen fit to stray.

On one occasion I saw the dog, Jason, looking decidedly worried when it lost its master. It rushed up to every fourball, examined us one by one and when he saw that David was not part of the party, he went off looking elsewhere. His "absence without leave" distracted David and his playing partner vowed that it cost them the match.

John Waters also owned a yellow Labrador called Polly. Likewise, this was attached to his trolley by a lead. The dog was perfectly well behaved and never gave as much as a whimper whilst John was either driving, playing an iron shot or putting. However, the dog was trained to a nicety inasmuch as it could always be relied upon to utter a whine or whimper when one of the opposition was about to drive or putt! No amount of reproval would persuade John not to bring his beloved dog onto the course.

Happily one sees others to this day like Nick White who has trained his dogs beautifully so that they accompany him and walk the course without causing any bother or distraction to the golfers.

The late Dr Dan Miller and his wife Jean often played as a foursome on a Sunday afternoon accompanied by their Dachshunds, Jack and Jessica, the latter often needing assistance by being carried down the first because of the long grass but afterwards felt free to romp away.

Lorne Smith, an elegant boulevardier whose good looks and dress are reminiscent of a 1930's matinee idol, as I have often reminded him as he was about to putt, is the owner of a black Labrador called Dexter who is often photographed with his master. Lorne is a more than useful low handicap golfer who takes the game seriously and is a frequent contributor to the Golf Club newsletter and writer on golf courses of distinction.

One Over Par

Some time at the end of the 1960's, the late Dickie Parr was a regular playing partner of a talented left-handed golfer at that time named Stuart Banks. They played together on Sunday mornings and in various Club competitions.

On one such occasion they entered the Lees Cup and found themselves drawn against another partnership, one of whom was, at least, strange in his persona, if not downright eccentric in his ways. At the time he was a master at a well known public school not far from Church Brampton and doubtless sought relaxation on the course from the turmoil of life at his school, and the pestilence of schoolboys!

Having introduced themselves, they played the first eight holes according to the prescribed format of endeavouring to score against bogey. All went on agreeably and quietly, although because of the large field on that warm and sunny May afternoon, it was necessary, as always, to keep moving steadily.

When they reached the ninth hole, the schoolmaster (although a golfer with a middle-ranking handicap) was having a bad hole and had already taken five shots in order to reach the green, whereas his playing partner was on in two.

The presumption was, therefore, that the schoolmaster would not putt in the interests of saving time. His partner was farthest from the hole and began to line up his putt, when a voice cried out "Hang on a minute, I wish to help you". The schoolmaster whose ball was relatively close to the flag turned his back on the hole and putted in the general direction where his playing partner's ball was marked. Messrs Parr and Banks not only expressed some surprise at this turn of events but were very properly concerned at the element of expending time unnecessarily.

Mild remonstration made not the slightest difference. The schoolmaster turned and said, "I am quite entitled to putt if I choose to do so" and without more ado, had done so. Clearly the purpose of this was to show his playing partner the line of his putt which was put to good effect. His partner faced with such a long putt might easily have three-putted, instead of which he left it stone dead.

So the round continued with a hint of tension in the air. When they reached the Clubhouse further discussion took place as to this unusual incident and the advice of the Club Secretary, George Mobbs, was sought as to whether such an unorthodox course of action was lawful and within the strict rules of golf.

For once in his life George was flummoxed. He pondered the matter and then said "I have never come across such a thing before but I will see what I can find out". George instantly went to work with the Rules of Golf book and sought further counsel from the Club professional, Robin Day. However, neither was able to come up with a proper ruling and as a result George said "It's an interesting, if abstruse, point and so I propose to ask the R & A to deal with the matter as a precedent, which they did and, which by now, was with the full approval of the General Committee.

Several months passed before the result of the R & A's deliberations was known. Finally the Secretary of the R & A wrote to George Mobbs saying that in all the history of the game, they had never come across such a happening as being recorded. Having considered all the facts of the matter, they were bound to say at the end of the day that what the player had done was lawful and within the Rules of Golf. They added the rider that they felt that it was not entirely within the "spirit of the game". The precedent is now, to this day, to be found in the Golfer's Bible.

Tom Spokes

Tom and Peggy Spokes were longstanding members of Brampton Golf Club. Tom's family had farmed Spencer land at Little Brington for several generations and their son, Robert, still occupies the family farm and he too is a member of our Club.

Tom and Peggy played mixed foursomes golf regularly on Sunday afternoons. One September they were playing a friendly foursome against another couple and upon reaching the fifteenth hole they found a small party picking blackberries, the fruit of the season. The party were close to the bridleway but were actually on the course, slightly off-limits. The two ladies said nothing but stood patiently waiting the drives from their respective husbands.

Tom Spokes, by his own admission, struck his ball a tad carelessly "off the toe" and the two men screeched a loud "fore" lest the ball fall near the ladies way out on the right. It did not do that but found its way very close to the blackberry pickers and rumour has it that with one bounce Tom's ball seemed to be enveloped by the folds of an elderly lady's skirt which caused much affront to the dignity of that particular lady.

The two lady golfers walked over to commiserate and make sure that no one was hurt but the aggrieved party was voluble in criticism. Thus the advice was given that perhaps it might be wiser to move away from this spot because of obvious danger and the fact that children were in the blackberrying party.

By this time the two men had arrived, Tom was concerned to find his ball after his wayward drive, having completely forgotten the blackberry pickers. Peggy Spokes explained the delicacy of the situation and Tom was at once at pains to make his peace. He started to stammer an apology in case his ball had frightened the lady. The lady said, in the broadest Northamptonshire vernacular, "Frighten me. You. Apologise. You did it on purpose"
No amount of remonstration could convince the lady that Tom was actually aiming at the green and not where his ball had fallen. He said with some resignation "I might have done better if I had aimed in your direction because the ball might then have gone on the green".
When they finally got round to playing the next shot, Tom found, luckily, that his ball was on nice green sward after having ventured beneath the lady's garment! What penalty did he incur other than the lady's wrath and indignation?

John Duffy
John Duffy was playing one day when a walker was strolling across the ninth hole "off tracks", along the stream in the direction of the fifteenth hole. John gently remonstrated with the stranger, quite courteously, and explained that golfers cannot always be relied on to hit their balls in a straight direction. He further explained that it would be far safer to stick to the bridle road or the public footpath, where there was a sporting chance of a rambler being seen by the golfers.
This advice was not accepted with good grace. The rambler said "I shall walk where I like and who do you think you are? Do you think you own the place?". John was thoughtful for a moment and replied "Well yes, in a manner of speaking, I do. My name is on the title deeds". This was an inspirational answer because as one of our Trustees, his name is there. The rambler had nothing further to say.

Raymond Tuckey
Raymond Tuckey continued to play golf over many years. After he had given up playing tennis he became a member of Church Brampton and played off a very low handicap regularly with Dr Jim Mitchell.
Despite the onset of old age Raymond continued to play, never making any concession to the fact that he was getting older. Indeed, in old age he absolutely refused to discuss the possibility of ever riding in a motorised buggy and was quoted as having said if he ever reached that state he would give up the game. He continued to play golf right up until he became ill, aged 90, when severely handicapped by a stroke.
Before his stroke, Raymond played each week and dominated the chosen quartet with whom he played. First, one had to be personally invited by Raymond which was an immense honour – it was somewhat akin to a letter from the Palace. Raymond wanted to be sure that anyone in the foursome was "suitable":

Raymond Tuckey

no mountebanks; specious talkers or those given to hyperbolical inexactitude were even mentionable.

One day I received a pleasant telephone call from Raymond inviting me to join his highly select Wednesday foursome, a golf format which was mandatory, despite whatever anyone else was playing at the time on the course. Raymond always carried a "pencil" bag of clubs and no longer walked with the tall military upright bearing of his earlier years. Indeed, he had developed a slight stoop. I was touched and mildly flattered to have been invited and so I readily accepted. Raymond's final words were "Be there on Wednesday morning promptly at 10.30 am".

And so it came to be. Week by week we formed up and played, always competitively, drawing lots for playing partners. Alas, Raymond no longer was able to play to his former exacting standards and silently, but with dignity, he would berate himself for any occasional personal lapse which became progressively more frequent. Heaven knows, the rest of us made our own share of mistakes.

On the first tee Raymond would remind us all, especially a newcomer, that we were playing Sunningdale rules whereby if anyone got two up in the match, a stroke was to be given on the next hole regardless of length and so on. This always ensured a modicum of equality throughout the game. The golf matches were played in a friendly and civilised manner.

One Wednesday, finding myself extremely busy with work, to my shame I confess that I forgot all about our weekly encounter. The reminder was delivered by Raymond personally by means of the Clubhouse telephone. In somewhat acid tones he quietly asked if it were my intention to be present!

As it was 10.29 am I unhesitatingly said "Raymond, I have forgotten our date but I can be with you on the tee in 20 minutes". This was said lamely and I knew that such a suggestion would not be tolerated for one second. "Please do not take the trouble", Raymond replied.

These foursome matches for me were over and in a sense, quite rightly so. I had committed the cardinal sin at golf for only the second time in fifty years but I knew that apologies, whilst graciously accepted, were to no avail. I subsequently went to see Raymond at his home and made a kind of peace. Now for most of us, my display of bad manners was something which is unacceptable. In Raymond's eyes it was a court martial offence!.

With some relief I learned several months later that John Waters was guilty of the same offence, save that he was sitting in the Clubhouse at the appointed time of the match, drinking coffee with his wife!

Some time later I related the shame of my fall from grace to Caroline, his stepdaughter and son in law, John Gale, who seemed to derive much merriment at my discomfiture.

John went on to explain that as a musician and conductor of orchestras, up to the time of his marriage to Caroline, golf was something totally alien to his lifestyle. However, it was not long before Raymond suggested, rather forcefully, that John should take up the game and that after taking lessons from the professional he would personally take him to our course and play with him.

John duly took a course of lessons from our professional and thereafter laboured on the practice ground until one day Raymond summarily declared that he would take John onto the course the very next afternoon.

John confided that he was in a highly timorous and agitated state on the first tee the following day. Somehow he struggled to keep his end up for the first seven holes, by which time this two ball had caught up a fourball who were putting out on the seventh green. They were obliged to wait before driving off at the eighth tee and John stood nervously waiting for the eighth green to clear when he reached his drive.

The fourball moved to the ninth teeing ground and waited with the clear intention of inviting the twoball "to go through". John then played his second shot which went as straight as an arrow at the flag and straight into the hole, to John's utter personal amazement and consternation!

Raymond was as taciturn as ever and did not blink an eyelid but simply said in staccato fashion "Good shot". The fourball on the ninth clapped, which caused John still further blushes. One of them said "You two must go through. We can see that you are star players". John thought to himself "If only they knew!".

Mrs Ros White

Mrs Ros White, Lady President 2005-07 relates:

Her late husband John, was wont to tell his wife Ros any yarns or amusing stories which he had heard from his golfing companions that day, after returning home from playing. One such story concerns the scattering of the ashes of a deceased golfer on the third hole of our course.

With all due solemnity, the gentleman charged to deal with this important duty on behalf of the family duly arrived on the course on the appointed day and at the correct time, armed with the necessary "casket". Several old friends of the deceased formed up with him and together they walked down the course to the third, politely waiting for a quiet moment when the hole was clear of players.

Thus, at a tranquil moment, he set about dealing with his office. Heads were bowed and with all due solemnity the scattering of the ashes commenced. However, the strength of a stiff westerly breeze had not been allowed for and the contents of the vase were swept away in the general direction of Mr Brian Rice's farm next door – now Brampton Heath Golf Club. Seeing the discomfiture of his friend, one of the party said "Well never mind old boy, you did your best and if you remember he was always out of bounds on this hole"

* * * * *

I have dealt with this important office on the course twice in my lifetime for good friends. I aver that no such disaster overtook my own execution of the duty.

"A Shot Too Far"

The George Row Club Golf Society was founded and from time to time visited various courses in the area to enjoy their pleasantness and test of golf. On one such occasion this particular Society was playing at Church Brampton and one of our own members, John Paterson, a former county golfer of very low handicap was participating. John was a tall, fit man until his latter years and had a powerful repetitive swing with a wide arc.

The order of the day was to draw for playing partners and John found himself as part of a rather dreary foursome. One of the four was a builder who was rather better at talking about the game, than his performance revealed. After a tedious afternoon and much ball searching, they eventually reached the eighteenth hole. John was all but on the green in two shots and the builder had reached a position just past the cross bunker, approximately a hundred yards from the green and turned to John who was his playing partner and in the middle of a yawn at the time and said in a strident tone of voice "I think it's a five iron. Would you agree?". John chose to look at his watch at that moment and whether the builder took it as tacit approval of his club selection or not we shall never know.

Anyone, even the most recent newcomer to the game, could not have failed to assess the distance as being suitable for about a nine iron shot at most. The player took his stance, had a practice swing and smote the ball as nigh perfectly as he could and it was last seen still rising as it cleared the Clubhouse roof. Bitter words of remonstration followed. The other three golfers moved silently and with resignation to the green, smiling, because they could see the end to a tortuous afternoon.

Ernest de Bell

This tale concerns Ernie de Bell who was a very interesting personality and an extremely clever man. By profession he was a scientific boffin, gifted and brainy, who found himself at the beginning of the war working for Plessey, then an important firm engaged in the communications industry, so vital for the war effort. Ernie thus found himself excluded from any call-up, as his job was classified as an important reserved occupation. After the war Ernie set up his own company and built up a fine business.

Passionate about sport, especially soccer and golf, Ernie was left-handed and had a most bizarre swing, and being rather tubby, his swing had to compensate for this particular physical feature. Ernie's swing was also rather long which resulted in a huge pirouette like a ballet dancer at its conclusion. As Lee Trevino once said as Open Champion "No one who ever had lessons would have a swing like mine!". Nevertheless, the swing was effective because Ernie played to a single figure handicap for a great number of years.

Ernie was a keen member of the St Botolph Golfing Society and kept up a constant patter or chat like machine-gun fire throughout the round of golf with his golfing companions. In the 1970's when Harold Wilson was Prime Minister it was decreed by parliament that double summertime should be reintroduced, as it was during the war years. Then in order to prolong the hours of daylight, both to assist industry and farming, the clock was put forward two hours in summertime instead of one. By so doing, it remained light until close on 11 pm during the long summer evenings and this was certainly helpful to agriculture in getting the harvest in during those times when harvesting was a much slower and more precarious process than now. In the wintertime, the clock only went back one hour instead of back to Greenwich Mean Time.

Of course there was a downside to all this, in as much as in Scotland and northern England it did not become full daylight during the shorter winter days until about 8.45 am.

Notwithstanding all the "whys and wherefores", Harold Wilson and his Cabinet decided that we should get ourselves as a nation in line with the other European countries and so for two winters the clocks did not go back in October. This very much affected the early morning golfers on Saturdays and Sundays.

Thus it was that the Committee, in their wisdom, decided that only foursomes golf should be played between November and February. On reflection, I personally feel that this was a very good move because it made sure that the whole field of Saturday and Sunday morning social golfers kept going at a better pace. In any case, I believe that we never seem to play enough foursomes golf at our Club, compared to others. Some may agree with this, some may not.

So it was that a large crowd would forgather at the first tee waiting for their moment to arrive to drive off and balls were put into the chute to determine the order of play but this could only be done when all four golfers stood by the tee in readiness. Ernie de Bell at this time regularly partnered the late Tony Dwyer, the County Veterinary Surgeon, who was a delightful Irishman and also a passionate and competent golfer. They were playing in the foursome format and as partners against the Captain of the day and the professional. It was agreed that Ernie de Bell should drive off from the first tee. Perhaps he was slightly over-awed by the large gathering of people and the few gently teasing remarks directed at him. Ernie struck the ball good and hard but it never became airborne and struck the concrete pyramid marking the ladies tee with some ferocity, shot up into the air and circumscribed a high arc before landing in the car park. Some comedian watching the incident called over to Tony Dwyer, "I don't fancy your next shot, Tony". The ball was retrieved and the match proceeded in a more normal and calm manner.

* * * * *

Ernie de Bell himself told me a tale of an occasion when he was playing in the Autumn Meeting. Ernie drove up the fifth hole, not particularly well and drifting to the fourth fairway, just as the players on the fourth tee were driving in the reverse direction. As Ernie approached and found his ball quite readily, he discovered a second golf ball lying only about six inches from his own. At this moment Richard Aitken, one of the golfers playing the fourth hole, walked over and said "I think that must be my ball". Ernie said "Well, there are two here and one of them is mine and the other must be yours". Richard said "I'm playing a Dunlop 65, number 3". Ernie replied "I am also playing a Dunlop 65, number 3". For a moment there was some confusion, both players wishing to ensure that they continued playing the correct ball and endeavoured to identify their own correctly. Ernie said, "Mine was a brand new ball on the first tee so it should be pretty straightforward". Richard Aitken then replied "Mine was also a brand new ball on the first tee". Ernie said "I can see that this one is my ball" and Richard by no means convinced that this was so, acquiesced.

Ernie played his second shot up the fifth fairway towards the green. Richard pitched his ball high into the air, dropped it on the fourth green but to his fury it ran over the back of the green and down the slope. Somewhat irritated by the whole business he found his ball in a perfectly good playable lie, pitched it carefully and holed out for a three. Thus for a moment he was elated and pleased with himself at having played such a good shot and was congratulated suitably by his golfing companions.

However his joy was short-lived because as he extracted the ball from the hole he found that it was defaced with a split which he had not noticed previously and which convinced him that it was the wrong ball. His predicament was made emphatically worse because the Rules of Golf, as they were then, precluded him from continuing further. He was obliged to disqualify himself there and then and retire from the competition. This was, of course, a source of some irritation, quite understandably.

Later in the Clubhouse, Richard and Ernie met up and Richard explained to Ernie what had happened and how he had been obliged to disqualify himself. Ernie was immediately on the defensive and said "Well, how can you be sure that the ball that you holed out was in fact mine and not yours?". The response came in an instant, "Because I never damage or deface my ball when I strike it". That seemed to settle the matter without further ado. No other comment was necessary.

The Rules of Golf have since changed and Richard would be allowed now to continue to play, having discovered he played the wrong ball. He would have had to have gone back to the spot where the confusion over the balls arose and replay from that point onwards, under penalty of two strokes and prior to teeing off at the next hole. Perhaps it is a case as the song lyrics say "What might have been is past forgetting!".

Clive Blackburn

One Sunday morning Clive was playing with his usual fourball comprising Tim Moore, Dudley Hughes, Dick Renshaw and himself. The men emerged on to the bridle road from what was then the tenth hole (now the fourteenth) to be confronted under the bridge by two young girls on horseback. Suddenly one of the horses reared up having been disturbed by something and threw the rider off its back who crashed into the brickwork of the bridge, opening up an enormous gash which clearly needed speedy medical attention.

This was in the early 1960's well before the advent of mobile telephones. Three of them gasped in disbelief as Tim Moore, a rather comical Yorkshireman but certainly no horseman despite his jockey-like figure, grabbed the reigns of the excitable horse and in one leap, jumped into the saddle and raced the horse back to the Clubhouse to summon an ambulance.

I recall being told this story myself by Dudley Hughes the following day who was still full of profound admiration for Tim Moore's spirit and coolness in taking the initiative but smiled because of the bizarre and amusing aspect of seeing this golfer on the horse so unexpectedly wearing his golf shoes.

Clive concludes by saying that the girl recovered and had not suffered serious injury.

From Peter Palmer

Members were few and far between after the war years and Peter was elected Captain, he says, because there was no one else available! The Trustees at that time were T E Manning (his uncle), Turkey Baillon (Spriggs father) and A J Fraser of the Phipps brewery.

Peter wanted to stage a gentlemen's Club dinner but this was thought by his elders not to be right for the County Club. So Peter says that he was precluded from presiding over the dinner. However, he persuaded his successor in office, Don Chamberlain, to have one, which he did. The dinner was held in the men's lounge for the first time with meat provided by Norman Buswell and cooked by the Club staff. A dinner has been held ever since. Peter went on to say that having served as the Captain in 1947, he was persuaded to do another year which he claimed was an anticlimax.

Peter also recalls the Drage brothers who have been mentioned elsewhere in this book. John and Bert Drage lived in the Red House in Chapel Brampton. Bert farmed and trained horses at the farm in Sandy Lane, Church Brampton, more recently occupied by Brian Rice, who later built Brampton Heath Golf Course adjoining our own land. It is popularly called in this day and age by certain of our members "Royal St Rice's".

Bert Drage was thought to be one of the finest judges of horses in the nation and walked with kings and princes and all the great and the good in his day, advising them and purchasing horses. One has to think that his sphere of activity predated the motor car which came in at the beginning of the twentieth century. He bought and sold racehorses and hunters (and this county was heavily steeped in fox hunting lore and that sport in general).

Bert took up golf fairly late in life and became a member of our Club. He wrote a privately published autobiography which I once read and it was a fascinating experience. He produced a number of daughters, one of whom married Jack Jeyes of the family chemist Philadelphus Jeyes, a member of Brampton, about whom I have written elsewhere in the narrative.

Peter reflects on the years when he was Captain, organising the planting of the spinneys between the first and eighteenth fairways, behind the first green and the fifteenth green. He says at the time the Club was very short of members but the Club still continued to impose strict limits about new members to make sure they knew how to behave!

Charles Catlow gave considerable help with the spinney planting and in other ways as he did to many Captains.

Peter says that he played a great deal of golf and of course became extremely proficient, participating in all the competitions, and once winning the Burn Cup defeating Raymond Tuckey in the final – to quote him "Against all the odds!". He is the father of our Club and as I write is aged 96 and still bright and full of life. He said as an aside, "I have so many happy memories, I feel I could write a book myself about them".

John Merry

John became a junior member of Brampton before the war years as a schoolboy. He is the son of the late J B "Chub" Merry, a well known auctioneer and surveyor who also found time to captain both the Saints' Rugby Football Club and the East Midlands and whose father had founded the first estate agents in Northampton. George Baldwin, a leading member who lived at Church Brampton and who was John's uncle, encouraged him to learn the game.

Educated initially at Northampton Grammar School and then Felsted and, following national service, John became an active player. In 1954, to his amazement, he found himself in the final of the Burn Cup. His opponent was George Marriott, an older man and a very successful, prosperous shoemaker and a rather more senior member of the Club. George Marriott turned up to play the Sunday final in a very grand car for those days – an Austin Sheerline, at a time when new cars were almost impossible to procure. George was immaculately turned out in plus-fours, tweed waistcoat, bow tie and cap, accompanied by his personal caddie. John himself was faced with turning up on the day by way of a bicycle, his only means of transportation, until his mother relented and allowed him to borrow her car for this occasion.

In those days, there was no question of a Finals Day with a field to follow and the accompaniment of a referee. The game was played in privacy, "head to head ", as were all the other rounds.

So they shook hands and drove off. John said "I felt that I was four down the moment George stepped out of his car". Very soon he was and by lunchtime the deficit had reached nine. George Marriott, as was his habit, took luncheon at the Clubhouse. John, as an impecunious young man like we all were then, decided to return home for lunch. In response to his father politely enquiring as to how the match was going, John replied "Not too bad, Dad, I'm nine down with eighteen to play".

Then back to the serious business of redeeming himself and the match. Alas he continued to fall further behind until the match ended abruptly on the old sixth (now our tenth) with the customary handshake followed by the long hike back to the Clubhouse. It was all over – John had lost his only match play competition final by 13 holes down and 12 to play.

Asked to recount some of his other golfing successes since the final, John replied "There are none. I peaked in 1954".

John spent a large part of his working career in Nigeria where he ultimately became the manager of a tannery processing 8,000 goatskins a day. (Imagine 8,000 goats loose on the course!). Later he started his own export merchanting business in Northampton. He usually has an amusing story or two to tell to anybody prepared to listen and especially to the Northamptonshire Golf Circus, of which he is a founder member.

For a time he resided in Cogenhoe at the home of our former Club President, Spriggs Baillon. Now John and his wife, Jean, live at Grendon.

Has anyone else ever recorded such a monumental defeat in the Burn final?

CHAPTER XXVII

Unusual And Remarkable Feats
And Odd Incidents

"A glorious, sailing bounding drive
That made me glad I was alive".

John Betjeman

Jim C Smith
Ron Hamlyn told me of a remarkable feat accomplished by Jim Smith in the years 1998-99. Playing off a handicap of 10, Jim achieved albatross twos on the par 5 second and par 5 eighteenth holes during the same round of golf. We are unaware of anyone else equalling this feat.

Andrew Marchant
A solicitor, long since retired but who practised in Olney, north Bucks and who was a very competent golfer, was once playing in a Law Society golf meeting at our course in the 1970's. At that time he played off a single-figure handicap and his playing partner was the late Tim Harley who related this tale to me.
Andrew Marchant's Stableford score up to then had been quite good but on the eighteenth tee he went for a big drive and hooked it rather badly out of bounds into Harlestone Firs (where our new 9a hole now stands). Andrew turned to Tim Harley and said "Oh bother it" (or words to that effect) and placed another ball on the tee adding that he would play "three off the tee". His second drive was a beauty and carried a long distance.
Walking up to his ball rather nonchalantly, Andrew took his stance and struck a fine iron shot straight at the pin and to their mutual amazement, the ball went into the hole. Thus he had scored a two off his second ball but of course it was recorded as a four on the score card.

Len Holland
Neil Soutar in the original narrative makes mention of a trick shot which Len Holland could play from a start position, somewhere between the present tenth tee and the fourteenth green, then not so thickly enveloped by trees. George Mobbs tells me that he demonstrated this trick shot to King George VI and Queen Elizabeth, the Queen Mother, when they were both playing members of our Club in the late 1920's as Duke and Duchess of York.
Standing on teeing ground higher than the arch of the railway bridge, Holland would play an iron shot directed to pass under the railway bridge by dipping in flight, but with sufficient slice as to land on the fifteenth green. However incredible this may seem, he performed the trick on many occasions.

Holing In One
Holing out in one gives a glow of satisfaction to any player who has accomplished this particular feat, especially at Church Brampton, where none of the short holes are

particularly low in yardage as they are on some courses.

Some golfers, and fine players to boot, never in a long lifetime of playing the game achieve a hole in one. Frank Roe was a case in point. He played golf for over sixty years but never once had a hole in one. Richard Aitken has accomplished the feat no less than nine times and has holed in one on all four short holes on the Brampton course, as did Sidney Drown during his playing career, thrice after his hip replacement and once before.

The late Dick Stevens holed in one on the twelfth hole and was shy and slightly embarrassed by the acclaim with which this feat was greeted upon his return to the Clubhouse. He said to me afterwards "Well at least it was a decent shot, pitched twice when it reached the green and ran into the hole!". I think that he was somewhat needled by the avaricious clamour as they thirsted for a drink as was demonstrated by his circle of friends, ever eager to tap the hapless victim by way of celebrating his accomplishment.

I recall one member, a very poorish golfer, to whom par and his score were mostly strangers, once holed in one on our third hole. It was said by a reliable eyewitness that the ball never went much above six inches above ground level from tee to green, but struck the flag hard and dropped into the hole. He was so proud of his feat that it was rumoured that he would put an announcement of the fact in the Chronicle & Echo.

* * * * *

Sydney Wittering wrote to me about the fact that he has holed in one on three separate occasions on our fifteenth hole. This was accomplished for the first time in 1978 and again in 1988 and finally in March 1990. On each occasion he used a six iron and is proud of the fact that he acquired from Thresher and Glenny Ltd two separate ties – "The Oneholer" after his first success and "The King Oneholer" after the second. As he says, the odds of achieving this must be astronomical.

* * * * *

Matthew Myers, the youngest of the trio of golfing boys of the Myers family, holed in one on the third hole at the age of seven.

George Mobbs

Graham Eric (alias George Mobbs) halved the third hole in one. This was in July 1939, during a friendly Sunday morning game, when George was aged 20 years. He was playing with his next door neighbour, Hubert Martin, a much older man who lived in the house adjacent to the Mobbs family home in Golf Lane, Church Brampton, and who eventually moved to Sussex. Hubert Martin was the Clerk to the Northamptonshire County Council and a gentleman of some importance in the local community. As a matter of fact, his house was later occupied by Mr J Alan Turner, his successor in this post, who was also a member of the Club and later still it became the home of the Towers family.

When they reached the third hole, George reached for and struck a six iron straight and true for the 160 yards to the flag which went straight into the hole and was seen by both players. Hubert Martin said "Well done. I don't think that I shall bother to play". George said "Oh please take your shot. You might as well and then we can walk to the next tee". To their mutual astonishment Hubert Martin's iron shot also went straight into the hole. Subsequently a letter was sent to The Times asking if this remarkable feat had ever been done before. The circumstances of the incident were explained in the letter and details of the two players were given.

Mr Bernard Darwin was then the golfing correspondent of The Times and he was the most eminent golf journalist and author of his day. The "response" was embodied in his Saturday column in The Times which set out the details of this extraordinary feat quite some time later. Mr Darwin explained that up to then, it had been accomplished, as far as was known, several times. But he went on to say, with a touch of humour, that to the best of his knowledge and belief, it had not been achieved before by a twosome involving a Clerk to a County Council!

As a footnote, the "Golfer's Bible" revealed some years later that this feat had now been recorded eight times up to then which seems even more incredible.

Mobbs "12" at the Tenth

On one occasion George Mobbs in his heyday was participating in the Newnham Cup and Neil Soutar was his playing partner. It was an unpleasant wet day. George had gone out in 39 for the first nine holes. When he reached the tenth hole (now our fourteenth) George found his second shot to the green bunkered and lying in a soggy, damp and sandy lie from which there could be no relief. What followed is explained in Keith Mason's piece on "The County Cup".

George played on valiantly until he finally holed out, recording a 12 on this particular hole. He told me that he rapidly calculated that to be back in 36 he would thereinafter need eight threes successively. In actual fact he scored six threes in a row and on the final hole he holed out in six for a gross score of 81. Not a bad achievement given the circumstances! Most of us would have torn up the card long before then.

George Gee – Five Under Par

It was a typical autumn day in November 2003 as George Gee set out to play a friendly singles match with Nick Godden. The weather was overcast but dry. The wind was no more than a gentle breeze from the south-east. The men's tees were well forward, the conditions were favourable, and George is a sound single-figure golfer. Nevertheless, there was no indication that anything unusual would occur.

The players reached the third hole and the pin was front centre at about 130 yards. George selected a pitching wedge and took his shot. After two bounces, his ball rolled four or five yards forward into the middle of the cup. A hole in one!

They came to the sixth hole. The flag was back left at 187 yards. George selected a five wood and struck it quite well, his ball finishing just off the green, short and left, some 22 feet from the hole.

Now if there is a weakness of any sort in George's game it is with the short chip shots and he comments "Luckily I was able to use the putter" and it went in for a birdie two.

On they went to the twelfth hole. The pin was left centre at 115 yards. Again George took his pitching wedge, finishing pin high, 12 feet from the hole. His putter was still working well and he holed it for another two.

George had two more holes to think about it. Then he stood on the fifteenth tee with what he describes as "A decidedly uncommon shot total for the par 3 in prospect". The pin at the fifteenth hole was front right, about 130 yards from the men's tee of the day, the wind left to right. George would have settled for anywhere on the green, plus two putts – and level twos for the four short holes. But no! A perfectly struck nine iron pitched two feet short and ran on two feet past the hole. Defying the tension, George holed it for his third two in a row.

That was it, one, two, two, two, a total of seven shots, five under par on the four short holes. Not bad for an afternoon's work at Brampton. Will such a score ever be equalled? Just possibly perhaps. Will it ever be beaten? Surely not while golf continues to be played on the County Course.

Another Odd Incident
Richard Catlow relates:
"I was playing in the January Medal, forty years ago. Conditions were foul. Playing the tenth hole after a good drive, I holed out with my second shot – a 3 wood. As I walked towards the green a messenger came on a buggy to tell all competitors still on the course that the medal was cancelled. Several holes were underwater including the tenth. "Completely impossible, the tenth" he said. I rather enjoyed that – achieving the impossible. Never before nor since … !

Peter Woods
Peter became a member in the 1980's. He was a former professional golfer and when he joined the Club he had applied for and obtained his amateur status once again but was still playing off scratch.

Peter was an agreeable man with a very sunny nature and frequently partnered the late Jack Humphreys in various Club competitions. On one occasion in 1983 both played as partners in the Autumn Meeting.

On the golf course Peter Woods could be very tempestuous at times and was not unknown to tear up his card at the slightest provocation. He might be at level fours and then three-putt a hole which put him in such a fury that he would instantly tear up his card. It was this uncertain temperament that probably prevented him from making the grade as a professional.

As they reached the seventeenth hole in this particular occasion on the second round, which would have been in late afternoon, they were at the tail-end of the field and they happened to bump into Jack and Kay Belson who were playing nine friendly holes in the late afternoon, long after all the participants in the competition had set off and thought that they might cut in at the seventeenth hole when they reached it. Quite naturally they stood aside to allow the Autumn Meeting field to go through. Being the friendly soul that he was, Peter Woods invited them, and indeed insisted, that they join Jack Humphreys and himself to play into the Clubhouse.

Thus what had started as an official singles match concluded as a mixed foursome. George Mobbs saw them from his office on the eighteenth hole and ever alert as to the possibility of irregularity and being a stickler for rules and etiquette, said immediately that this could not be right and conferred at once with the professional, Robin Day. Both had to look up the rules which presented some difficulty as it was such a bizarre and unusual situation. Thus George decreed that no prizes would be awarded that evening until such time as this affair had been properly sorted out.

The following day they got to the bottom of it and both Jack Humphreys and Peter Woods were disqualified on the premise that every match must stick to the same format as that at which it had started. It was an unequivocal rule that a match could not change in midstream, so to speak, from a singles medal to a mixed foursome, whatever the circumstances. As far as George knows, this is the only time in his experience of Secretary that such a thing occurred.

CHAPTER XXVIII

Those Who Did Their Bit

"We band of brothers".

William Shakespeare

Northamptonshire Regiment

I chanced on a copy of The Journal of the Northamptonshire Regiment, (the old county regiment - 48th and 58th foot) dated September 1958 which made interesting reading in part, inasmuch as the regiment no longer exists. The regiment had to face the severe government cuts and changes with so many others over the past fifty years since the end of World War II. Many of our own members served with the regiment during the war and even afterwards doing their national service.

That particular journal carried a report of the annual match of the regimental golfers against Northamptonshire County Golf Club played at Church Brampton. A report of the match and those who participated is shown below.

Many names are familiar and a few of our own Club members made up the Northants regimental side including, I notice, Brigadier Bobby Osborne-Smith and Charles Mumby. Alan Allebone was heavily involved as an officer in the Territorial Army having served with the regiment during the war years. Young Peter Rushton played for our own Club side having served as a gunner officer during his national service. He appears to have been the youngest club representative. I am told that this annual match took place over many years and was a popular part of the Club's social golf calendar. As a matter of separate interest, J B Akehurst, who was then a young officer in the County Regiment, went on to become a General.

Extract from The Journal of the Northamptonshire Regiment, 1958

The annual match against Northamptonshire County Golf Club was played on Sunday afternoon at Church Brampton under somewhat boisterous and rainy conditions.

The combination of what sailors would call grand sailing weather, and three days concentrated social pleasures proved too much for some of the regimental team.

It is suggested that the next year's training programme should provide officers serving with the battalion with at least one week's course to enable them to tune muscles, eyes and temperament to the better use of the golf clubs.

We would like to record our thanks to Harry Lees for raising the team which beat us so soundly and to the Captain of the Club for the excellent tea and hospitality given us after the match.

The result:

Northamptonshire County Golf Club

R B Douglas, C G Gledhill	1
P Rushton, A M Harris	0
S H G Humfrey, H A Lees	1
R A Palmer, A Pepper	½
D J Barber, J C J Legge	1
T F Gammage, D Chamberlain	1
S F Kennedy, G F Branch	1
	5½

Northamptonshire Regiment

R Osborne-Smith, H N Drake	0
C J N Longmore, C E G Mumby	1
J R Britten, J B Akehurst	0
J H Johnson, D E Taunton	½
A Allebone, E M Goodale	0
P F Keily, H H Moore	0
J P Growse, T C S Knox	0
	1½

A Soldier in Ulster

Having volunteered for the Territorial Army, George Mobbs found himself as a private soldier initially in the Northamptonshire Regiment in company with many of his friends. The Regiment was moved to Northern Ireland, even then a hotbed of Republicanism. Eire under the Premiership of Eamon de Valera was certainly anti-British and was supportive even of Hitler. Together with his cabinet, a message of condolence was sent in March 1945 via their Ambassador in Nazi Germany commiserating on their misery, desolation and imminent defeat. Thus it was necessary for the British to maintain a strong military presence in Northern Ireland.

By that time George had already been promoted to Sergeant. Meanwhile, back home his Mother had, by chance, met Lady Cynthia Spencer whilst watching the cubbing with the Pytchley Hunt in company with various other local ladies. It was Countess Cynthia Spencer who gave her name to the Hospice at Manfield Hospital and is remembered for her beauty, gentility and compassion, displayed in her nature throughout her life. She was chatting to the various ladies and enquired of Mrs Mobbs as to the wellbeing of her sons who were all called up at the time. "Tell me about Humphrey" she said. Mrs Mobbs reported that Humphrey was in the Royal Artillery and had settled down well. "And how about George" she continued. "He has been posted with the Northamptonshire Regiment to Northern Ireland" replied Mrs Mobbs. The Countess said, "Well, isn't that strange - we're just about to go to Northern Ireland. My Father (the Duke of Abercorn) has been made Governor General of Northern Ireland and we are shortly to visit him. It would be nice to see George at some time". No more was said.

Some weeks later the Brigade Major sent for George and said "Sgt. Mobbs, you've been ordered to go to the Governor's house. Get your best BD and best boots on". George was conveyed by a truck and driver to keep this important appointment, was duly dropped off at the imposing front entrance to this grand house and duly rang the door bell. A querulous Major Domo opened the door and said "Can I help you?" George explained that he'd been invited to tea with the Governor's wife whereupon the Major Domo enquired as to his name and whether George would like to wash his hands before entering the drawing room. Upon hearing the name Mobbs, he enquired whether by chance George was in any way related to Edgar Mobbs the distinguished rugby player. When George replied in the affirmative he was immediately shaken by the hand and duly treated with great civility.

Thus it was that George entered the drawing room and was invited to join the Duchess of Abercorn for afternoon tea. Cucumber sandwiches and suchlike were somewhat different from regular army fare I imagine at that time. George duly departed, fully requited when it came to the time to leave and return to the Barracks.

* * * * *

WOSB (An Acronym For War Office Selection Board)

George speaks nonchalantly of further army days. After serving a couple of years in the ranks of the Northamptonshire regiment I was sent to WOSB to see whether I possessed so called "Officer qualities". Once there, I duly reported and was interviewed by a Brigadier resplendent with red tabs on his collar and a red band round his service cap etc. who almost immediately fired his first question at me by saying "Mobbs.........yes Mobbs ....are you by any chance related to Edgar Mobbs, the Rugby player?" "Yes sir, he was my uncle", replied George. A few more questions followed in a desultory kind of way, then the Brigadier said "Well Mobbs, I don't think there's anything else. Best of luck to you". George makes light of it but soon found himself at OCTU (Officer Cadet Training Unit) where he met up with Norman Buswell, some months ahead on his training course, who was soon to become a gunner officer and commando.

George was commissioned into the Royal Artillery himself and was soon sent off to Nigeria in West Africa. In due course, General Bond sent for him having recognised his name as being familiar to him as a golfer. George most certainly had played with the General's son in Public School's golf. Thus it was that the General invited George to make up a four at golf, an invitation which was readily accepted to George's great satisfaction!

Jesse Lionel Harrison

In the late 1930's Lionel had qualified as a solicitor and joined his brother, the late Cyril Harrison and father, Frank Harrison, at Shoosmiths and Harrison, 20 Market Square, Northampton.

Just pre-war, Lionel volunteered for the TA and joined the Northamptonshire Yeomanry under their Commanding Officer, Lieutenant Colonel J G Lowther DSO (father of Sir John Lowther, Lord Lieutenant of Northampton for many years) and was mobilised before war broke out. Whilst on battle training manoeuvres on Salisbury Plain, Lionel had the misfortune to be accidentally shot by "friendly fire" which put him in a military hospital at Guildford for very many months during which time he lay on his back watching the Battle of Britain in the high summer of 1940. Later discharged, Lionel was commissioned and served until eventual demobilisation.

During the war years Lionel married Beryl (daughter of Alfred Garrard) a past Captain of Brampton and herself also a past Ladies' Captain of the Club. Lionel was a very hard-working and successful lawyer and a person full of fun and personality. He played bridge, poker and other games of chance with much subtlety, skill and shrewdness. Lionel was a golfer who participated in and supported all sections of the Club. A familiar figure with Beryl on his buggy after illness forced this state of affairs on him, Lionel was popularly known as "Speedy Gonzales" because of his racing driver technique in the buggy!

Lionel donated to the course several hundred Norwegian spruce saplings from his home at Overstone. They were planted in various places on the course and are now fully mature trees. The copse between the fourth green and fifth tee is an example of this benefaction.

Dennis Laverick

Dennis served in the Royal Navy as a dental officer during the war. Seeing him in the Clubhouse one evening, I remarked in a rhetorical way that on the previous day I had been the guest of Sir Murray Fox at the Worshipful Company of Wheelwrights, one of the City livery companies in London. I explained that I had arrived in London and undertaken some business, which concluded earlier than I had anticipated and that I had used the spare hour and a half by visiting HMS Belfast, the battle cruiser moored on the river Thames and the only ship of the line of the city class in existence.

Dennis immediately said that he had served on a city class cruiser and his ship had accompanied The Belfast on the occasion of the Battle of the North Cape at the end of 1943 which was the last major set piece battle of capital ships in World War II, in this particular hemisphere. I told him that I had observed that the dental surgery was at the top of the ship on The Belfast and he explained that this was so and that when the ship was at action stations it became a casualty clearing station and the dental officer and his assistants had to act immediately as assistant medics.

On the occasion of the Battle of the North Cape a full scale action followed and their ship was engaged in the exchange of heavy gunfire. Dennis said that their ship had been hit on a number of occasions and severe damage was done with a good many casualties and loss of life. Men in a bad state were brought up to his surgery and they were busily occupied in dealing with the wounded. All of a sudden there was a loud bang and a rushing sound as one might experience standing on the platform in the London underground as a tube train rushes past and not scheduled to stop at that particular station. No one said anything. They were all too preoccupied with what they were doing and were extremely busy. When the battle was over they saw that there was a huge shell hole in the outer plates of the ship and another one at the far side of the surgery. Later they were told that an armour-piercing shell from the Scharnhorst had hit the outer works of the British cruiser, screamed through the surgery boring its way through various partitioning divisions and exiting on the far side of the ship before it finally exploded in the sea. Dennis said casually "God help us all if it had exploded when it entered our surgery". Such was the quiet modesty of the man that one would never have associated such an occurrence with him.

Dennis's dental practice was in Newland for a time in the centre of Northampton. During the war he married a pretty Wren Officer, Daphne, who has been a much respected Lady member of the Club for many years, Ladies' Captain and past Lady President, who died in 2007.

Charles Norman Buswell OBE MC and Bar, Croix de Guerre

Norman Buswell was a delightful man and a popular member for many years and Captain in 1970. After the war Norman took over the family business in retail and wholesale butchery from his father and took it to dizzy heights with the help of his two sons Roger (also a member of the Golf Club) and Michael. The company was eventually sold. Norman was a liveryman in the Worshipful Company of Butchers and a former President of the National Wholesale Butchers Association. He was a person of infinite charm and sunny nature.

During the war, Norman served with the Royal Artillery and the Commandos and had the misfortune to be taken as prisoner of war in the North African campaign in 1942 and found himself incarcerated in a POW camp in Italy. In September 1943 when Italy capitulated and Mussolini and his fascist regime were ousted, the British prisoners of war were ordered by the senior officers, rather naïvely, to stay in their camps for the time being, the Italian guards having laid down their arms. This "honeymoon period" lasted but a trice. The German army were having none of this and immediately took over the camps, seeking to round up any escapees. All were to be sent by train to Germany.

Norman found himself, with many others, ordered at gunpoint onto a train which took them northwards to Germany. Three of the men decided, very bravely, to break out and escape if they could. Covertly, Norman procured a knife from somewhere at some stage. The three intrepid comrades comprising a brother officer, a Russian and Norman, asked consent to use the lavatory on the train which was moving quite rapidly at nightfall. A German armed guard accompanied them. It was there that Norman killed the guard and with the help of the other two, threw the body from the train. They then jumped off the train in the darkness and took to the hills, each going their separate ways. Norman was given sanctuary by nuns and experienced many other adventures after he had thrown in his lot with the Italian partisans fighting the Germans in the mountains. Most of these were communists who had hated the fascist regime for years. All suffered extreme privation and hardship. Norman walked 700 odd miles southwards through the Apennines until he finally reached the British lines for which he was decorated with the Military Cross. Once repatriated and after well deserved leave, he returned to normal duties and was later involved in the D-Day landings and went on to serve under General Dempsey and won a bar to his Military Cross and was awarded the Croix de Guerre by the French.

* * * * *

One of the most pleasant aspects of Norman's Captaincy was when he presented a baron of best English beef on the occasion of the annual dinner when he was in the chair, so to speak. This was roasted suitably at the East Haddon bakery, then still extant, conveyed to the Clubhouse and carved and served to all those attending.

* * * * *

Norman was the personification of a gentleman and very well liked as was his wife, Margaret, sister of Lord Boardman, solicitor, MP, Cabinet Minister and later chairman of the National Westminster Bank.

The then Club Secretary, George Mobbs, told me an amusing tale when Norman assumed the Captaincy of the Club. It was George's practice to advise all new Captains to fix, not only a date for the annual gentlemen's dinner the following November, but also to make sure that suitable arrangements were made for booking the best guest speaker they could find. It was necessary to do this well ahead because the best are always in demand and committed far ahead and thus difficult to secure. This was sage advice from George.

At that time Selwyn Lloyd had just been made Chancellor of the Exchequer by Harold Macmillan. As it so happened, this coincided with Selwyn Lloyd's election as Captain of the Royal Liverpool Golf Club, Hoylake - the famous course and scene of several Open Championships. Norman decided that Selwyn Lloyd would be a good choice of speaker but sadly they were unacquainted. Norman dashed off a letter, unfortunately on his home stationery, inviting the Cabinet Minister to speak at his Club dinner. Norman signed his letter "C N Buswell, Captain".

With hindsight it would have been far better to have used Golf Club stationery as this would have cleared a great deal of mystery, ambiguity and misunderstanding from the letter. In the event it triggered a somewhat brusque response from the invitee who regretted that "He was unavailable on the date at your unnamed Golf Club". The letter was addressed to Captain Buswell (shades of Captain Mainwaring!). He looked elsewhere and found someone more accommodating.

Robert Arnett Grigg

Robert is one of our "band of brothers" who has shown fortitude when so many others would have quietly given up playing. In 1991 Robert developed macular degeneration of his eyesight causing a gradual deterioration, leading to badly impaired vision. Nevertheless, Robert has continued to play several times per week with the seniors, despite other health problems which beset people of his age group.

Born in Bagshot, Surrey, Robert went virtually from school to the army in 1940 and was soon sent to the Honourable Artillery Company OCTU at Bulford and thereafter commissioned into the South Staffordshire Regiment.

In 1942 Robert embarked for the Middle East and found himself with the Sudan Defence Force and soon after in the Western Desert fighting with the Free French out of Kufa where he came across the famous Long Range Desert Group, operating behind the German lines. So on to India where his regiment were part of General Orde Wingate's "Second Chindit". Robert served under Brigadier "Mad Mike" Calvert. When Wingate was killed, the American General "Vinegar Joe Stillwell" assumed command. Robert was wounded and flown out, later becoming ADC to General Sir Geoffrey Scooner.

After the war, and a year's sick leave for recuperation, Robert studied Arabic at the Foreign Office language course in Jerusalem which led to his appointment at intelligence headquarters, Middle East. A posting to Ethiopia preceded his retirement with the rank of honorary major. After demobilisation, Robert took up farming in Devon, before turning to a business career.

In 1946, whilst on enforced and prolonged sick leave, Robert took up golf at Liphook,

Hampshire, and achieved the lowest handicap of six in his playing career.

Some time Captain of Pinner Hill Golf Club in north London, Robert's company moved him to Northampton in the 1970's before shortly afterwards posting him to Scotland.

Upon retirement in 1984, Robert returned to this county and rejoined NCGC. After the late Ken Hunter, Robert ran golf for the seniors, until his eyesight began to give him serious trouble. Even after being warned off driving his motor car, Robert attempted to ride by bicycle to the Club from his charming bijou converted chapel cottage at Pitsford, until he realised that this was more hazardous than jungle warfare!

Today we see an immaculately groomed and gentle warrior, striding the fairways until the motorised buggy was adopted as his only concession to old age. His ingrained golf swing (impaired vision or not) still enables Robert to press on, playing off a handicap of 20.

Those of us privileged to know him, consider that such acquaintance enriches our lives.

Richard Francis Watkins

Dick Watkins, having joined AC Palmer & Co, Chartered Accountants, under the leadership of RA (Peter) Palmer, soon became a member of the Golf Club followed by the role of Honorary Treasurer for a number of years, with the consequent attendance at Committee meetings and finally the honour of Captaincy of the Club.

Dick was always the most charming of golfing companions and the game introduced him to many new friends, of whom I was one, who found him the most agreeable companion. He was always passionate about golf and of the Club in particular and was a much respected Vice-President. Indeed, only the onset of Parkinson's Disease prevented him from accepting the honour of Presidency of the Club which was his due.

He was educated at Clifton College and virtually as he left school he was called up into the Royal Air Force where he trained as a pilot in Rhodesia (as it then was) and for whose people he retained abiding affection.

Having got his wings and returning to the UK Dick was trained to fly four-engined Halifax bombers. His first role was in flying out agents to occupied Europe, especially France. The SOE (Special Operations Executive) agent had to be dropped by parachute, which was a hazardous business for all concerned and involved extremely difficult navigation. Dick told me once that very often they had to bring their passenger back home because they simply could not find the dropping zone because of poor visibility, low cloud and suchlike. Later they were converted to towing gliders – not a very attractive job as the glider, heavily laden with men and arms, slowed the towing aircraft down to almost lethal speed. This involved him in the Battle of the crossing of the Rhine in the spring of 1945.

Once the war was over in Europe, Dick was flown out to India to take up bombing operations against the Japanese but mercifully the dropping of the atom bomb ended the war promptly and saved many lives.

After the war, Dick qualified as a chartered accountant and came to Northampton as an assistant accountant working for Peter Palmer at A C Palmer & Co in Sheep Street. Soon afterwards he became a partner and later, of course, Palmers merged with Coopers & Lybrand.

Dick was a gentleman through and through. Married to Dorothy (who worked at Bletchley Park during the war, where they cracked the German Enigma Code), they had twin daughters and a son. Dick was a great oenophile who spoke with authority on the subject of wine. He played in a regular fourball for many years –called "The Wonderful World of Golf" (after a TV show of that name) – the participants were the late Norman Buswell, the late Jack Belson, the late John King (who was Dick's adjutant in the RAF at one stage) and Dick himself. Later Neil Soutar joined them. They made a point of playing the best courses all over the country.

Dick was one of the men of the greatest stature at the Golf Club in the post-war era.

R T Mason

R T Mason was the son of a bank manager in Rugby and became a member of our Club prior to 1939. George Mobbs met up with him after the war when they both played in the Halford Hewitt. R T Mason was a reasonable golfer and achieved some fame as a war hero when he personally commandeered and drove a train through Japanese-occupied territory to Singapore during the terrifying debacle of the British Army's humiliation and defeat at the hands of the Japs in the early months of 1942, after the Japanese perfidious and treacherous attack on Pearl Harbour and the British Colonies.

His main occupation after the war was that of Golf Club Secretary. He served in this role at several smart clubs including Ganton in Yorkshire and later became the first Secretary of the new Woburn Golf Club in the late 1970's.

Edward Ronald Knapp CBE MA

George Short wrote the following article which was published in the Spring edition of The County in 2006. The article had been written the previous December. I have added two additional items concerning Ronnie Knapp.

"Ronnie was born in Cardiff in 1919 the first child to a loving family and under the care of "Madame Good Fortune" who maintained her care and influence throughout his whole life, and later referred to as "GF".

He was educated at Cardiff High School, where his athletic prowess led to honours in sprinting and rugby, playing for Welsh Schools and later Cardiff RUFC.

With school-days behind him Ron was called up and chose the Royal Navy, which permitted him to follow a Mechanical Sciences degree at Cambridge. Whilst there he played four times against Oxford (no Blues in those days), for the last of which he was Captain. In the same year he captained a side which won the Middlesex Sevens, both contributing towards selection for the senior Welsh side to play England.

Following his exploits at Cambridge, Ron became a temporary probationary sub-lieutenant working on a "new" invention called radar. This "new know-how" having a close affinity to his degree, led to his posting to HMS Aurora - a 5000 ton cruiser but this appointment proved rather difficult to achieve. First he chased to Glasgow, having heard that she was refuelling there but not true, she went directly to the Med. A troopship carried him down around the Cape for a stop at Durban, then on to the Red Sea and Egypt, and a slow train to Alexandria.

Meanwhile Aurora had reached Malta so, renewing his efforts, he took a speedy minelayer towards Malta, which was 'Stukered'. Forced to abandon ship, he was rescued by HMS Southwold (GF) and escorted back to Alex.

Hitching a ride in the Southwold which was escorting a supply ship to Malta and having 'stood off' Malta, the ship received more attention from enemy aircraft, blowing a hole in her side, splitting her in two and sinking her. Ron and a colleague decided to swim for Malta but were fortunately picked up by a minesweeper (GF) and put ashore at Valletta where he at last joined the Aurora. (Join the navy to see the World?).

The Aurora then sailed back to the UK for a refit in Liverpool and during this time two remarkable events took place: one, celebrating home leave at the Adelphi, Ron happened to be at the next table to Mae West ("Come up and see me sometime"), and secondly, considerably more important, getting married to Vera his long time girlfriend, and so began a period of sixty-three years of happy married life (GF).

The next brief for the Aurora was to escort a couple of convoys bound for Russia (no tropical kit for this!) and for this Ron qualified for "The Russian Medal" triangular in shape, and presented to him years later by his postman with the words "Congratulations Comrade!".

Aurora returned to the Med in order to intercept and destroy supply routes feeding Rommel's Afrika Korps and later to support allied landings in Sicily and Italy.

It was about this time that Aurora had the honour of having King George VI on board from North Africa to Malta, but her end was near and, following severe battering from the Luftwaffe, she was decommissioned in Italy, Ron returning to the UK only to be appointed to the US Naval Research Group in Washington DC as a lieutenant commander, using his expertise in radar, and there he stayed until the end of the war.

So, after such an amazing war service (GF) Ron returned to civilian life to be recommended to British Timken by his university appointments' board. There, after a couple of years 'on the floor' it was forever upwards, culminating in his appointment as Managing Director which led to his civil honour of CBE.

After a number of temporary residences, Ron and Vera settled down in The Elms, a wonderful home set in two acres of beautiful gardens, orchard, tennis court, kitchen garden and two greenhouses. Here their children Ian, William, Vanessa and Lucille grew up to form a closely knit family, all with university degrees and highly successful careers. It is a rare occurrence when some of the members of the family and their children are not visiting home for the weekend to receive a warm welcome from their proud parents.

It is realistic to suppose that as Ron has such acreage to care for, he must be a keen gardener. He has been described as a compulsive gardener whose skills are known nationwide, for only last year a photograph of red, white, and blue varieties of potatoes appeared in a gardening magazine. If it is a seed he will grow it, showing a wide range of plants in his vegetable garden - these of course are decimated when 'the family have been'. His orchard provides a regular supply of apples to staff and friends at our golf course.

This leads on to Ron's sporting life. As we all know he was one of the Saints' stars, playing as a fly-half or other positions in defence. He recalls an occasion when, running in to score one of his many tries, he left his torn shorts in the full-back's hands leaving little to hide his embarrassment. His exploits as a young rugby player are legendary and his fun-loving nature led him into another of his escapades of riding pillion on a motor bike inside the Salon ballroom, but then realised that instead of a Thursday night hop it proved to be a Hunt Ball! On a serious note he captained the Saints in 1949 and also turned out for East Midlands and Vikings, serving on various Committees, then Chairman and President. He is still an ardent supporter and sits in the stands with his memories.

In the 1960's, turning from tennis and squash he had an urge towards golf, from which he derived much enjoyment, but his style was cramped when some heart trouble restricted him to nine holes only. He has a regular partner (opponent) playing perhaps three times a week and together they have formulated a new system called 'Knapp Rules' which include such things as 'Mulligans' from any tee, provisional Mulligans if there is a doubt about the lie, 'nudges' of up to ten yards if the lie cannot be improved readily, and "Medicals" which allow a ball to be lifted from a hazard if there is a risk of breaking a leg when climbing out (or losing the hole). All this contributes to a highly social game (he does like to take the money!)."

* * * * *

Ronnie Knapp also told a story concerning himself. He was an avid gardener and in his retirement spent many hours beautifying the garden surrounding his home at Old Duston within an eight iron distance from the British Timken headquarters of the company, for whom he worked for so many years.

One day, whilst dressed in his gardening glad rags, a lady walked past and glanced over the fence at him kneeling and beavering away. The lady, walking her pet dog, smiled as if to approve his labours. A few minutes later the lady returned and Ronnie was still busily engaged in his gardening efforts. The lady paused and stopped and engaged Ronnie in conversation over the fence. She said that she had always admired this garden as it was always so immaculate. Ronnie immediately rose to the situation and knew that he had been mistaken for a gardener/handyman employed to do the work. "Thank you Madam" he said, "I like to do things nicely". The lady paused and then with some hesitancy said "Do you have any spare time and would you be available to do a few hours for me? I have recently moved here, down the road, and could do with a little help". Ronnie beamed and immediately responded by saying "Yes, Madam, I think I could spare an hour or two". "Oh, that would be nice" said the lady, "Would you mind telling me what you charge?". "Ah now" said Ronnie, "That presents me with some difficulty. You see I leave that to Vera, the lady of the house, and she always allows me to sleep with her!". The lady with her dog were seen beating a hasty retreat in the opposite direction! Ronnie was still chuckling as he told the tale the next day at the Golf Club.

I am advised that Ronnie was placed in his coffin wearing his Royal Naval duffle coat from his heroic war years. Ronnie always used to joke that he donned that particular item of apparel when he was shipwrecked. The coat was given to him by the bosun of the minesweeper which rescued him from the sea. When they were finally rescued and got ashore, the duffle coat was duly cleaned and remained in Ronnie Knapp's possession until the end of the war.
The coat always hung in the cloakroom at the family home and Ronnie's wife eventually got fed up with the sight of it and suggested that it might be time to put it out for a jumble sale or donated to a charity shop. This suggestion was brushed aside with instant dismissal by Ronnie. He said "We can't do that, it doesn't belong to me. It belongs to a brother sailor who may turn up at any minute to come and reclaim it!". This was some twenty years after the end of the war. It was, therefore, more than appropriate that this should end up as his shroud.

INDEX

**Page numbers in bold refer to
photographs**